Where We Started

a novel

Arthur Dobrin

Nsemia

First Edition: April 2020
Published by Nsemia Inc. Publishers (www.nsemia.com)

Edited By: Sally Boyani
Cover Concept & Illustration: Author
Cover Design: Linda Kiboma
Layout: Bethsheba Nyabuto

Note for Librarians:
A cataloguing record for this book is available from
Kenya National Library Services.

ISBN: 978-1-926906-91-1

Dedication

To all those who have labored, struggled, suffered and loved to create the United States.

Acknowledgements

Many thanks to Rich Green who helped with editing, Barbara and Mel Haber who listened to oral readings as the writing of the book progressed and especially my wife, Lyn, who helped every step of the way with her boundless encouragement and expert skill as an editor. A special thanks to Christian Hayden and Don Johnson, who read early versions of the manuscript and Jonathan Lande for his help in directing me to scholarly historical articles. I am grateful to Michael Franch, who helped keep track of historical accuracies

Table of Contents

A New World

KWASI

Blue

FROM HIS HUT by the beach, Kwasi watches canoes from the forest bring captives to the Komenda holding warehouse. He has been in the palaver house many times to complete the sale of his ironware, but he has never been inside the fort itself or in its adjoining barracoon. He hears, though, that in that compound men are shackled to one another while women and children walk about freely. It is in the barracoon that slaves are examined, bought by an agent and taken to a waiting Guineaman, a merchant ship reconfigured into one that transports human cargo.

From his beachside forge, Kwasi watches naked men and women herded on to canoes and paddled out to a waiting ship. Once Kwasi saw a woman jump into the sea, leaving behind only a pool of blood in the shadows of fins of circling sharks.

The boom of a British cannon salutes the dawn and announces the end of day. This provides Kwasi with enough confidence to work his metal by daylight and sleep throughout the night certain that the guards and the guns would repel the Dutch invaders encamped a mile down the shore, if they are to attack.

As an itinerant blacksmith, Kwasi has lived in several areas before settling in Komenda. He was born in Ntwaaban village into an ironworkers' clan and, like all the men in his village, produces farm instruments and warriors' weapons for the rest of his tribe. They also forge bracelets, necklaces and waistbands to ward off evil spirits, giving birth to essential objects.

Kwasi is amongst those whose life is mediated between the sacred and the profane, an intercessor into the unseen world, the maker of essentials from earth. The awe and fear they inspire led to their isolation from all but their own clan.

Kwasi's father taught him the art of metalworking. And when Kwasi reached puberty, he was apprenticed with a little father. Through two rainy season cycles he gathered wood for charcoal making for his mentor, his father's brother. After the second yam festival, he was permitted to assist by holding the blacksmith's tongs, repair bellows, and stoke the forge. He wasn't yet allowed make anything other than personal charms.

The repetitive and exclusionary nature of a blacksmith's work kept Kwasi away from things that held greater appeal. He would prefer going to the weekly market to flirt with girls with glistening legs and budding breasts; he envied the other young men who had spears and shields to call their own and went on raiding parties to rebalance the forces of the universe.

"You'll never be a proper husband to your forge, Kwasi, unless you pay attention," he was chided.

His little father continued to postpone the day when Kwasi would take the next step in his education as a smith. The longer it was postponed, the more restless Kwasi became. He did what was asked of him but paid scant attention to the subtleties and details. He couldn't distinguish birdcalls or read cowry shells when they were tossed. His interpretation of dreams was mundane. After many seasons of desultory work, Kwasi was called by the village elders and told by them that he needed to leave. He had prowess enough to forge utilitarian items, but they saw no prospect that he would master the skills needed for the spirits.

Kwasi was given tools from the big father. In his sacred bundle for protection Kwasi packed blue beads, a bird's claw, a piece of dried vine, a teal feather from a kingfisher, and cats' teeth. For several seasons Kwasi moved around the interior, living on the margins of his tribe. He watched many marched by his home, hands tied together, to the place where people lived on winged houses, homes that walked on water, those captured by pillaging marauders or in war, some tricked with promises of visiting fantastical places, others spirited by an agent.

Kwasi was never in danger of being taken by Fante slave traders or red-skinned slave agents—his ritual scars signaling his status as a member of a blacksmith clan kept them at bay. By engaging freely with slavers, Kwasi learned rudimentary English and heard about the fort on the coast. After trekking throughout his region, bringing his arcane skills from village to village, Kwasi wended his way to the coast and settled in Komenda. Whatever anxiety he had about being so close to slavers was lifted when looked at the blue water wider than any river or when he viewed the vast blue sky unhindered by overhead trees. He was the only African who didn't live in the fort; every other black was a slave waiting for transport, working in the fort or warehouse.

Kwasi built a small furnace and before long developed a sustained trade with the Europeans along the shore. They are in constant need of metal goods and his wrought iron products satisfy agents, government officials, soldiers and merchants. He aids captains in repairing their ships battered from a long voyage. Here at the fort, as the only resident blacksmith, he is essential for repairs and reconstruction. And his wares bring him enough wealth to bribe Europeans whenever necessary and to pay for his necessities.

A dozen languages swirl in Komenda. Kwasi easily converses with those who speak a Fante vernacular, as he did in his mother tongue. He has more trouble with English but manages to carry on his business without a translator and had picked up rudimentary Dutch.

What Kwasi hasn't anticipated is the loneliness that came from living in a strange land. Kinsmen now and then come to Komenda and are a welcome respite, but aside from these calls, Africans stay away from Kwasi. For some any association with an ironworker is taboo; others steer clear because of his magic—because his furnace makes only tools for Europeans or household items, it is clear to them that his powers aren't used to heal or appease the spirits but instead are designed to bring misfortune. Kwasi lives in a space that no African would tempt. That he is worthless as a medium of the spirit world, he keeps secret.

His rough skin, coated in white ash from his furnace, keeps European bookkeepers and tradesmen at a distance, deepening his alienation.

When Kwasi repairs the fort surgeon's saw, the doctor, Coombs, offers to assuage Kwasi's solitariness by procuring a woman for him. Kwasi rejects the offer of a shipping-slave. Upon their arrival at the coast, the women were feeble and anything but desirable. He doesn't want to be near anyone who has been in the barracoon waiting to be transported to a floating house. It is a cursed place ravaged by fevers and plagued by death.

Although Kwasi concocts medicine to keep from contracting the flux and other illnesses by combining seeds, leaves and bark from the towering kapok tree on the edge of the forest, he doesn't trust that any compound he can make will be strong enough if he were to lay with a woman from the holding pen.

The surgeon makes another proposal.

"She is a few shillings more," the surgeon says. "But she is healthy. I've examined her myself. She has worked here and she has never been sick."

KWASI BRINGS ANTOBAM, a fort-slave, to his home. Her beaded necklace rattles as she stands next to his bed. When Kwasi removes his trousers, she shrieks, breaks for the door and races back to the fort. Kwasi lets her go.

The surgeon finds the incident amusing and says to Kwasi that he won't charge him for another go.

"This time she's a gift. She won't run off. She knows her place. I've made sure of that. You'll find her ready. But I think you need to wash off if you don't want her so wild. You scare me half to death with that detestable ash covering your body. Are you sure you ain't a ghost, boy?"

"Let me know the day before you bring her," Kwasi says.

Kwasi locks the cabin door this time. She whimpers and closes her eyes as Kwasi removes her dress. He stares at the letters RAC raised on her shoulder. He has never seen anyone branded before. He runs his rough hands along her back and down her thighs. She doesn't resist.

Kwasi arranges with the surgeon: repairs of his surgical instruments in return for the girl once a week.

Kwasi says to the girl, "You are Antobam."

"Yes."

"Your father didn't protect you," Kwasi tells her. Antobam, he knows, meant the 'girl born after her father's death.'

Over the next several months she goes with Kwasi to his cabin without protest. Her fear of being with a blacksmith hasn't disappeared altogether but her fortune hasn't turned worse. She thinks that in some ways it has improved: at the fort, Europeans leave her alone and she can sleep in Kwasi's cabin until dawn on the nights she is taken. And she finds that there is comfort in being in the company of an African man from her own tribe.

As they lay together, she tells Kwasi, "The first time raiders came to my village they kidnapped the men and left the women. My father, my little fathers, my brothers, they were all taken. We had heard about such things but it had never happened to us. We didn't know where they were being taken. There was a white man with them. I had never seen a European before."

Over several months she tells him more.

"For a few moons we women lived alone. We were afraid of everything—the forest, hungry spirits, another raiding party. Then men from nearby took us to their villages to protect us and we came back to life."

She never volunteers to tell her story. Antobam needs Kwasi's prodding. She tells him this part as she is scrubbing thickened ash from his back:

"They came again, the slave traders, to our new village. They were different now. There was no European with them. I don't know what they said; I don't know where they came from. This time they snatched everyone. Not just the men. Everyone. But the babies were left behind. We could hear the babies crying as they tied us together and marched us through the forest."

Sometime later, she explains what happened when they arrived at Komenda.

"At this place Europeans bought us from the captors. They put us in the barracoon. There were others there already. We waited in the courtyard until a ship appeared. Two weeks. This ship wasn't in need of repair, so it left quickly."

"But you are here."

Another night Antobam says, "I don't know why I was separated from the rest. But I was. One morning dugouts took my kinfolk to the big boat but not me. My mother begged and cried for me. But it did no good. A soldier took me away from my mother and brought me to the fort."

She tells Kwasi how lucky he was that he had magic to keep Europeans from taking him as a slave.

"I heard that African wizards had no power over Europeans."

"My power is my skill. I am useful to them. But my charms are strong," he added. Kwasi fingered his necklace. His bundle remained in a secret place. "They offer protection."

She asks if would make her a charm.

When he sees her next, Kwasi gives her a piece of metal the size of a coin inscribed with a crosses and hatches. Antobam then tells him that two seasons ago there had been a grometto from the fort who had run away with his wife and child.

Antobam begins to cook for Kwasi. She pounds maize meal into flour, puts it into a clay pot fashioned by her own hand and adds warm water. She sets the mixture beside Kwasi's furnace. When the dough has fermented, she skims off the top, kneads the remainder, and drops it in boiling water. How she has gotten the peppers, tomatoes and onions for the sauce Kwasi doesn't ask.

As they sit outside his cabin eating *kenkey,* she tells him more of the story of the runaway family.

"A grometto," Antobam explains, "is an African who works for the white men and receives a wage for his labor."

"They're free, like me?"

"You can come and go as you like, work as much or as little as you please. Not the same with them. He had a wage contract. The husband repaired canoes. The wife had a mat at the market where she sold fish. The husband also spoke the Asante language. They came from Elmina. So they could also speak the language of the Dutchmen. The grometto lived inside the fort when I was sold here."

Each time she prepares a meal for Kwasi, she reveals a little more.

"They ran away as if they were slaves, but they weren't," Kwasi says.

"An agent talked to the husband. He said the floating house wanted him to work there. There weren't enough slaves in Komenda and they needed to go to Elmina to purchase more. The big boat would then go to America."

"He didn't go, but why did they run away?"

"He was afraid that he would never return and he would be sold when they arrived in the other world. Other free Africans were tricked this way. So he took his family and fled down the coast. Scouts pursued them as soon as they discovered the family was missing. In two days they were returned to Komenda. They were tied as though they were slaves."

"I've never seen the family. Where are they now?"

Antobam says that the agent met the family when they were returned.

"The ship had not yet cast off. It was still in the harbor."

Kwasi breaks off a small piece of fried fish Antobam has prepared that day.

"The family was brought into the fort amidst much arguing. The agent and Mister Holmes, the big man in charge of the Royal Company then, and the grometto had words, many sharp words between them."

Kwasi sips his palm toddy from a calabash.

"Later that day there was bangs, loud noises. I heard them myself. At first I thought the cannon had fired. But it was after dark. And the sound was in the section of the fort where we lived, not the barracoon, so I peeked out from my doorway. The moon was full. I saw the woman and child on the ground. They were dead."

"The agent shot them," Kwasi interjects.

"No. I saw the husband with the gun in his hand."

"*He* killed them, the grometto."

"Then he shot himself in the head," Antobam says.

The fort-surgeon no longer arranges Antobam's nocturnal visits, although Kwasi continues to pay him for each night she come. Before the beginning of the next season, the understanding between Kwasi and Antobam resembles that of husbands and wives in Ntwaaban where each continues to live in separate houses. She cooks for him and he makes jewelry for her to trade at the market. The trinkets are very popular. With her profits she brings Kwasi strong soap and sometimes cooks with millet instead of maize for the *kenkey*.

Expecting that his life would be without children when he began his itinerant life, Kwasi is delighted to find fate had kindly intervened. Now he needs to bring Antobam to his village where the child could be properly raised. No good can come of Antobam remaining in Komenda. Who would perform the naming ceremony? Who would teach the child the proper ways? Kwasi's charms are impotent against the stronger magic of the English.

"I'll bring you there myself."

"This is impossible. We'll be caught."

"I know the area better than anyone at the fort. They won't catch us before we arrive at Ntwaaban."

"Why do you think I'd be safe at your home? No place is safe from slave traders."

"Have you ever seen anyone from my region as a slave? No. Why? Because the British protect us because we help them against the Dutch."

No argument moves Antobam. If she doesn't want to flee, it is useless. But he is convinced that she won't remain a slave, either. He needs to bring her home.

Kwasi persuades Antobam that with the money that each of them earned they would be able to purchase her freedom. Antobam agrees. She forgoes buying English cloth from a floating house and instead takes to mending everything; she cooks only with vegetables she grows in her garden and bargains harder in the market. She accepts the cooking pot Kwasi makes for her; at the market the following week she sells it. Soap is a luxury but Antobam doesn't display her fear of sleeping with a ghost-like man.

Neither does Kwasi complain that she seldom cooks millet *kenkey* for him or that the pepper sauce lacks fire. He works at his furnace throughout the day, even when the sun is overhead, resting only when the sun is low in the sky. Besides his work selling metal goods to the RAC and repairing items for the Guineamen, he produces trinkets for Antobam to sell. Each time a ship arrives, Kwasi brings their blue glassware and secretly buries the beads and bottles under the door and bed, and places pieces over the door.

When Kwasi finishes a knife, he brings it to the fort for sale. Having closed the deal, he says to the factor in charge of the slave collecting, "I want to buy Antobam."

The Englishman looks at Kwasi for a moment, "Why would you want to do that? She does all the work now. Isn't it better to pay Coombs his commission?" Holmes asks.

"That will never end."

"The price for a young girl like her is steep."

"There isn't another fort-slave for buying."

"You don't need a fort-slave. Wait for the next coffle to come from the forest. There's sure to be a wench for you to purchase."

"They arrive in no condition for me to choose. Antobam is well-broken. She's the one I want."

Holmes' price, Kwasi knows, is an opening gambit. Not wanting to show his eagerness, he says, "I'll wait for the next caravan to arrive. You may be right. There will be a girl there to suit me that I can afford to purchase."

Kwasi waits for Holmes to approach him.

"She's good, that Antobam. You'll agree to that."

Negotiations proceed in a desultory fashion—the factor happy to keep Antobam as a fort-slave and Kwasi wanting not to show his hand.

In the middle of the rainy season a slave caravan arrives just two days after a Guineaman drops anchor.

"Are you certain there's none here you want?" Holmes asks.

Kwasi glances at the group standing in the rain as the surgeon examines them. Two pubescent girls were amongst them.

"None appeals to me as much as she does. Antobam knows all my tastes."

"I'm sure she does," the factor says. After a long silence he adds, "You aren't going to get Antobam, you know."

Thinking that the flush of money coming from the sale of fresh slaves would make the factor ready to close the deal, Kwasi is ready to meet Holmes' prior offer a few shillings shy. Between the two, Kwasi and Antobam have accumulated enough money to satisfy Holmes' price. Kwasi makes a bid again, certain that he would accept it.

Not only does Holmes reject it, he ends the negotiations with the remark, "She's worth more than I knew. You are a conniving Negro, Kwasi. But I'm no fool. You are not going to get away with such trickery."

Holmes doesn't need to explain. Kwasi has waited too long to make the purchase and it is now clear that Antobam was pregnant.

The next morning, as Kwasi stokes his furnace, the enslaved are marched to the shore. He watches as Antobam files by him, placed in a long canoe with six others and paddled out to the waiting ship. From a distance he can't tell which of the Africans ascending the rope ladder on the schooner's side is Antobam.

Sail Away

THE NOISY whistle 'pu-pu-pu-pu-ku-ku-ku-ku' of the kingfisher awoke Kwasi in the middle of the night. This was the first time he heard their call since building his furnace in Komenda. These birds usually inhabited the forest waterways but during the dry season they made an occasional visit to the coast. The rains had not yet let up and the gray skies were to continue for three more weeks. But there was no mistaking what he heard.

The avian visitors from Ntwaaban were welcome guests. For the first time since Antobam's delivery to the Guineaman, Kwasi felt his resolve returning. The black face, back, and shoulders; the white throat, the red legs, the blue wings and tail—he saw it all before opening his eyes—the beak nearly as large as its body, the upper mandible bright red, the lower one black. During the day Kwasi had seen kingfishers dart along rivers, in the mangrove swamps and lagoons feasting on termites, crabs, beetles, wasps, frogs and fresh water fish. Kwasi once saw a kingfisher attack a hatchling crocodile.

Kingfishers nested in pairs but this nocturnal commotion disrupted the silence with the crescendoing call of hundreds of birds. The whistles that at first comforted Kwasi turned into the alarming clamor of tchup, tchup, tchup, tchup. Through the gaps in the grass roof, he saw the luminescent wings of chirming birds illuminate the sky blue as brilliant as the shallow ocean water.

The sky brightened to gray with the rising sun and the tchup, tchup ceased, the cries replaced with the songs of littoral birds. No one else in the trading post mentioned the night clamor and Kwasi didn't bring it up.

With the arrival of a brigantine the following day, Kwasi gathered dirt from the fort's graveyard, stole a pin from Holmes' jacket and broke it in half. He then mixed the dirt and pin pieces with white ash and dried rat skin. Kwasi put the potion in a blackened goatskin cache and at the proper time would drop the bundle into his household fire.

Usually Guineamen were destined for the Caribbean or Brazil, but when the ship's first mate, David. Snelgrave, came ashore, he made it known that the brigantine *True Blue* was bound for the northern colony of New York. No slave ship would cross the Atlantic without a full load, but this ship held no more than 120 slaves, half the amount plied on other ships, so he was hoping they would be able to sail to America with this being the only stop along the Gold Coast.

This was the first Outward Passage for the *True Blue*. Like others before it, it called at Komenda not only to buy slaves but also to employ skilled Africans for the return journey. Half a dozen of its sailors had succumbed to illnesses at sea. Captain Johnson knew when he left New York that many of his crew would either die or they would desert in one of the Guinea ports. Johnson wasn't surprised by the losses; the American owners, like everyone in the shipping business, built it into the cost of doing business.

Convicts, beggars, drunkards—"*refuse and dregs*," one captain called them; "*degenerates*," Johnson wrote in his diary—comprised much of the crew as it left its home port. Aside from a seasoned first mate and two other officers, those were the only men willing to sail on a slaver. For Johnson, these men were disposable. The captain, on his first voyage on a Guineaman, was told that seamen from the African coast were more reliable and cheaper than the colonists. Africans willing to work aboard weren't difficult to find, he was advised. Adventure and profit were adequate enticements.

At the factory, Snelgrave traded for slaves and gold, offering textiles and guns in exchange. He took the lot, including the children. They all appeared to be healthy. None, though, were skilled. In markets, he bought palm oil, beeswax and peppers. Near the fort, he inquired about available African seamen who would be taken as freemen.

"What's more I need skilled craftsmen." For two weeks, the crew hadn't had a dry thread. They were stinking from moldy clothes rotting on their backs. "I am in desperate need of a tailor."

No African in Komenda volunteered for service on the brigantine. The *True Blue* would have to continue to larger forts on the coast to get its fill of crew and slaves.

Snelgrave came to Kwasi's forge.

"The blacksmith died yesterday as we ready to drop anchor," Snelgrave said to Kwasi in Pidgin English. The first mate tested the point of a knife handed to him by Kwasi. He examined the other items scattered around. "All yours?

Kwasi agreed.

Snelgrave tested the blades of a couple of spontoons propped against a tree. He bought both pole-arms and a cutlass.

"I want to interest you in joining the *True Blue.*"

"Where are you sailing to?"

"If you don't get our fill here, we'll stop again. Our home is New York. The ship was constructed there and we are returning there with our cargo."

Kwasi let the mate talk. "I have *arrangoes*," Snelgrave offered, taking from his satchel a handful of barrel-shaped beads half the length of his little finger. Each had a hole drilled in the middle and several were held together with a thin wire.

Kwasi turned the beads in his palm and returned them to the mate.

"They lack clarity," he said, suppressing his desire to own them.

Snelgrave told Kwasi he would buy from him all the weapons and shackles he had ready.

"The wage is a good one," the mate added.

If Holmes knew that Kwasi was leaving Komenda, the fort's big man would make his life difficult. Since Kwasi's ironworking was critical to the outpost, without him Komenda would be more vulnerable to the Dutch. Kwasi guessed that Holmes would claim that he was a slave and offer to sell him to the *True Blue* at an exorbitant price. If the captain bought Kwasi as a slave from Holmes, the windfall would provide the head of the fort enough money to find another blacksmith for Komenda. And if Johnson refused to purchase him, Holmes would have one less freeman to contend with. Both outcomes were appalling.

Kwasi could smell burning flesh as he imagined the iron pressed against his skin, but still he replied to Snelgrave, "I do well enough here."

He learned the way of hard bargaining from Antobam.

"I know you have heard that some commanders cut off legs and arms of those who are willful. That's not the way of this brigantine. The captain runs a Christian ship. He isn't hard hearted."

Kwasi told him that this life on the coast was all he wanted. The sea had no appeal to him.

"I'm not a seaman. My legs are meant for land. I like the songs of birds. There are no trees in the Atlantic, I've been told."

THE OMENS PLACED BEFORE Kwasi were clear, benevolent and pointing him in the same direction. His mind was set. When all the haggling, selling and buying was complete, he approached the fort before sunrise and placed the black bundle outside the wall of Holmes' quarters. He then went to the beach and washed himself in the water. He poured sand over a coconut coir and scrubbed the front of his body. To clean his back, he rubbed against a tree trunk, rolled in the dirt and rinsed again. His body was clean when slavers arrived at the shore to embark on canoes for the first of the several shuttles to the anchored ship.

"I need to speak to the captain," Kwasi informed to the head paddler.

The paddler knew the blacksmith's power and was reluctant to let him on the boat. Kwasi handed the African a metal bracelet as he climbed into the boat. A sack of beeswax and peppers was placed at the feet of the rear paddler. Five men, two women and two children, all naked and shivering in the rain, crouched in the center, their gaze focused on the floor of the boat, their hands cuffed in a braided cord. Kwasi tried to remain upright with the three rowers but lost his balance as the canoe bobbed in the foaming waves. He held on to the sides as he put himself amongst the slaves.

Wobbly from the ride over the breakers, Kwasi had difficulty climbing the *True Blue's* rope ladder to the deck. Captain Johnson remained in his cabin while Kwasi spoke to Snelgrave. The transfers would be complete by the end of the day, the mate told him. They were already preparing the sails. The slaves were untied, and then shackled and manacled, right wrist and ankle of one to the left wrist and ankle of the other. A chain was reeved through the shackles and locked to a ringbolt on the upper deck. Under a temporary thatch covering built for the respite of the sailors from the tropical sun, the captives remained chained as another group and then a third arrived, each comer then shackled in the same manner. Although the barracoon was emptied, the hold was less than half filled. The ship was also in need of more crewmen. Kwasi took his chances; his missing wouldn't be reported until they had left port.

Kwasi agreed to the terms: 20 shillings a month while at sea and a bonus of 5% of the price of the oldest female slave when they landed. The mate produced a piece of paper. He read the provisions to Kwasi and had him mark the paper with an X.

The anchor had hardly been raised when Kwasi witnessed the strong hand of the commander. Unaccustomed to their accents, all Kwasi could make out was one sailor say, "soft African wench," as he leaned over one of the slaves. Another seaman shoved him aside. Punches were thrown and several crewmen pulled them apart.

For the first time Kwasi saw Captain Johnson.

"I won't tolerate wanton rudeness on my ship," Johnson declared to the assemblage. "Tie this one to the starboard shroud." The sailor's shirt was removed and his hands were bound to the thick rope. "And give this one the cat." One of the mates, with a pistol jutting from his belt, handed the sailor a long whip with nine tails, each tail having three knots.

The crew and the slaves watched.

"Two lashes," he said.

The first raised welts, the second drew blood. "Wash him," Johnson commanded. "Fetch a pail of seawater and clean the back you just bloodied. When you are finished both of you clean the lower deck to ready it for these Negroes."

Men were separated from the women and children in stowage. A comely girl was taken to the captain's deck and given a cabin next to his.

The brigantine sailed for a month on a coasting voyage, keeping close to shore, making it first stops at Elmina. At Cape Coast they were delayed as Johnson met with the captains of a half-dozen other slave ships. The council meeting had called together all the captains around Cape Coast to deliberate on the fate of a slave.

Following the meeting, the Guineamen were circled around one ship. Johnson brought all his slaves to the upper deck, as had the commanders of each of the other slave ships.

"The Negro killed a white man," Snelgrave said. "While the seaman was below deck, the slave struck him on the head."

A rope was tied around the ankles of the African and he was hoisted high enough to be seen from all ships. As he squirmed like a fish at the end of a line as it is pulled from the water, the air rang with the sound of a musket. He was still dangling when Kwasi's brigantine set sail for Fort Nassau. They brought on several more slaves and engaged more crew. Although there was still more capacity, Johnson decided to leave with the human cargo, mahogany, gold dust and crew members he now had. The risk of fevers to the white men while still close to shore was too great and the trip to Benin too far.

The *True Blue* made for the Middle Passage with 118 slaves and twenty-three seamen from America, Malabar, Prussia, Britain, the African coast and Sweden. Aside from Kwasi, there were two other free Negroes, both from Spain. Of everything that he experienced during his lifetime, none was worse than the three months on the confines of the brigantine. A task that Kwasi loathed but couldn't refuse was cleaning the slave quarters. Every day he emptied two large tubs of urine and excrement; twice a week he scrubbed the area with sand and fumigated it with vinegar and tobacco smoke.

Although Kwasi was directed to break up fights amongst slaves, he wasn't issued a knife or pistol. He carried out the daily searches for tools that might be used as weapons; he clipped slaves' fingernails to prevent them from becoming daggers.

Despite provisions enough for the human chattel for the trip, Johnson kept meat and beans away from the enslaved for the first two weeks. He wanted to cull the weakest before reaching the point of no return, so he wouldn't be responsible for their cost.

While white sailors took turns scrubbing the deck and cleaning the captives, Kwasi and the Spanish Negroes were required to do both duties every day. The slaves were brought on deck—the men shackled, the women and children free—and Kwasi and the Spanish Negroes washed dirt, mucus, sores and dried vomit from their hands and faces. Then Kwasi followed the ship's surgeon to interpret for him as the doctor made his daily inspection of the slaves. Once during the journey they confronted a woman who was starving herself by refusing to eat. Kwasi pried her jaws open with a scissor-shaped *speculum oris* and then poured gruel down her throat.

After the inspection the slaves were fed the first meal of the day: maize or yams served in bowls with a pannikin of water. A full-body wash followed their breakfast, a task made easier since no slave wore clothes from Komenda to New York. The shelter over the deck had been dismantled once the ship left port for the open seas. Weather permitting the afternoon was time for what the sailors called "dancing" and what the surgeon called exercise. Kwasi watched the entertainment—the women and children roaming the deck in continuous movement, the men clanking their chains as one of the African sailors played a one-string fiddle—until the day when one girl stopped to rest and a sailor in charge brought a simple whip across her arm. Her mother leaped to her daughter's aid by pushing the sailor to the deck. The woman was quickly restrained, tied to a spar and whipped with the knotted cat.

Sharks trailed the brigantine after the first body was tossed aside, their fins cutting the water. The fish had learned from Guineamen before *True Blue* that more meals would follow.

When the ship turned north to sail up the American coast, Johnson released the food he had been hoarding. Now was the time to give stews of meat, beans and rice to restore their strength and appearance before arriving at the slave market.

Before reaching its destination, twenty slaves and ten seamen had been buried in the deep: two died from starvation at the outset, one woman jumped overboard with her child, a few men didn't recover from punishment received for insubordination, the African cook was shot dead by Snelgrave, who then had her purchase price deducted from his wages. Others, including the ship's surgeon, died from fevers.

They sailed along the New Jersey shore with its long stretches of beach. They then entered into a tidal strait and then an enormous bay that divided into two rivers as they headed north past Half Moon Battery and along the East River, a continuation of wharves filled with ships on the Manhattan side and finally anchoring at Cruger's Wharf by Fly Market Slip. A row of houses lined the street alongside the slip with the largest at the south corner of the inlet.

Never could Kwasi imagine a place so large with so many people, living houses as tall as trees, ships clustered like a school of fish, a river wide enough to drown the most practiced swimmer, more noise than the sounds he heard in his lifetime gathered in an hour.

The goods were off-loaded as Kwasi stood on the deck with Snelgrave. He watched the slaves quivering as they stood chained together. And for a fleeting moment he thought he should join them.

Snelgrave turned to him and said, "Not a bad journey. There's a good profit here coming straight from the Guinea Coast."

Two men wearing hats and long coats approached the slaves. A discussion ensued and the enslaved were filed down Water Street.

"They'll be auctioned at Meal Market. The captain will do well, the bastard. The woman deserved to be shot," he said. "But a fine will do to avoid a trial."

Kwasi didn't understand what fine or trial the mate was referring to.

"You got yours?"

"All that was agreed to."

"Then buy me a drink, will you? There is a tippling place that isn't far."

Kwasi suspected Snelgrave's motives but being on his own in a place so overwhelming large seemed no safer than being with the mate. In a few streets they arrived at a rude tavern at Hanover Square. Filled with sailors and local people, Kwasi sat on a bench beside Snelgrave. Kwasi ate while Snelgrave drank. Ships' agents moved amongst the crowd making offers to sailors for the next schooner out.

"Interested in sailing again?" "Maybe sometime. Not now," Kwasi replied.

"A merchant ship this time. That's what I'll sail. I've had my fill of Guineamen." Kwasi watched him swallow another double bowl of ale. "The African coast is vile."

In the garden behind the tavern a cockfight was arranged. Snelgrave bet on a winner, leaving Kwasi to pay for the bill for both.

"Good luck," he said as he walked into the darkened city.

Snelgrave, Kwasi learned, took command of a ship that left New York for the Gold Coast.

Fires Everywhere

KWASI CARRIED few things with him when he debarked from the *True Blue*: a sturdy jacket and a pair of trousers from the dead surgeon that Snelgrave presented to him; shoes Kwasi had removed from a mate before the sailor was tossed overboard; a *navaja*, a folding knife from one of the Spanish Negroes, a purse made fat by doubloons he discovered in a loose plank in the bulkhead when scrubbing the deceased surgeon's cabin.

As he walked through the darkened New York streets looking for a place to sleep, he kept his hand firmly on his Spanish knife. Nighttime was always full of danger, never more so than when alone in an unfamiliar place.

Kwasi couldn't tell where the voices were coming from—the laughter, the singing, the arguing arising from every corner, from above the street, from below. Ships rubbed their sides against the piers like spirits groaning in the forest; and there were barking dogs and yowling cats. Where lanterns lit the street, he kept away, not wanting to be seen. Kwasi was going to keep as far away as possible from everything until he learned where he could be protected.

But he needed to sleep. He saw a barn that appeared to house tools but no animals. He pried the door open and climbed up to the loft, covered himself with straw and curled into a ball.

Exhaustion overcame fear and later he awoke, shuddering, to the sound of roosters. Nights in Africa during the rainy season were cold but not like this. Not even on the *True Blue*, with his clothes heavy with rainwater and spray and the wind blowing, did the cold dig into his bones like this.

Kwasi climbed down from the loft and saw the henhouse. He hoped the chickens wouldn't attract too much attention to him as entered the pen. He picked up a couple of eggs, wrapped them in his handkerchief and walked away quickly.

As the sky lightened, Kwasi looked for a sign. He heard a rasping caaw!-caaw!-caaw! and saw black birds descend on the carcass of a piebald cat. He waited until the birds were finished tearing the animal apart and then snapped a tooth from the cat's skull and placed it in his sack.

Birds with rust breasts fed on the ground, and he could hear birds chirping but couldn't see them.

Not even the sky was blue that day, as the dull morning, as gray as the river water, grew only slightly brighter as the day progressed. Kwasi removed from his bundle the crucifix gotten from the Spanish sailor and hung it around his neck.

He walked along the streets, from the fort to the wharves, stepping aside for the white people he passed, not knowing what language to use for the blacks. When he reached the first farm, he turned back to the city.

He hadn't eaten since the night before. He stopped in an alley to eat the eggs he had put away. He cracked the shells with his teeth filed to sharp points. He had never eaten raw eggs before.

Kwasi stopped in a cooper's store to ask for work.

"No, I'm no one's slave," he assured the cooper. "I arrived yesterday on the *True Blue.*"

"The slave ship." "Yes, from the Gold Coast. But I'm a free African man. I would be far from here if I was an escaped slave from the ship."

Kwasi finally convinced the cooper with his ability to speak English.

"But you're Popish," the cooper said.

Kwasi looked puzzled.

"I'm from Komenda," he replied

"That, around your neck."

Kwasi touched his wooden amulet.

"I'm a skilled blacksmith," he said, showing the cooper his rough hands. He pointed to the scars on his cheeks. "These are the signs of my work."

"I won't take a Catholic."

"It was given to me on the ship."

"Remove it then," the cooper said. "It is against the law to teach the Popish religion. The penalty is execution."

Kwasi removed the crucifix and put it the bundle with the bloody cat's tooth.

FEARING THAT SPAIN WAS LAUNCHING an invasion against the English colonies to the south of New York, British troops in the city were redeployed, leaving only a handful of soldiers barracked at Ft. George and untrained militiamen for protection. After working for the cooper for a few months, Kwasi found work better suited to his skill, at a blacksmith's shop. He quickly adapted to the different style furnace and became a valuable employee. He slept in the room in the back of the store. "Can you make these?" the blacksmith asked, gesturing at Kwasi's *navaja*. "I've not seen anything like this. It will be popular, I'm certain."

Kwasi knew he would do better if he owned his own business, as he had in Komenda, but he was stymied in purchasing a vacant store in which to put a furnace— Negroes were barred from owning real property. This was one of the regulations that rankled him. Another was the ban of buying food from black farmers. Since Negroes were forbidden to sell their produce, he had to buy his fruits and vegetables from whites at the market. The ban on mingling with slaves in taverns he ignored, as the sheriff had no interest in enforcing the law that was so widely flouted.

By Christmas, when the snow began to fall day after day without let-up, covering houses two stories high, Kwasi made his first folding knife.

Then cold, unlike any experienced by the colonist, descended on New York. Working the furnace kept Kwasi warm but as soon as he stepped away from the glowing fire he began to shake. He shared the observation of the *Weekly Journal's* correspondent who said, "While I am writing in a warm room by a good fireside, the ink freezes in the quill pen."

More than ink froze. Narrows and channels choked with ice. The North River was solid as far as Poughkeepsie. People and even an occasional horse walked across the water from Manhattan to New Jersey. Kwasi couldn't stay outside long enough to put on a pair of ice skates, an item in demand in the blacksmith's shop by Dutch families.

The cold's grip had wrung the city into near submission. No provisions could reach New York until the end of March. By then there was little food to eat and several poor residents died from lack of firewood. Traffic came to a halt, streets were deserted. "Look for yourself, Kwasi. We haven't had a patron in a week. I can't pay you until I get money myself. But you can stay in the room. There'll be no charge. And as soon as I am able, I will resume your pay."

"I'll find somewhere else," Kwasi said, knowing full well that he would die before finding shelter.

"You can eat with my wife and me. I can't do more."

The blacksmith needed him, Kwasi was now certain. He was in a good bargaining position.

"No charge for the food."

"No charge," the blacksmith conceded.

THE SIEGE OF BRUTAL WEATHER lifted but life didn't return to normal. Kwasi first noticed the difference when he returned to his favorite tavern. It was as though the months of confinement needed to be made up for with bawdy drunkenness, as though every night were making up for the snowed-out Christmas revelry. Kwasi had never gotten used to the white man's alcohol; his only concession to drink was cider. He went to the taverns for the company and entertainment. As for drink—better to use his money for moving to another city. In Philadelphia and Boston blacks could own property, he learned.

Soon after arriving in New York, Kwasi had asked if anyone had seen his woman from the Gold Coast. The long winter finally convinced him of the futility of his search: Antobam had gone to another world and was beyond redeeming. As if it were a consolation, a patron at the blacksmith told Kwasi that he could have a woman for the night, and for right price he could even rent a white woman, one of the indentured bar maids at the Black Horse. Leasing a woman Kwasi found to be repulsive. The winter confinement also created a kind of madness in Will, a watchmaker's slave. Every time Kwasi came to the tavern, Will would be there, drinking more heavily than most. Kwasi would rather avoid the man who bragged about participating in an uprising in Antigua.

This night the more Will drank the more he lauded someone named Cudjoe, in Jamaica, who led a group of freed slaves in the mountains.

"They'll wind up like you," someone at the table said. "Next year you'll be drawing water with them at the well. They'll be just like you—a slave!"

Will shoved the table aside, squeezing Kwasi against the wall, and stood up. He shouted above the din.

"You is all cowards."

"*You* is the fool. Keep your voice down and your seditious opinions to yourself. I don't want my head mounted on a spike."

"You deserve your chains."

Kwasi pushed the table away from him and began to leave.

"And you is the worst coward. You won't even listen."

Kwasi tightened his strong fist.

"Keep your mouth shut, Will. You'll get us all hanged by tomorrow."

"If you keep your knife in your pocket, you may as well be dead." Will jumped on a table. "And the rest of you, if you keep your guns under your pillows, what good are they?"

"Don't you doubt they won't kill us all."

"You're already as good as dead."

"It's slavery that's as good as dead," a mulatto said. "Our shackles will soon be removed."

"You'll be long sleeping in your grave before that happens." Black Horse's owner, John Hughson, who had been in the adjacent room, burst in.

"Enough, Will," the white man demanded. "The law has big ears. Get out before all of us will regret the night. You ain't in your right head."

No one bore Kwasi ill will. So it surprised him when Quack confronted him after Will left.

"I saw you looking," Quack accused Kwasi. "When all eyes were on Will, you was looking up and down my Irish beauty. You do anything with Mary, I'll kill you."

"You can have her. There are other beavers in the dam, black ones, more to my liking."

As Quack towered over the seated blacksmith, Kwasi reached into his pocket to hold his knife.

"Will was enough trouble, Quack. Cool down. The white woman is nothing to me."

The publican intervened.

"Come back, Quack," Hughson said. "We're not done. It's enough that I have all you Negroes congregating and drinking. Don't make more trouble, Quack. Let's finish our work."

He reached for Quack's arm.

"I'll do business with you, but get your hand off me, white man."

"We're both businessmen, Quack. Nothing more."

Everyone in Black Horse knew the kind of business they were engaged in—the slave bringing in stolen goods, then Hughson reselling the items to shipmates just before they left port or to households on Long Island. City officials suspected the thief and his fence but never had sufficient evidence to convict either.

And then the city began to burn. From the blacksmith shed, Kwasi saw smoke billowing from the direction of Half Moon Bay. The alarm bells rang. Kwasi ran towards the fire. At Ft. George he joined the bucket brigade, assisting fire engines with leaking hoses. There was nothing to be done to save the fort. The governor stood outside the walls half-dressed, without his wig, his charred furniture still smoldering. The house collapsed and sparks flew over the walls and soon the chapel was consumed, then the army barracks, the armory and the secretary's house—nothing left but ashes and smoke. As Kwasi and the firefighters were returning up the cobbled Broad Way, an explosion in the fort's gunpowder magazine rocked the earth.

Fires were commonplace enough that Kwasi didn't give the Ft. George conflagration much thought until the next one, a week later, that razed a warehouse along the East River on April Fool's Day. What followed caused Kwasi to join with others in suspecting more: a cow stable burned; Ben Thomas's house burned; a haystack fire spread to an attorney's house; the fire at Sergeant Burn's house was doused before damage could be done; then the fire next to the Thomas house. On another day, four alarms were sounded, leaving a waterfront warehouse in ruins, a storehouse useless and rendering two dwellings unlivable.

The city was aflame and suspicions pointed to a Negro conspiracy when a firefighter pursued a fleeing black man.

"A Negro, stop the Negro," he called.

What Kwasi heard in front of the blacksmith shed was "The Negroes are rising!"

Kwasi assured the blacksmith he knew nothing about a planned uprising or any of the men who may have started the fires. That he had suspicions he kept to himself.

Before the day was out, six black men were arrested. This didn't satisfy the citizenry. There had be a wider conspiracy. One hundred pounds offered to a white person who could lead them to a conviction; twenty pounds to a slave whose tip lead to a conviction. In addition, the slave would be made free, his master compensated twenty-five pounds. A free Negro, mulatto or Indian would receive forty-five pounds.

Forty-five pounds would be enough to open a shop of his own. The temptation to report Will or Quack was great, but he would receive the reward only if they were convicted. And if they were released, his life would be in jeopardy.

Before he decided that he would tell the sheriff about Will, another wave of arrests swept the city. Hughson and Quack were amongst those standing trial. One of the indentured tavern girls said she heard Quack say, "When all this is done, I will be governor and Hughson should be king."

The day after one of the accused testified to Spanish Negroes setting fires, a constable arrested Kwasi.

"That's him," the blacksmith said. "Ask him to show you his knife. It's Spanish. And look in his room. I saw a Popish cross there myself."

Kwasi shared the jail cell under City Hall with Will. It quickly filled so there was barely enough room to sit, all men but for two women.

Quack was convicted and taken from his cell. Kwasi and the other detained men were taken to follow Quack's wagon that trundled to the scaffold site. By the time they reached Little Collect, a huge crowd had gathered. Kwasi stood beside Will as they saw Quack chained to a wooden post and kindling gathered at his feet. The crowd shouted for the sheriff to hurry and finish the work. Quack begged for mercy.

"I set the storehouse fire with lighted charcoal," he said. "And put a lighted stick under the shingles of the governor's house."

With his back to the stake, Quack continued to name others involved in the plot.

The crowd wanted no part of mercy. They told the sheriff to get on with it. As the sheriff lit the pile, Kwasi closed his eyes. The smell of burning flesh made him sick. The cartful of detained returned to City Hall. Quacks body remained on the scaffold until the birds and rats left only bones.

Kwasi, squatting in the middle of the crowded cell, saw Will take a knife from his boot. He hunched down further so that Will would have to climb over others before reaching him. Will stood with his back to Kwasi and his face to the barred window. He raised the knife above his head and plunge it downward. Will collapsed to the floor and hours later his body was removed by the jailer.

Allegations tumbled faster than the jail could accommodate the accused. More than one hundred were packed in the basement jail. They heard that Hughson had been hanged and gibbeted.

In mid-summer the jail doors were opened. He along with dozens of others was placed on carts again. But they were not tied this time and, instead of heading north to the Collect, they went east to the docks where they were being sorted. One group boarded a ship bound for Newfoundland. Kwasi was taken aboard another sloop. By this time the city had hanged twelve and burned eleven. He was one of eighty-three transported from the colony, the only African-born man.

Kwasi didn't know his destination.

SALLY

The Snow Penguin

SALLY MACSWEENEY leaves her sub-tenant farm at Athnowen with little trepidation. She has thought about sailing away for months as she watches her mother, two sisters and one brother die during the endless, bitter cold unlike any other winter in memory. Storage proves useless to protect the meager crop of potatoes; they are destroyed before spring. Compounding the adversity is the failure of the oats and other tillage crops and the death of the milk cow. In early winter they had herring and river fish provided by the landlord, but none since the great freeze.

Blocks of peat placed around the one room mud cabin keep at bay the hollowing winds that blow without stop. Still, even lacking a window or chimney, inside has never been so cold. Eight huddled bodies lend little warmth.

Sally's father has left the farm in hope of finding work in Munster's counties where, as before, he would be given a half acre of land in exchange for labor. He leans upon his spade the day before he leaves him, faint from want of food. The children will care for themselves, he says, for he can't any longer provide for them. As the oldest and there being no boys, Sally will be in charge until he returns, he says. Sally doesn't believe that he will come back.

She is right. He may have died from starvation or perhaps has indentured himself as thousands have done, to leave behind a brutish life that would never get better—no sub-tenant's life did. As soon as the farm is improved, taxes will be increased. It is better to raise just enough to feed the family. The Duke of Devonshire's estate is better managed than most but when Sally's father discovers that he will be unable to pay the tax, as small as it is, on the November gale day, a law officer is certain to appear with a notice to leave the stony farm.

Fantastic tales from the American colonies reach Sally, each story beyond comprehension, all beyond her belief. But as faith has carried her across the tribulations of this life, she thinks that faith will carry her across the turbulent waters to the new world.

After her father's disappearance and púcas begin to haunt the nights around the hut, Sally is certain she will join many others and emigrate. These shape-shifting spirits have been frequent visitors in the townlands since the English Undertakers, the wealthy colonists who established the Munster Plantation, arrived. The spirits sometimes appear as protectors, other times as mischievous beings. Because this fall there hasn't been enough in the harvest to leave the púcas their share of the crop, Sally knows it is a púca that beckons her. She wakes her siblings and brings them to the doorway. All the children agree with Sally—there is a goat bathed in moonlight. All the other ruminants are dead, but only Sally hears her name in each bleat.

During the day she spots a large rabbit at the top a rock outcropping.

One night she refuses to come out of her house when enticed by a black horse with a flowing mane and piercing, golden eyes that shine as bright as noonday sun. The púca gallops on top of the limestone boundary wall. 'Let me take you to the river, come ride me,' but she won't be fooled by so clearly a lie. This creature, she knows, would drown her and devour her.

She won't be taken against her will but will rely upon her own feet to carry her to the water.

If a spirit decides to follow her to the sea and wreck her sailing ship against the rocky shore, as they sometimes do, that was a chance she is ready to take.

Púcas can live only in Ireland, Sally believes, so she will be safe from them across the ocean. Or if one does manage to conceal itself on the ship along with its passengers and sailors, she is certain it would show its benevolent side and protect her, just as the spirits have chased many English tenants back to their own country years before.

The allure of the continent on the Atlantic's far side is great. She knows for certain that one Englishman brought ironworkers to a plantation and that the Gaels now owned the land themselves. And cottiers like herself, Sally believes, have acquired estates with deer parks and established themselves as gentry beyond their lot in Ireland. Her progeny will one day have their own townland in America.

Still dangers lurk. There are pagans who eat their captives and Africans as dark as a crow.

Unlike her father who said that he would return, Sally walks away without a goodbye and has no intention of coming back.

SALLY STOPS BESIDE *THE PENGUIN*, a snow, as it lays in Corcaigh port, at Lot's wharf, as goods from America are offloaded on the quay and the vessel is made ready for the return trip to Philadelphia. The vessel has plied the Atlantic several times arriving in Ireland laden with lumber and tobacco. This year Éire has little to offer—Irish beef in tierces, a few firkins of butter but no linen or salmon or clover seed. In substitute for the paltry offerings, the island provides labor, on this snow forty-nine men, women and children.

Gabriel Butler approaches Sally on the pier with the prospect of a new life—a future of limitless prosperity— and she reluctantly agrees. When she overhears someone refer to the ship as a 'snow,' Sally is hesitant. Although rivers have frozen over for seven weeks and an ox has been roasted on the ice, there has been no snow and the ground is bone dry. The thought of being bound on a vessel full of snow for the ocean journey, even if at the end it would be in the clement Caribbean, makes the memory of the year past even keener. Is the vessel's name a sign to her, a warning? There is no thought about returning to Athnowen. Seeing an abandoned newborn being eaten by a pig is enough to ensure she wouldn't go back. But perhaps it is best to wait for another ship with a more auspicious name, one whose bowsprit doesn't resemble anything as much as a raised spike.

"But I've got no means," Sally says. She wants to stare at Butler, a man of such corporeality. Unlike the rawboned men she knows, he looks hale and thriving. His clothes have no repairs. Her face flushes as she stands before him with an uncovered head, her cap left behind in the hut. How could her stomach hurt, she wonders as she glanced at Butler's fleshed jowls, when her bowels have been emptied by dysentery?

Butler assures her that money is no matter. Instead of being dismissed because of her penury, to her amazement Butler offers an advance of £100, the cost of the travel, and tells her that she can repay the debt over the next three years once she was in the colonies.

Sally is near accepting the offer that seemed as though a blessing from God had descended upon her but she stops herself. She raises her eyes furtively and notes that the solicitor's frock reached to his knees, an uncommon cut for men on the quay. Púcas were known to shift to human forms, with pointed ears and tails giving away their true character. Butler's ears appear normal but she suspects what he had hidden behind.

When a gust of wind whips Butler's coat upward, revealing the upper part of his trousers, Sally turns to run from the dockside.

"Wench," he says sternly as he grasps her by the shoulder, "don't be foolish."

"I don't want to go!"

His fingernails pierce her thin skin. She feels the shoulder dislodge from its socket.

"What will a maiden like you do? I can send you to the workhouse. I am on the Board of Governors."

Sally looks blankly.

"Is that what you want? There is only punishment for vagabonds like you."

Sally is mute.

"I also can see that there will be no further relief for the parish you inhabit. You wouldn't want that, would you?"

The púca has given her fair warning. She is uncertain how to take it.

Her attempts to wrench free are constrained by the pain that radiates down her arm.

"I'm no vagabond."

"Such obstinacy. You'll be brought to goodness despite yourself or you will walk the streets to lead a wastrel's life, I warn you. You'll be a dissolute woman. Look around. You will regret your decision if you stay. I've taken on board one convict and I can easily replace him with you."

Sally squirms under his grip.

"Take her." Butler motions to a sailor standing on the larboard side of the *Penguin*. "She'll be the last. There's no more. She has nothing to bring."

The shipmate takes Sally from Butler's clutch and brings her to the steerage. With his quota filled, Butler has no more to do with her and leaves for one of many taverns along the wharf.

Sally can't stand upright as the sloop rocked. Below deck she stumbles beside a sleeping man reeking from the familiar aroma of smoke and the boiling wash of poitín. Her father's face flashes before her but even in the dark she can see that this man was much younger than the man who abandoned her home. As her eyes adjust to the dark she sees men and women spread on berths. She hears babies crying.

She places herself on planks far from single men, between the berths of husbands and wives. One husband sits at the foot of the small bed, the other's wife places herself across her husband's body. The emigrants' chattel is scattered about them; items are tied securely to posts, knobs, rafters and hooks.

Sally isn't the only child on board but she is the only one without human attachments. Her sole possession is her dress.

A flurry of activity sounds above: the pounding of feet moving around the deck, ropes untied, calls from ship to shore, sails unfurled and then the movement of the vessel slipping out to sea. Before the port dips behind the horizon, Sally closes her eyes, expecting not to wake and soon knowing the flames of hell.

Throughout the seven-week journey Sally stays close to families for protection. She learns that the *Penguin,* a square-rigged ship with two masts that was one of the smaller vessels in the harbor, is filled with those who came out of necessity and those out of choice. She is the only one brought against her will, the only one without papers indicating a debt. "I'm a weaver and my husband is a school teacher," Jane Kirwan tells Sally beside whose bed she had prostrated herself. Others are skilled workers of various sorts. One is a pardoned convict, referred to as a 'king's passenger.'

"We're the ballast for the ship," Jane's husband, Martin, says. "We don't have sufficient money for the passage, but it will be paid for when we arrive and we'll repay the debt with our service when we reach Pennsylvania."

She has not heard of Pennsylvania and thinks it is one of the islands in the Caribbean where many Irish had gone before. Over the next few weeks Sally comes to understand where they were headed and learns about the system that brought most of the ship's migrants to America.

"We are redemptioners ourselves," Martin Kirwan continues. "Not everyone is. But we are. There will be relations, or someone they have sent, who will be waiting for us when we arrive in Philadelphia."

Jane tells Sally that when the bond was paid they will be given land that will be their own.

"We have a letter from Mr. Kirwan's brother. Read it to her, Martin."

He takes out folded papers.

> *It is a beautiful panorama of forest and plain spread out in all their beauty that meets you everywhere. In the not very far distant future this will become the happy home of intelligent, God-fearing people.*

Not all seventy-five passengers are in such an arrangement. Others have negotiated the terms of their passage with an agent and entered a contract with the master of the ship. The captain, Robert Morris, would resell the contract to a buyer upon the ship's arrival in the colony. They will then be in servitude for the terms of the original contract, for three or more years, until the debt incurred has been acquitted.

"And you, Sally, did your guardian arrange to sell you?"

"No," she answers.

"You aren't yet of age to enter into a contract by my eyes."

Sally doesn't understand the comment.

Martin continues. "Where was the magistrate who arranged for your indenture without a guardian's approval? Did he give you papers?"

"No," she said. "No magistrate was involved with me. I'm not a vagabond. Why should I have seen a magistrate?" She told him that she had been grabbed against her will. She had no contract, no paper agreement detailing the terms of her service.

"The merchant threatened to exchange me for the criminal he said he had taken. But I didn't want to come on this ship."

Martin tells her that the young man she is referring to had been pardoned by the court for his breaking and entering a factory storing hard cheeses destined to London on the condition that he would serve as an indentured servant for seven years in a quarry. If he violates the terms of the agreement, Martin explains, he will be returned to Ireland and hanged.

"But for you, Sally, what you say means you will be a servant, not an apprentice, according to law. You won't be free until you come of age. There will be no instruction for you. Lodging and washing will be provided for you, but you will be property until then."

Jane worries for Sally. She examines Sally's arm purpling from her injury. Tearing a piece of cloth from the bottom of her own dress, she creates a sling to support Sally's damaged shoulder. As Sally lays at the foot of Martin and Jane's berth that night, Jane asks, "We can claim you as our daughter. Would you like that, Sally?"

Sally says nothing. She hasn't heard Jane Kirwan's proposal or that their own daughter had died the year previously. Sally is asleep from exhaustion. Jane takes her silence for agreement.

Martin begins to teach Sally to read. She quickly learns the alphabet and acquires the ability to read simple words and rudimentary sentences. As long as there is light and persistent weakness doesn't overcome her, Sally applies herself under the schoolteacher's guidance.

THE FIRST FEW DAYS ARE singularly quiet in the steerage. Lethargy pervades everyone except for the man from Ulster who says that while he was no preacher he would hold daily prayer meetings on deck with the few Presbyterian and Anglo-Irish passengers and crew to maintain their spirits. When Martin is too tired to teach her from his lesson book, the Ulsterman, who sees that Sally has no crucifix hanging from her neck, helps her read with the aid of his Bible. Sally doesn't know that anyone other than a priest could possess or even hold one. He teaches her simple prayers to recite herself. She prays that the púca will leave her alone.

Not long after the ship is at sea passengers grow sick; lice multiply and crawl from their skulls and onto their skin. The day after Sally's fever breaks Jane scrapes the parasites from Sally's armpits with a knife and shaves her hair to her scalp. During one storm, immigrants moan and pray when mountains of waves crash across the deck and passengers tumble over one another, releasing what little contents their stomachs and bowels contain, as the snow rolls for two days during vicious gales.

In the journal he keeps, Martin writes:

> *During the voyage there is on board terrible misery, stench, fumes, horror, vomiting, many kinds of sea-sickness, fever, dysentery, headache, heat, constipation, boils, scurvy, cancer, mouth-rot, and the like, all of which come from old and sharply salted food and meat, also from very bad and foul water.*

A mother with a nursing infant is the first to die, before the ship is halfway to Philadelphia. There is no other mother with milk to spare. As the Ulsterman commends their souls to God's mercy, the corpse and the sniveling infant are sunk in the water.

More deaths follow.

> *There is want of provisions, hunger, thirst, frost, heat, dampness, anxiety, want, afflictions and lamentations. Yesterday, just as we had a heavy gale, a woman in our ship, who was to give birth and could not give birth under the circumstances, was pushed through a loop-hole in the ship and dropped into the sea, because she was far in the rear of the ship and could not be brought forward.*

Twice a week small quantities of warm food are served. Like many others, Sally thinks the provisions inedible. There is no choice but to drink the thick, black water full of worms, however.

One day Jane restrains Sally from jumping into the turbid sea after Sally sees a mother leap into the ocean after her deceased child. Martin writes. *"Many people whimper, sigh and cry piteously for their homes; most of them get homesick."*

In another entry he notes, *"Scores necessarily die and perish in such misery, and must be cast into the sea, which drives their relatives, or those who persuaded them to undertake the journey, to such despair that it is almost impossible to pacify and console them."*

By the fifth week, matters become more desperate. Martin writes, *"We are compelled to eat the ship's biscuit which had been spoiled long ago; though in a whole biscuit there was scarcely a, piece the size of a dollar that had not been full of red worms and spider's nests."*

Nearly half the passengers are dead before they reached Pennsylvania. If a relative remains, they will now also have to serve the indentured time of the deceased.

While at sea, there were events in Ireland which passengers heard about months after landing: rioters broke into food stores in Dublin, stole bread from bakeries, and sold pilfered grain at discount prices to the city's hungry. Soldiers from the Royal Barracks killed several rioters. In Drogheda, a mob removed the rudder and tore the sails of a ship filled with oatmeal that was preparing to leave for Scotland. A counting in Ireland revealed that thousands of barrels of stored grain were stored on the estates of English farmers.

The weather in Ireland that followed the *Penguin's* departure is bleaker than the previous year. Blizzards batter County Cork in autumn. A brief warm spell follows with terrific rainstorms washing away the season's meager harvest. More riots erupt as famine and fevers worse than what Sally had known in Athnowen ravage Éire through the winter months. If the thought of returning home has entered anyone's mind, it is dispelled when they receive such news.

Land is first sighted at night, with a fire burning in a wooden, whale-oil lighthouse atop a dune, as a beacon warning against foundering on the rough shoals. The captain knows they would not be the first to be wrecked upon the shore.

In the morning, America's promontories come into view. Those who are able crawl from below and shed tears of joy. The Ulsterman offers a prayer and the Catholics make the sign of the cross.

Martin and Jane are among the few that haven't been widowed during the voyage. Half the migrants are in the ocean grave. And of all the children who have departed from Cork on the *Penguin*, Sally is the only one to survive when the snow lowers its sails at its first call in the colony.

There is little to be seen as they wait offshore, just dunes higher crested with coarse grass that is higher than the sails of the ship. An officer and a mate climb into a longboat and row to land. Just to the north are a few houses and the tops of masts can be seen in an inlet. Within a short time the crew returns with another person. Instead of debarking, as the passengers had expected, the snow lifts anchor and they continue to sail.

Morris isn't going to navigate these waters alone. He, like every ocean-going captain, has reads published report about the dangerous shoreline and the sinking of ships on their final leg of the ocean voyage.

The passage from the Virginia Capes to Philadelphia is littered with broken ground, sand pits and shoals, creating such a treacherous sail to Philadelphia that it is necessary to get a local pilot from the colony to steer them safely up the river to their port. Without such aid, the *Penguin* wouldn't be the first to have successfully crossed the Atlantic only to be snared in the hazards, stranded or split within walking distance of redemption and profit.

To Murderkill Hundred

BEFORE DOCKING, the *Penguin* anchored near Province Island, at the confluence of the Delaware and Schuylkill Rivers.

Dr. Nazaro, an inspector from the Pennsylvania colony, boarded to examine the passengers and crew that awaited him on deck. The doctor walked amongst them and stopped before Sally, her body caked with grime and her pale skin marred with ulcers. He looked at Sally's dress that came halfway down her thighs; he noted the sling. She looked feverish.

The inspector backed away from her and leaned against a capstan, staining his frocked vest with grease. "It is the shoulder," Martin offered before the inspector could talk to Sally. Several passengers separated Sally from Martin and Jane. "It is on the mend."

"Is she your daughter?" the doctor asked.

"She is."

Martin pressed his way closer to the inspector who wore cinnamon colored breeches with puffs tied at his knees. Martin was too fatigued to be embarrassed about his own appearance. Sally's appearance was poorer than Martin's but after the exhaustive journey the difference wasn't so great as to cause skepticism on Nazaro's part. Martin, too, looked like a peasant.

"She seems feverish."

"No, she is not, sir. I assure you it is only her arm that is the bother. It was injured during the crossing. Nothing more. She has no contagion."

49

That she may be permanently disabled and not what had been bargained for when she left Cork was of no concern to the doctor. Her reduced value would be sorted out at Market Wharf as the terms of the contracts were confirmed and accounts settled.

After considering Sally's medical condition, the doctor concluded there was no reason to remove her.

"Is this everyone?" he asked Captain Morris.

"There are two below," Morris responded. He held on to his tricorn to keep it from blowing from his head as the wind snapped the snow's studding sails. "They are ailing and couldn't come on deck."

"No others?"

"The fevers were few."

Nazaro removed his hat as he descended the ladder to look at a nailer and a sawyer both of whom burned with fevers. The inspector, although accustomed to such malodorous spaces, gagged—the open hatch had not yet let in enough fresh air to be fumigated. Standing at the foot of the ladder, he ordered the tradesmen removed from the snow to be quarantined at the island, in the Pest House. They would remain there until either they recovered or died. The stench from the shrub-covered island, where a hospital to house sick immigrants was under construction, wafted to the ship, leaving little doubt as to the fate that awaited them.

In the port of Philadelphia, the merchants boarded the vessel. Redemptioners stood aside as the others examined for their physical state and questioned about their skills.

More bustling than the port in Cork, the quay in Philadelphia was filled with ships that dwarfed the *Penguin* and the wharves groaned with plunder none of its passenger had seen before. There were merchants, seamen, stevedores and agents hauling and haggling, examining papers and filing forms; the air hung heavy with the smell of varnish, pitch, pine tar and turpentine. Cables and chains smacked and clanged against the forest of masts.

"I'm wanting the butcher and millwright," one merchant called.

There were requests for upholsterers, butchers, barbers, coopers, bricklayers and breeches makers.

"A cordwainer. I need a cordwainer."

"Who wants a joiner?" Morris asked.

A nailer, joiner, currier and two saddlers—all advertised— had died in transit.

"I'll take a soap maker."

Negotiations continued all the morning. In the afternoon, redemptionists waiting with their chattel on deck were claimed.

WHEN ALL THE VOYAGERS had debarked, the Kirwans and Sally remained as the only human cargo.

"Where is your surety?" Morris asked Martin. "There's no one here to claim you."

Jane, feeling faint, clasped Sally to her side.

"He will be here."

"I heard you tell the inspector this vagabond is your daughter." Morris couldn't admit to having the girl who had been snatched onboard, taken against her will and without papers. That practice was now illegal, although often indulged in, but if he were caught, the captain would have to pay a fine on top of losing the cost of her transport. By Kirwan claiming her as family they did him a favor. "I will accept the truth of that when I receive the payment for you and your wife. There must be payment for three when you are redeemed."

"You needn't worry. You will receive the proper amount," Martin said.

"I can assure you I will. But until that time when I have it in hand, all of you will remain on the ship. You won't be going ashore before the payment is complete."

Martin was aware that if no one claimed them within two weeks, they would be sold as indentured. That's not why he left Ireland, to be put into another's debt.

"How am I to inform my cousin to get your money if I am confined and can't bring him?" Martin asked. "There must have been confusion. I think he's waiting at another quay or perhaps the date he has for our arrival was incorrect. I think that perhaps we had unexpected winds and arrived early."

"We were two days late in schedule."

"Won't you let me find him? There is no good for either of us if we aren't redeemed."

Capt. Morris ignored the request. In the past redemptionists absconded into the backcountry, allegedly in search of their benefactors, creating a loss for a captain and a ship's investors.

Morris calculated and decided that Kirwin was wrong; it was in the captain's favor that the family not be redeemed. If they remained unclaimed, he would be free to negotiate a better price with an agent and keep the difference of the greater cost. His bargaining powers, he believed, were as prodigious as he ability to command a ship. There was little possibility that Kirwan would jump the *Penguin*. A man alone could manage but not with a wife and a child in tow.

For the first time in weeks their food on the snow was edible. They eagerly ate the Indian corn bread and vegetable gruels given to them twice a day. This was more food than Sally had seen in a year.

"Do you know why we've come, Sally?"

"To eat," she said.

"Yes, but more. Our relatives have prospered and the land is very beautiful. I have with me a letter they've written."

Martin took out a sheaf of papers and slowly, as he continued to teach Sally to read, read the letter aloud.

It is not the grandeur of rocks, cascades and romantic glens, but it is the beautiful panorama of forest and plain spread out in all their beauty which meets you everywhere.

Sally didn't understand all the words but the very sound of Martin's voice soothed her.

Jane placed Sally's hand in her own. Sally held the Bible in her other. They sat under the shade of a furled sail as Martin read to them.

The stone house, in which the Widow Piper now keeps tavern, is a good substantial two-story house. The stone house at the Branch is also a very fine house, a large, square, stone building for a distillery.

On the second morning Jane found Sally near the ship's prow with a Bible on her lap.

"Where did you get that, Sally?"

"From the man who taught me to pray."

"He gave it to you?"

Sally pressed the book against her chest.

"Take ahold of my rosary. I forbid you to read from it. Give it to me."

Sally wouldn't let go.

"No harm, Jane," Martin said. "She makes no sense of it yet. We will get her a crucifix when we settle and bring her to church with us. Until then, let this do. She is learning to read."

When Martin and Sally dozed in the afternoon, Sally ran her index finger along the lines of the Bible, picking out the words she could read.

Later in the day, Martin read from the letter again.

A quarrel occurred last night out at the Spring amongst a party of drunken Indians, during which, four of their cabins were set on fire, and burned to the ground.

Sally listened intently.

The first time she saw them Sally mistook the men on the docks as chimney sweeps but when she realized these were the Africans she had heard about, she ran to the vessel's starboard side. And now this letter brings news that Indians are setting fires at her prospective home. Beyond a doubt púcas had crossed the ocean with others from Ireland.

"Is something the matter, Sally?"

"No," she said.

Martin placed the page behind the others and continued to read.

These savages will give us trouble yet. I have no confidence in the friendship of these savages, and have always felt that we have been warming a viper which will someday show us its fangs. Our only safety, in my opinion, depends wholly upon our vigilance and the preparation we make in our defence.

Despite the grim weeks at sea, Sally chose not to sleep on deck with the Kirwans, but go below to the steerage, closing the hatch behind her, shutting herself in the dark and curling into a ball, pulling her dress down to cover her legs. She held the Bible tightly.

She had not been asleep very long when whinnying startled her. Two shafts of light pierced the darkness. The púca!—there it was, in the hold alone with her. She felt its moist breath and heard the rhythmic slapping of its tail against the boards. Sally bolted to the ladder and when she pushed the hatch open, shielded her eyes from the rising sun.

From the deck Jane looked down at Martin on the quay who was engaged in conversation with a stranger standing next to a horse and wagon.

"Come down here, girl," Morris commanded. Sally joined him on the dock.

"I can't take her."

"But we can't leave her here. She's alone."

"I have enough for you and Jane. Not three."

"There must be a way. I'll pledge the money," Martin said turning to the captain.

Morris shook his head.

"You are released upon payment. If there is money for the girl, she can go. I don't deal in credit."

"She just a child," Martin said to his cousin. "She'll be a good addition to the village. She's of good character."

"Character or no, she's no good." He scrutinized Sally. "Her arm makes her useless."

Martin made one more attempt to persuade his cousin. "This isn't my choice, Martin. If I had known you had a child before, I could have made arrangements with others in Shippen. There could have been money enough. But I don't have more to pay. There is a contract and that is the amount I have." He turned to Morris. "Will you take a pledge from me?"

The captain shook his head again.

"I sail back to Ireland before I'll see your money. With so many lost," he explained, "profits are already at the margins."

The Kirwans asked for the chest to be given to them. When it was brought on deck, they discovered that it had been broken into and nothing was left. Everything of value they had brought with them was gone. Demanding that his goods be returned was futile. Martin took the chest and heaved it over the side and walked to the buggy.

Jane took out a cap from her bundle and placed it on Sally's head.

"Thank you, Miss," Sally said.

Jane tied the bow under Sally's chin.

Martin handed Sally an envelope.

"Here are the letters. You can continue to learn from them. Keep them. You will be able to find us."

Sally placed the letter in her Bible.

Martin and Jane climbed into the wagon and drove down the rutted, dirty Water Street without looking at Sally. The captain waited with her until the redemptionists passed the storehouses and turned the corner at MacLeod's ship-chandlery.

AS SOON AS THE KIRWANS disappeared, Morris engaged an agent on the wharf. Gathered near the soul driver were more than twenty men, their legs tied to one another, their hands tied to each other.

"£100," he said, with Sally beside him.

The agent, Joseph Hayward, rejected the price out of hand.

"She's young."

"Her arm . . ."

"That will heal," Morris tried to assure him.

Sally's had no fever, so the soul driver looked closely at her.

"Take off your cap."

Sally removed the hat.

"Her scalp has lice," Hayward said.

Morris didn't respond. Scarcely a migrant arrived without parasites.

The agent looked into Sally's eyes and then examined her legs and bare feet. Sally winced as he grabbed her shoulder.

"That is permanent damage," the agent said as he released his grip. "She'll be almost impossible for me to sell."

Morris lowered his price again.

"Do you have papers for her?"

"They were lost."

"I can't properly register her then. She is worthless if I am caught."

Morris reduced the terms once more.

Hayward turned to walk away without a counter offer. Morris took him by the sleeve.

What final conditions the captain and the soul driver agreed upon Sally didn't know.

With the sun at its apogee, she was tethered to the others on the wharf and the group began their trek from the city. It was a slow walk until the sun set. Sally had some difficulty keeping up with the stronger men. Occasionally Hayward gave her some water and biscuit. The group stopped for the night and bivouacked beside a tavern that also provided food and lodging for travelers. Hayward left them tied to one another, went inside and returned with food to the servants from the ordinary. After seeing that everyone was secured for the night, he returned to the inn.

As he sat with a pint of rye whiskey in front of the open hearth waiting for his dinner, another traveler joined him at the plank table.

Hayward told him his business.

"I'm bringing them to Cumberland Valley. There are contracts there but if you are interested, I can transfer one to you."

"No. I have no need for a servant. I am on the move too much. But we are in the same line of business, in a way."

"And that is?"

"I bring back runaways. So perhaps you can be of assistance to me," the man with the bulbous nose said to Hayward. "Where did you say you was coming from?"

"Philadelphia."

"Then maybe you have seen the two I am looking for. One's a Shropshire man, about 26 years of age." He continued to describe a tall slender man, long visage, brown hair, wearing a felt hat and blue jacket.

Hayward thought for a moment and said that he hadn't seen anyone matching the description.

"No help, I'm afraid."

"If you take up and secure him," the soul catcher said, "there is a five- pound reward. And reasonable charges will also be paid."

A third traveler, plainly dressed, joined Hayward and his tablemate in the smoke-filled, crowded taproom. From Valentine Cogwill's unstylish brown jacket, a waistcoat free of edging—his clothes lacking ostentation whatsoever—Hayward concluded that this supper companion was a Quaker.

Cogwill's hat, the brim uncocked, remained on his head throughout the evening.

As soon as Cogwill sat, he was handed a flier with a description of the two runaways. He read it carefully, giving it some thought.

"I've seen no one like this," he said.

During the conversation, Cogwill told his tablemates that he was returning home to the Lower Counties.

Hayward asked several direct questions, which he declined to answer. But Cogwill did offer, "I had seen elders in Philadelphia to discuss forming a new Monthly Meeting, in Duck Creek, where I live."

Hayward wondered if he could interest Cogwill in the girl. The Quaker, he knew, would deal fairly and there would be no question that if he arranged credit with him, it would be paid without quarrel.

"I have one outside to sell. Perhaps you need a young female." He explained, "Having a girl in my convoy will be too much trouble for me in the weeks to come. I'm afraid she won't last even half the distance to Baltimore." Hayward lit his clay pipe. "I'll sell her to you at bargain price. You will do me a great favor if you take her off my hands."

The Quaker thought about the proposition. Before going to Philadelphia, he had planned that upon his return he would employ a servant girl. His neighbor had one and he was ready to buy out her contract and employ her himself. But just before leaving for Philadelphia, while the neighbor was at a meeting, the servant girl locked all the doors in the house and hanged herself.

Cogwill thought a better deal could be struck with Hayward in the morning, so gave no indication of his interest. After Hayward and the pursuer finished a pint and a long pipe of tobacco, they retired upstairs to divide a bed for the night. Cogwill slept outside in his wagon.

After his breakfast of buckwheat cakes, fried venison and cider, Hayward met the Quaker. Hayward offered Sally once more and seeing how eager Hayward was to exchange the contract, Cogwill drove a hard bargain and at the end of the negotiations, Sally was untied and now was in his indenture.

Hayward came away £3 richer than he had been that morning. Before leaving, the minder counted the numbers in the bivouac to discover that during the night, one of the Irishman had slipped through the ropes and went missing. Hayward's fortune was now diminished and he returned to Cogwill to re-open the arrangement. He interrupted the interchange between Sally and the Quaker.

"My book," she cried. "I want my book. Where is it?"

"You have no book. You ain't going running off on me. Stay here."

Hayward said he wanted more money for the girl.

"We haven't yet given me your hand. The deal is still to be made."

"You are not right. Your word is the seal. There's nothing more to be said."

"That was before I knew I was one short. The conditions have changed."

"Your conditions aren't my concern."

Cogwill ignored Hayward's entreaty. He turned his back on the agent and took Sally by her hand.

"What's your name, girl?"

She didn't answer.

"What's your name?"

She remained silent.

He asked again more sternly this time.

"Sally."

"Sally what?"

"MacSweeney," she said.

"Let's go, Sally MacSweeny."

Cogwill attempted to lift Sally onto the back of his bay. Looking at the waiting mare, she squirmed to loosen

Cogwill's grip. Her thin body shook so hard Cogwill feared she would break a bone.

"Come."

"No," she insisted.

As he lifted Sally onto the pillion behind his saddle, she cried from pain and muttered 'púca.' Sally clung to the strange man as she felt the horse shift from side-to-side as Cogwill left for his home in Murderkill Hundred. She stared at the man's back so she wouldn't see the horse's black mane or its flanks between her legs.

There were no papers for the girl and Cogwill would need them when he returned to the Lower Counties. When they reached New Castle, Cogwill visited the office of a lawyer.

"I need you to draw up papers as to her provenance," he said. Cogwill placed his coins on the table. Even with this expense, Sally came as a bargain.

On her journey to her new home Sally shut her eyes at the sight of Africans walking on the roads and working in fields beside English-looking men. She wrapped herself tightly in the blanket Cogwill provided. She heard noises in the nearby woods that she had never heard before and when the ghastly caw of a thousand crows darkened the sky for hours like dirt thrown into a dug hole, Sally tossed the woolen covering over her head hoping the world would disappear.

Five Can't Catch Me

ROLLING HILLS gave way to flat country on the second day of the trip, strange land alive with growing and moving things. There was no famine here, no bodies along the paths.

There was a brief but torrential downpour, then sun and flies and the steam off the horse's back. At first Sally swatted the flies from her eyes. Finally too tired to engage in an endless task, she allowed the flies to settle on her face.

The forever-dense greenness of forest, shadows and shafts of sunlight, tawny swamp water, unseen animals rustling in the underbrush—even at the end of the two-day journey, the wonderment of the landscape kept her awake. Mosquitoes left blood splatters.

"Púca," she muttered.

"What?"

Sally didn't answer.

At last they turned into a lane that passed through a mottled landscape of fallow and cultivated acreage that stretched from the front of Cogwill's brick house to a distant grove by a creek. Barking dogs brought Elinor to the porch to meet her husband. She first saw Valentine and the young woman by the paling fence. When they pulled up to the house, Cogwill lifted Sally off the horse and placed her on the ground. He dismounted, threw a blanket over her shoulders and approached his wife. Elinor hadn't expected to see anyone else with him.

Valentine and Elinor stood facing each other for several minutes without saying a word. Elinor looked over her husband's shoulder to see the wan girl tip forward in the saddle.

The woman's robust appearance frightened Sally and when she did speak it was with the same reproving quality that Sally had heard English women speak in Ireland, not at all like the lady on the *Penguin*.

"I've brought a new girl for you," Cogwill said as he took a step up to be closer to his wife.

"Do you think I need assistance?" Elinor asked.

"You can use thine freedom, good wife. This girl will be of assistance to you."

Elinor looked at the curled girl covered with a blanket.

"You will hire a girl for me if I need help. There are many idle hands this time of year. We don't need to assume a new contract."

"She will be steady with you and you can teach this one what you desire. It will be good for you to have another female around."

"I do fine without one," Elinor said. Despite Valentine's sincere acceptance of the Inner Light, not every man succeeded in taming his animal spirits.

"Since we hired out Belinda," Cogwill persisted, "you have had less time for charitable deeds."

"Then bring me back Belinda."

Cogwill reminded her that it was she who didn't want the Negro any longer and it was because of her insistence that he hired her out.

"She has a short contract. Two years and she will be returned."

He then presented the financial concern.

"Until then the rent I get for her is enough to buy the needed equipment to expand the farm, and is far more than the cost of this girl's contract. This girl's freedom dues," he said gesturing towards the carriage, "are in five years' time. I have a bargain in her."

Elinor dismissed her husband's remark with pursed lips. She doubted Valentine's business acumen but kept her tongue to herself. Besides, contrary to her husband's notion that having a servant girl would allow her to pursue more spiritual interests, she was more liberated with Belinda gone and her children grown with families of their own. She didn't want another girl to train and supervise and worry about.

A black man had come from the barn when Cogwill arrived. Catching sight of him from under her covering, Sally pulled the blanket more tightly around herself and mumbled a prayer she often recited.

"Stand up, girl," Cogwill demanded, as Sally had slumped to the ground.

Sally didn't move. Cogwill reached for her and she clutched her chest.

"You can't sit there all day," he said as he stepped back from her. "You have to stand up. The horse needs to be to be watered and rested. Do you want to sleep in the shed?" He reached for her again, pulled her up and she flinched. As soon as Cogwill let go, Sally fell to the ground and curled herself into a ball.

"Leave her be," Cogwill said to the slave. "She frightened. This is all very new to her. Take the horse. I'll take care of the girl." Cogwill turned to his wife and said, "I've gotten her for a very good price."

"Not good enough," Elinor said, looking at Sally, who was slowly straightening her body and rising to her feet.

"Four years' service at a bargain price is a good deal."

"Whatever the contract, you get the better of it," she said looking at the boney, shivering girl. "Indecent she is, too."

65

Elinor scrutinized Sally's legs and arms and at the tear at the top of her dress that that exposed her upper chest. "Cover yourself, girl."

"All she has is on her back," Cogwill explained. "Some clothes will make the difference."

Sally listened to the conversation but her ears were too stuffed with fright to make out what they were saying.

"She'll be a good servant. Give her time. She's just debarked from Cork. It's a difficult journey," Cogwill said. "Take her in graciously, good woman." He turned to the man holding the horse's reins. "Peter, when you are done prepare the attic room for the new girl."

"Yes, master," Peter responded. The muscular man with receding gray hair took the bridle and led the horse away. Mosquitoes replaced the flies that followed the horse to the barn.

"Does she have a name?" Elinor descended from the porch.

"She doesn't say much." Valentine avoided answering directly. "That's a good sign. She esteems quiet and modesty."

Elinor wasn't assured by Valentine's assessment.

"But she did tell me her name on the way here. I think she said her name was 'Sally MacSweeney.' With her Celtic tongue, it is difficult to understand."

"What is the name on the deed?

Cogwill ignored the question.

"That's what we'll call her unless she decides one day to talk again and tells us otherwise."

Finally Elinor took Sally by the elbow and led Sally into the house. Here were many rooms, a shingled roof, wooden floors, glass windows and no children. This room, she learned, was for cooking and eating. In the kitchen an iron pot hung above an open fire. Elinor placed the girl at a bench, ladled venison made with peas and cabbage stew into a pewter bowl. She was unsure it was for her to eat. She waited for a prayer but there was none.

"We will offer our thankfulness for the meal and for each other," Elinor said. "Take my hand, Sally MacSweeney."

When Sally didn't reach out, Elinor took her hand and placed it in hers.

Sally waited for grace to be said but there was only silence. They remained that way until Elinor released her hand. Sally looked at the steaming food.

"Go ahead," Elinor said.

Sally looked at it tentatively and then devoured the meal.

"There'll be more," Elinor said.

After Sally settled in a more content but still wary state, Elinor called Peter.

"Shave her head before she is put to bed."

Elinor walked with Sally and Peter outside. Isaac, another slave, took out his knife while Elinor grabbed her hair. Sally shrieked and squirmed under Elinor's grip. Isaac spoke to her soothingly and began to sing. Sally calmed as Elinor held her tightly. With Sally's head shaved, she scrubbed her head, neck, arms, legs and feet with water and soap. Elinor then brought her to the attic and showed her straw ticking on the floor. While Sally had slept below deck on the *Penguin*, she had never slept above another room.

Perhaps it was the unfamiliar noises kept her awake despite her weariness. Or it may have been a púca having followed her from the ship into this motley land.

"THE TRIP WENT WELL, ELINOR," Cogwill said as he sat at his desk in their bedroom preparing his daily diary entry. He was in his nightshirt. Elinor was in their bed.

"It was a good trip, Elinor." He told her a little about his business in Philadelphia and his discussion with Friends about the state of the meeting in Duck Creek. He then told her about the religious fervor sweeping the city.

"Preacher Whitefield has arrived from England again for one of his evangelizing missions. He preaches every day in the city. He says the whole world is his parish. His enthusiasm is boundless."

"Did you see him?"

"It couldn't be avoided. Some say his look is associated with divine blessing. As far as I could see, it was a tic that made him cross-eyed. But I must admit that although he is slender, there is about him something imposing."

"And the crowds. Are they as large as last time?"

"I should say larger and they are as enthusiastic as he. I saw fainting and swooning. His words strike like lightning. Children are converted to his ministry."

"Children?"

"Yes, children, Elinor, children who can't know what they are saying."

The shadow of Cogwill's shaking head moved across the wall above their bed.

"The children preached, Elinor. They went so far as to reproach the adults. The insolence was galling."

Valentine picked up his quill, twisted it in his fingers, then replaced it on the desk the size of an open book.

"But they don't know what they are saying. How can they? They're only children. But they shout them with complete conviction. They look more for the words than the substance."

"Were Friends with you when you listened to the preacher?"

"Yes. A few of us went to hear."

Cogwill paused, reflecting on the experience.

"He no influence on us. But with the young and Negroes, Elinor, he is especially favored by them. It's their innocence. Preacher Whitefield's intentions are good but his notion of faith in opposition to good works is mistaken. Salvation is found in what we do."

Elinor let out a deep breath. The bed creaked as she pulled a thin cover up to her chin.

"Yet what he is doing is also good. I see that, Elinor. Religion is the topic of every conversation because of him. He's mistaken in his beliefs, yet a piety runs through his exhortations. And I have seen the wicked altered, men struck beside me. With my own eyes I have seen them turn from sin."

Elinor's eyes closed.

"I'll join you shortly," he said to her. "But there is danger in this, Elinor. The dread he is filling them with makes them outrun their Guide. Elinor. This isn't Light but fear that moves them to spasms."

When he heard Elinor's wheezing, he ended his soliloquy. He picked up his quill and by the flame of a candle he made his diary entry:

Now what can appear more dreadful to their childish apprehensions than being told of a dreadful eternal Hell, scorching, blazing, fiery brimstone ready to overtake them, sure damnation, certain destruction and unavoidable desolation, where they must forever dwell with devils, fallen angels, damned spirits, fiery furies, forever burning, tormenting, and never, never, to be released?

Cogwill rested his hand for several moments as he rubbed his temple in a circular motion. His eyes shut momentarily and then penned his final observation:

Even a parrot may be taught to speak some few words, but he cannot give any rational account of the cause of those words. Why? Because he is destitute of the power of reflection and so incapable of understanding the difference between causes and their effects.

ROOSTERS, TRILLING MOCKINGBIRDS and warbling redbirds weren't enough rouse Sally at dawn. She remained in bed, finally asleep after clouds shrouded the full moon, until Elinor woke her at sunrise.

"Come down, girl. There's work to be done," she told Sally as she stood by the hatch door. "Here. These are for you."

She put a bundle on the floor. In it was an underdress spun from the Needful Portion's flax plants.

"Put it on. Your shift is disgraceful. Takes it. And here are a pair of Negro shoes," she added, "almost like new." There was also bonnet and told her she must always wear except for sleeping.

Sally put on the clothes Elinor brought. When she arrived downstairs, the strings of the bonnet hung down.

"Tie it, girl," Elinor instructed. Sally's headgear had always been a cap; she didn't know how to tie a bow. By the end of the day she had mastered the skill.

Elinor brought the servant girl to the kitchen to prepare breakfast. It had become apparent to Elinor that Sally would need many lessons, so she prepared the food as Sally watched.

Peter came in from the barn. Two other Negroes, both older than Peter, one bent, the other limping, came up from their sleeping space in the cellar. Their skin seemed to Sally to be as hard as leather, their faces scarred from pox. The men were several years older than Cogwill. In her eyes they were as big as the largest seaman on the *Penguin*. The men arranged themselves on barrels in the smoke-filled room and placed crates in front of themselves to put their plates upon. Peter took a spoon from his pocket and put it beside a plate. Daniel and Isaac removed knives.

Sally instinctively grabbed Elinor's arm and hid behind her, more afraid of the men than she was of the gruff woman whose clothes were heavy and respectable.

"Don't be afraid. They won't harm you," she said, pushing Sally to stand beside her. "They are good boys." Elinor told her that they have been in the family since they were born. "My good husband inherited them."

Sally wasn't certain what was being said and it wouldn't have made any difference if she had known that Cogwill had sold several others to boost his income.

Sally continued to cling to Elinor's sleeve. The mistress brought her to the hearth and instructed her to put ham, Indian bread and honey on the cutting board and bring it to the men.

"Come with me," Elinor she when she was finished serving "Sally MacSweeney. Is that your name, girl? Well, someday you will tell me otherwise if I am wrong."

"Yes, miss. That's my name."

"Good. Then, Sally MacSweeney, arrange the table in the dining room." She looked at the girl with arms swollen from bites. "The room there," she said, pointing to the adjacent room with a table with four chairs.

Sally didn't know what to do and stood without a word.

"Mr. Cogwill said you was a bargain. I see why."

Valentine came down from his bedroom and Elinor ordered Sally to return to the kitchen to get their breakfast.

"You will eat here, with us. When we are done, you will clear the table. The washtub is outside. And when you are finished, go upstairs. The first chore is to empty the chamber pots in the pit by peach trees behind the house." Elinor saw the blank look again. "A peach is a fruit. You will see them by the chicken yard. When you are done, I'll take you to the field. There is hoeing to do. You dost know how to hoe, don't you?"

Elinor handed her a hoe.

"Do you know what to do?"

Sally nodded.

"I have something for you to give to Peter," Cogwill said, handing Sally the package that had been hung over the horse's side.

"What this?" Elinor asked.

"A violin," he said.

She tightened her eyes as she scrutinized the package.

"You know I disapprove," she said.

Cogwill tamped down his ire. Religious matters were his concern, not hers.

"I don't know how Peter has learned to play it without assistance but he does it well. I've heard him scratch on the one he has made himself. One string."

"One string too many. You shouldn't indulge him."

"It would be better if he found the Light in quiet, I know, but his fiddle playing is diverting."

"It's contrary to the spirit," Elinor interrupted. "He doesn't need to pleasure himself but find the spirit. How will he find the Light in such an indulgence?"

"Don't begrudge him a new fiddle, wife. I bought this one for him from a maker in the city. It has two sets of spare guts."

"Let his old one break and that will be end of it."

"Not so, Elinor" Cogwill insisted. "He'll make another for himself."

"It's contrary to quieting the flesh," Elinor reproached her husband.

Cogwill tightened his fist behind his back.

"You shouldn't be encouraging the agitation."

Cogwill was more worried about a different kind of agitation: the trouble along the North River. He would keep from her, as long as he could, the news about the conspiracy that burned down New York. He heard it from Friend Hicks, from Long Island, who had conveyed it to him. Concern deepened that such a Negro uprising would emerge elsewhere in the colonies. The memory of the Cato's Conspiracy three years earlier in South Carolina was still fresh in his mind. Keeping Peter pleased in a little thing was a pacifying thing, Cogwill thought.

"Let's not judge, Elinor. He has found Christ his own way. Judge not."

"You are right, husband. But giving to the flesh this way is wrong."

Elinor knew their exchange had ended when Cogwill said, "You have the new girl to take care of. Come, Elinor. Let's pray together that he will sing in the spirit and the new girl will come to the Light."

Elinor took Sally to the garden where they found Peter in the chicken yard tossing Indian corn kernels to the birds. Pigs, sheep and cattle roamed in the pasture, wandering as they pleased. Peter had just returned from the pine forest where he set traps for wolves that plagued the county, snatching wandering pigs in the woods and even invading the farm itself.

Isaac and Daniel were in the adjacent garden tilling the ground, pulling weeds and singing. As Daniel called, Isaac responded—

Five can't catch me

And ten can't hold me

Hoe Emma hoe

She works harder

Than two grown men

Hoe Emma hoe

I can 'ginny bank

'ginny bank the weaver

Hoe Emma hoe

This white girl

Make the day pass quick

Hoe Emma Hoe

Mesmerized by the syncopation of the downward thrust of the hoes regulated by the chanting of two black men, Sally didn't notice that Elinor had returned to the house. Sally placed the package on the ground between Peter and herself. He looked at her. Finally she said, "This is for you."

"What is it?"

Sally shrugged her shoulders, unable to look at Peter directly.

"Put it in the shed," he said.

As Peter spoke directly to Sally, she turned to run back to the house, leaving the violin on the ground, her loose-fitting shift slipping from her shoulders. Her left shoe flew off as she stumbled up the steps to the porch. Elinor took her by the hand and brought her back to the garden.

"You are to care for Sally MacSweeney," she instructed the men.

She handed Sally a hoe, but Sally's injured shoulder prevented her from lifting the tool above her head. Seeing her struggle, Elinor told Sally to return to the house. There was work there less onerous but just as needed.

In her cottage at home, Sally spread her palette on a dirt floor. She picked up the broom and began to sweep. She set it aside when she noticed a book on a small table. She recognized that one word on the cover was the same as that on her lost book. She had it opened when Elinor returned, quickly returning it to the table.

"Are you stealing the holy book?" Elinor asked, her face flushed with anger.

"No, ma'am. I'm looking at it. That's all. I'm no thief."

"Do you know what this is?"

"I know that I had such a book until it was lost."

"It is difficult for me to believe you owned one. Where would you get a Bible of your own?"

"On the ship that took me here. A man gave it to me. He was giving me lessons."

"Spiritual lessons, I hope."

Elinor picked up the book and asked Sally to read from it. She managed a few words but had difficulty making out the letters in shapes she hadn't seen before.

"You can read."

"Little," Sally said.

"Come with me," Elinor said, her sternness softening to consolation.

Elinor led Sally upstairs to the bedroom. There hanging from a peg in the wall was a wooden board with a page laminated in sheep horn and held it for Sally to look at. Across the top of the hornbook was the alphabet.

"What are these?"

"Letters," Sally said.

"Read them to me."

Sally recited them correctly.

"And this?" Elinor challenged, pointing to the words on the parchment board.

She could read only a few words.

"Do you know its meaning?"

"No, ma'am."

"It says, 'Truly I tell you, whatever you did for one of the least of these brothers and sisters of mine, you did for me.' Do you understand?"

Sally stood with her head slumped.

"Would you like to learn more, Sally MacSweeney?" Elinor asked. "It will be good for thine spirit."

Valentine was pleased that Elinor had decided to teach Sally.

"Educate her away from vain arts and inventions of a luxurious world," he reminded Elinor, though he needn't have. "Teach her what she needs know about the spirit and profane life."

Valentine and Elinor shared the belief that education was a practical matter necessary for everyone.

"Daniel was in the field today," Elinor said. "He is too old for the work."

"This will be the last year for the tobacco. It's worn out. The remainder crops will be easier."

"He is in poor condition."

"Yes. I've noticed and I've been thinking about him."

"With the new girl servant I can't use Daniel for the house work. He's become a burden."

"I'll find something for him."

"I think the time has come to grant him his freedom. Other Friends are manumitting their slaves."

"In the Philadelphia Meeting there is increasing talk in this direction. A few preach very strong about our Christian duty. But the Meeting is far from united."

Cogwill poured water over his hands to wash off the soil.

"It is easier for the city merchants to say. They can more easily manage" He rinsed again. "But what can we do with Daniel?"

"Let him go."

76

"He's old. How will he care for himself? What's more, giving him his freedom dues is no longer ample. There is the new £30 indemnity bond we must pay the county for his upkeep if we let him go. It is an oppressive law. But our finances, Elinor, are parlous. We'll have to find some fit for him here."

"Perhaps we can write to our son to take him from us. He has known Daniel all his life and is fond of him."

"This wouldn't be good for Daniel to leave for Virginia. The journey is too arduous."

Elinor said, "Perhaps Daniel can buy his own freedom sufficient for the bond." Cogwill shook his head.

"I will write all our slaves' freedom in my will. Until that time, we have a duty to perform."

Elinor took her husband's hands and they stood silently together waiting for the Light to break and give them guidance.

Meetings and Gatherings

AT HER FIRST MEETING, a year after being taken to the Cogwills, Sally sat amongst men and women in drowsy silence. She still hadn't grown accustomed to wearing shoes and she slipped them off and hid her feet under the bench. In Athnowen, mass had been conducted in the stone parish church by a priest wearing vestments, the church no bigger than the Cogwills' house, a building filled with incense, bowed heads, candles, wafers and wine.

A lantern hung from the rafters in the Meeting House, the only light. Twenty people sat in the one-story plank house owned by Widow Needham, without stirring. Where was the priest? Why no genuflecting?

After more than an hour Elinor stood to testify.

"Am I my brother's keeper?' What have I to do with the welfare of another? If ye love God, we must also love our neighbor."

A woman addressing an assembly of men shocked Sally, who didn't know whether to flee or hold onto Cogwill's jacket. She quickly put on her shoes.

"Christ the light of the world, is certainly in us, unless we are reprobates; if we are reprobates the fault is our own." Sally couldn't follow what her mistress was saying, as Elinor continued the oration for many minutes. Sally heard her say, "Is there even a servant lad or a servant girl that hath continued neglected and their minds left to wander at will?"

Cogwill sat next to his wife with his eyes closed. Beads of sweat trickled down his forehead.

Sally thought her mistress's reprimand was meant for her.

Contrary to Sally's worry, Elinor's sermon wasn't directed at her but at a Friend, Joseph Young.

"He has given way to a libertine spirit," Elinor said to her husband after walking for more than a mile to home.

Sally listened to them, a few words spoken now and then punctuating the silence.

"Yes, and he refuses to make a public acknowledgement."

Sally heard Cogwill tell Elinor that at the next business meeting of the Friends, the men would decide whether to disown Young.

Later in the month Sally learned from Peter that the man in question wasn't an indentured servant, as she had inferred, but an owner of a small farm in the hundred.

"Then how can he be disowned?" she wanted to know.

It was, Peter explained, that Friends disapproved of his behavior.

"He was at a public house playing hustle-cap."

She let him continue. She had never heard of hustle-cap but thought it was probably one of the games she had seen sailors play on the ship.

"He stripped off his shirt to fight with another person. I can't say I know which was the worse offense." He said that if he were disowned, he would no longer be a Friend.

That wouldn't be so bad, Sally thought. She preferred the smell of incense; she thought that singing could lift the spirit. She had also seen many seamen without shirts and some black men in the fields without theirs. "Why would he be disowned?"

"The Friends like things strict. They say there is a light that tells them the rules they got to follow."

SALLY HAD LEARNED TO TRUST the Negroes at the farmstead and felt at ease with them. And with the summer heat and so many bondsmen and freemen living in Murderkill Hundred, she sometimes thought her snow had sailed to Africa, not America. Sally didn't understand the different constrictions under which the Negroes lived in the Lower Counties but it didn't matter to her. She thought that those in servitude were like herself and when their contract expired, they would be given their liberty to live like other freemen.

Sally had also come to see that the púca that had followed her across the Atlantic was benevolent after all. Rather than being harassed and haunted by the night visions she had previous had, the púca in her garret thrilled her.

After months of Sunday Meetings with the Cogwills, Sally had asked if she could accompany Peter to the trading post at Fullerton's Tavern, a gathering place along Beaver Dam Branch. Elinor told Sally that a meeting with Friends would be better for the spirit. Sally had heard that a Sunday gathering at Fullerton's brought together laborers and farmers from Murderkill and surrounding hundreds. Being with Peter would be better than another soporific day at a Meeting.

When Peter told her he was bringing his violin with him to the tavern, Sally decided this was the time for her to go.

"The conscience is yours, Sally MacSweeney," Cogwill told her. "I cannot force you to do what the will won't allow. We cannot tie ourselves to any duty before the Spirit moves us."

Elinor warned Sally against the temptations awaiting her. "Peter will care for her," Cogwill assured her.

On the walk to the tavern by the creek, Peter wore a jacket over his cotton shirt, tow cloth trousers and hemp shoes. Under Sally's dress was a linsey petticoat; she preferred to walk barefoot to the tavern. Peter regularly went to Fullerton's to buy fish, oysters and clams, farm implements, wrought nails and bricks. Crushed shells mixed with sand used for mortar at Needful Portion also came from Fullerton's store. Cogwill had given the Negroes at the trading post permission to sell their items to Peter.

Peter assured Sally that there was no need to worry about the law. Although more than six Negroes weren't allowed to meet without fear of punishment, the law was never enforced at Fullerton's.

Before arriving at the tavern, Sally heard a beating drum, then, more insistently, laughter and singing. Slaves, free Negroes, indentured servants, barefoot men who lived in the forest, and tenant farmers were at the tavern. For the next several hours Peter played his imported violin outside while others danced, downed tankards of cider and perry. Sally learned to enjoy the peach and apple brandy that made her feel the way she did when the púca visited.

Peter finished playing and went into the tavern where he bought a freshly caught fish from the creek behind the building.

Sally recognized a man from a Friends Meeting tossing a halfpence at a mark on the ground. Others did the same. She watched them put more coins into a hat. One man shook the hat and the coins tossed onto the ground. The man who had tossed the coins took all the halfpence that came up heads. The remaining coins were put in the hat again, hustled and tossed on the ground by the second player. He then collected all the halfpennies that turned up heads. This continued until all the coins in the hat were gone.

"He's a man from the Meeting, isn't he?" Sally asked Peter.

"Yes," Peter whispered to her. "That's why he was disowned."

"*He's* the man that Mrs. Cogwill preached against at the Meeting?"

"Master Young. He's here most Sundays. Every once in a while he goes to the Meeting. For some gambling gets into the blood. The gambling, fighting—he has a mean temper—and removing his shirt was too much for the Friends to tolerate."

"Will they beat him?"

"Quakers never do that. They'll welcome him back if he repents. But it don't look like he's ready to do that. What he wants is not to lose all his money," Peter laughed. "Those Meetings ain't for me, either, though I don't like gambling. And fighting is for younger men."

Sally nodded in agreement.

"I love my playing and dancing too much to get the light they preach on. It's in my blood, too, this moving about. Those Quakers don't know anything about amusement, though I am grateful for Master Cogwill getting this violin for me."

Nearby a man held a gourd covered with an animal skin that had three strings stretched over an attached stick; another rattled a beaded gourd. A third Negro beat on a hollow log. Sally couldn't help but stare at one of the dancers whose sharpened teeth were exposed in his broad smile. She held onto Peter when Kwasi walked to her. She didn't understand what he said as he spoke to Peter.

"I was arranging for some items to buy from him," Peter said. "He is a good iron worker."

"He is peculiar looking with those sharp teeth and marks on his cheeks."

"He came fresh from Africa, as a free man," Peter said.

"Indentured, like me. He purchased his freedom?"

"No. He was always free. Never belonged to no one." Sally asked for an explanation of Kwasi's peculiar history but Peter didn't have one. How the African arrived in Delaware was a mystery, Peter said. Some claimed he was in New

York before coming to the Lower Counties. Others said he had lived in the West Indies.

"He lives like a swamp man," Peter said. "He comes out from the swamp only on Sundays or when he had items to sell."

Peter joined the circle dance when the music slowed. When he returned to Sally, she asked him more about the man.

"He has two furnaces in the swamp, one for iron and one for bricks. He's the person who makes the iron pots and utensils for Needful Portion. Fullerton sells his bricks but I buy the wrought iron from him."

Before returning to the estate, Sally watched Kwasi engaged in conversation. He caught her staring at him before she could turn her head. He looked directly at her and bared his teeth. Sally smiled in return.

NOT TO PROVOKE HER employers' displeasure, Sally met with the Friends the next few Sundays. During that time, Peter asked the Cogwills for permission to have Sally accompany him on his next trip to Fullerton's Landing.

"She knows what is needed in the house," he explained to Elinor. "She'll be of some assistance to me."

In the time between sowing and harvesting, Cogwill was inclined to let her go. Elinor was more skeptical. She was familiar with the rumors regarding the tavern and thought it was a dangerous temptation. By mid-August Sally had gone to the trading post twice with Peter. The first time she stayed close to Peter's side as he negotiated with Kwasi. As they were about the return home, Kwasi spoke to her directly.

"This is for you," he said.

"Go ahead, Sally," Peter urged. "You can take it."

Sally held a wire-wound necklace of black beads with blue in the center.

"It will protect you," Kwasi said.

Sally began to finger the beads the way she had seen others handle their rosaries.

"This man is strong," Peter said to Sally on their way to Needful Portion.

"Why does he have ash on him and the scars on his face?"

Since Peter had never seen Kwasi's kiln or talked to him about the scars, he explained it to her as best he could.

"Keep the beads with you, Sally, it will protect you," he advised. "But don't let the master or mistress see it."

"I have no pockets in my garments," Sally said.

"Then let it stay in your room."

The Cogwills' hopes that the Light would penetrate Sally's spirit gave way to resignation. They no longer urged her to attend meetings. Weather permitting, every week she went to Fullerton's Tavern with Peter.

Sally spent a few pence on food; men paid for her mobby. She enjoyed Kwasi's company as he told her about New York, Barbados and the Guinea coast.

"You want I'll tell you a story," he said to her as they sat outside on a large rock. Kwasi threw a potato into the fire.

Sally raised her eyebrows in agreement.

"There was this rabbit. You know what a rabbit is?"

"I once saw one outside my house before I came here," she recalled.

> You know rabbit is clever. Very clever. But he is also lazy. He is so lazy he got others to do his work for him.
>
> Rabbit watch bear dig up the ground. He watch ox put water on the vegetables. He watch deer pull out weeds. He watch and laugh and laugh and laugh at all their hard work while do nothing.

Just when the cabbages is ready to be picked, he jump out in the dark night and pick the food for hisself.

He does the same next time cabbage is ready for picking. He laugh and laugh at the other animals with cuts and calluses on their hands.

Other animals get downright mad at doing all the work but not getting the harvest. They don't want to kill rabbit. That won't be any good. So they put out a muskrat trap. The trap will snatch rabbit by his tail and cut it off—

Kwasi raised his hand and slice the air—

    —just like that.

Snap. The trap sounds like a shot from my pistol.

Sally wanted to ask him about the pistol but she let him continue.

In the morning bear and ox and deer, they look for where they put that trap. And right where they put it sure enough there is something in that trap. Just like the hard-working animals planned, rabbit's tail stuck in the trap.

Rabbit has no fluffy tail now, just something like a little stump. Rabbit don't mind so much that he don't have his tail but he is sacred. Rabbit, he gathers brother rabbits for some kind of meeting. Not a testifying meeting but like a business meeting. They get around and he presents to them.

He says to them, 'They have my tail, so they know it's me, that I'm the one doing the stealing. They be coming to get me and beat me bad.'

The other rabbits, they give him no sympathy at all. Just the same, he is a brother.

'I have a plan to fool them.'

'Tell us your plan. Tell us how you going to outsmart the animals.'

'They angry at me. But that means they be angry with all of you. One rabbit the same to them. Makes no difference. So here is how we fool them: all of us cut off our tails. That way they won't know who it was that did the stealing.'

I said at the beginning that rabbit is clever. What I didn't tell you is that you can be clever and *stupid* at the same time. So you know what rabbits do? They take their knives and stand in a circle back to front and they cut off each other's tail until none of them got tails no more. Everyone now got a stump and no tail.

Kwasi laughed.

"So that's why rabbits got no tails," he added.

Looking at Kwasi's pointed teeth, Sally asked, "Why are your teeth sharp like that?"

Kwasi ran his finger along his front teeth. He wanted to tell her more about learning to work the furnace at Ntwaaban, the Komenda factory, Antobam, birds and the sailing ship. Instead, he replied, "When an animal threatens me, I open my mouth. You ain't scared though, are you?"

"No more."

"Good," he said. With his bare hand, Kwasi picked the burnt potato from the fire, cracked the skin and broke it in two. He gave a steaming half to Sally.

"Potatoes at my home are white," she said, looking at the yam.

"Like you."

"These are better. They're like honey."

Kwasi noticed that Sally used only one arm.

"I was hurt, so I can't hardly use it anymore," she explained.

"I have something for it," Kwasi said.

The next time at the trading post, Kwasi had ready a poultice made from the roots of plants he had gathered in the marsh.

"Come here," he said, holding a paste in a clay bowl, "let me look at your arm."

Sally tried to raise her. She tightened her mouth as Kwasi moved near.

"Let me see."

Sally didn't move as Kwasi stood next to her. He smelled of smoke and ash. He touched her neck with his rough fingers and slid his hand under the collar of her dress. She jerked as he pressed gently on her shoulder joint.

Kwasi removed his hand and put a dab of ointment on his fingertip. She placed it under her nose.

"Take a deep breath," he said.

She felt herself getting dizzy.

"Now I'm going to rub this on your sore place," Kwasi explained as he put his hand down her dress. She watched his face and couldn't turn away from his eyes that were shining like lanterns. She wouldn't look at his hands. As soon as he touched her crooked bone and rubbed in his ointment, Sally felt its cooling relief and breathed in the aroma of peppermint. Kwasi had her sniff the poultice, then dabbed a drop on her forehead. He said something to someone she couldn't see in a language she didn't understand.

"Take this," he said, "and put this on every night, where it pains."

Elinor disapproved of Sally dousing herself with fragrance, telling her that perfumes belonged to the priestly liturgy of the Roman Church, but when she saw that Sally had regained mobility in her arm, she accepted the truthfulness of the servant's claim that it wasn't for vanity that she used the poultice. And as Sally was always in the company of Peter at Fullerton's post, Elinor didn't ask her who had prepared the medicine. She was glad to have a more useful servant girl.

Cogwill had decided to replace his Indian corn with wheat for the following year, so Sally walked in the dug field planting seeds. As winter approached, she husked and shelled Indian corn and drove with Daniel to sell the excess ground meal at the trading post. There was harrowing and weeding to be done. When days grew longer again the wheat crop sprouted and there was task of repairing and building paling fences keeping the free-roaming livestock from getting to the shoots.

WORK SLOWED AFTER THE two-week intensive July wheat harvest, a welcome pause, although the heat, unlike anything Sally knew in Ireland, was enervating. She was lethargic in the house and struggled to keep up with Peter on the Sunday outings to Fullerton's Landing, and, on couple of occasions, she was too tired to make the walk to the tavern with him.

Sally had never felt this way before, not even on the voyage across the Atlantic, but Elinor's suspicions were validated when Sally's swollen belly bulged under her shift.

The shame of Sally's unwed pregnancy led Elinor to refuse Sally permission to leave the farmstead. She kept her indoors so that not even a visitor to the farmstead would see her.

Cogwill questioned Isaac and Daniel and was satisfied of their innocence. They were as surprised as their proprietor.

"What do you know, Peter?"

"She was in my sight at Fullerton's. Nothing more."

"You don't believe this is a virgin birth. Have you gone elsewhere?'

"No, sir."

"She was always under your eye?"

"Even a good dog wanders," he responded.

"Where did she wander to?"

Despite their servant's egregious transgression, they were ready to keep the child until they reached the age of freedom and leave matters there. Neighbors weren't as liberal.

When she gave birth to a boy, the child's legal status was in doubt and needed to be settled. Sally was summoned to court. Punishment was necessary for flouting the rules of civilization. The law proscribed sexual relations between the races "to ensure the preservation of virtue and chastity among the people of this government and to prevent the heinous sins of adultery and fornication."

The second charge against Sally left no doubt. The baby was a mulatto. While she wouldn't explain what had happened, she did confess that she once was afraid of the African man.

"His teeth and the scars on his face," she said. Sally's body shook as she spoke.

"Did you see markings on any other parts of his body?" one judge asked.

From the Cogwills Sally had learned the power of silence.

"What did you do with this Negro?"

She said they ate together and that he comforted her with medicines.

"Did he force himself on you?"

She said she didn't understand his question. The judge asked if she did anything against her will.

"No," she answered.

Having bastard children was all that was needed for the jurors to convict her of fornication. That she had consorted with a Negro was also proven. However, she was nearly a child herself and the court wasn't without mercy. The judges decided she deserved leniency. Her term of indenture would be extended two years and the court would forgo imposing the £10 fine.

They tied Sally to a whipping post. She received twelve lashes lightly delivered, after which she stood in the pillory for two hours. The Cogwills took her home. Blood soaked Sally's back, her legs too weak for her to stand upon. Cogwill insisted that she be bathed but Elinor wouldn't let a Negro touch her.

"Then you must do it," Cogwill said. "Who will take care of her child if she isn't able? The child is innocent. He isn't responsible for the sins of his parents."

Elinor washed Sally roughly.

"If your body is clean," she said, "then perhaps you will see the Light."

Kwasi's case was more difficult to adjudicate. First, it was decided that as a freeman the case wouldn't be held in a Negro court but would be tried by the same judges and jurors who had heard Sally's case.

As a Negro, Kwasi wasn't allowed to bring testimony on his own behalf but could only answer questions posed to him by the judges. From Sally's case, they had several facts against him. His explanation about giving her a necklace and salves of his own preparation was sufficient proof of his pagan ways. While not part of the case, his idolatry and witchery were marks against him.

After thirty lashes, Kwasi stood with both ears nailed to the pillory. Four hours later he was untied and his ears cropped low to his head. His crimes were of such magnitude that the court nullified his free status.

An ironmaster and merchant bought Kwasi from the county for £30, plus court fees, and brought him to the Deep Creek Iron Works. Here he extracted bog ore from the marshy ground, chopped trees to turn timber into charcoal and, then at the ironworks, tended the furnace turning the mineral to low-grade iron. While English workers often fell ill with fevers, Kwasi remained immune. His biggest fear was the water moccasins and other snakes that lived in the fallen timber.

Two years later he was sold to a cooper from Lewis Town who, recognizing Kwasi's value as a blacksmith, brought him to his coastal home. After living in the forest and working the swamp at Deep Creek, a hut by the shore was a relief. He enjoyed the sound of the surf and salt water soothed his many welts and sore bones. Although the pigs that roamed behind the dunes could provide meat enough for every day, Kwasi confined his diet to fish and beans.

Kwasi's blacksmithing, good enough for him to become known in the hundred, left him with a small amount of money. Within ten years he would be able buy his freedom from the cooper.

One late February a storm stranded a ship with more than two hundred slaves. The ship anchored for a week during which time Kwasi helped with repairs.

In March, while washing himself in the ocean, Kwasi was caught in a riptide, pulled into the water and drowned. He had never learned to swim.

Deciding they were unable to control the girl, Elinor at first refused take her into the house. She tried to persuade her husband that they needed to transfer Sally's contract. She wouldn't have a fornicator in her house.

"We can't turn her out now. I will find someone to take her contract when the child is weaned. Before that, there won't be a buyer."

Elinor relented but for two years Elinor merely tolerated the mother and child. When the baby had begun to talk, Elinor insisted that Cogwill rid the farm of the two of them.

"No one will take a mother and young child," Cogwill objected.

"Then separate them"

The boy was indentured for thirty-one years to a husbandman in Nanticoke Hundred. The farmer said he would take the boy to his wife who was unable to bear children.

Between the two contracts, Cogwill recouped his investment in Sally and was pleased with the profit. It made no difference to him to that there was no wife waiting for the man who now held the boy's contract. Neither did Cogwill care to know that the man wasn't a yeoman farmer. Upon arriving in Seaford, Sally's son was sold as a slave to Denton Swain, who renamed the boy Bell.

On Plum Alley

AS SLAVES DIED and weren't replaced, or were manumitted outright while others were freed upon the death of their owners, or decided their own fates by walking the freedom, the number of freed black men and women in Delaware nearly equaled that of those kept in servitude.

Moved by the considerations of biblical teaching, the Cogwills had drawn new wills freeing their slaves upon their own death and so were bewildered when Isaac and Daniel were gone one day. The men had never complained about their lot. The Cogwills had often said how fond they were of the men. In all the years with them, the men had never been mistreated. Whatever punishment was meted out was deserved and justly deliver. Not once had they physically beaten them. The Cogwills distributed the farm's provisions fairly, provided clothing for all the seasons and gave them adequate shelter. When ill, they treated them no less than they did themselves. In all they did, the Cogwills exhibited a charitable disposition.

What reckless thoughts had been put into their heads at the goings-on at Fullerton's?

Sentiment for immediate manumission was widely expressed in Meetings, a position the Cogwills tepidly supported publicly but didn't share privately. Spiritual change could be radical, but social arrangements needed time to change.

When asked to explain why they wanted their slaves returned, the Cogwills said that they were moved by Christian charity. They cared for the welfare of two old men who, they said, were unlikely to have sufficient funds to care for themselves. What's more, they added, Peter was wasting from loneliness and wanted the companionship of his life-long friends. By bringing them back to Needful Portion, they were being charitable to everyone concerned.

> RAN AWAY from the subscriber, a Negro Man named ISAAC, about 5 feet 8 inches high, very round shouldered and small, bowed legs; had on when he went away, a very good hat, a new pair of buckskin breeches, a new jacket of home-made cloth of a dark brown colour, a great coat of the same kind, almost worn out. Whoever takes up said negro, and secures him in some jail, so that the owner may have him again, shall have THREE POUND reward and reasonable charges paid by me.

The second advertisement read:

> RAN away from the subscriber, living in Murderkill hundred, Kent county, an indented servant Negro Man, named DANIEL, about 125 lbs., 62 years of age, about 6 feet high, walks very currsey, had on when he went away, a tow shirt and trowsers, and a whitish colored cloth jacket with metal buttons. Whoever takes up and secures said negro so that his master may get him again, shall receive THREE POUND reward, and reasonable charges paid, if brought home.

Peter's melancholy grew worse. None of Elinor's ministrations could restore his vigor. One morning Cogwill found him dead in the barn beside the horse.

After a meeting in which being a slaveholder was compared to being a leprous person, Cogwill vowed not to engage in the sinful habit again. Reason that issued from the preacher persuaded him.

"Our fellow-creatures have equally a right to the purchase of redemption by our Savior's blood. It is but adding sin to sin by holding them still longer under the galling yoke."

Denunciations of holding another person as property were increasingly heard at meetings. This time Cogwill could no longer deny the appeal. Light, like he had never known before, illuminated his soul.

To fully acquit himself of sin Cogwill offered Belinda's renter a deal: he would sell Belinda to him at the cost of one year's rent, if, as the new owner, he agreed to manumit her when the contract expired. The renter accepted the terms.

It was more economical, Cogwill had calculated, to be rid of slaves and indentured servants. He would hire labor as needed. Providing food and shelter for non-productive workers between seasons was bad business.

Despite her husband's keeping worldly news from her, Elinor was aware of the disturbances and plots in the province. Along the Nanticoke River soldiers had recently intercepted a planned massacre by Indians donning war paint and boiling poison intended for English wells. And she knew about uprisings by slaves in various colonies. There had never been trouble with Daniel or Isaac but there was something unnerving about their willful attraction to vanity and pleasure. The material world of darkness held them in its thrall. They, like all God's creatures, had been born in the Light but they rejected righteousness; they had been born saved but chose licentiousness. There was no way of knowing what the next step into darkness would bring.

Elinor often wanted to tell them when they worked in the field to stop the pagan songs. Sing hymns, if you must sing, she wanted to tell them. Elinor refused to imagine what took place at the trading post. As she thought about her husband's purchase of the violin, she wondered if he was partly responsible for the disgrace that had unfolded at Fullerton's.

DURING THE TIME THAT Sally nursed her infant, her arm recovered its strength. Her wounds had healed leaving only small welts across her lower back.

Two years after the trial, Cogwill approached Sally with the decision to transfer her contract to a bachelor in the northern part of the province.

"Mrs. Cogwill don't like me," Sally said.

"You are a burden."

Sally began to tremble.

"I will do better. Give me one more chance."

"You must go."

"I want to stay here," she importuned. "This is a good place."

"No, it's not, Sally. Not for you. The temptations are too great. You have proven yourself wanting. Look at the trouble you've caused."

"Let me stay with you," she persisted.

"You can't stay, Sally. The shame's too great. I have found somewhere else where you can find your way to God. Too many here won't let you do that. You have been marked forever here."

"I don't want to be hungry again, sir."

"You won't be hungry."

Sally knew to stop. The more she contested the more Cogwill would see her as self-willed. She bit her lip and twisted her fist into her hip.

"My child will stay here with you?" she asked. Cogwill hesitated.

"I will care for him."

Her child was playing with a corncob when Sally left with Cogwill for Roger Prettyjohn's home. She didn't look behind as the buggy left Needful Portion behind.

AS THE PROVINCE'S CAPITAL, New Castle needed Prettyjohn's printing services. Broadsides, legal documents, advertisements, books—all this and more were turned on the press in Prettyjohn's workroom, leaving him little time to care for himself. This was a gentleman's town where men outnumbered women. Prettyjohn had little spare time to pursue the few eligible females, most of whom showed no interest in his ink-soaked appearance.

The county seat clattered with sounds she hadn't heard since debarking in Philadelphia. Fullerton's Tavern would be lost amongst the buildings that numbered close to a hundred. Most striking about the town were the many black men and women walking about freely.

For several months she searched for Kwasi, looking at every black man his size and age, but she never asked anyone if they knew an African man with sharpened teeth and ashen skin.

If Sally had arrived one year earlier, she would have been placed in a house much like the log and plank constructions common in Murderkill. But Prettyjohn's new house was brick, one amongst the dozens of new brick houses that followed the principles of geometry and proportions espoused by architects in England.

Prettyjohn's house on Plum Alley stood close to the Strand. A red door led directly into the five-bay, two and a half story house with shuttered windows. On bright days, a square fanlight helped light up the parlor. Inside were plank floors, a fireplace and in the kitchen a cast iron pot in which Sally cooked their meals. The exposed beams across the ceiling of the bedroom were much like that of her attic room at Needful Portion. The furnishings were simpler than in Murderkill, except for the decorative lintel that spanned the fireplace.

For the first time, Sally slept in a bed, used a cotton blanket and feather pillow. She slept in an unfinished room adjacent to Prettyjohn's. Only the river breeze mitigated the smell of ink and paper that wafted from the basement.

Every so often she thought of her child and imagined him in a house like this, perhaps in Philadelphia. She was troubled, though, at the thought of him being mulatto and wondered what his lot would be like. She pushed aside the harsher imaginings. For a while he visited her at night, assuring her that he was safe. When he no longer appeared beside her bed, he also faded from her memory.

Hardest for Sally at the beginning was living with a white man who had stained-black hands and arms and whose forehead was purple with ink. Lye soap helped some but he could no more return to white than Kwasi could fully remove the ash that turned his skin pale. Her new master's hands were swollen and he constantly coughed from breathing in the ink mist.

Prettyjohn took on Sally's contract because needed someone to do domestic chores. At the price he paid for her services, he didn't expect she would be experienced and was delighted that she had rudimentary cooking skills. She prepared shad and cod, oysters and clams, all in abundant supply.

"You don't eat much yourself," Prettyjohn observed as he refilled his plate. "Don't you like it?"

"It's not proper . . ." she began, intending to say that gluttony was a sin.

"You're a servant girl, but that doesn't mean that you need to go hungry. There's enough here for both of us. I don't want you looking as though you are ready for the almshouse."

At first, Prettyjohn appeared to Sally to be gluttonous but she quickly came to a different opinion: the Cogwills' abstemiousness was a mistaken belief. She had seen enjoyment of the flesh amongst the Negroes and now with Prettyjohn and thought that if God punished with scarcity, he must also reward with abundance.

Prettyjohn took her to the town market and bought vegetables, grains and a slaughtered chicken. On other days he selected a wild bird, other times beef, pork or mutton. Sally cooked as best she could, but often Prettyjohn expressed his displeasure.

"These can't be done the same as the fish," he said.

"I'm sorry, sir," Sally apologized. "That all I know how to do."

"You'll learn," he told her.

When Prettyjohn saw Sally looking a book he had on his workbench, he asked if she could read.

"A little," she answered.

"Here. Read this to me," he said, handing her a book that he had purchased to use as a model for a book that he would publish.

Sally struggled with many words.

"Do you want to learn more?" he asked. "How to read better?"

She nodded in agreement.

"Then I'll teach you myself," he told her.

Before retiring, Prettyjohn sat with Sally, using the broadsides and simpler books that overflowed throughout the house. She responded to his instructions as eagerly as she took to eating and learning to prepare different kinds of food. One day he handed her a set of papers she hadn't seen before.

"What is this?" she asked. "These aren't sentences."

"They are from an English lady, Sally. I bought them in a Philadelphia shop. I thought you would like to see them. They are recipes, a plan on how to cook. They are instructions to follow."

"I can cook," she said, worried that he was going to let her go.

"Yes, you can. People can build houses on their own, log houses, small ones, like those found everywhere."

"My house in Murderkill was brick."

"Just so."

What does a brick house have to do with cooking? she wondered.

"Then you must know that for such a structure you need an architect's plan."

He caught her puzzlement and explained the function of an architect.

"That's what this is, a plan for better cooking, to help a woman make more tasty dishes."

Prettyjohn read aloud the note at the top: "*Every servant who can but read, will be capable of making a tolerable good cook.* And you are a tolerable good cook. And now you can read from this, too."

She looked at it again. She needed Prettyjohn's help with only a few words, where the print was smudged.

Prettyjohn continued: "*And those who have the least notion of Cookery cannot miss of being very good ones.* You will be the best cook in New Castle. I plan to reprint one recipe at a time, to sell for two-pence. But I won't reprint any until you have mastered it first."

Prettyjohn explained to Sally that he was going to move his printing press and publications to another building a few streets away. He would use the parlor for discussions and add a special Sunday night where Sally would serve the latest from the cookbook.

For the several months, they perused the book. Their first recipe was for Chickens Chiringrate:

> CUT off their feet, break the breaft-bone flat with a rolling-pin, but take care you don't break the fkin; flour them, fry them of a fine brown in butter, then drain all the fat out of the pan, but leave the chickens in. Lay a pound of gravy-beef cut very thin over your chickens, and a piece of veal cut very thin, a little mace, two or three cloves, fome whole pepper, an onion, a little bundle of fweet-herbs, and a piece of carrot, and then pour in a quart of boiling water; cover it clofe, let it ftew for a quarter of an hour, then take out the chickens and keep them hot: let the gravy boil till it is quite rich and good, then ftrain it off and put it into your pan again, with two fpoonfuls of red wine and a few mufhrooms; put in your chickens to heat, then take them up, lay them into your difh, and pour your fauce over them. Garnifh with lemon, and a few flices of cold ham warmed in the gravy.

"This high dish may be too much, don't you agree?" he asked Sally.

She understood what he meant as they tried dishes from the British lady's recipes.

They followed recipes for small birds and various animals. They rejected dishes that were too difficult to prepare. Some ingredients weren't available in the market.

"Later, when we are successful, Sally, we'll hire an assistant. But until then, you have to work by yourself."

They finally settled on simple, unusual and tasty dishes.

Once the press was moved out of the house, Prettyjohn invited select men for Sunday discussions.

Sally served a new dessert to go with coffee and brandy as men gathered to discuss the latest political events. Prettyjohn then opened his house for Sunday dinners. He was certain that it was Sally's food that made this event the most popular in the city.

Women that Sally had come to know asked how she had made the pudding, Prettyjohn sold them recipes that had already proven successful. A demand developed for future recipes. They were sold out as soon as they were printed.

Sally's reputation grew with each dinner served at Prettyjohn's: sauces for turkeys, roasted rabbit, boiled leg of lamb, veal roll, duck with green peas and onions, goose ragout, barley soup, rice made the Indian way, broiled mackerel, fried eels and flat fish, and a dozen different kinds of pies. She pickled barberries and black walnuts.

Sally's skill in the kitchen was matched by Prettyjohn's business acumen. Sumptuous meals attracted the most influential people in Kent County to his home. Parlaying the dinners to his advantage, Prettyjohn's first negotiation was to buy the Horse Head Inn, a building fifty yards north of his house. The tavern was one of the several in New Castle, but under Prettyjohn's direction it became the prime center for daily discussion and business transactions. Soldiers, common sailors and privateers patronized the Cave, but his clientele was literate and influential. Not the swagger of ruffians but serious discussions by gentlemen addressing political matters and the relations between the colonies and Britain filled Horse Head Inn.

In addition to the Sunday dinners, Sally prepared breakfasts of eggs and boiled milk and light meals through the day at the inn. The printer kept Sally from the side room of the Horse Head that filled with smoke and men playing whist or dice from the earliest morning hours.

Some visitors spent little money in the tavern—two dishes of tea with bread and butter all afternoon—but travelers splashed out on food and drink.

Prettyjohn's aim wasn't to turn a large profit from the tavern but to make it prime meeting place for Delaware's most influential citizens. His plan proved correct: through acquaintances he received a license from the Levy Court to print a daily newssheet of legal and shipping notices that provided him with a steady and lucrative income. He employed an apprentice as a rag picker to make the paper on which all his publications were printed.

Following tips given by patrons, Prettyjohn bought several properties in New Castle and a tobacco farm in Kent County, which in turn he rented to tenants.

The night a sloop docked on its way north from Jamaica Prettyjohn stayed at the tavern until dawn negotiating for part shares in the Boston slave ship. By midnight, Sally decided to retire. This was the first time she had been alone in the house overnight. She went to window to draw the bedroom curtains when she saw two lanterns swaying on the ship's deck. In the stillness stirred only by the sound of hooves on paving stones she heard the clatter of chains from the ship's deck.

She shut the window before a púca could enter.

She said nothing about the night to Prettyjohn. He wouldn't understand.

The following night voices from the slaver were louder. Sally clearly heard the rhythmic beating of metal on an anvil. A horse whinnied. As Sally went to close the window, light from the twin lanterns flashed before her eyes.

Sally ran to Prettyjohn's room where he had been reading in bed. His wig rested on a stool beside the bed. A candle burned on a small table. He pulled up a coverlet.

"I'm afraid," she said.

Prettyjohn asked of what but she couldn't say. She couldn't tell him about the horse or the light or a black man in chains staring into her window from the street below. She climbed into his bed. Prettyjohn didn't move until she placed herself closely against his side. He put the book down and they remained this way until the candle guttered.

Prettyjohn lay still for several minutes, feeling her settle, then took her into his arms and stroked her hair. She fell asleep, twitching now and then, and kissed her on her forehead. He had never seen someone so frightened.

Freedom's Struggle

BELL

In The Hollow of a Tree

BELL'S MISFORTUNE can be traced to his having disturbed the bird's nest that day in the woodland. That's what Robert's father says after Bell nearly drowns in a creek. Robert Panquash, Bell's friend, tells his father what Bell has done when they were out fishing: as they were putting oysters and a turtle in a gunny sack, they saw a vulture fly out of a hollow of a tree.

Six days a week Bell works in his master's field or grinding and packing flour at the mill by the rapids; Robert lives in a wigwam on the creek's clay side with his parents.

The two boys watch the bird soar into the sky and disappear into the distance. Bell is certain that the bird has left in search of food and won't return soon. He has seen vultures circle high for hours before returning to their nests.

"Let's go look," Bell says.

"Mothers watch," Robert warns. "She won't leave the baby for long."

"There's no baby yet."

"Just the same. She'll be back to protect her nest."

"She's as far away as Maryland by now."

"Vultures can see as far away as the bays." Bell laughs.

"Not even these buzzards can see that far."

He looks up and points. The sky is filled with summer clouds. There are no raptors, as there often are, with the large red-headed vultures wobbling with raised wings and above them a flock the black-headed vultures circling, waiting to descend on a carcass.

"She's gone now," Bell says softly.

Robert responds, "You can't see her. But she has eyes that see for miles. She sees everything."

"Maybe there are eggs in the tree, like you said."

"If there are, you got to leave them. She'll peck you to pieces."

Bell dismisses Robert's concern.

"You like chicken and turtle eggs. These must be good, too."

"The bird eats dead things. The eggs won't be good."

"One thing's not got anything to do with the other. That's a big bird. The eggs must be sweet."

"You heard how these bird hiss," Robert continues to argue. "They don't sing or call like other birds. You know that, don't you? You hear them. There's no sweetness in vultures. They're spirit birds."

Bell pays little attention to his friend's warnings.

"It will tear you into small pieces for its dinner, if you get it mad at you," Robert continued to warn.

"Go away," Bell says dismissively.

"I'll tell you something more: I heard vultures like black meat," Robert joked, trying another tactic to dissuade his companion from acting foolishly. He didn't tell him that it was a *pèthakhuwe* his father had told him about, and if provoked, might kill them both. If left alone, the same buzzards would keep them safe from the horned serpents that lurked in the ponds and fed on humans.

The boys are between a field and a marsh, at the fringe of a pine forest. It is Sunday, a day without work, the time that they spent together, in the woods, trapping game. They have been doing this as long as they can remember. Robert teaches Bell how to plait his thick, red-tinted hair and tie it with a strip of deer hide.

ONE DAY AFTER TRAPPING small animals, Robert told his father that they had seen a white bear in the forest.

His father asked, "Did the bear have fur or hair?"

"It was far. I don't know."

"I saw it," Bell said. "It was shining like ice."

"Did it climb a tree?"

"No."

Robert's father grew visibly worried.

"That was no bear but a man-eater," Panquash said. "It's an awful creature. The Creator told us to kill everyone before they take all our food or we will starve."

Robert listened intently, as he always did when his father imparted such information.

"There was a bloody battle to rid us of the scourge," his father continued. "Every warrior came with hatchets and clubs and arrows. That was the end of the creature. Remember when you see the blood red cranberry that the Creator reminding you of the battle where we killed it."

"So what I saw wasn't the man-eater, because they are all dead," Bell said.

"It could be one," Panquash said. "It is said that one escaped. Last year one was seen by the river in Long Neck." After hearing about this recent sighting, Robert's father and several relatives took their guns and went to the forest to hunt for the stiff-legged monster but couldn't find a trace—no footprints, no spoor, no broken tree limbs or cracked animal bones, no track whatsoever.

IF SWAIN KNEW THAT BELL associated with Robert, he would have forbidden it. The Panquash family was widely suspected by whites of sympathizing with Negroes and aiding their escape into the forest far removed from European settlements.

Relations had worsened between the colonists and the Indians since Robert's birth, the year the Shawnee chief arrived at Panquash's house with twenty others from his tribe. The Shawnee chief said he had made a pact Britain's enemies, the French and Iroquois, to rid the peninsula of the English and wanted the Indians on the Chesapeake's Eastern Shore to join him.

Panquash told the story to Robert many times:

A band of Shawnee came with Chief Messowan said, "The Shawnee won't be driven any more. The English are cunning. They can't be trusted. They take our land and they say they give us new land. Then they take this land. Everywhere we go they take away what they left to us. You are our grandfathers and they take from you. I tell you, the Iroquois are prepared to attack the English and we must join them. The French will be joining us, too. Bring together all the people here, Panquash. We'll band together. We won't be driven anymore"

The Shawnee band stayed a week and returned to their home on the Susquehanna. Messowan was a wise chief. Others head his wise words. He invited people from Rossakatum and Assacatum and all the Lenape from their lands to gather at Winnasoccum. The Nause Waiwash, the Choptank, the Pocomoke and the Assateague arrived for a war conference—men, women and children all came, deserting their homes, gathering around bonfires and drums.

Simon Aldequeck brought his followers, Captain John came with his; Hopping Sam from Locust Neck and his villagers joined them. John Wittonguis, Jeremy Peake, George Pokahaum and Bastobello were all present on the island in the swamp, miles into the darkness amongst the cypress trees. Each man arrived carrying his bow and brass-tipped arrows; a few had muskets. In a hastily constructed arsenal they stored their guns, powder, shot and a thousand arrows as they listened to orators for days exhorting the gathering to join forces in war.

Hopping Sam said, "They took our land and gave us a reserve. They expulsed us again. They promise and they lie. Their word is like the clouds of a dandelion seeds in the wind. Who now lives at Naugatuck and Stropping, where have our villages gone? Then they took our new land and removed us to a small place. What will be left of us when there is no more hunting? What will we eat when the small land that remains is only sand?"

I made a plan and said, "You Shawnee will come down the bay, you will sleep in the woods by day and travel by night. Half of us will attack the English to the east and the other half will attack them to the west. The redcoats are small in number. The Iroquois and the French will land on the coast. They will be our allies."

We put feathers in our hair and dyed our faces scarlet and painted our torsos in red and black stripes. I hung around my neck a pouch decorated with porcupine quills; a man wearing a mask, whose name he kept from even me, brewed poison in a pot.

A week after the war camp meeting gathered in the swamp, Swain and his neighbors noticed that no Indians had been seen for days in the region. Similar reports came from Chesapeake Bay; the same was true along the Delaware coast. If it were only men who had disappeared, their absence would have been dismissed, as a hunting party perhaps. But not a single woman or old man or child was left in the county.

Upon receiving the alarming news from the white colonists, the governor ordered the royal soldiers to the swamp to block all escape routes. Many were arrested and brought to Annapolis for trial.

"They signed a peace treaty," Robert once told Bell after repeating the story that he had often heard from his father. "The English held Captain John and forced him to sign the treaty. One by one they agreed. There was no choice to sign except to stay in jail. But from then on we could no longer choose our chief without the governor's approval. We could no longer own a gun without the governor's approval. And again our land was made smaller. Most clans left; they took their canoes to join the Iroquois. My father stayed. A few others also stayed."

BELL WONDERED WHY Panquash stayed in the neighborhood but he didn't ask and Robert never volunteered. One time Robert overheard his father say that it didn't matter where they lived but Robert didn't know what he meant by that.

"Come," Bell said as he began walking towards the hollowed tree. Robert followed him. They glanced skyward. No birds. Bell climbed the tree and reached down into the cavity. His arm was too short to reach the bottom of the tube. He signaled to Robert for help. At first his friend refused but Bell insisted.

"Hold me," he insisted. Robert grabbed Bell's feet and lowered him head first into the opening.

Bell groped in the dark with his extended arm and felt the cool smoothness of an egg.

"There's an egg in here!" he called to Robert. "Pull me out." He clutched the egg to his chest as he was carefully lowered. He held the egg for Robert to see. "Look."

Robert ignored Bell and pointed skyward. In the distance Robert saw a speck of a bird making its way in their direction.

Robert began to run; Bell followed, holding the egg in both hands as the two darted into the part of the forest with dense canopy and thicker undergrowth.

The vulture darted towards the boys but was deterred by the heavy vegetation. Robert led them across the forest floor, the vulture's cry becoming more distant. They remained hidden until the sky began to dim. When they emerged, Bell raised the egg above his head in triumph. Robert began to trot down the footpath. Bell began to chase after him. Robert turned when he heard a snap and his friend yelp.

The egg lay splattered on the ground beside his sprawled friend. A bone jutted from Bell's ankle.

Panquash admonished Robert for disturbing the nest of the clan's protector.

"The boy is as evil as his master," Panquash said as he explained why Robert was forbidden from seeing Bell again.

The broken ankle hobbled Bell and left him with a limp. That year an oak limb fell near him; floating embers set his hair on fire; milk spilled from a bucket when his stumbled on a fallen twig. A fever and hemorrhagic pustules nearly took his life. And in the spring a water moccasin bit and killed a woman slave when she and Bell were gathering cranberries.

BELL USUALLY HELPED LOAD Swain's flat-bottom boat with a cargo of tobacco and bog ore, but he always stayed behind. This time Swain had Bell board with him and two slaves as they meandered across the branches and creeks towards Angola Neck. Two men sat with oars across their laps as Swain sat in the stern, the boat drifting downstream with the current. Bell strode the walking-board with a setting pole taller than himself, which he used to push against the banks to keep the Durham boat from running aground.

They off-loaded the cargo and Bell watched the men argue about the price of the shallop Swain wanted to replace his Durham.

"Half now," the shipwright demanded.

"One third, another third upon completion of the framing." "In the new year," Zebulon Dyer countered.

"Before winter."

"I could not get her done sooner than April by any good carpenter."

Disagreement also broke out about the price of the bog ore.

"The quality is poor and it is overpriced. I'll do better with iron from Pennsylvania. Half your asking price."

The truth, Swain knew, was on the buyer's side. It was time to shut down the furnace.

The shipwright and Swain reached an agreement that was beyond Bell's hearing.

Bell and the men turned the Durham around and the rowers took their seats ready to guide the boat upstream. Swain looked at Bell, who immediately sat down on a plank seat.

Swain looked at Bell again and pointed to the sodden ground.

"There," he said.

Bell alighted. Mud ran through his toes as he stood there.

The men placed their oars in the creek. Swain swatted scores of water bugs with his hat.

For a nominal one pence Swain had added the boy in as a bonus when negotiating the price of a bateau with the shipwright. He had concluded that Bell was hapless and worthless to him. There was greater value in establishing goodwill with the buyer by giving him away without charge than getting a pound or two from the sale of the slave boy.

Months later, Swain learned from Panquash that Bell was under a curse. The slave owner was glad he didn't know that Bellhobble had been damned when he rid himself of the boy. Swain wasn't sure that with such knowledge he could have in good conscience gifted Bellhobble to someone else.

Wreckers

HERE IS THE STORY that Robert heard from Panquash who heard it from his father:

One day white fog will arrive with the rising sun. That is what the prophet said. We waited for fog all winter and spring. There was no white fog with the rising sun. The prophet was never wrong, so we watched for white fog with the rising sun all summer and fall. But for years no white fog came with the rising sun.

On the sixth year a huge bird with white wings arrived in the morning fog. We spread thousands of beaver and otter skins over the waves for the Great Spirit to walk upon. But the white men didn't step on them. They considered the beaver pelts and otter skins; they admired them and took many. They asked us for land no bigger than a cow's hide. We gave it to them. We welcomed them. The whites gave us many things in return: knives, axes and water the color of mud that burned like fire. Along with the whites and rum came bloodshed.

Because the story explained the arrival of whites but not that of blacks, Bell had nearly forgotten the legend Robert had related to him until he arrived at the cove in the area some still called Whorekill and saw for himself a big bird with white wings hovering above the water. Another bird lay on its side, a creature larger than an entire volt of vultures, its white wings clipped and lying beside its body.

Black and white men worked on the inert bird, attempting to keep it alive, it seemed. This ship's captain, like many others who sailed the barrier shores, hadn't been able to avoid the hidden spits and shoals that ran like deadly snakes' tongues ten miles out to sea. The *Prosperity* was luckier than countless other vessels. The ship remained upright and merely lost its rudder when it ran aground. The brig from Philadelphia, on its maiden voyage, hadn't even entered the open sea when it halted on a shallow trough no deeper than five fathoms and needed to be towed into the Dyer Shipyard, where it was careened and under repair when Bell arrived.

Zebulon Dyer owned the shipyard on Shipcarpenter Street, employing freemen, indentured servants, an Indian and slaves. He also had been appointed overseer of the highway, an office he leveraged to his advantage by acquiring tracts from bay to bay, although it wasn't at all clear whether Maryland or Pennsylvania had authority over these hundreds. For Dyer, the uncertainty regarding jurisdiction was like the roiling ocean waters, a place of opportunities for those ready to seize them.

Dyer put Bell to work as a hauler, bringing the needed pieces to workers for the repairs and construction. Bell saw men looking at papers with marks upon them. By the end of the year, he could decipher the numerical code and bring the proper piece of timber whether it was oak for ribbing, locust for trunnels or pine for masts whether planks, knees or futtocks. He learned what joiners and carpenters needed before they asked for their tools and material. And when an oxen-team arrived, Bell helped raise sternposts into place, then handed the ship-carpenter his tools as the skilled workman bolted the ribbing to the deck beams. Bell took wood from the steaming facility to be sawn and then helped stockpile the aged wood.

"Take this," one carpenter said, handing Bell a wedge to be inserted into the kerf. A couple of months later the bottom sawyer had Bell grip the whipsaw with him for the additional strength.

"You is clever," the top sawyer said and instructed Bellhobble in cutting plank boards into the proper thickness.

When Dyer was assured of Bell's wit and dependability, he sent him to collect salt from a shallow well a mile away, a task that was Bell's alone. There from the top of the 70 feet dunes he saw white birds far bigger than those in the shipyard. They were remarkable, floating on the horizon, with many sails of different sizes. In time he learned to distinguish those coming from Europe or the Caribbean from ships on shorter voyages. Bell could tell merchant from war vessels, and could distinguish the flags of many countries.

Every now and then, when work at the shipyard was quiet, Dyer allowed Bell to go to the market to buy plums or huckleberries, or cockles to be used as bait by fishermen.

Known simply as Bell when he arrived at Angola Neck, the workers in the shipyard—sail and mast makers, rope makers, caulkers, and haulers—agreed that as a boy one name would do, but he was nearing manhood and deserved a second. But it was Dinah and Tony who gave him his additional name.

"You are staying here," Dyer told Bell when he first arrived.

This was his slaves' house in the pine forest. The husband and wife, although not legally recognized as such, simply called him Bellhobble. But the yard workers preferred Yaller, but to Dinah and Tony 'Bellhobble Yaller' didn't make sense. Maybe if it was 'Yaller Bell' but they rejected that, too, neither of them ever having seen a yellow bell. Tony suggested they add Dyer, just as he had acquired his master's name when he was born.

"If he was born here," Dinah said, "then we'll call him Bellhobble Dyer. But who knows where this boy was born? Maybe you asked him."

"I asked. He don't know. But everybody at the shipyards like him."

Sip, their daughter, a couple of years older than the newly acquired slave, commented on Bellhobble's limp. They accepted Sip's proposal: 'Hobble,' an apt name for the boy. The yard workers dropped Yaller and Bellhobble Hobble became his name. It was Tony's fellow sawyer who fixed the two names, making Bellhobble a single word. Everyone, even Dyer strung them together, like Redcoat or catfish.

"Why's your hair like that, Bellhobble?" Sip asked.

Bellhobble shrugged.

"Come here," she said and touched his shoulder-length braids.

"Teach me how to do this," Sip said. "Here. Take this." She handed him a wooden pick. "You help me with my hair, I'll do yours for you." She removed her kerchief.

Bellhobble wasn't sure he wanted her assistance but didn't know how to say no. In a short while, he liked having her wash his hair and having her near him.

There were now three in the log cabin, one room that was kitchen, parlor, bedchamber and hall.

Dinah gave Bellhobble a tick to sleep upon. She placed it on the floor beside Tony. When Bellhobble moved his bedding next to Sip's palette, no one objected. Sip and Bellhobble slept on their sides, his back to her front. She placed herself with her chin on his head and her arm draped over his hip. Many nights Bellhobble placed her hand between his legs. She held his nib between her thumb and forefinger until it stiffened. He quickly fell asleep as she rocked him and rubbed herself against him until she quietly shook and soothed her.

When Bellhobble left in the morning with Tony for the shipyard, Dinah and Sip washed clothes, hoed and weeded in a clearing. They brought water from a branch and managed the cattle and pigs. They kept a portion of the money from the clothes they made that Dyer sold.

Some speculated that Bellhobble was, in fact, a mixed Indian and white and that Dyer shouldn't be holding him as a slave. Bellhobble wondered if perhaps the story was true. The legend of an Irish born woman who married a slave and raised a family was widespread. Their children weren't permitted to intermarry with their pure white neighbors, so they associated with the remaining Nanticokes in Sussex, explaining why so many children in that hundred came in many hues.

ALTHOUGH THE BOY PROVED USEFUL at the shipyard, Dyer was having second thoughts about acquiring another slave. The prospect of acquiring a slave without charge had been too tempting. While he hadn't regretted his decision, Dyer reasoned that it would be to his benefit to remove Bellhobble from his assessment and employ him as free labor instead on a seasonal basis. By claiming fraud— he hadn't been told he was mixed blood—he would avoid incurring the tax he would have to pay for manumitting a slave.

"Swain duped me into taking him," Dyer explained in his plea. "My ignorance is sincere, as you can determine by the circumstances. I should have realized what he was when I first saw him wearing his hair in the Indian manner. But I have no pecuniary interest in him. There is no money to be returned to me. I only want the rightful manumission of this boy Bellhobble, for him to live free."

The court examined the bill of sale for Bellhobble's purchase and found no basis for Dyer's petition. Nowhere was there an indication that Bellhobble was anything other than what the contract stipulated, a Negro slave.

If Dyer wanted to free Bellhobble, the court would facilitate the transfer of status requiring a posting of a bond.

"But if this boy proves unable to care for himself, Mr. Dyer, be aware that he will continue to be in your charge."

While Bellhobble was a quick learner, being lame, Dyer thought, he might well become a wastrel, and so declined to manumit him.

As soon as the case was over and Dyer returned to the neck, conversation returned to more important things: protection from pirates and privateers.

ZEBULON'S FATHER HAD BUILT a small lighthouse at the cape, its care now fallen to him. No more than a raised stone platform with a metal shelter that shielded an oil lantern, it was the only warning to ships' captains along the stretch from Hatteras to the mouth of Delaware Bay. While of some use, the beacon atop the dune line was inadequate to prevent ships from foundering along the shoreline. The lighthouse flame was small and the wind often extinguished the lamp fire. The structure needed frequent rebuilding; sometimes whale oil had been spent.

Residents in Lewes Town had reason to worry: there been an attack at Bombay Hook, and French privateers took several ships in the Delaware Bay. Dyer heard that French pirates seized a Chesapeake brigantine. Not having a local pilot to guide them, the captured ship ran aground and floundered while the pirate ship slipped away unscathed.

Dyer went to the beach with his father to look for plunder. A single barrel of cider bobbed in the surf, the rest of the flotsam twisted and useless pieces of cargo and ship matter. Bloated bodies littered the beach. One seaman, a shirt his sole covering, wandered towards them. His father let the delirious sailor die.

Dyer and his father scoured the beach for weeks. They found a few reals and a couple of gold escudos. They took good pieces of wood to the shipyard.

The county sheriff reported that "several evil-minded persons have contrary to all law and justice" taken possession of items from the wrecked ship for their own use. Suspected of having stolen material and carried it home, the sheriff questioned residents in Lewes Town. Nothing was found to implicate the elder Dyer or his son. The Spanish coins were hidden in the forest and what decent wood they had salvaged was already part of a flat bottom boat in the creek.

William Dyer assured the sheriff that if he did find anything of value in the future, he would without hesitation report it to the authorities. And if there was the slightest suspicion that a neighbor had plundered, the elder Dyer vowed he would inform the sheriff about the lawless wrecker.

"We've had more than our share of marauders," he told the sheriff. "It is from my own effort and pocket that the lighthouse, such as it is, is maintained by my son and me. I am not a wrecker, sir."

WHENEVER DYER WENT TO the lighthouse, he brought Bellhobble with him. Although he was lame, the slave was strong enough to assist with the sails on the shallop. Dyer steered the small boat across Rehoboth Bay, then waited as Bellhobble climbed the steep dune to re-set the base of the stones, replenish the sperm oil in the near-empty lantern and swap a new glass shade for the often broken old one.

Two weeks had passed since Dyer and Bellhobble had last maintained the lighthouse. The backlog of repairs had been taken care of and Bellhobble was certain that with the lowering clouds Dyer would take him from the sawpit to make the lamp ready before the storm would settle.

"You better get going soon, Bellhobble, before the storm," the top sawyer said. "This looks a hurricane coming down."

Bellhobble left the sawpit to find Dyer.

"What do you want?" Dyer asked as he continued to read the papers on his desk.

"Just waiting to go fix up the lighthouse."

"If there's no more sawing, there's work elsewhere."

"Yes, sir."

Bellhobble returned to the sawpit as the wind picked up and the sky blackened. A pilot schooner's lines were secured to the dock cleats, a pungy under repair was battened and every boat in the cove had its sails furled.

"Put away the tools," Tony told Bellhobble.

Bellhobble went from station to station as the tradesmen made their places sheltered from the storm. When the workers secured all the loose objects, they left the shipyard. Bellhobble followed Tony to their cabin.

Only God could understand the capricious nature storms— the worst hurricane in anyone's memory devastated the area and prostrated Lewes Town, yet little damaged Dyer's shipyard. Coastal dunes were reduced to swales; where the land had been flat, sand banks climbed forty feet high. Beach grass tore away like hair taken from a scalp. In the forest trees toppled but Tony's log cabin proved stronger than plank houses. Lewes Town lay prostrate.

Dyer, with Bellhobble and several men, went down to the beach. The wreckage they found wasn't like anything found before. This was a frigate, heavily armed and laden with treasure. Dyer and neighbors decided that an unannounced military ship had planned an attack against the British crown and so therefore should be treated as an enemy. Dyer called them pirates.

"They will have no succor from me," he said. He also would deny them shelter. "They gave none when they raided."

Others had more sympathy for the handful of survivors and accompanied them to Lewes Town to await county authorities to arrive,

A small portion of the ship sat humped on the beach like a turtle's shell. Dyer cut a hole in the hull and lowered Bellhobble on a rope into the darkness to search for treasure. Nothing was found on a body that hissed putrefied air when Bellhobble poked it with his knife.

Over the next several days wreckers collected copper pots, iron tools, packets of tobacco that had been kept dry in wrapping, many pieces of mahogany planks worth thousands of pounds, rigging and belts. Only one of the two hundred small arms seemed worth salvaging. Dyer gave one to Bellhobble and told him to bury it in the forest, along with the bayonets that were found. Between them, the wreckers had found two hundred pieces-of-eight scattered across a mile of beach. They gathered the coins together and buried them in several locations.

Months after the storm a court case opened in Annapolis. The captain, who had been one of the survivors, presented his complaint. Whatever was found on the beach belonged to the Spanish king.

"We were part of a treasure fleet," the captain explained. "One ship was the admiral's ship and carried the president of Hispaniola."

"What did it contain?" he was asked.

"Three hundred chest of silver, sugar, copper, hides, cochineal and indigo."

"That ship is reported to be in the Carolinas," the judged said. "It is safe. The crew has been saved."

"Thanks God for that. The zumaca was he admiral's vessel. The Hispaniola governor was on board."

"And yours?"

"We had horses. We dropped anchor within sight of the bluffs. The flukes dragged along the sandy bottom but didn't hold. Each swell we drifted closer to the beach. We kept the stern to the sea to prolong our drift. The mainmast, foretop and mizzenmasts were gone. We took on more than seven feet of water in the hold. I ordered all twenty guns tossed overboard. Wind and swelling waves drove the frigate into a trough between a sand bar and the coast. Several sailors hoisted our small boats but they were crushed to pieces before they could be manned. Many tried to swim but all were drowned."

"How did you make it, captain?"

"We lashed together a raft. We carried with us a good deal of money and other things of value."

"They and a few men and me survived. On board we had chests of silver, cochineal, hides and sugar."

The court agreed with the captain's plea but by the time the sheriff arrived in Lewes Town to enforce the law, demanding that everything that had been salvaged be accounted for and turned over to him, much of the material gathered from the beach had been smelted or repurposed, sold or hidden.

The sheriff explained that since England and Spain had signed a treaty, the goods properly belonged to King Philip and the monarch's representative wanted his property returned.

The Lewes Town citizens dismissed the argument as frivolous. The year before the hundred was ordered to form a militia to defend against the harassment of French and Spanish marauders but not a single battery had been built to protect them. The town's plea to the colony for permanent defenses, but it fell on deaf ears. They needed English frigates off their coast to intercept privateers and pirates before they landed. Muskets should be arms of last resort and certainly were of no use against canon broadsides.

"The captain claims valuable properties were taken by him to the shore. If not returned, this is larceny," the sheriff said. "All goods are those of the king's own Royal Company."

"There were worthless things on the beach. The sea chewed up everything. It was a terrifically fierce storm. If there is anything of value, it is out at sea, not here."

"The captain's petition says otherwise. He claims there are valuable properties here. He brought them himself on a raft. It was all there when you found him."

"We saved his life," Dyer retorted.

"Maybe so. But you have no more right to the wood in the bay than the English have to the mines in Mexico." Reprisals by Spain were a real threat without appeasing the Spanish monarch, he explained. "You are putting the colony's shipping at risk."

The sheriff searched the salvers' homes. When the wreckers walked with him on the beach, they helped the official uncover a score of silver pieces. Over the following week the sheriff questioned every suspect in the hundred. The sheriff had only one lead. It took him to the forest. There he found a pistol buried beside Tony's house. While every white man was required to keep a musket and rounds of ammunition for his militia service, possession of a gun by a Negro was outlawed since the time of the conspiracy to burn New York. Authorities feared foreign enemies but equally an insurrection by their own slaves.

Tony protested that he knew nothing about the pistol. Not wanting to lose his service, Dyer intervened.

"I was with the boy at the beach the day we went down," Dyer said. "Tony is a good worker and law abiding."

"The boy took the pistol, then," the sheriff said, more a decision than a question.

"I don't know who else, if not him."

"You do what you will with the boy," the sheriff said dismissively. "He is more a danger to you than to the colony. He's a local concern. Bring him to be tried in your Negro court. You need to be concerned about yourself."

Before leaving the sheriff served Dyer with a summons to answer in Annapolis. Several months later he received a second summons. Dyer ignored this one, too. There wasn't a third demand.

The Lewes Town magistrate had no interest in enforcing a directive from the Maryland colony; he favored Pennsylvania's claim to the area. Dyer wanted no part of any court.

Upset about Bellhobble's carelessness in not keeping the pistol better hidden, Dyer punished the boy himself. The penalty for a Negro owning a gun was twenty-one lashes on a bare back. Not wanting to further compromise the boy's physical abilities, Dyer stroked him half the amount and allowed Bellhobble to keep on his osnaburg shirt during the whipping. Dinah replaced the shredded garment with one made with her own hand.

No Longer a Slave

WAGONS ROLLED into the city carting the rank bodies from the massacre. Angry wagoneers left the mutilated, rotting remains of pioneers in front of merchants' and government houses. A woman, from Shippen, had a bullet hole in her head; her husband had been scalped.

Ready to defend themselves, the frontier settlers were desperate for assistance from the province. Great Britain had encouraged the colony to muster a militia but the provincial legislature was reluctant. Pacifist sentiment was strong in Penn's proprietorship. But without assistance, the western farms couldn't be sustained. The remains made the point.

> The humble petition of the subscribers, inhabitants of Lurgan township, in Cumberland county, amicably unite in a company, under the care and command of Mr. Alexander Culbertson;—Showeth, that inasmuch as we Dwell upon the Frontiers our case is Lamentably Dangerous, we being in such imminent Peril of being inhumanly Butchered by our Savage neighbors, whose tender Mercies are Cruelty; and if they should come upon us now, we are naked and Defenceless; being in a great Measure destitute of Arms and Ammunition.

> It is the only kind Providence of God that restrains them. And in these sad and lamentable Circumstances, we betake ourselves to your Honor's compassion, as to a kind and lamentable Father of whose tender concern for us we are well assured.

> May it therefore please your Honor, in your great wisdom and goodness, to Commiserate our unhappy

case, and strengthen our Hands with such a Quantity of Arms and Ammunition, and upon such terms as your Honor see fit, and your Dependent Petitioners, as in duty bound, shall ever pray.

The bodies left on the streets moved the council to provide funds for the construction of forts and settlers were also assured that a militia would be raised to defend against "the cruel incursion of the French and barbarous Indians, who delight in shedding human blood."

The necessity of a tax divided opinion in Lewes Town, as did the British bill permitting the enlistment of servants. Dyer argued that although he would be compensated for the time a servant spent in the militia, it would still cause financial harm.

"I have invested much in training apprentices," Dyer said with a mug of cider in his hand as he stood on the dock, "and now when they are most productive they will be gone from my service. The compensation is by no means adequate. And where will I replace them while they're gone? Good servants are scare as it is. It's an unjust burden." A neighbor argued that the raising a militia was morally wrong, a position expected from someone of the Quaker persuasion.

Dyer continued, "I tell you, if recruiting officers go ahead and sign up apprentices and servants, there will an insurrection."

"Let them take free Negroes," one resident said. "Let *them* march with the militia."

"Never give arms to niggers!"

"Agreed," Dyer said.

"But there's much servile labor to be done in the military. No need to arm them. There is also watch service."

"Not even a club or hatchet in their hands."

"Yes. It's a hazardous position we put them ourselves in if the darkies are around with so arms."

"That's all well and good," another said, returning to a previous comment. "But drummers and trumpeters won't do, music doesn't win wars. We need to procure proper militiamen. We can't allow the massacres to continue. Who will be next? Who's going to protect us against the next French marauders on our shore? They're coming. They're certainly coming again."

The Quaker responded, "The consequences of taking Negroes will be the introduction of slaves to provide your missing labor. The province will have to import slaves to replace them. Slavery is an abomination and evil that must be eliminated." He paused to regain his composure, unwilling to provoke Dyer. "This regulation will weaken the colony and prevent the increase of white inhabitants."

Dyer thought there would be a benefit to the threats and turmoil. Preparations for war would increase the demand to outfit a naval patrol. To his surprise, he discovered that his business barely benefitted. Shipyards in Philadelphia were better positioned than his to take advantage of the new interest in military expenditures. His yard was designed for fishing vessels and shallow draft boats; it was too small to accommodate warships for refitting and repair, no less building, although he hoped he might get a contract for gunboats. He couldn't expand his yard works. The problem was that Lewes Town was too shallow to provide a safe harbor. Citizens of the hundred had to acknowledge that business was shifting upriver to New Castle, Wilmington and Philadelphia.

Shortly afterwards Dyer received a letter from his cousin, Joel Hambright:

> *The enemy came down upon Penn's creek, killed, scalped and carried away all the men, women and children, amounting to twenty-five in number: and*

wounded 1 man, who fortunately made his escape, and brought us the news, whereupon the subscribers went out and buried the dead, whom we found most barbarously murdered and scalped.

We found but thirteen, who were men and elderly women. The children, we supposed to be carried away prisoners. The house where we suppose they finished their murder, we found burnt up; the man of it, lying just by it. He lay on his back, barbarously burnt, and two tomahawks sticking in his forehead.

I am exceedingly sorry that the legislature has not seen it practicable to send two hundred fusees for the Road-cutters. John Potter, the sheriff, tells me that his son and a few more ought to set off to-morrow with forty head of cattle to support the Road-cutters and Captain Hogg's men, but the people are so alarmed about the Indians that he cannot think it safe to venture them out unless he can intercede with twenty or thirty of his neighbors to guard them.

Hambright beseeched his cousin for help on his frontier farm. With the promise of a bounty for each Indian scalp brought in by the military, he explained, there was also a shortage of farm hands, as many able-bodied men in the township had joined the British forces in battle against the Indians and their French benefactors.

Dyer replied promptly, writing that he was greatly moved by his cousin's melancholy state and, like him, he, too, was greatly concerned about the French threat.

"Inasmuch as he is a reliable lad who is not yet a journeyman, I will lease to you without charge one of my bondsman. You will find him of average intelligence and passably skilled in carpentry. He is an honest boy," Dyer wrote.

In exchange for a year of Bellhobble Hobble's service, the shipwright added, was an equal share of any bounty received for Indian scalps. At $130 for a male scalp and $50 for each woman proposed by the legislature, Dyer calculated that his munificence could also be good business.

DYER INFORMED BELLHOBBLE THAT the following day, he was to bring to the shipyard a bundle with his belongings.

"There is a packet ship and I'll be taking you to Philadelphia with me."

That afternoon Bellhobble and Sip sat on the sandy ground by the backdoor. An oriole sang in a pine tree at the forest's edge. Bellhobble said, "I didn't tell you this before. Once I did a bad thing."

She waited.

"I was with Robert. He told me not to do it. But I did it anyway."

Sip looked at the ground.

"I disturbed a vulture's nest. The birds are sacred. I didn't know that. But Robert warned me. I did it anyway. Because of what I'd done I have been cursed."

Sip lifted her head and took his hand.

"It has come on me again, this curse. I thought that I had left it behind but it is still with me."

Bellhobble examined Sip's hand that contrasted sharply against his own.

"Look at this. Our two hands," Sip said, raising them to her chest, "are like colors of the singing bird."

"Maybe we can fly away together," Bellhobble's voice as quiet as the bird's.

Sip rubbed their hands against her cheek, waiting for him to explain.

"Turtle Nose is sending me away. I know that's what he's going to do. He's going to sell me. I begged him to let me stay. He grabbed a club when I talked to him, so I didn't protest any more. It's the punishment for what I did."

"What did you do to make him angry?"

"Nothing. I always do what he asks. It's the curse that brings me bad fortune. The vultures. I'm as good as some of the hired workers and apprentices. It's not my work."

"Maybe you is too good," Sip said a bit sharply. "Turtle Nose can get a fair price for you. Don't be so keen at what you do. There's no profit in it for you, Bellhobble, only sweat."

"I thought my leg was damage enough to make me worthless.

"You're too eager."

"I don't want to go away from this place."

That night Bellhobble and Sip pledged themselves as husband and wife.

Departing Lewes Town before sunrise the following morning, the packet ship with Dyer and Bellhobble sailed up Delaware Bay to arrive in Philadelphia before dusk.

Dryer knew why the wagons were gathered for the frontier. He had seen the advertisement from Ben Franklin in the newspaper stating the need for "one hundred and fifty wagons, with four horses to each waggon and fifteen hundred saddle or pack horses, are wanted for the service of his majesty's forces."

On Market Street Dyer bought dried meat, then stopped at the Sign of the Conestoga Wagon to find a driver heading west. Behind the inn smelling of coffee and sweat there was a livestock pen, and a place for slaughtering and dressing pigs. A half a dozen colonial wagons were being loaded.

"Yes. I'm on my way to Blue Ridge. Not far from Penn's Creek. I have no room to carry anything for you. The wagon is fully booked."

"I am sending my bonded boy to aid my distressed cousin. Can you transport him? He'll be of help."

"This boy here? He can barely walk. He'd have to ride."

"Don't be fooled by his limp. He's clever and can do what labor you need."

"Yes," the driver, John Smith, said, "I can take on your boy—what's his name?"

"Bellhobble."

"— for a shilling a day until delivered."

He bargained with the driver and when they reached the agreed upon price, Bellhobble settled under the canvas covering. He sat amongst fifty bushels of grain, half oats, half Indian corn.

"GET OUT FROM THERE! No one rides inside."

The red-wheeled wagon with blue sides and arching, white canvas covering lumbered out of the city as part of a convoy to the Appalachians. The teamster walked alongside the left side of the horses, his hand close to the brake handle, while Bellhobble sat on the lazy board, a plank pulled from under the freight wagon. Several times a day Smith mounted the wheel horse for relief. Bellhobble and the driver slept on the sacks of grain in the enclosed wagon.

They followed the King's Road to Lancaster, where blacksmiths repaired what had been damaged on the highway and the Conestogas were re-provisioned. Outside the borough severed Indian heads on spikes lined the road. When they forded the Susquehanna at Harris' Ferry, one wagon slipped on a rock and tipped on its side. The teamster, pinned under a flailing horse, drowned. Bellhobble jumped from the lazy board to help push the wagon upright and then loaded the dead driver's body in the wagon. They buried the body before the vultures could descend, then continued westward.

They met a score of white men, women and children heading on foot in the opposite direction, towards the river.

"It's not safe up the road," one of the marchers said. "Six people were scalped not more than four miles from here. The Indians have fired our barns and houses." The band's leader explained that they had left their farms and Indian corn behind and were heading to Lancaster where they could be better protected.

Indian attacks on whites weren't news to the wagoneers; they had seen the mutilated bodies dumped on the Philadelphia streets. But it was the first that Bellhobble heard about such atrocities.

"Where can we find the general's troops?" Smith asked.

They had no answer for him.

The convoy's teamsters conferred with one another about the advisability to continuing their trek. Six drivers decided to return to river's east side and took the marchers with them. Bellhobble's teamster and three others decided to press on.

A letter of testimony read in court, when the teamster was released as part of a prisoner exchange with the Indians five years later, explained what happened next.

> *I returned up the road, in the company with one Arnold Vigoras, a back countryman. Three Indians had made a blind of bushes, stuck in the ground, as though they grew naturally, where they concealed themselves, about fifteen yards from the road. When we came opposite to them they fired upon us, at this short distance, and killed Mr. Vigoras, yet their bullets did not touch me; but my horse making a violent start, threw me, and the*

Indians immediately ran up, and took me prisoner. The one that laid hold on me was a Canasatauga, the other two were Delawares. One of them could speak English, and asked me if there were any more white men coming after? I told them not any near that I knew of. Two of these Indians stood by me whilst the other scalped my comrade: they then set off and ran at a smart rate, through the woods, for about fifteen miles, and that night we slept in the Allegheny mountain, without fire.

When Dyer learned of the fate of the wagon train, he wrongly assumed that his slave had been slain. But Bellhobble, like Smith, had been spared. While Smith had been run off into the forest, Bellhobble was taken by other Indians waiting in the woods who, after two days walk and feasting on roasted groundhog, brought him to their encampment surrounded by laurel thickets. One warrior, his face painted vermilion and clad only in a breechclout, let out a long yell to announce that he had brought a captive with him. The villagers returned the yell, which was answered with celebratory gun bursts in a nearby village. Two ranks of villagers stood ready for the prisoner.

"You must run between them," he was told. "They will flog you as you pass." With that, he kicked Bellhobble so that he fell to the ground. He picked himself up and was hit on his back with the side of a tomahawk. Bellhobble ran between the Indians as they beat him. He couldn't see when sand was tossed in his eyes.

Why he wasn't beaten to death after he fainted, he found out later. The English-speaking brave stood beside him as a woman washed his wounds with brandy.

"Why didn't you kill me?"

"You aren't English. You aren't their color and your nose is flat. You wear your hair like one of us."

"I'm a slave."

He told him about Robert but kept secret his disturbance of the vulture's nest.

"I don't know my mother or my father. I've never known them. I was sold when I was very young."

"You are Susquehannock. No longer a slave. You live with us. Your name is Onskat. One. I am Chinnohete. I was born in the snow. You are the only one with yellow skin. Onskat."

The gauntlet run by Bellhobble had been the first step in a rite of passage into the tribe, a replacement for Chinnohete's brother who had been murdered by the French.

After the initiation, Chinnohete's parents accepted the captive as their own child. He and Chinnohete were made fully brothers.

By the stream, the chief held Bellhobble's hand as he made a lengthy speech that Bellhobble didn't understand. When the old man finished, Bellhobble struggled to free himself from two women who held him firmly and then stripped him of his clothes.

"Don't be afraid," Chinnohete laughed as the women dragged Bellhobble to the water, plunged him in and rubbed him vigorously with grit. The women removed him from the water and walked him shuddering and naked to a large house where the villagers were waiting with fresh clothes: moccasins, leggings adorned with ribbons, a ruffled shirt and porcupine quills and red feathers for his hair. Bellhobble, now Onskat, was presented with a pouch made from a cougar filled with dried sumac and tobacco leaves. By the end of the ceremony he also possessed a flint and touchwood for fire.

Chinnohete plucked the hairs from his brother's head, leaving only three locks, two tied around a beaded band, the other braided and held in place with a silver pin. His upper body was pained in various colors and gave him bracelets for his right arm. They pierced his nose and ears and plugged the holes with blue stones. The chief spoke again and Chinnohete translated.

"He said that you are now one of us and have nothing to fear."

Chinnohete taught Onskat how to set beaver traps and recognize the spoor of deer and bear. He taught him how to fire a musket; he helped make him a bow of his own. When the men went on long expeditions to hunt for meat, Onskat remained behind with Chinnohete. Women and girls gathered haws and nuts; Chinnohete and Onskat brought them turkeys they shot in the nearby woods. Within several months, Onskat could speak as well in Chinnohete's language as Chinnohete could speak English.

The following winter Chinnohete took Onskat to a cabin a day's walk from their village. The men had been away for more than a month and hunger was beginning to grab everyone's stomach. For the first time Onskat had been on a hunt for a large animal.

Each time they approached a deer, the crunch of snow under their feet scared the animal away before they could shoot.

Chinnohete pointed to an elm tree. Scratches from bear's claws led their eyes to a large hole in the crown.

"It's sleeping for the winter," Chinnohete whispered.

Onskat wanted to tell him not to disturb the bear in the tree. But he wouldn't tell him about the curse that was on his own head.

Onskat found a long, straight branch to give to Chinnohete along with a pouch of dried wood. Chinnohete tied a hook to one end of the pole and secured the pouch to his waist. He climbed from limb to limb with the pole until he reached the opening. Tying the dry wood to the hook, he lit it and poked the smoking branch into the burrow. Chinnohete scrambled down as soon as he heard snuffing. He grabbed his gun, waiting for the bear to chase after him. Seeing the bear's nose, Chinnohete aimed his gun but it was too dark to aim properly. He then picked up his bow and when the bear fully emerged, he killed it with his first arrow.

They skinned the bear, roasted its liver in caul fat, ate until they were full, then cut as much meat as they could to carry back to the village.

Chinnohete stopped Onskat from taking a further step. The brave picked up a quill from the slushy ground and turned it slowly close to his eyes.

"It's filled with rattlesnake poison," he told Onskat, holding it close to his brother. He turned the quill upside down and liquid dripped from the point. "It's a trap set by the Catawba."

As they walked through the brush, sweeping the ground before them, Chinnohete told Onskat about the French and English at war with one another, about the many tribes that had been pushed from ancestral grounds into the area where they now walked, about their land taken by chicanery and violence, the shifting alliances between Indians and whites, tribe and tribe, allies one day, enemies the next— Chinnohete speaking too quickly for Onskat to understand, the details too much for Onskat to comprehend. But he knew from Chinnohete's demeanor not to ask a question.

From the woods they could smell smoke.

A lone dog whimpered.

Chinnohete and Onskat crawled on their stomachs to the perimeter of their village.

"Come," Chinnohete said, leaping to his feet. Onskat followed him into the forest. They dropped their heavy sacks of meat but when the winter sun set running was too dangerous. They covered themselves with leaves and snow, rested against a tree and awoke before dawn. By a rill they sat on a raft they had fashioned from branches and floated down the cold stream until coming upon a bend clogged with ice. They ran across frozen fields as far as the big river, paddled across on logs and continued until they reached a Conestoga compound. Here lived the remnants, numbering twenty, of a prior generation who had signed the Treaty of Friendship with William Penn and were now under the protection of the sheriff of Lancaster County.

The brothers conveyed their news and were taken in by the villagers.

Dyer read an account of happened in the *Gazette*:

On Wednesday, the 14th of December 1763, Fifty-seven Men, from some of our Frontier Townships, who had projected the Destruction of this little Common-wealth, came, all well-mounted, and armed with Firelocks, Hangers and Hatchets, having travelled through the Country in the Night, to Conestoga Manor. There they surrounded the small Village of Indian Huts, and just at Break of Day broke into them all at once. Only three Men, two Women, and a young Boy, were found at home, the rest being out among the neighbouring White People, some to sell the Baskets, Brooms and Bowls they manufactured, and others on other Occasions. These poor defenceless Creatures were immediately fired upon, stabbed and hatcheted to Death! The good Shehaes, among the rest, cut to Pieces in his Bed. All of them were scalped, and otherwise horribly mangled. Then their Huts were set on Fire, and most of them burnt down. When the Troop, pleased with their own Conduct and Bravery, but enraged that any of the poor Indians had escaped the Massacre, rode off, and in small Parties, by different Roads, went home.

The universal Concern of the neighbouring White People on hearing of this Event, and the Lamentations of the younger Indians, when they returned and saw the Desolation, and the butchered half-burnt Bodies of their murdered Parents, and other Relations, cannot well be expressed.

The Magistrates of Lancaster sent out to collect the remaining Indians, brought them into the Town for their better Security against any further Attempt, and it is said condoled with them on the Misfortune that had happened, took them by the Hand, comforted and *promised them Protection.* They were all put into the Workhouse, a strong Building, as the Place of greatest Safety.

The governor ordered judges, justices, sheriffs, constables, civil and military to arrest the murderers from Paxton County.

Whereas a Number of other Indians, who lately lived on or near the Frontiers of this Province, being willing and desirous to preserve and continue the ancient Friendship which heretofore subsisted between them and the good People of this Province, have at their own earnest Request, been removed from their Habitations, and brought to the County of Philadelphia, where Provision is made for them at the public Expense; I do therefore strictly forbid all Person whatsoever, to molest or injure any of said Indians, as they will answer the contrary at their own Peril.

JOHN PENN,

By His Honour's Command, JOHN SHIPPEN, jun.

Secretary

GOD Save the KING

Confined to the workhouse for their protection with the others whose lives had been spared because they had been outside the village at the time of the raid, Chinnohete and Onskat sat without speaking for a week, scarcely eating the boiled squirrel and bread provided by the government.

A company of Royal Highlanders positioned nearby for additional protection, were useless, as an account in a pamphlet printed by Prettyjohn's press made clear:

> Notwithstanding this Proclamation, those cruel Men again assembled themselves, and hearing that the remaining fourteen Indians were in the Workhouse at Lancaster, they suddenly appeared in that Town, on the 27th of December. Fifty of them, armed as before, dismounting, went directly to the Work-house, and by Violence broke open the Door, and entered with the utmost Fury in their Countenances. When the poor Wretches saw they had *no Protection* nigh, nor could possibly escape, and being without the least Weapon for Defence, they divided into their little Families, the Children clinging to the Parents; they fell on their Knees, protested their Innocence, declared their Love to the English, and that, in their whole Lives, they had never done them Injury; and in this Posture they all received the Hatchet! Men, Women and little Children— were every one inhumanly murdered! —in cold Blood!
>
> The barbarous Men who committed the atrocious Fact, in Defence of Government, of all Laws human and divine, and to the eternal Disgrace of their Country and Colour, then mounted their Horses, huzza'd in Triumph, as if they had gained a Victory, and rode off—unmolested.
>
> The Bodies of the Murdered were then brought out and exposed in the Street, till a Hole could be made in the Earth, to receive and cover them.

Despite another proclamation by Penn offering a two-hundred-pound reward for the capture of each of the three ringleaders, the vigilantes, emboldened by their raid and mutilation of the Indians at Conestoga, marched to Philadelphia, demanding more than protection from the Indians—they wanted them eradicated. Along their march route village church bells rang warning people of the approached armed mob. Now hundred and fifty strong, they halted when they arrive in Germantown upon hearing that a militia had been mustered in the capital to intercept them. Doors in the town were closed and shops shut tight. Not soldiers but civic leaders from Philadelphia accosted them and engaged the vigilantes in street-side negotiations.

The leader of the city's delegation maintained that the Indians at Conestoga were unarmed and their attack without justification.

"The village was full of spies," Matthew Smith, the leader, claimed. "The savages were providing material to the French Indians. If the government fails to protect us, we won't let ourselves be slaughtered."

Franklin wanted to know why they were armed, if their aim was to petition the legislature.

Smith offered a reason that no one believed: "We are going to conduct the Indians out of the province who are on the island by Philadelphia. We ain't going to harm them."

The standoff in the street lasted several hours, until a deal was struck. The gang dispersed with the promise by Ben Franklin that their grievances would be read before the colonial legislature. Smith was given a pass to continue to Philadelphia to publish the settlers' demands.

Not ready to take sides in the debate about the province's response to Indian troubles, Prettyjohn printed pamphlets on both sides of the debate: the Quaker party, insisting on continuing to live in the spirit of Christian peacefulness; the frontiersmen calling the Quakers hypocrites whose sympathies were misplaced.

When the pro-Quaker party was swept out of office in the election held later that year, Dyer's worries about his business increased. Three years later, when it was obvious the shipyard would never recover, he manumitted Dinah and Tony, calculating that after paying the county tax for their upkeep, it was still in his favor to hire Tony as a day laborer. Sip and her baby, Mingo, he sold for a pittance to a plantation called Young Man's Chance, in the southern most of the Lower Counties.

NICHOLAS

Varnished and Feathered

AFTER THREE miscarriages and the deaths of two infants, Sally turns away from Nicolas when he is born. She stays in bed for a month while she hires a free Negro as her baby's wet nurse. After regaining her strength, she remains indifferent to her son. Sally refuses to leave her bedroom or remove her nightclothes. She sits silently as a servant brushes her hair.

Worried about his wife's lassitude while at the same time seeing opportunities in the burgeoning town to the north, Roger Prettyjohn has moved his family to Wilmington, where he petitions for a full license to sell wine, beer and spirits. In his appeal, he explains his reasons for wanting to engage in the tavern business in a new town. His wife needs a more salubrious atmosphere, he begins, and then quickly moves on to explain the financial need: an investment in a Boston ship has proven near disastrous—the slave ship lay at the bottom of sea off Antigua. His investment in the tobacco farm proves equally damaging, as the cost of tobacco production in the face of falling price put him on the brink of insolvency. Wilmington needs an establishment such as he would create, Prettyjohn says, a gathering place for genteel residents. It will not be another tippling house for sailors and vagrants. A friend from New Castle supplies written testimony that Prettyjohn is fully qualified and a man who will keep "no disorderly house." In front of the justices, Prettyjohn proclaims his willingness to serve the community. No witnesses are called against him and the magistrates grants him the license.

WITH THE ASSISTANCE OF A LOAN, Prettyjohn found space for his press in the cellar of a burger, and, one block away, rented a two-story brick building, on High Street, for his residence and tavern. He and his family occupied the cellar, while the upper stories were used as a coffee house, bar and lodging. His most lucrative endeavor was the annual publication of an almanac, which he sold widely throughout Delaware and Chesapeake,

Within two years after having relocated from New Castle, Pretty, as now everyone called him, had saved enough from his printing business and inn to add an addition to the house for his family. Sally planted sunflowers and hollyhocks for the front and lilacs and roses for the side garden and behind the house a vegetable garden. A buttonwood tree grew by the street.

The Pretty Tavern, with its overhanging sign of a buxom woman, remained at its original site.

Sally had recovered from her depression and assumed control of the household. In her cellar were potatoes and roots, casks of vinegar, barrels of sauerkraut, strings of onions, and bundles of herbs, hampers of dried peaches and apples, shelves of jars filled with sauces. In a few years, the cellar also contained a cask for Madeira for Pretty and his friends and a barrel of Marsala for Sally.

Pretty encouraged Sally to follow the advice in the *London Pocket-Book*, but she had no interest in thickening her hair with powders and pomades. However, she did own two chintz dresses that she wore with hoops, often with an apron that billowed from her stomacher and covered her petticoat.

Pretty and Sally were concerned with their hygiene. They adopted the latest method for their morning toilet: soaking a rag in snuff and rubbing their teeth clean; bathing once a week; but no matter what he tried, Pretty couldn't remove the deep ink stains that dyed his hands near black.

Pretty recognized Sally's business acumen and turned over much of the tavern's financial affairs to her. With her old injury making her arm all but useless, she supervised two Negro hired-girls around the house and in the kitchens, reading the recipes aloud, watching them they she added ingredients in correct proportions.

As his reputation and wealth increased, so did Pretty's belly, which rivaled that of any gentleman's in the county. Merchants', tradesmen's, lawyers' and judges' wives sought out Sally's company, eager to please their husbands as much as she did hers.

"An afternoon tearoom would be a good addition," Pretty said. He pointed to the success of Betty Jackson, the free black woman married to the butcher Hans Shadd. Shadd, a former Hessian soldier, had fought in the French and Indian Wars. His wife had a tearoom in their French Street house. From the first-story balcony a stairway led to a platform in the crotch of a willow that seated a half-dozen women. The expansive view of the Delaware River made it a popular place with Wilmington's ladies during the summer months.

"I know her cakes," Sally said. "They are the best of its kind."

"You can do better," her husband said.

"I have taken seeds from her flower garden. The idea of flowers on the dining table is hers."

Despite Pretty's encouragement, Sally, apprehensive about her ability to hold her own in conversation with other women, ignored her husband's suggestion. Her decision to reject tea was fortuitous. Shortly afterward, Wilmington's citizens viewed the sale of tea as unpatriotic.

While new thoughts and accumulated grievances began to cleave families and friends, Pretty fostered comity by dampening discussion about English rule, independence and slavery in his salon. Discussions on a philosophical level were tolerated but it was impossible to keep politics at bay.

"Two wagons left Duck Creek," a patron announced to the gathering one day. "They had cargoes of sugar, piece goods, rum, coffee. On their way to Chestertown a tax collector stopped them and demanded to see their papers. As liberty men, they didn't have what he asked for."

A lively discussion about British taxes ensued—to ignore them, to boycott certain goods, to pay the tariffs and duties under protest, allow Committees of Inspection and Observation to act in enforcing boycotts and morals.

Not having a part in the creation of the tariffs was a position everyone shared.

"We are free men and insist upon being treated as such."

"The collector put the drivers under arrest," the patron continued, "and told them to follow him to the nearest tavern where he stopped for several drinks. The drivers went back to their wagons while he was in the tavern and drove off. With their cargo, the wagons were slow and the collector on his horse easily caught up with them. Word of the arrest spread in the hundred. Men gathered and formed a group to capture the tax collector themselves. When they got him, they brought him to Oliver Gallop's mill."

He waited until he had everyone's attention.

"They varnished and feathered him and sprinkled him with water from a duck hole. They held his head under the reeking water until he saw the merits of our cause and damned the ministerial sons of bitches."

"Liberty and Duck Creek forever!" Everyone raised his mug in salute.

"The collector promised to resign and was told to report to Lord North with the warning that if he had been in his place, the treatment would have been far worse."

"Drinks for everyone," a traveler announced. "Liberty! Liberty!"

Not all wished the king well on this round.

It was a good day for business.

When Pretty's silence on political matters raised suspicions by staunch Americans that he was a secret agent provocateur of the Crown and by Tories that he was a revolutionary instigator, Pretty said that he was a half-way man, a patriotic American Briton, a statement enough to blunt sharp edges thrown by some and not to spoil Sunday appetites, where he tried to keep conversations around matters such as whether to yoke wandering pigs.

Pretty also did his best to keep neutral in his business: he printed essays and speeches on all sides of the debates, presenting arguments for conciliation and confrontation, articles by Whigs and Tories, proponents of voluntary manumission and those advocating mandatory abolition; broadsides for and against ending the slave trade, and defenders of the chattel slavery; he accepted work if the credit was good and the arguments not seditious. Most of his income was derived from advertisements, many of which offered rewards for returned slaves, a few for their sale.

Although Pretty valued his acumen as a businessman, he recognized that he wasn't a naturally gifted thinker. Wilmington had its fill of college graduates and houses with libraries and while he didn't aspire to their intellect, he brought such gentlemen together at his tavern, men who wore two watches—one hung on each side from a silver chain adorned with colored tropical seeds—, watch keys and seals, although such ostentatious display was coming under criticism by some in the Assembly. A few older gentlemen continued to wear large wigs made of white horsehair. Pretty kept his own clothes simple and his hair tied behind. He, like all gentlemen, was clean-shaven.

Pretty liked to think of himself as righteous, nearly in a Quaker fashion; he aspired to be remembered in the way a death notice he printed eulogized a mill owner: *"If it is even possible to suppose that any one man was more separated from worldly affairs, more willing to perform deeds of charity and benevolence, less guilty of bad thoughts of capable of bad action, than any of the rest of his kind, we should have upon—."*

He also expected that remaining even-handed and modest he wouldn't be driven to make a choice. He could take advantage of whichever side prevailed.

RECENTLY A QUAKER elder in the county had refused to accept Colonial scrip on religious grounds—the money was used to support a militia. His conscience couldn't countenance the use of force even in the cause of defending one's liberty.

He was brought before the Committee of Inspection and Observation, which denounced him as a traitor. The committee demanded that friends of liberty refuse to do business with him: millers wouldn't grind his Indian corn, and shallopmen wouldn't transport his grain. The schoolmaster sent his children home.

Nicholas gleefully watched as a sign was fastened to the Quaker's back:

ON THE CIRCULATION OF THE CONTINENTAL CURRENCY DEPENDS THE FATE OF AMERICA

To the beat of a drum, the farmer was marched through the town streets with a jeering crowd in tow. Nicholas struck the old man several times with rotten eggs.

Pretty planned for a keener intellect for his son. He wanted Sally to educate Nicholas, but it became evident to him that she didn't want to have anything to do with her son. She acted as though he were a stranger in the household and, except for a few unavoidable interchanges, she never spoke a word to him.

Pretty hired a tutor for Nicholas. And when the courthouse was extended to include a school wing, Pretty enrolled Nicolas there to learn about historical and scientific subjects. Each weekday Nicholas climbed wooden stairs on the outside of the building to his schoolroom, but he had no interest in developing his mind. He frustrated the schoolmaster, paying scant attention to the humdrum lessons. Nicholas would rather stare out the window at the smokehouse than lower his eyes to look at a page. When his eyes closed, the schoolmaster kept him awake with a rap to his head.

Residents referred to the jail as the 'smokehouse,' a name given to it because smoke from coals burning for warmth in the cells dishes leaked through the prisoners' brick walls. The only available light for those awaiting trial, vagrants or disorderly persons came through a one-foot square iron grating. Behind the cage stood the stocks and whipping post. It was impossible to keep the children in the room when they heard the beating of the drum when a prisoner was being released from the smokehouse.

At the first drum beat, Nicholas dashed down the staircase and across the square. A crowd had already assembled on the steps of the jail. As the door opened and the constable emerged with the prisoner, a vagrant, Nicholas began to hoot with the rest of the crowd.

"Forward!" the constable shouted and the drum began a steady beat. The prisoner was pelted with rotten eggs and vegetables. Nicholas scooped what he could from the gutter and threw pebbles, mud and animal excreta. The procession continued to the Brandywine Bridge, the drum beating, the man, a discharged prisoner from a Philadelphia prison, dragging his feet and begging for mercy.

Back in the classroom, the teacher berated the pupils for acting like rabble. He warned them that they would face worse circumstances themselves if they lacked self-discipline. The rigid Presbyterian schoolmaster called each pupil to the front of the room where he hit their knuckles with a willow switch.

One day when Nicolas was driving his father's one horse cart carrying newssheets throughout the hundred, Major Molliston, a British officer with a reputation for meanness, stopped him.

"Whose cart is this?" the major inquired. The cart was simple but new, painted black, the seat unvarnished and without supporting springs. On the harness were brass buckles and rings.

Nicholas answered, "My father's," and no more passed between them.

When Nicolas told his father of the encounter, Pretty told him to tell that he was going to offer the cart to the major for a certain sum of gold.

"But it's worth twice that amount," Nicolas objected.

"The soldiers will take the cart when they go away and I will get nothing for it."

"Ask for the proper price."

"Then I will get none."

Molliston agreed to Pretty's asking price. The cart was sent to the major and Nicolas went to collect the payment. Before returning to his father, Nicolas went to his room to exchange the gold coins for Delaware scrip he had kept hidden there.

"Here," Nicolas said, as he handed his father the tender.

"I demanded gold!"

"This is what he gave me."

"You shouldn't have taken it."

"Then he would have taken the cart with no payment at all," Nicolas retorted. "You said so yourself."

Pretty had no objections to various pastimes if they appealed to the higher sentiments. He, like all virtuous men, had been repulsed by the promotion at Philadelphia's Bull's Head tavern to gaze on a "wonderful female child with two heads, four arms, four legs, etc." A man and a woman seeking lodging always raised suspicion. He did his best to recommend rooms elsewhere, but when business was slack, he convinced himself that the couple were husband and wife.

Although dancing bordered on the licentious and wasn't encouraged at his inn, he didn't object when it did break out.

Only once did he regret his decision.

"I am seeking lodging for my wife and me. She is a Quaker and I want a place where there are none."

Pretty assured him that few Quakers attended his tavern.

The couple sat at the long, oval table with the other patrons.

"My wife was once a good dancer and singer," the guest complained. "Now all she wants to do is preach. Her new-found Quaker convictions are robbing her of her liveliness. And me of a good wife."

He told them that by moving to Wilmington, he hoped to cure her of Quaker preaching. His wife sat without expression, her cap neatly tied, her hands folded on her lap.

"I want to dance," he said. "She won't dance. But I want to dance. Is there a musician?"

"I'll fetch my fiddle," another patron announced. He began to play and the husband grabbed his wife's hand. Fear crossed her face but she didn't protest or resist.

"Come, my dear, shake off that gloom. Quit being a stiff Quaker."

The husband pulled his wife around as anguish shadowed her face and tears filled her eyes. The fiddler abruptly stopped.

"Leave your wife alone, sir."

The musician returned his instrument to its case.

The guest and his wife resumed their place at the table.

"Bring her to my town in New Jersey," another guest offered. "She'll soon be cured of her Quakerism."

Pretty did what he could to keep the high tone he set. Other publicans had been brought before magistrates for running bawdy and disorderly houses, places that attracted idle and debauched men. They were no more than dens of vice, sufficient reason to have removed him from the trade. Franklin called them "rookeries of vice as notorious as Helltown."

The Boston Histrionic Academy, fresh from an appearance in Baltimore, came to New Castle. Its manager approached Pretty about presenting the group for what the manager billed as a lecture.

No tavern in the county had presented this form of lecture, a discourse from an esteemed traveling troupe that was novel to Pretty, who was persuaded that it was certain to attract a crowd of decent people seeking spiritual improvement. As he had met success with Sally's meals, he saw the importance of innovation and accepted the manager's proposal. Unlike other taverns, Pretty had rejected gambling, billiards, gamecocks and boxing at his establishment and banned the use of rum, but lectures on moral uplift fit his temperament as much as the young ladies' vocal recitals he had introduced at the Horse Head and continued here. Quakers protested musical entertainment and attempted to sway him to give up the performances, but as a subscriber to no church, he easily tolerated these indulgences.

The manager convinced Pretty to offer his inn for the histrionic society. Tickets would be sold in advance and Pretty would keep half the income. Chairs would be provided for the ladies and benches for the gentlemen.

Nicolas posted handbills around the borough and rode as far as Red Clay Creek to announce the event.

The Pretty Tavern Wilmington Delaware

On Monday, June 10th,

at the Public Room of the

Above Inn

will be delivered a series of

Moral Dialogues

In Five Parts

Depicting the evil effects of Jealousy

and other bad Passions and Proving that Happiness can only spring from the pursuit of Virtue

Excited by the prospect of adding this attraction, Sally presented a new dish to Sunday's menu.

As plans were finalized for the night, Nicholas heard the troupe's manager tell his father, "I am glad to inform you that the esteemed Mr. Douglass, a triumph in New York, will represent a noble magnanimous Moor called Othello."

"Represent?"

"Yes. Represent."

A steak pudding.

MAKE a good cruſt, with ſuet ſhred fine with flour, and mix it up with cold water. Seaſon it with a little ſalt, and make a pretty ſtiff cruſt, about two pounds of ſuet to a quarter of a peck of flour. Let your ſteaks be either beef or mutton, well ſeaſoned with pepper and ſalt, make it up as you do an apple-pudding, tie it in a cloth, and put it into the water boiling. If it be a large pudding, it will take five hours; if a ſmall one, three hours. This is the beſt cruſt for an apple-pudding. Pigeons eat well this way.

"Explain what you mean."

"To show."

"To lecture, you mean?"

"Words, of course. Great words recited in a most effective way."

Pretty, his right hand in his waistcoat pocket, waited for more information.

"This is a new form of instruction, Mr. Pretty, a most informative method of elucidation and elevation. Sermons are appropriate for church, lectures are delivered in academies, but this is entertainment in the service of instruction for ladies and gentlemen in a fine establishment such as yours." Pretty waited for him to continue. "As a gentleman yourself, Mr. Pretty, a man of noble discernment, you are in no need for further explanation, I assume."

"No, I don't. But you must assure me that it is suitable for ladies of fine taste."

"No doubt, Mr. Pretty."

All the seats were occupied and before the lecture began Pretty calculated his profit. Not more than a quarter-hour into the presentation, Pretty realized that he had been misled. A few women left, soon followed by their husbands, who wanted their money returned. At the end of the first act, Pretty confronted the manager.

Pretty himself had printed a statement from the Association of Nonimportation, Nonexportation and Nonconsumption adopted by Congress laying out standards of behavior for patriots.

"True Americans should forgo every species of extravagance and dissipation," Pretty quoted to the manager. "Horseracing, gaming, cock fights. And exhibitions of plays and shows. Plays and shows! Do you understand? That's what you have presented here—theatergoing! Not a moral lecture. You are a deceitful man."

As they argued, more patrons left the room.

"You are a prevaricating scoundrel."

"You insult my honor, sir. But I forgive you. Give me my due and we'll leave."

"I won't pay you for a false delivery."

"If we stay any longer, for certain you'll be hauled before a court by the week's end for presenting what you call a show."

Pretty needed to put an end to the argument. It was best to demonstrate that he stood on the side of virtue.

At this point, Sally intervened.

"Have Nicolas get the money from the sale of the cart. He knows where it is kept."

Nicholas went to the house where he retrieved the money his father had hidden in a mortise in the frame of the house and returned with the Delaware ten-shilling notes. Pretty took the money from him and gave the manager a fistful of paper scrip.

Natural Rights

THE **SOLDIER USED** his cut and thrust sword as a walking stick, a "tremendous instrument," as Nicholas called it, bending and straightening with each stride the sergeant took.

The soldier, the first Nicholas could remember seeing, had arrived in Wilmington years before Sgt. Molliston, as the head of a company searching for a deserter. Nicolas and his friends trailed the soldiers as they went house-to-house looking for the defector. The English found him sitting in the parlor of a boarding house near the river. Clark had been in Wilmington for a couple of years and employed as a laborer at a farm supply store, a man who kept to himself and was respected by everyone. Whether the citizens knew that Clark was a deserter was unclear to Nicolas; he had never heard anything about the man's background.

The soldiers tied the prisoner at his wrists and paraded him to Pretty's Tavern. They planned to shoot him the following day. Suddenly a delegation of the borough's gentry, headed by a sheriff whose face was always covered by a green scarf to hide his cancerous sores, confronted the English soldiers.

"What do you want with him?" the sergeant asked, as he put his leather tankard on the plank table. He wiped the foam from his mouth with his sleeve.

"That you set this man free."

The soldier took his sword from the table and returned it to his scabbard.

"He walked away from his post. He is a deserter."

"Are you sure you have the right man?"

The deliberations lasted through supper and into the night, the sheriff speaking coolly and deliberately to Molliston, making the legal and humanitarian case for Clark's release. Pretty and Nicholas stood by the bar as the talks unfolded. By dawn the sergeant expressed his admiration for the sheriff and they toasted King George.

Clark's freedom had been purchased by the sheriff's delegation.

"Send me the bill for the food and drink," the man in the green scarf told Pretty as he departed the tavern with Clark following a few steps behind. The company of soldiers left Wilmington soon after.

When the birds sang and the crows cawed, a new crowd arrived for coffee, news, scheming and gossip. Nicholas eagerly filled them in on the night's events.

Pretty decided that the cost of food and drink was his contribution in buying Clark's freedom. Besides, Pretty reasoned, many business debts had been deferred indefinitely during the unsettled economic times that hung over the colonies. The chances of collecting the money weren't very good, he knew. Better to ignore the debt and be thought generous than to fruitlessly chase after a few pounds that may soon turn out to be worthless.

When the Committee of Inspection and Observation directed every white man between sixteen and fifty to enlist in one of three militias in the county, Pretty assembled with the trainbands, the men without uniforms directed to protect the neighborhoods who mustered in the town square once a week. Several free blacks volunteered to serve. They arrived at the town square with their muskets but were rebuffed. No one wanted to repeal the law barring blacks from bearing arms, a statute in place since the Negro insurrection in New York a generation before.

POLITICAL LINES HARDENED: a holder of a few lucrative offices in the county sailed for England, as did the minister and schoolmaster in the neighboring hundred; several large landholders from the southern counties joined the officers ranks of the British army.

Pretty refused Nicolas's urging to lie about his age to the committee in order for him to enroll for duty, not for the home guard, the volunteers or the Continental regiment. Until Nicolas reached the proper age, at least one more year, he would have to submit to simply admiring the smartly turned out soldiers in the uniform militias—blue coats with metal buttons, white waistcoats and breeches, white stockings held up with black garters. Half-gaiters covered the lower part of their boots and on their heads they wore round leather hats with a high, front peak and a ribbon around the crown.

Each soldier—trainband, volunteer or Continental—was required to possess a powder horn, a bag of balls, a firelock with a bayonet and a half-pound of powder. Although many white men owned guns, they needed to learn the fundamentals of military discipline. Pretty printed a manual of arms: hold the weapon on the left shoulder, forefinger and thumb on the left side of the stock, the other three holding the stock. The manual also contained the dozen steps needed to load, ready, aim and fire.

Nicolas urged his father to join a proper military force but Pretty wouldn't be cajoled by his son. He will do more for the cause of liberty by running his businesses and paying his taxes, he explained with irritation.

"They need money to keep . . ." he continued, when Nicholas interrupted with, "They need men. Let Negroes do the work and men defend our liberty."

Nicolas's opinions were more vocal than his father's. While Pretty tried to accommodate Whigs and Tories, a neutrality becoming near impossible to maintain, he failed to contain his son's truculence. More distressing was his frequenting dramshops.

"Our boy has the night mares," he told Sally. "He comes home stiff as a ring-bolt most nights. He has become a common drinker and a disgrace."

With her husband's turn of phrase, Sally could hear a black horse whinnying in the vegetable garden and if she were to peak through the window, she knew, she would see its luminous eyes. The spirit hadn't visited her in years but after her husband's complaint about Nicholas's drunkenness, the púca revisited her regularly during stressful times.

Trying to block out the sound of the púca, she said to Pretty, "I am going to cover our whitewash. There is paper for lining the walls for sale in Philadelphia."

Pretty encouraged Nicholas to drink at his own tavern rather than dramshops and throughout the winter his son complied.

After a difficult season, spring came as a relief. As was his custom since opening the tavern in Wilmington, Pretty brought in a small tree from the forest shorn of limbs, except for the top that looked like a knob. Adorned with flowers and ribbons, the pole was erected in front of the tavern. On the first day in May, Sally hired additional barmaids to manage the annual influx of fishermen and fish peddlers to the borough who had adopted the holiday as their own. While they drank and played various games inside and out, those young men and women who hadn't gone to the nearby fields danced around the festooned pole.

Capt. John Caldwell and his company of Continental soldiers, on their way back to Dover after defending Lewes Town from an attack by a British ship, happened to be in the borough that day. The company of nearly 100 joined the carousing throughout the town. Pretty ignored the cockfights Caldwell staged behind his tavern with blue hens, the captain's gamecocks that always traveled with him as part of his troop.

Not until Nicholas came home besotted long after the town quieted did Pretty realize that his son had been gone all day. The next day, Shadd complained to Pretty about Nicholas. Shadd's German accent made it difficult for Pretty to follow but he heard that Nicholas had slashed the butcher's daughter's skirt with a razor. The garment was beyond repair. Pretty didn't bother to confront Nicholas and gave his neighbor money to buy his daughter a new dress. The incident was forgotten until the end of the summer when the Shadds' daughter was sent to relatives in Baltimore.

"I was never with that nigger girl," Nicholas insisted when confronted by his father.

Pretty responded to the butcher's charges by accusing him of being a Tory.

"You've hunted and fished with the British soldiers," Pretty claimed, "and you've supplied the enemy with provisions, haven't you?" Pretty charged the butcher with accepting silver and gold, not Delaware scrip, contrary to law. Pretty had no proof of any of his charges, but Shadd didn't deny them, either. Given the butcher's reluctance to unequivocally support the cause of liberty in the last year, it was easy enough to raise doubts as to his patriotism. The penalty for treason was severe but usually resulted in nothing more than a public rebuke and fine, enough, however, to unsettle a person's business.

Shadd apologized to Pretty for raising the matter and Pretty quickly forgave him.

"Will you permit me to drink a glass of wine with you?" the butcher asked.

They walked to the tavern where Pretty poured them each one glass, then another and told him that the drinks were his gift to a man of good character.

"To cause of liberty!"

Shadd remained at the bar with Pretty as more patrons came in. The conversation turned to the coroner's Negro who had disappeared the day before.

"Runaway?"

"It serves Jones right, that Tory sympathizer. His Negro was following his lead in joining the British."

Once again, as it had been for the last several months, an invective was launched against Virginia's royal governor, Lord Dunmore, for his declaring:

All indented servants, Negroes, or others (appertaining to Rebels) free, that are able and willing to bear arms, they joining His Majesty's Troops, as soon as may be, for the more speedily reducing the Colony to a proper sense of their duty, to this Majesty's crown and dignity.

Rumors, believing by many, claimed thousands of slaves had flocked to the governor's headquarters and whites in the colony were arming themselves against a black revolt.

"Jones's negro had no cause of complaint. Perhaps now Jones will see the error of his ways and join our cause."

"The Negro Jones," an abolitionist interjected, "was following the best offer, not Jones's Tory ways." He raised his voice to speak over protests: "He heard the call of liberty but from a false source. If you don't want to put our own lives at risk, take the opportunity now to set your own Negroes free."

"You're right. But you can say that, but I can't afford to do it. The Assembly will have to make it easier for me to manumit them."

The arguments continued:

"Every man has a right to be free. It is unfair and unjust to deny them otherwise. It's man's natural state."

"They're unconscious of liberty and incapable of enjoying it."

"Yes, now. They will someday earn it. It's our duty to educate them. But not before that time can they be freed."

"Slave holding is a violation of God's commandments. We must do unto others as you would have them do unto you."

"The person who manumits his Negroes does an essential injury to the neighborhood where he lives. You have seen the free blacks. They have an aversion to work. They steal and rob in order to get their substance. There'll be no end to it."

Shadd began to rise from his seat. Pretty put his hand on his forearm.

"That man's wife used to come to Betty's tearoom," he whispered. "He knows my wife."

Pretty continued to hold on to the butcher's sleeve.

"No one will remove my liberty," the burgher with the green scarf insisted, putting an end to the quarrel. "I affirm the natural right to my property, as do all men."

"We won't be enslaved!" another shouted.

Pretty, who had been quiet throughout the debate, still feeling the sting of dishonor caused by Nicolas, scized upon the comment and, raising his glass, proclaimed, "To liberty!" to which everyone assented.

Pretty didn't see Shadd for several weeks, not until the came to the print shop again. Pretty set aside pulling the press to talk to the Hessian. Once more Shadd's comments were about Nicolas.

"Your son confronted me yesterday," he said. "He came to my shop and publicly insulted my wife. He called her most foul names."

"He never heard such things from me," Pretty said.

"He accused Betty of unspeakable thing. Vicious and untrue things. He then turned it on me and said that I was spreading lies about him and my daughter. I never said a thing about this to anyone except you, Mr. Pretty. No one. My wife and I aren't that sort of people. The matter is settled between us. Not my wife or me has said a word. There is no advantage in us doing so. But he didn't believe me and called me most offensive names."

"Send him away."

"I did. I did it pleasingly, although it was difficult to hold my temper. But he came back later and began again, in front of purchasers."

"I admit he is difficult."

"This time he challenged me to a duel."

"What?"

"He said his honor was at stake. That I had impugned him with malicious slander. As a gentleman—he called himself—he said he was challenging me to meet him."

Pretty wasn't sure he understood him correctly. The more agitated Shadd became, the heavier was his accent.

"He wants to meet you in a duel?"

"At Cranes Neck the day after tomorrow. What is your boy thinking? I was a private in the army, not an officer. Does he believe that he's a gentleman? He's a publican's son and I'm merely a butcher."

"Yes. Quite so. Nicholas is full of pretensions and fancy. Of course," Pretty added with something less than conviction, "you are not going."

The butcher shook his head.

"How could I? But he won't let go of me. He is tenacious. You have to deal with him. Something must be done."

"Yes, of course."

Pretty told Shadd he would inform Nicholas that he, the butcher, was contrite for any misunderstanding and that he meant him no dishonor.

"I will keep a watchful eye on him."

Nicholas's disdain for his father's chastisement was palpable.

Pretty didn't tell Sally about the arrangements he was making for their son and on the day of Nicolas's departure to his cousin's plantation, she rose early and went to the kitchen, where she remained, to supervise the baking of cakes, something she hadn't done in a long time.

The Shadow of Twilight

GIVING HIS SON A HORSE made Nicholas's removal to his cousin's plantation not the ordeal that Pretty had anticipated. Pretty never told his son that had written to his cousin in Sussex, the most southern county, requesting that he take him for an agreed upon sum until he reach eighteen years of age. Letters were exchanged throughout the winter, sometimes taking as long as a month to arrive. By spring an arrangement had been reached.

When told that he was to live with his cousin Draper Lockwood, after being assured that he wasn't being sent to be an apprentice but an assistant and that he would be given the brown horse as his own, Nicolas readily agreed to go. He was eager to be away from his father's watchful eye, although he knew nothing about his cousin except that his tract exceeded five hundred acres.

His father handed him four bundles as Nicholas mounted the mare. He placed two bundles holding his belongings in front of him and two behind. Pretty then gave him a pistol that Nicholas placed in a holster in front of the saddle.

From the open window by the oven, Nicholas smelled the wafting aroma of baking biscuits and pies. He wanted a few to put in his saddlebag but he wouldn't make a request. Sally heard the hooves clop on the cobblestones as her son rode out of town.

Not long after his departure, events had taken place in Wilmington that he didn't learn about until that fall, when Pretty's letter was received. The farmers succumbed to Washington's orders to his generals: "If there should be any mills in the neighborhood of the enemy, and which might be liable to fall into their hands, the runners should be removed and secured. Grain, too, should be carried out of way, as far as circumstances will admit. Horses and stock of all kinds, lying contiguous to the enemy and within such a distance, that there may be a probability of falling into their hands. These must be driven out of their reach, and all wagons and carts removed that that might facilitate the movement of their baggage and stores."

My Dear Cousin:

I write you this letter about the considerable sensation in the town for a few days after Nicolas left on his journey to you. Gen. Washington and a reconnaissance party arrived and the General, with Generals Lafayette and Greene spent two nights at my neighbor George Forsythe's house on West Street. A dozen others on his staff stayed at my inn.

The Continentals are in good spirits. From what one soldier told me, several of the British ships are mired in the mud. Gen. Washington's estimate of the number of British troops was not high. The Free English are well prepared to defend Philadelphia.

There is a spirit of optimism and defiance amongst the militia. They brought back from the Elk River a British boat with all four oars. Before leaving the river, they fired on a British galley and now have entered it into the patriot's cause. Whoever may have voice for the Tories is silent now.

Upon leaving Forsythe's house the following day, Gen. Washington settled his bill of £12.6s. I will have to send a bill to Congress for the expenses incurred at my establishment.

Your affectionate cousin Roger Preddy

Although Pretty thought that while news came slowly to Sussex County, his cousin may have known about the revised policy of accepting of blacks in Washington's Continental army. Pretty didn't want to add to the alarm already felt around Dunmore's proclamation knowing that his cousin owned more than twenty slaves and must necessarily have been anxious about the state of affairs on his farm. While Dunmore's Ethiopian Regiment had been disbanded, a new company of Negro soldiers, the Black Pioneers, had been established and was positioned in Philadelphia. Like the Ethiopians, they wore their motto 'Liberty to Slaves' emblazoned on their uniforms. As many as a hundred slaves, men and women from the southern end of the peninsula, it was said, had been given their freedom by a British ship off Cape Fear.

During his stay in Wilmington, Washington had created a special corps of light infantry composed of marksmen from several Continental Army companies in Delaware. As the general prepared to leave to town and reestablish his headquarters to better defend what appeared to be an impending assault on the nation's new capital, he addressed the citizens that stood in front of Forsythe's house.

"The season loudly calls for the greatest efforts of every friend to his country," said the tall soldier plainly dressed in a gray coat. The plea wasn't enough to change the county's position on blacks in the militia: while they were accepted into the Continental army, they would be barred from taking up arms under the direction of the county militia.

Pretty stood beside Shadd as they listened to Washington. Shadd muttered something.

"What did you say?"

"The generals are too presumptuous. They don't know Hessian jaegers well. They are established soldiers. They begin their training as boys. They are the best soldiers. Disciplined. Look at these men," he said pointing with his chin to the motley group gathered in front of them.

The Continentals were well turned out but the militias were very much the citizens they were— disordered, disheveled, eager.

"Von Knyphausen is commanding," he whispered.

The three generals mounted their horses when Washington concluded and the entourage left the town to rejoin the assembled Continental army to the north.

The newly formed infantry company stayed behind a while and then took up positions near Iron Hill "to give every possible annoyance to the enemy," as Washington had instructed. The British had sailed up the Chesapeake to capture the country's new capital, just as they had successfully taken New York. The deployment of Continentals was to delay the British long enough for Washington to gather his troops at Brandywine Creek to defend Philadelphia from an attack from the south.

Gathered on the square, the minister addressed the mustered troops: "We have gathered together—God grant that it may not be for the last time. Under the shadow of a pretext, under the sanctity of the name of God, invoking the Redeemer, do these foreign hirelings lay our people. Might and wrong may prevail, we may be driven from the field—but the hour of God's own vengeance will come. How dreadful the punishment. When we meet again, may the shadow of twilight be flung over a peaceful land. God in Heaven grant it."

NICOLAS PICKED UP SNATCHES regarding the flow of the war on his way to Young Man's Chance but the further he went from Wilmington the less frequent but wilder the stories became. He tried to overhear travelers' conversation, as he set down his blanket for a night outside a tavern.

Nicolas traveled over marshes and forests, through a few towns surrounded by farms; he forded creeks wide and narrow, following few maintained roads and many cart tracks. As he came into a large clearing on the fourth day after leaving home, the putrid smell from a tanyard caused a wave of nausea to overcome him. He covered his mouth and nose with a cloth. He saw a heap of oyster shells next to the noisome pit. Two men were carrying a hide from the river to pile atop other skins. Another man wore a shirt with the sleeves rolled down to his wrists. He was sliding a knife over a hide stretched over a beam. The tapping of the tanner's mace traveled clearly across the field. Even from his distance Nicholas could see that the naked chests, arms and hands of the men coming from the water were mottled. Whether the men were white or black he couldn't tell from where he watched. Later, when he would oversee these slaves, he would learn that the urine baths in which the ox hides were soaked burned and bleached and corroded their skin.

My Dear Cousin:

News of the war in our neighborhood I am certain has reached you by now. I am writing to inform you that whatever rumors you may have heard are not exaggerated.

The newly formed infantry company and our militia took up positions on either side of the road by Cooch's Bridge towards Aiken's Tavern. The militia had laid a trap for the British and the redcoats were ambushed as they came up the road. The militia fought in the woods like Indians and killed many British soldiers.

The skirmishes lasted throughout the day. The Americans stood until they ran out of ammunition. When the Hessians charged with swords and bayonets, the Continentals retreated as they had no bayonets on their muskets. The British secured the bridge and the Americans returned to Wilmington.

Nine waggon-loads of wounded were taken from the field to be taken to Head of Elk. 20 Continentals are dead.

I have learned of these events because the troops have taken lodging in my tavern again. This would be good business, if they paid their bill. However, I could see that there is scarcely money for ammunition, weapons and artillery. The militia is poorly outfitted. I also expect that in the not distant future there will be another tax imposed by the Assembly to support not only the militia but also to aid the Continentals in defense of the other states.

I hope you understand the difficulty this has created for me. I am a man of my word and mean to fulfill my pledge to you.

With all humility.

Your cousin Roger Pretty

NICHOLAS SHOUTED TO THE MEN requesting directions to Mr. Preddy's house. They directed him to the far side of the woods. There he found a hip-roofed house made of cedar logs. On the grounds of Young Man's Chance, besides the tannery, Nicholas was shown a water-powered mill and a blooming furnace that made the air around smell of charcoal. Over the next few days, his cousin showed him fields given to Indian corn, tobacco and sugar cane; they rode past the fourteen slave cabins in the forest. The tract straddled the place where one creek flowed eastward into the Delaware and the other westward into the Chesapeake, so he was able to send lumbered products to either bay. As they rode together, Preddy introduced his slaves to the new overseer on the property.

My Dear Cousin:

Please excuse this letter for it is once again without the enclosed payment I promised you for my son's upkeep. Matters here are more frightful than anyone anticipated.

A few days after the encounter at Cooch's Bridge, the troops left our borough to join Washington's army. On the morning of the 8th, a sign appeared but at the time I didn't know in which direction it pointed. As the roosters crowed, the black sky burst with green and purple swirls like paint being thrown across a screen. It amazed everyone who saw it. My wife knows how to read these things, so I woke her and brought her to the window with the curtain drawn back to see the dancing lights. "The light, the terrible light," is what she said. When I saw her face I knew which side God would favor.

Four days later a detachment of British and Hessians arrived in town. They arrested our state president while he was in his bed for the night and have him imprisoned him on a ship in the Delaware. They raided public offices and seized all the state papers and certificates relating to loans. They left with all the public money.

I thought the British were done with the borough. I was wrong. They returned and now occupy the town, plundering whatever they can. Several of my own items have been taken. Worse, waggons full of wounded and sick came in from the Brandywine battlefield, where as you must know, the Americans suffered a great loss, to take my inn as one of several buildings seized to be used as a hospital.

I attempted to negotiate terms for their occupancy with the captain in charge. He accused me of being a traitor and threatened to send me to the prison ship. I don't know how long the British and Hessians will remain here. What I do know is that as long as they are here, there will be no income from my tavern, a loss that I cannot long sustain.

I am certain you understand the difficult position in which I now find myself. I beg your indulgence once again and pray that you don't think of me as a reprobate. As soon as I am able, I will fulfill my obligation.

I believe me sincerely your affectionate cousin Roger Preddy

AT FIRST FEELING DISGRUNTLED about being sent far from the center of excitement, Nicholas surprisingly found the plantation to his liking. He did miss the soldiers on parade, the sailors and ships in the river, dramshops, gambling, dances and games. The appeal was several-fold. Lockwood, a widower, was not at all like his father. He had about him a sense of ease that he didn't claim but adhered to him without advertisement.

Nicholas found that whatever else he was doing, his thoughts returned to Lockwood's daughter, Gertrude, a girl of no remarkable features except for the large pot mark in the center of her forehead was the same age as himself. Mostly this was to the advantage of the slaves he oversaw, as Nicholas's mood was sunny when conjuring Gertrude or remembering the smell of her. He couldn't help but think of her.

Lockwood didn't reply to his cousin's letters. Pressing him for the money was useless. Everything in the northern part of the state was in turmoil. He counted himself fortunate that the fighting was at a distance. His business faced west and south. New Castle County may as well remained part of Pennsylvania, he thought. There was the scare of runaway slaves mixing liberty with revenge, but as long as he treated his slaves well, he had nothing to fear. Matters were more peaceable than ever on the plantation since he had gotten rid of his most recalcitrant slave by offering him freedom for his service in the militia in lieu of his young cousin's.

My Dear Cousin:

I pray this letter finds you in good health.

Pretty couldn't continue. Every explanation for the delay in sending the money appeared to be an excuse. He knew his cousin wouldn't believe him, so he didn't bother to finish the letter.

Pretty was in his print shop when five Hessians broke in with fixed bayonets. They said they were arresting him for being a spy.

"I'm no spy. This is ridiculous. Who made this slanderous accusation?"

The Hessians smashed the press; they piled all the broadsides, pamphlets, handbills, advertisements, announcements and newssheets outside. They broke his bench and pulled down shelves and with the wood taken from his work station lit a fire that consumed all that remained. The soldiers brought him to a war ship in the bay where he was kept for a week with biscuits and water, in a room large enough only in which to sit. After being transferred to Philadelphia for trial and held there for two days in the new jail, charges were dropped and he returned to Wilmington.

Sally calmly listened to her husband explain his absence. She didn't say a word as Pretty released his thoughts in short rushes over the next hour.

Summer still lingered and the window in the bedchamber was open. He looked at the stars most of the night and could hear the laughter of soldiers on the street. Sometime before dawn he had fallen asleep. When he awoke, Sally was already attending to the food at the tavern. The servant girls had been dismissed, so she prepared simple dishes for the soldiers herself. Sally always presented a bill for the food and occasionally an officer would leave a few pounds in specie. At least it wasn't Continental scrip. And there was always the hope for more.

She found the recipe for egg pie she had been looking for, a dish she was certain would appeal to the Hessians.

MAKE a good cruft, cover your difh with it, then have ready twelve eggs boiled hard, cut them in flices, and lay them in your pye, throw half a pound of currants, clean wafhed and picked, all over the eggs, then beat up four eggs well mixed with half a pint of white wine, grate in a fmall nutmeg and make it pretty fweet with fugar. You are to mind to lay a quarter of a pound of butter between the eggs, then pour in your wine and eggs and cover your pye. Bake it half an hour or till the cruft is done.

Sally added one more ingredient not found in the book: she stripped the leaf blades from the stalks of rhubarb plants stored in her cellar and cut them into small pieces.

The night Shadd ate dinner at the Pretty Tavern with the occupying soldiers, Sally told him that she had prepared an egg pie that was especially appealing to Hessians. By morning three soldiers were dead. Shadd took a week to recover.

The British withdrew their troops from Wilmington in November but not before Sally was hanged for murder. With her dress pulled from her shoulders it was the first time since her whipping that anyone had seen the twelve scars across her back.

Ratsbane

RUNAWAY FROM the subscriber, on the 23d ult. a
Negro Lad named Fortune, about eighteen years of age,
of a brownish cast, and much pitted with the small
pox, is slender made, and about five feet seven or eight
inches high, is very fond of dress, generally wears a
small round hat bound with silver lace; one of his eyes
are sore and much inflamed. Whoever will apprehend
said Negro and bring him back to Young Man's Chance,
Sussex, Delaware, shall receive Two Guineas reward paid
by Draper Lockwood. N.B. All persons are forewarned
harbouring or secreting said negro at their peril, as in
case of conviction they will be dealt with accordingly.

"Perhaps I won't get Fortune back," Draper Lockwood told
Nicholas, picking up a poster from the sideboard. "But it is
easy enough to broadcast the notice, so I lose nothing but
a few shillings if it comes to nothing. My guess is that he
has gone to Maryland to join the British army. But he won't
get far. Gen. Howe won't allow slaves to join the Provincial
forces. And if he decides to join the Maryland Loyalists, he'll
rue the day, I tell you. Colonel Chalmers is an acquaintance
of mine. This would be a day of great *mis*fortune for the lad
if Chalmers lays his hands on him. The colonel will dutifully
return my property to me after having wrung the rubbish
from the lad's head."

This was the first extended conversation with his cousin
since Nicholas's arrival. Lockwood's, his daughter Gertrude,
and Nicholas usually sat in polite silence. Nicholas looked
at Gertrude's brown hair that fell to her round shoulders.

Nicholas also admired Lockwood's hands that were free from ink stains that tattooed his father's hands.

"Are you a Whig or Tory then?" Nicholas asked. "From what you say, it isn't easy for to me to understand which way you lean."

Gertrude tried to stop the conversation.

"Have you ever been to Philadelphia?" she asked. "I've never met anyone who's been there."

Lockwood interrupted before Nicholas could answer.

"You know, until two years ago, it wasn't clear to which province this area belonged, Delaware or Maryland. Now that's been drawn, some of us have property on both sides."

"You, too?"

A black woman brought in tea and a girl removed the dinner plates. Nicholas smelled the tea and replaced the cup on the table.

"It's old Bohea," Gertrude said.

"I don't care for tea," he said.

"This tea's been stored for several years."

"I prefer something stronger," he said, trying to impress Gertrude.

"There is a parcel on Maryland side," Lockwood said, unaware of the Nicholas's attention to Gertrude. "It's separated from the rest of the plantation. No more than ten acres. It is rented out and I get a small sum for it. It isn't worth much. I'll sell it soon."

Lockwood put in several spoonsful of sugar and stirred the tea vigorously. He lit a pipe and filled the room with the smoke of it.

Nicholas eyed the pipe.

"Do you smoke?"

"I do," he lied.

Lockwood continued his discourse on Sussex history: "Governors from both provinces neglected us for centuries, Nicolas. That was to our advantage. Penn and Calvert's abandonment left us free and honed our sense of liberty. It was as though we were in a state of nature. Ungoverned. No one interfered with our business. As long as they could agree with each other as to where we belonged, neither put their thumbs on us. I desire it will remain this way. Everyone wants liberty and peace. We once had both. Being left alone is a blessing."

Nicholas began to cough.

"Can I get you anything?" Gertrude asked.

"No, no. I'm fine. But I am wondering, sir, which side you favor."

Gertrude tried to change the subject again.

"Is Wilmington a big city? Is there entertainment there?"

"The Americans and the British have their claws in us now" Lockwood said forcefully, "but in truth I tell you neither has our interests at heart."

Nicholas, his coughing subsided, pressed: "Do you want us to stay with the king or go?"

"Congress says there are plots and conspiracies of treason. The southern counties are under suspicion."

"What about you?"

Nicholas's head spun. He didn't know if it was the seditious nature of the talk or the new-found vice.

"Reconciliation," Lockwood responded. "Blood will have more blood, nothing more."

"I don't think there can be compromise with tyranny," Nicholas asserted.

"Why don't you tell me about Philadelphia," Gertrude said.

"Let's drink to liberty. Sip!" Lockwood called. "Which do you prefer, Nicolas? Claret or spirits?"

Nicolas gestured towards the tinted bottle, not knowing which drink it contained. "

"You are free to make your own choice," Lockwood said.

"Yes. But I can't have both at the same time."

"I admire our new Delaware president," Lockwood said. "He represents both the Whig and Tory complexion of this state."

Lockwood directed Sip to pour them each a glass of wine. Gertrude took port, surprising Nicholas that she drank alcohol.

Lockwood raised his glass.

"Long live . . ." he hesitated as Gertrude's pale face grew even whiter. "You know it's s a capital offense to pray for the king in Delaware, Nicolas. Don't worry. This isn't a prayer I am giving but a toast. Raise your glass with me." He smiled at his cousin. "Caution is preferable to rash bravery. So I say: Long live those whom the Lord has made it our especial duty to pray for!"

Gertrude laughed at her father's joke. Nicholas didn't know what to do. He looked at her. When she noticed Nicolas's smile, her cheeks turned pink and she placed her hands over them.

"How are you getting along with the darkies, Nicholas? Let me know if there is discontent amongst them. A smoldering fire can quickly consume a forest. You must get them to like you."

Nicholas finished the claret.

"What happened to Fortune, the one in the runaway notice?"

Sharper shrugged his shoulders.

"The Indian corn in another's ground seems more fertile than our own, an enlightened man once wrote," he said, once again attempting the quote from a magazine he subscribed to. "Some darkies think they can do better elsewhere. It's a fool who thinks so."

Lockwood finished his drink. Nicholas watched as Gertrude excused herself and left the dining room. Sip came in and cleared the table.

"There is one thing, Nicolas, Leave your pistol at the house when you go out to look after the boys. It's not fear that will keep them straight. Tenderness and mercy will take you far."

"It's for me, for my own protection."

"That's not necessary. Treat them right and they'll be right with you, same as with anything. But I'll give you a gun for hunting, if you like. Take one from the rack in the sitting room. My gift to you for your work here. It's yours. Come with me the next time I go out with the dogs. Have you ever shot a hog?"

Lockwood added the long rifle with the walnut stock to the list of Nicholas's expenses that would be sent to his cousin.

HEEDING LOCKWOOD'S ADVICE, Nicholas removed the holster from his horse and went unarmed throughout the plantation. The only place he didn't oversee was the malodorous tannery and the only slaves he didn't meet were the men who worked there. He found the sight of them abhorrent. Nicholas didn't tell his cousin that he avoided the pit and their cabins. But Nicholas never reeked and Lockwood knew why. It made no difference to Lockwood. The men were skilled craftsmen and did all the work given to them. Besides, where were to go if they decided to run? Hounds' noses weren't needed to smell them out. And men that were mottled like the backs of marsh ducks couldn't hide.

"Most of the slaves' songs are groans and howls," Nicolas said to Gertrude after coming in from the field. The longer he stayed at the plantation, the more infatuated he became with her. He liked looking at her white hands as she sat at the spinning wheel, her soft voice above the whirr as the cotton was spun, her eyes that mostly looked away but occasionally caught his gaze.

"They sing to ease their load and sometimes to amuse themselves," she explained.

"This must have been the amusement kind. Something about a captain and a light horse. That's all I could understand."

"Did you ask them?"

"No."

"You could have. They would have told you."

"No, I'm no friend of theirs and they shouldn't think so. Why? Do you talk to them in the field?"

"Sometimes I do. I visit at a cabin. There's nothing to fear."

"I'm not afraid of a nigger. Unaccustomed is what I am."

"I don't know the song you heard," Gertrude said.

"Do you sing?"

"Would like to hear one?"

"Yes."

"When I first sang this song, Father got angry. But now he sings it himself. It's amusing." She sang as she spun: "The captain of the brave light horse/ began the insurrection/ his videts flew on every course/ to spread the wide infection/ lang do lang diddle."

"You have a sweet voice." Nicholas looked her directly in the eye. "But that wasn't it. I understand your words, but they don't explain the meaning."

"Ask father. You ain't afraid of him, are you?" she teased.

Nicholas couldn't get angry.

"I don't know the meaning either, only that it's about Tories."

He just wanted her to talk. It didn't matter about what. He wasn't listening to the words.

When Nicholas asked Lockwood about the song Gertrude sang for him, His cousin responded that just before Congress declared independence, Tories sent a petition to the Committee of Inspection and Observation. The Whigs destroyed the petition and put the farmer who delivered it in a pillory.

"The petition was legal and legitimate. The Assembly should have accepted it. The poor man's offense was opposing independence. And he wasn't speaking for himself but was the messenger for the majority of the landowners who favored keeping the existing state of affairs. Those favoring separation from Great Britain were in the minority. Three of four were loyalists."

Nicholas couldn't see the connection between the song and his cousin's anecdote but he had grown used to Lockwood's grousing

Lockwood continued: as a result of the illegal response of the Committee, two hundred signers marched on Dover. They planned to burn the town and hang those who had offended the farmer. They gathered on the north and south side but the plot was leaked and the Tories were turned away.

Nicholas's interested had been piqued.

"Were any killed?"

"Not a shot was fired. It was all rubbish. Two reverends told them to go home and they went."

Nicholas thought his next question was impertinent but asked anyhow.

"Were you one of them?"

"I told you I am for reconciliation."

"The Whigs launched their own raids against the Tories. They raided their homes and took their weapons. The Whigs are now in charge."

"So the Tories were jailed," Nicolas said, as if it were a fact.

"No," Lockwood corrected. "The Tories petitioned for a pardon. The newly formed Assembly granted it and even returned our guns."

"Yours?"

"It is easy to be accused by one side or the other. They are a pack of fools. Ratsbane."

"Who are?"

"All of them. Let's just go on about our business and stay out it all."

WITH WINTER'S ARRIVAL the sawmill ran as long as the water didn't freeze; the blooming furnace burned most days. Sawyers, carpenters, blacksmiths, all the slaves remained in their cabins. Until spring's arrival, when the tobacco fields would once again need constant attention, the men slaves split wood, worked on buildings and fences, while the women shelled Indian corn, assisted Gertrude in the house and made sure the stored Indian corn was kept free from rats. With his rifle, Nicholas kept wild pigs away.

During the winter days, Nicholas would often sit next to Gertrude on a settee.

She opened the family Bible for him to read:

Mary Manlove and Draper Lockwood married on the sixteenth day of October 1745, in Lewes Town.

Nine births: Thomas, Margaret, John, Comfort, Nancy, Rachel, Stayton, Mason and Gertrude.

Two marriages, Nancy to Elias Sturgis; Rachel to Piercy Webb.

Deaths were enumerated: Thomas, departed this life from a bilious fever after eight years, five months twenty days, ten hours; Comfort departed this life after twenty-two days; Mason departed after ten hours. Stayton departed this life at five years when his cart turned over.

Mary Lockwood departed this life February 6th, 1773.

"That was my mother. In the morning she complained about a sharp pain in her head. At 9 o'clock she had a convulsion. All morning she cried about her head. In the afternoon she had another convulsion that left her speechless. She lay this way for nine days until it pleased God to take her into his safe keeping."

Another night Nicholas asked: "Where is Margaret? You've said nothing about her."

"She disappeared when the war started. We cannot conjecture a reason why she left. One morning she was gone. She had taken some items with her, that's all. She had once said to me that she loved a soldier, but she confided nothing more. There hasn't been any correspondence from her. We are hoping that when the Tories stop interfering with mail delivery, we'll soon receive a letter bringing us news."

"She may be a bad correspondent and is in good health."

"If only God would grant that wish."

"And John?"

Gertrude looked downward in distress.

"He joined the Delaware Blues."

Nicholas was taken aback and blurted, "He's with the Continentals?"

"Yes. He went to New York with the regiment."

"What did your father think of him joining the rebellion?"

"He's not spoken about it since."

"Yes?"

"We received a letter but not from him. A friend kindly wrote to us from New Jersey after the British routed Washington's army in Long Island. The British captured John in New York. He thinks he is on one of the prison ships in New York harbor."

She showed Nicholas a letter reprinted in a Baltimore newspaper describing the battle on the heights:

The Delawares and Marylanders stood firm to the last; and after a variety of skirmishing the Delawares drew up on the side of a hill, and stood upwards of four hours, with a firm determined countenance, in close array, their colours flying, the enemy's artillery playing on them all the while, not daring to advance and attack them though six times their number and nearly surrounding them.

"Don't speak to Father about John. I know he has given up hope. There is misery on prison ships. No one who goes in comes out. A soldier is more likely to die on one than in the battlefield."

Gertrude seemed comforted by the thoughts of the deceased and missing and when she and Nicholas were sitting side-by-side she often opened the Bible's pages to her family's record.

The unremitting sadness that hung about Lockwood slowly lifted over the years as he spoke about himself to Nicholas.

"The Committee sent a notice to me last year after they received a report that I opposed the acts of Congress. You never know what your neighbors think. It's been hard to find an honorable man. I keep my opinions to myself, so this was a baseless charge and nothing came of it."

Lockwood then asked Nicholas if he should uproot all the tobacco.

"I need too many for an acre, Nicolas. I can't handle more than twenty acres with the slaves I have. Too many worms and pests. That weed needs constant care. Indian corn is more lucrative.

"And the sugar cane doesn't seem like a good proposition, either. I tried it as a little experiment. I am also going to close the furnace. There's foreign matter in the bog ore. Not many want it anymore. I want to plant more peach and apple trees. I'll have Sip put in more flax. There's a market for good linen in Virginia. I can expand the distillery for spirits."

Nicholas thought about the dramshops in Wilmington.

"The little barley has done well. I should sow more. Rye, too. I'll make a pot-still. A neighbor tells me the return on barreled whiskey is more than on barreled grain. With rum difficult to get, I think I need to get into the business. The pine forest to the west is virgin. So is the oak. We can clear it. What do you think?"

Nicholas didn't know whether his cousin was talking to himself out loud or truly soliciting his opinion.

Later, Lockwood asked Gertrude about the welfare of the slaves she had visited in the cabins and Gertrude answered by saying that a few of the children were bothered by inflammation of the lungs.

Another night Lockwood told Nicholas that he had been betrayed by Leatherberry Barker's wife. She told the committee that he had advised neighbors to muster to defend themselves against the patriots.

"You know me, Nicholas. Does that sound like me? Take up arms? But there was one more bit of rumor. Barker said I declared the Congress to be unconstitutional."

"But it is," Nicholas interjected. "That's a fact."

"Be that as it may, I wrote to the committee stating that I refused to appear before them. Nothing came of it and I haven't heard from them again. Others similarly charged in the county have signed letters of recantation after being threatened with tar and feathers."

The days grew longer than the nights again and the ground was being prepared once more. The oxen pulled the wooden plough, hoes turned over clumps of sod, seeds were planted.

"These men who spin our heads and threaten our existence," Lockwood complained. "They're incompetent and lack all judgment. They know nothing of administration or justice. They arrested a neighbor the other week. He had given a Continental officer one hundred and ninety-nine counterfeit thirty-dollar bills. He confessed and the magistrate released him. *Released?* The man was guilty. If you release him, then do away with the law under which he was arrested."

"Mercy, perhaps," Nicholas offered.

"Incompetence. And you, Nicholas, listen to me: don't stray from the plantation. The militia has taken to impressing men. Even the Delaware Assembly has told them to stop this abuse. Still, the Kent County jail is filled with deserters."

Nicholas became indispensable for the maintenance of the plantation. Following his cousin's advice, he took a firm but kind hand with the slaves. One or two died from illness and a few were born in the next couple of years. Another's leg was mangled in a churning mill wheel. Even Fortune returned to Young Man's Chance. A small iron brand was forged in the furnace. One day it was made red hot again and a 'Y' two inches high was seared above the eyebrow over his sore right eye.

The endless war made its presence known in the farm's deterioration. The orders for lumber had declined; while iron was in demand, getting the metal to buyers was difficult and costly—Royalist along roads and navigable waterways captured goods and kidnapped crews that they carried off to

British ships in the bay. Lockwood tore out that last of the tobacco plants. Wheat and Indian corn rotted in the fields. Loyalists waylaid traders' riverboats if the goods meant for patriots; or patriots confiscated goods for the own use if the intended buyers were British.

Lockwood confided in Nicholas that he was not able to meet all his debts and obligations.

"I don't belong to any church, Nicholas, but I've given liberally to all. I can't afford to be generous any longer. The problem was not only the disruption of supply routes but, equally serious, the depreciation of the dollar.

"We may as well burn the paper to keep us warm for all a Continental is worth."

When Nicholas asked to marry his daughter, Lockwood answered quickly.

"You're too young," he said emphatically, catching Nicholas by surprise.

"You trust me with everything."

"Not my daughter. Not yet. You have your oats to sow."

"I once envied the men in their uniforms," Nicholas said. "Living at Young Man's Chance is adventure enough, I've learned."

"You're already like a son to me. And in a few years, when we will know one way or the other where we all stand, you will in fact become one in law. I know the two of you love each other. Gertrude talks to me about you. But patience is a virtue."

Gertrude was as eager for marriage as Nicholas. Whatever the conversation with her father, she turned it back to Nicholas, never expressing her desires but always describing his strengths and his great assistance to her father.

After months of praise and admiration of Nicholas from Gertrude, Lockwood decided it was better to direct their passion in the proper channel and agreed to their marriage.

The banns were read in the Dover church and when the marriage was consummated, Lockwood wrote a new will before the Justice of the Peace in Sussex County: that his just debts be paid and discharged; to his son-in-law Nicholas Preddy, his sole executor, he left the entire tract of Young Man's Chance and all his goods, chattels and credit; to his daughter Gertrude the tract of land in Maryland and Fillis, a female slave.

"To my said son-in-law I leave my Negroes. I instruct said son-in-law to treat the Negros with kindness and compassion and to consider the manumission of same Negroes when they reach an age of superannuation provided they have behaved as Free ought to."

To his son John, "who joined the Delaware Regiment against my wishes," he left one American dollar.

Lockwood's complaints mounted in inversion ratio to his declining means.

"No taxation without representation," he declared after receiving notice that a new supply tax had been levied. "What good is representation when the tax is theft. The Whigs vote to favor themselves. The money raised is to protect their merchant interests of the north county. We are going bankrupt us farmers and now they are imposing more taxes!"

Lockwood's face burned as bright as the kitchen fire, it seemed.

"The men around Nanticoke Swamp have the right idea."

"They're raising a militia against the state," Nicholas said. "That's what a rider told me yesterday when I was out. I told him to go away."

"He came by here, too. He took several of my guns."

"You ain't favoring them, are you?"

"I don't favor penury. Do you, Nicolas?"

"You've preached reconciliation," Nicholas said.

"When the snake rattles its tail, there is no reasoning."

"What are you suggesting, father?" Gertrude asked.

"If you know the right thing to do and don't do it, it is a sin. It isn't right to deprive a man of his sustenance."

The farmers collected arms from sympathizers or by raiding the homes of Whigs and stealing their guns. They organized themselves into a brigade, set up a training camp in the swamp and planned their strategy. Unable to obtain sufficient powder for an immediate attack, they delayed. Learning of an insurrection by disgruntled farmers, the state sent the militia to stop the 'Black Camp Rebellion.' Within three days hundreds were in jail, their stolen weapons returned to their rightful owners.

A committee arrived at Young Man's Chance to question Lockwood about his gun.

"This is yours."

They handed the rifle to Lockwood.

"Was it given or taken?"

"It was missing," he answered.

They told Lockwood that thirty-seven men were sentenced to death for their part in the uprising. The rest were levied fines of up to £10,000.

"No charges will be brought against you, though you must be careful, Mr. Lockwood."

They were ready to leave when they told him they were going to administer an oath of allegiance.

Lockwood agreed: "I do acknowledge the United States of America to be free, independent and sovereign states, and declare that the people therefore owe no allegiance or obedience to George the Third, King of Great Britain and I renounce, refuse and abjure any allegiance or obedience to him."

"I owe allegiance only to my family and obedience to God," Preddy explained after the committee left. "And it is evident today that at this moment after five years the United States are free from Great Britain despite my own opinion as to its advisability. I said nothing that I didn't believe."

The pledge, however, wasn't sufficient to prevent the Kent County Levy Court sending a notice stating that because Lockwood had not paid his taxes since 1778 his property had been seized. The entire tract was to be sold at vendue if the arrears were not paid within a year.

One day while riding across his plantation to look after his cattle, Lockwood's horse stumbled on a submerged log in a marsh. He was brought back to the house covered in mosquito bites. He had congestive chills for a week, until he weakened and died from lung fever.

Gertrude entered the date of her father's death in the family Bible, not the last time she would make such an entry.

Nicholas cleared the lien on Young Man's Chance with the sale of half the property and five slaves. Gertrude kept her parcel of land in Maryland. They worked harder than they ever had and by the turn of the century they felt secure in their positions.

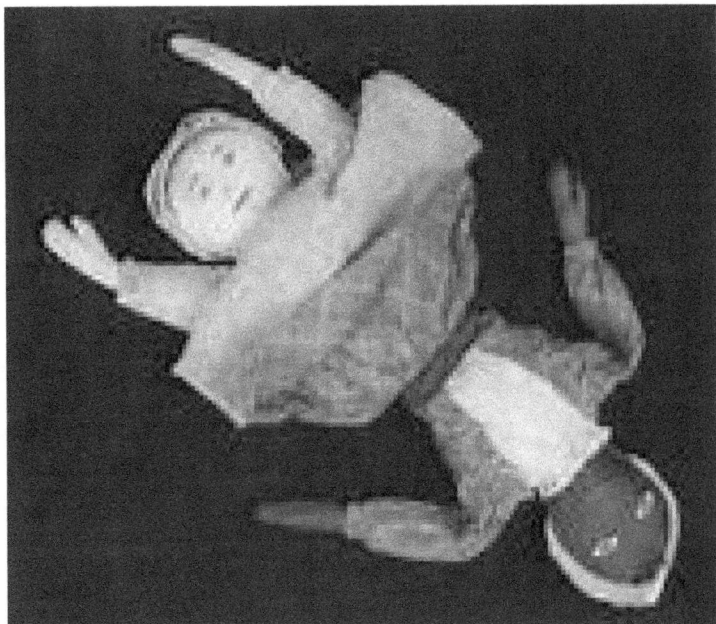

Tribulations and Wonders

MINGO

Branded

LARK STANDS ON THE wooden plow, her bare feet balanced on the curved beam that juts out over the soil being turned. If a coastal resident had seen her riding this way, he would have said she was the figurehead of a ship pointing the way like a black dove.

She leans forward to place her weight at the front of the beam, helping to push the blade deep into the soil. Suthy steers the yoked oxen from behind while her brother Mingo, a year older than herself, walks ahead of the oxen to clear a path for the plowing. When the moldboard clumps with soil and the debris brings the plowing to a halt, Suthy scrapes the blade clean.

"Geeup," Suthy calls, and the plowing resumes with the soil being lifted and turned and furrows dug to prepare the field for sowing.

Weeding hoes are used to break the remaining clumps left in the field after the cross plowing and harrowing. When the preparation is done, Lark, Suthy and Mingo take corn kernels and push them into the built-mounds with their fingers. In summer they use their hoes around the corn stalks to keep them free of weeds.

Lark uses a sickle but not the scythe, a tool recently introduced to the farm to remove corn blades from the stalks in late summer. A scythe is too heavy for her to swing. Soon after summer's end, she picks the ripened corn, while Mingo and Jacob load the cereal onto a cart and bring the harvest to the corncrib near the house.

In the fall they husk the corn on a moonlit night. As they work, they sing, a singing that can be heard in distant fields, on other plantations, as all the husking in the Chesapeake is done on the same appointed time, the songs coming through the pines, from across the swamp.

> Jinny was my darling
> Jinny was the gal
> Oh, Jinny was my darling
> Jinny was the gal
>
> Git away the corn, boys
> Git away the corn
>
> Jinny said she loved me
> Jinny was the gal
> Jinny said she loved me
> Jinny was the gal
>
> Git away the corn, boys
> Git away the corn.

Nicholas Preddy calls the bondsmen's cadences "droning, monotonous and repetitious," but has learned to appreciate their utility and understands how the chants and shouts are investments in his slaves' contentment. When the shucking bee is done, they eat roasted pig, fried chicken, sweet cakes. They drink apple brandy, buttermilk and coffee.

Preddy retires to his house. When he is asleep, the black community continues to carouse by their cabins. They dance around the lightwood fire; the fall air turns crisp and they warm themselves against one another. Preddy sleeps through the sounds of banjos, drums and voices.

Frank, who is too old to cut lumber and drag logs, and Paris, whose hands are forever raw from tanning, now are herdsmen who watch after cattle, sheep, pigs and the many oxen kept for hauling. These men, too, join the annual festivities.

OUT OF BREATH FROM HAVING run from the tannery, Paris called to Sip by the kitchen door.

"Get the master."

Nicholas Preddy, who ran the farm since his father-in-law's death, stopped twenty feet from Paris to keep his stench away.

"I think I might have killed a white man."

Paris was hauling a hide from the creek to the tannery, he explained, when he saw the forester. The man had hair knotted as thick as vines and was half-clad with clothes that barely clung to his gaunt frame.

"He was lifting a cut of leather from a drying pole."

"Yes."

"It was one of the thieves who live in the swamp," Paris said. "I'd only seen the shadow of him before. But that was him. He looked like he lived on rodents and made his home with muskrats."

Confronted by Paris, the forester yelled, "Nigger." He picked up the fleshing knife on the ground and lunged at the tanner.

"I took my pistol and shot him. He would have killed me with his knife."

"A pistol?"

"Yes, sir. I keep one."

The revelation didn't surprise Nicholas. The two tanners lived on the plantation's edge with the wilderness beside them.

"It's high time someone's killed that thief," Nicholas said.

"I don't know if he's killed. His leg's got a hole in it as big as a silver dollar."

"You left him there?"

"I didn't know what else to do. I didn't think he's going far."

Nicholas said, "We've all been wanting to get these weasels for a long time. They've been living in the swamp and stealing like niggers themselves. I'm grateful for what you've done, Paris. I think he's the last of the swamp men. Take me to me. I have to make sure he's done."

Nicholas stayed far behind Paris as the two of them went to the tannery. The forester wasn't where Paris had left him, but there was a trail of blood that they followed to the tanning pit. The forester had dragged himself from the drying hides and passed the shack. Nicholas gagged as he pulled out a kerchief to cover his mouth and nose. Paris looked down into the tanyard.

"Down there," Paris called to Nicholas who sat on his horse. Nicholas dismounted and forced himself to approach the pit. From a distance, he could see the body lying face up in the in the swill of urine and feces. His eyes were closed. Neither Nicholas nor Paris could tell whether the forester was breathing.

"See if he's alive."

Paris rolled up his pants and stepped into the pit as he often did.

"I don't know. Can't be certain. Seems that way."

"Trample the swamp snake," Nicholas instructed.

He pushed the body down with his feet until it disappeared under the brown muck.

"Cover him," Nicholas said, pointing to the pile of crushed oyster shells. "The body will soon be eaten by the acid. He doesn't deserve a better burial."

Nicholas retreated to his horse and waited for Paris to finish the job. The slave walked fifty feet behind Nicholas as they returned to the main house.

After telling his neighbors that Paris had rid them of the thieving rogue, Nicholas regretted it.

"I don't know, Paris," he said. "There may be trouble for you if you stay. You're going to be arrested. Some don't like Negroes, especially bondsmen, using guns. One of the neighbors is going to let the word out and the sheriff is sure to come for you. You'll be lashed or hanged."

Paris listened carefully, but he wasn't afraid. He had thought that no would miss the recluse.

In a month's time, Nicholas gave Paris more instructions. Paris would enter the pit again, take the remains from which all flesh had been eaten away by acid and bury the bleached bones in the muddy bottom of the swamp. When another swamp man would stumble on the bones, it would serve as a warning that their lives were worth no more than a Negro's if they continued to steal from the plantations.

"You'll be taken to the courthouse in Georgetown and then who knows what will happen to you."

Nicholas needed to protect his interest.

"You'll be safe if you go to Mistress Gertrude's parcel in Maryland," Nicholas told him. "There's a tenant there now. He could use your labor."

But leaving Young Man's Chance wasn't necessary. No one reported either crime—a slave's owning a gun or the murder. The hundred's farmers had agreed: the thief who made his home in the cypress roots had been more of a menace to them than a loyal slave with a pistol.

Relieved that the incident hadn't gone any further, Nicholas said to Paris, in appreciation of his deed, "When you are fifty years of age I will grant you your freedom."

Paris thanked him but declined the offer still more than ten years off.

"Where would I go to?" he asked. "Children run from me when they see me. Men and women run even before they see me. I can't rid myself of the stench, not ever. It's part of me. The smell has gotten into my bones. No one lets me on his premises. I can't even sit in church. I listen from a log outside."

Nicholas thought about the almshouse newly constructed in Kent County and wondered if he would be liable for another tax if Paris went there.

"Let me stay here. It's all I know."

Paris's requested that he begin work tending the expanded herd of sheep.

"I won't be much use to you much longer in the tannery," he said. "I can hardly lift or hold anything anymore."

"Except your gun," Nicholas laughed. He then agreed to Paris's petition.

Lark brought a pot of duck stew to Paris's cabin. She left it at the door and called to him, "My momma says to tell you, you did a good thing ridding us of that no count witch. He was putting spells on us."

ONE NIGHT SOON AFTER THE DEATH of the forester, Sip told this story to the children of Young Man's Chance:

> Have you heard the one about Buh Lion and Aunt Nancy? One day Aunt Nancy, she says to Buh Lion 'I'm gwine to throw away my knife and when you see me throw mine away, you must throw away yours, too.'
>
> Aunt Nancy, she takes something and throws it far away. Buh Lion takes his knife and he throws it away.
>
> When they reach the field to eat pine, Aunt Nancy has a knife. She is eating pine but Buh Lion has none to eat. Buh Lion, he sees Aunt Nancy eating pine. His stomach is crying from hunger.

Aunt Nancy, she laughs and laughs and says to Buh Lion, 'You're a fool, like you got the brains of a chicken. No man without a knife eats pine. Why you throw away your knife? You ain't got a knife, so ain't eating no pine.'

During the cold months, Sip used a spinning wheel and loom in a side room of the main house to turn flax and wool into threads and yarn. If there was surplus material after sewing shirts, jackets, overalls for the plantation's bondsmen, it was sold to markets in Sussex and nearby Maryland. As she became more efficient and Lark began to assist her, she made enough clothing for town markets.

As the oldest female Negro, it was often at Sip's cabin that the children would come to listen to her tales. When Lark's chest began to bud, Sip told this story to her alone one night before falling to sleep:

Have you heard the one about a woman who has a daughter? The daughter be engaged to marry many times but she won't marry no how.

'The men ain't my sort,' she says.

One day a well-dressed gentleman comes and proposes. But she has a brother who is a witch. He says to her the man was a snake.

'No, he's no snake,' the girl says. 'He's too well-dressed to be a snake.'

The brother, he is going home with them riding under a carriage as a lizard.

At the first place somebody asks, 'Mr. Snake, give me your collar.'

At the next place somebody asks, 'Mr. Snake, give me your jacket,' and so on until the well-dressed gentleman shows hisself plain as a snake.

They get home. He locks her up but can't kill her until

he gets a thing called 'bump.' He goes to the woods looking for it.

The mother-in-law, she says to her, 'The man you is gwine marry is a bad man. He has already killed one wife and he is gwine kill you.'

When snake comes out of the woods, brother lizard is taking her on his back to land. Snake can't get her because she is near land. Snake goes back home. He takes a stick and hits the mother-in-law on the head 'til he kills her.

BY THE TIME LARK TURNED A YOUNG woman Gertrude brought her in from the field to help her mother. Sip watched after Gertrude's two children while Lark helped prepare meals and keep up the house. The extension on the house was only temporary: an unused cabin put on a skid and pulled by oxen to be set on the opposite side from the kitchen. Sip would treadle while Lark furiously wound the ball from the spindle before it tangled on the floor.

Wind the ball, wind the ball,
Wind the ball, lady, wind the ball,
Don't care how you wind the ball,
Wind the ball, lady, wind the ball.

Soon Lark surpassed her mother in weaving and sewing skills; her clothes sold readily to neighboring farms. If they made more than the market demanded, they kept the clothes to sell themselves to poor whites. The money from these sales was theirs.

Still, in spring Lark was needed in the fields of sky-blue flax; she was also responsible for sweet potatoes, peas and other vegetables from the garden.

Lark and Mingo saw their father several times a year, when he came to the plantation. He had hired out to a Virginia plantation for fifteen silver dollars a year. The rent Nicholas received for his carpenter was more than he could realize by having him live on the farm. New sheds could wait, slave would make do with cabins being eaten by termites. Gertrude wanted a new table and an expanded cabinet but that too could be postponed. She would be happy with a covering for the table and a small rug for the floor. As for carving bowls, spoons, rollers and pins—it was cheaper to buy them from his neighbor's carpenter than to keep Adam around.

The children never learned Adam's given name, calling him, as did Sip, 'Papa.' During his visits to the plantation, Lark stayed at Auntie Vergie's cabin while Mingo stayed in a slave house with Suthy and two other adult males.

Adam talked to Nicholas about not wanting to work at the Virginia farm. He wanted some place closer to Sussex County.

"Master Carter pays me very well for your services, far more than I can get for you in Delaware or Maryland. And with the portion I give you from the rent you'll be able to purchase your freedom in a few years' time. Be frugal and save."

By Adam's reckoning, he would either have white hair or none by the time he had enough to buy his liberty.

Each time Adam left, Sip cried as she watched him walk down the road. The dogs trotted next to him as far as the first bridge. By the time they returned to the house, Sip's tears stopped and she returned to her spinning.

At the turn of the century Adam didn't visit Young Man's Chance nor did he come the following year or the year after that. Nicholas said nothing to Sip about Adam's absence and if Sip knew why her husband's visits ended, she never revealed it to Lark or Mingo. All they knew was that there was a day when Sip told them that they wouldn't see their father again.

"Who's going to lay this body when there ain't no body to lay?" Sip asked. "Who? The ain't no body. He's spirit and he's bound in jail no more. He ain't no one's but his own."

She then began to wail and run in circles around the house. She removed her headkerchief and yanked her hair hard enough for her to hold a few tufts. She tore the top of her dress exposing her shoulders and left breast.

Mingo was embarrassed by his mother's sudden burst of mourning; Lark was frightened at first, then joined her as other slave women came to their cabin to keen until sunset. The next morning the women swept the yard clean with an Indian corn shuck broom and placed yellow flowers beside Sip's door. That day she built a foot-high mound behind the house under a pine tree, took a large clay pitcher, a cracked blue bottle and an oak spoon made by Adam and placed them on the little hill. Paris brought oyster shells from the tannery and Sip didn't mind the smell of him as he stood near her. She took the crushed shells from him and covered the dirt mound.

For the whole of the next year each time an item broke in her house or a thread unraveled from her clothes, Sip added it to the mound. Mostly the hill consisted of things once touched by Adam's hand. If a pine needle fell from the tree on top of the mound, Sip removed it and placed it in her ticked mattress. There was always a cup of water for Adam by the table after breakfast.

"It's a good thing where he's gone to," Fortune told Lark. "I know what happened and I come to pay my respects."

"He's gone home."

Lark couldn't remember Fortune ever having spoken to her before. He worked alone at the furnace and at the end of the day he returned to the cabin far from the others. He built the log building alone when he returned, a shed with one door, no windows, no porch, a bench against a wall for his sleeping plank, and fireplace.

"No, Lark. He's not gone home. He's been called home."

Lark saw Fortune only when Nicolas called all the slaves together for a gathering.

She tried not to stare at the large 'Y' above his brow but her eyes on their own kept locking on the scar and the eye under it that remained half-closed and shriveled. He wore a conical liberty cap and a frayed jacket that at one time had been Draper Lockwood's finest. Nicholas permitted the revolutionary cap because it now had become a symbol of anti-Federalism, a position Preddy had come to favor and which Fortune knew nothing about. Fortune had worn it since returning to the plantation. For him it was a rakish advertisement of it earlier meaning—freedom. No one had seen him without it. Some said that was the reason he never set foot in a church.

"Master Nicholas, he put that mark there. When I come back. That way I'm his for sure and he can prove it. That's what he said. But I know it was teach me a lesson. To put fear in me."

He took Lark's hand and had her trace his disfigurement with her forefinger.

"It don't hurt. It don't hurt you to touch it, either," he said, as Lark flinched as her finger grazed the hardened skin. "My eye was bad before this. It made it a little worse."

Lark knew the brand had been put on him years ago— something about him having run away from Young Man's Chance. Perhaps the men talked about it; maybe Mingo knew what happened to Fortune.

"You want to know why I come back to the devil's place, don't you?" he asked.

She hadn't heard the expression before but she thought of the tannery. But Fortune worked at the furnace. Maybe

211

the heat, she thought. Preachers had come to the hundred several times and she heard from others that they talked about a place called hell where people were burned.

Lark tightened the knot in the back of her white headkerchief and looked at Fortune in agreement for him to continue.

"You need to know why I go away."

When he was a young man, he told her, there was much talk about liberty and manumission. Every day the number of freemen grew larger. And every day they spoke about how the English treated the Americans without respect.

He said he went to master and said that he wanted to be free. Quakers and other Christians were preaching freedom for black men; it was being argued in the State Assembly. Many farmers in New Castle were freeing their slaves.

"He laughed and said it was foolishness. But I didn't think I was foolish. So many times I went to him."

Preddy told him that if he had enough money, Fortune could buy his freedom.

"My mouth would be as empty as a tree hollow by the time I had enough, I told him. He said if I work harder he would hire me out some of the time to earn money. But I couldn't work anymore than I did. Then I said, 'You get a loan to buy something. Give me a loan.' His face turned the color of a hog's liver and he walked away."

No one in particular told him about the British offer to free slaves who joined their military.

"I didn't even know if it were true. But I needed to go."

Fortune walked to Philadelphia where every day a runaway would join the corps, one man to replace the death of another from disease.

"I remember my swearing, I would hear it every day with a new recruit: I do swear that I enter freely and voluntarily into His Majesty's Service, and I do enlist myself without the least compulsion or persuasion into the Negro Company commanded by Capt. Stewart, and that I will demean myself orderly and faithfully, and will cheerfully obey such directions as I may receive from my said captain, or the officers under his command, that I will continue to serve His Majesty in all such services as I may be employed in during the present rebellion in America. So help me God."

Fortune proudly wore a 'Liberty to Slaves' badge, although others had to tell him what it said.

"We were told to attend to the scavengers in Philadelphia. We were street cleaners and removed the nuisances dumped into the streets."

"Did you fight?" Lark asked.

"No. The Pioneers—that's what they called the black troop—we didn't have guns; we had strong backs."

"I stayed with them a short time. Then someone said that I had run away from Master Lockwood's plantation. They said that Master Lockwood was a Loyalist and they wouldn't take a slave from someone who was loyal to His Majesty. One minute I was a free man and the next I was a slave again.

Worse. I was a runaway. I heard what they done to a runaway. They put four horses to him, one to every limb. They cut the horses and each horse carry a piece of him. I thought I was going to be a bunch of me."

Instead, Fortune was returned to Young Man's Chance.

"Master Lockwood, he now was master. I expected Master Lockwood would put a rope around my neck. But he didn't. He brought me to the furnace and had me forge an iron with a 'Y' on it. When I finished it, I put the poker in the fire again until it was red and gave it to him."

Fortune stopped and turned away from Lark. He touched his face and after a minute turned back to look at her.

Lark wanted to know if he wanted to run away again.

"For what?" he asked. "To remove dog shit from the streets. But I've done something here. Drained some swamp and trenched the land. And my father did this before and before him his father also worked for a Master Lockwood from a long time back, to the beginning of time, Chesapeake time."

Fortune calmed himself down.

"We the ones that make this plantation something. We— me and Master Lockwood—we both sucked from the same pap. Me and him we drink the same white milk. I've done something here."

Lark stares at Fortune as he sat on his haunches.

"Master Lockwood, he presses the scorched iron against my head and then he gives me my own piece of land way out in the pines. 'You is free to sell eggs and pumpkins and whatever else you grow on the land,' he says to me. And from then on he lets me hire myself out from time to time and I get to keep a part of the money for myself. He says the person who hires me has to give me a new pair of European shoes and a hat each year. Master Lockwood also gave me two guinea coins. He says he gives it to me for returning a valuable slave to Young Man's Chance."

Fortune unwraps a handkerchief and shows Lark the gold coins.

"These are mine. They're precious, just like this place. They both mine."

Aunt Hany, Mistress Hester and Alexander Brown

HANY MARVEL frightened Lark. The old black woman lived with her husband Benjamin as free black tenant farmers at the south end of the plantation where cedar and oak trees met a partially dredged swamp. Lark seldom went to that section of Young Man's Chance; it was the spirit borderland of vines, brown waters and mossy beards dangling from trees. The place smelled sweet and fetid at the same time.

The Marvels' cabin was in a sorry state, a one-room log dwelling, whose roof was rotted, molded and a quarter gone. The chimneybreast, Lark heard, had collapsed one night when their son slept in front of the fireplace. The bricks crushed him to death. The fallen bricks were then sold to Mr. Lockwood and Benjamin propped up the remainder of the breast with a lumber pole to make a tolerable chimney. The roofs of outhouse and the corncrib had long ago blown away and most of the nails in the barn were loose or lost. Not since their manumission by a Kent merchant and taking up tenancy with Draper Lockwood did they add a single item more than they brought with them.

Hany wandered from her shed from time to time and Benjamin would have to search for her. Mostly she didn't go far, although it might take a while for her husband to find her if she walked into the swamp. She no longer could find her way home by herself. She sometimes walked into Nicholas Preddy's main house to sit beside Sip and Lark. Everyone knew that before the end of the day Benjamin would fetch her. Gertrude had no objection to the old woman walking in unannounced and sitting with Sip and Lark as she saw that she that the woman was harmless and was no distraction to the mother and daughter.

Hany sat mute as she watched mother and daughter go about the household chores.

"Get her some cornbread and milk, Lark," Sip directed.

The free black woman smiled as the two women cleaned, prepared and cooked in the kitchen for their master and mistress. With Hany in the parlor mother and daughter's chatter ceased. The whirring spinning wheel and Lark's stomping on the loom's treadle filled the silence.

"She's witched?" Lark asked her mother.

"She ain't right," Sip explained. "It happens to folks when they get old. But she ain't witched. No reason to be scared of her, Lark. She won't even kill a pestering mouse."

Sip's assurances did little to allay Lark's worries. And she wondered whether her mother had been wrong about Hany's affliction the day Suthy came to her mother's house to ask if she had seen the old woman.

It happened this way—

There hadn't been a visitor to the Marvels' shed for more than a month, not since the weather had turned raw. Benjamin thirsted for the companionship of words. Despite his difficulty in walking and needing to lead Hany by the hand, Benjamin slowly made his way to the sheds near the main house. He stopped at the windowless cabin occupied by Mingo, Suthy, Jacob and Frank.

The men sat on a chair, two stools and the floor while Benjamin placed a blanket around Hany as she lay on a floor near the fireplace. Indian corn and wheat whiskey, which Preddy had provided for them during the harvest season, was brought out. When the men drained the bottles, Mingo brought out the preferred peach brandy made from his own still.

They spent the time joking, telling stories, sitting quietly drinking the whiskeys, passing along news and rumors in equal proportions until the daylight grew weak.

"I've got to go water the hogs," Benjamin said as he lifted himself with the use of his cane. "Again."

He walked out the door and behind the cabin, looked around to see that no woman was near and then relieved himself in a double-streamed trickle.

He came back and shuffled across the darkened room. Suthy took him by the arm and sat him on the chair.

"You sure a long time, old man," Suthy teased. "Did your walking stick freeze?"

"Sure, but you know my eyesight's not so good," Benjamin responded, "but that gal out there that took ahold of my stick sure did seem familiar to me, Suthy. She freezed me so stiff the hogs had to wait their turn."

"Ain't that so," Mingo laughed.

Benjamin looked around the room lit only by the flames from the fireplace. After a minute he could make out the figures in the room but didn't see his wife.

"Hany," he called.

Hany didn't answer.

"Where's Hany gone to?" he asked.

"She got up after you left," Frank said. "She's not outside when you went?"

"I heard her say she was going to wash," Suthy said. "That must have been . . ."

"Ain't no one out back but me," Benjamin said.

"She can't go too far," Mingo said. "Maybe she's at Sip. She goes there when she comes here."

"Last time Hany was here was summer," Sip told her son. "She' not here today."

"She's got to be somewhere near," Mingo said.

"Maybe she went to the main house. Go, Lark. Maybe she's looking to sit with us over there."

Lark went to the house to ask the mistress if Hany was there.

"What's the matter, Lark?"

"I'm looking for Benjamin's wife," she explained.

"Why would Hany be here? I've always seen her with you."

Lark explained that Benjamin had brought her with him to the compound but she wandered out on her own.

On her way back to the cabins, Lark heard a commotion. There was a gathering of Negroes in front of her mother's yard.

Hany wasn't found in any house or in the woods, creek or swamp but at the bottom of common well, the shaft next to it holding a bucket.

Lark, with a dozen others, gathered by the door of the main house on Tuesday to listen to the testimony before the coroner's jury from three witnesses regarding Hany's death. Although Mingo and another Negro were the first to find Hany, they weren't called to testify. Only Benjamin and two white landowners were summoned to offer their comments. Standing by the window, Lark heard what the Sussex County Coroners Reports later recorded:

Daniel Davis: I happened to be on my way to visit Nicholas Preddy that day and was passing Mingo Preddy's cabin seeing people gathered about the well. I made up to see what was the matter and I beheld Hany, Benjamin's wife, down the well dead. After looking down the well a little I sat down sat down by the fire in an empty slave cabin until I was called to assist in drawing her out. I saw no marks of violence. I have been sometime acquainted with Hany, Benjamin's wife and according to seeing her in recent years she seemed to be somewhat deranged or in her dotage and I really believe that she put herself in the well purposefully.

Nicholas Preddy: About three o'clock I went out of my house when Mingo called to me to go and assist in drawing Hany Benjamin's wife out of the slaves' well. I ran to the well and I beheld her down the well dead and I assisted in drawing her out and saw no marks of violence. I have been acquainted with her about twenty years and I consider her to have been somewhat doty recently but from the marks on her feet on the ground by the well that I saw if scraped back from the well I believe it was accidentally done.

Benjamin Marvel: About three o'clock my wife Hany was with me at the house where Mingo stays. After some time talking among ourselves I wanted to water my hogs. I came back and Hany was gone. I looked for her in Mingo's house and outside here and there. I heard the well bucket rattle a few minutes after I went out and I thought she was drawing water but I could see nothing of her and when I came near the well I looked down the well and beheld Hany at the bottom. I called them that Hany was in the well and as soon we could get assistance we drew her up and I saw no marks of violation. I consider that she was much doty as she was about seventy-five years old. I believe it was accidentally done.

But Lark knew there was something more. Mishaps and deaths are never random but were the visible signs of a latent cause that lay below.

LARK COULDN'T STOP THINKING about Hany. Not long after the accident, she had reason to look for the forces that led to people's troubles.

A neighbor, Elizabeth Cattell, visited Young Man's Chance. Lark listened from the pantry to the neighbor confide in Missus Preddy as she prepared tea to serve with stewed peaches. Lark knew that Elizabeth's daughter had been buried a month ago after dying in the bed she shared with her mother.

"I don't know why Hester did it," Elizabeth said. She wiped her dripping nose with the sleeve of her dress.

Lark turned her head slightly in the direction of the dining room to catch the conversation.

"She was born in pain," Gertrude consoled.

"You're right. She cried for months after she was born. Nothing I could do stopped her. I tried to hold her but she wouldn't let me. When she was old enough to talk, she said that her skin pained her all the time. Everything hurt her."

"She never talked when I saw her. Did she ever talk?"

"Some. She was quiet that way. She even stopped talking to me for periods of time. Mr. Cattell, he got so angry at Hester he beat her. I said to him, 'That only makes her hurt more.' He said everybody is in pain but that don't mean they should be acting like her. He didn't know what else to do. He said he was going to shackle her to the ring on the wall like a slave. I wouldn't let him do that. So he hit her again. He said the devil got into her and he was going to drive Satan out."

Lark waited for the visitor to explain why her daughter had been born into such a condition, if she didn't think it was the devil's doing.

What Lark had heard from others might explain it: the lady was the daughter of a large landholder in Maryland and married into a Sussex farm family that had meager resources. Why did her father send her down in life? What was it that the woman brought with her that haunted the family? It was something other than the devil, something bigger in a way.

No explanation satisfied Lark.

"At last the child is now free from pain," Lark heard Gertrude condole with her visitor.

"So I've prayed."

"Lark," Gertrude called. "Where's the tea?"

Lark brought in the new cups with handles and poured the women their pale infusion that smelled of violets.

"The milk, Lark," Gertrude said.

"Yes, mistress," she said and returned with a pitcher.

"Go tell Mingo to feed the mules, Lark," Gertrude directed.

Lark walked to the gate that fenced in the yard and stopped there to listen to the women through the open door. From the distance what Lark heard was a muddle. They used a word she didn't know. She thought she heard the woman say that Hester "drank it every day."

When Lark asked Sip about it, her mother said that the potion was a tincture made with a powder favored by white people.

"Master Nicholas drinks it every once in a while," Sip explained. "It eases pain, I hear."

"Too *much* easing with Miss Hester," Lark responded.

"Master Nicholas keeps it locked up in the cabinet and won't let anyone touch it but himself. Not even his son."

Lark would have known more about what had happened to Hester if she had known about the testimony kept in the county courthouse. In the Coroners Reports she would have found:

> I heard her go to the dresser, I heard a bottle or cup fall, and I thought she had been taking some peppermint, for she me told me in the afternoon that she was sick in the stomack. I saw her come into the room take off her dress and go to bed. The room was so strong of laudanum that it made me sick and I had to leave.

That still wouldn't have answered Lark's question—she understood that too much laudanum could kill a person, but why is it that some drink the potion and don't die?

LARK WAS GIVEN ANOTHER REASON to speculate about the hidden cause of adversities the day she went to Seaford to sell clothing she and her mother had sewn. Lark bundled dresses and shirts in a gunnysack and placed it in the wagon that Fortune loaded with cedar planks he had cut. The wagon belonged to Alexander Brown, one of the many freemen in the area and the owner of a successful business transporting goods across the state.

It was more economical, Nicholas calculated, to hire Alexander and rent his wagon for a day than it was to send one of his male slaves away with one Nicholas's own wagons.

Alexander, with Lark sitting beside him, guided his ambling mule over corduroyed roads that only recently had been made suitable for carriages. Countless waterways etched the landscape like arthritic fingers, slowing their journey each time they needed to ford the stream. When they reached Seaford, near the Maryland border, Alexander soon found Preddy's cedar buyer while Lark went to the several houses where she had sold her goods before. By mid-afternoon she was done and returned to the store where they had parted. The wagon was there but Alexander wasn't. She waited until dark when she finally climbed onto the wagon bed and curled up to sleep.

Roosters woke her. She propped herself against a sideboard waiting for sunrise.

"You seen Mr. Alexander?" she asked the storeowner. "That's his wagon. I came with him and I need to go back to Young Man's Chance."

She spent most of the morning accosting people as they came to shop.

"He got into a fight yesterday afternoon. I saw it. A Negro man light complexioned, like you, and wearing a blue jacket?"

"That's him!"

"He was arguing with a white man, a blacksmith from hereabouts. They was arguing right here in the street. The Negro was telling the blacksmith he was a free man and to leave him alone. The blacksmith grabbed his jacket and the Negro didn't hesitate a second and punched him back."

"Hit him?"

"The blacksmith's companion was standing nearby. He shouted, 'No nigger hits a white man,' and he jumped in and knocked the black man down. They kicked him from both sides. Then they tied him up and threw him in a farm wagon."

"Where's Mr. Alexander now?"

"I don't know. They drove him off."

"They took him away?"

Since it was illegal to sell slaves out of state, he explained, free Negroes were being kidnapped in the neighborhood and brought into Maryland to be sold to planters in the South for as much as $500 each.

"Those two men, I've seen them before. They live right on the border, a house where the line runs right through it, one part in Delaware, then other in Maryland. Whenever the sheriff comes to arrest them, they just step over the state line into another room. They've been catching Negroes like this for some time." He looked at Lark. "You better watch yourself."

"I'm not free."

"Lucky for you. They won't dare take someone's property. There are so many freemen here they're easy picking."

"I need to get Mr. Alexander."

"He's gone by now. I bet they sold him straightaway to buyers from Virginia."

A townsman drove Lark back to Young Man's Chance in Alexander's wagon. He then purchased the horse and wagon from Alexander's wife.

Alexander's wife, Mariah Brown, sent a letter to the Delaware Abolition Society to have them investigate her husband's kidnapping. An agent visited came from Dover to visit with her. He then appeared at Young Man's Chance to talk to Lark. She described the man in Seaford who had told her about the kidnapping and had taken her home.

"I intend to bring your husband back," the agent said. "The Justice of the Peace will look into bringing the two men to trial. They are vicious criminals, that gang."

When Mariah Brown saw Lark in the market several months later, she showed her the letter she received from the agent. At the dry goods store, the proprietor read the letter to them. The agent had traced her husband to Norfolk. He regretted to inform her that three days before his arrival, Alexander had been sent to Florida on a slave ship. The men were brought to trial for kidnapping.

The reprobates who manstole your husband have been prosecuted twice before but the propensities of the juries to lean on the merciful side of the question, when the crime is committed against a black person, is so strong that the accused were acquitted. The jurors believe a free Negro is better off as a slave. I am sad to say that justice could not be done.

AUNT HANY, MISTRESS HESTER, ALEXANDER BROWN—the question was the same: why them? Of all the people who walked by the well, why was it Hany who fell in; of all the people who drank laudanum, why was it Miss Hester who died of poisoning; of all the freemen in Sussex, why was it Alexander Brown who was kidnapped?

The church offered one answer, her mother another. Lark thought that maybe the two answers were really the same. Or that neither was the answer at all.

Bats of the Wilderness

MINGO OFTEN took Master Nicholas's and Gertrude's son, William, with him as he carried out minor affairs for Young Man's Chance. William enjoyed the liveliness of Dover and Wilmington. More so, he liked carrying out his father's instructions to keep an eye on Mingo.

One time when he returned from Wilmington, Mingo reported to his companions about a show featuring a black man who turned white.

He hadn't seen it himself, he said, but he had spoken to someone who had.

"Master William saw it?"

"No. But he knew someone who did."

"It's not possible," Lark protested. "No more than a blue bird wakes up one day as a red bird."

Mingo insisted on the story.

"Maybe it was a white man who washed off some mud."

"No. That would be a trick. An easy one that everyone could see."

As proof of the amazing personage, Mingo presented a poster he had cadged from William.

"Read for yourself. It is certified. By Joseph Holt."

"Who?"

"William says Holt was a captain in the Continental army. Holt says so himself. And he says Harry Moss served with him and was a person of good character."

"Let me see it," Lark insisted, as she took the broadside from Mingo. She unfolded the sheet and began to read. "It says, 'A great curiosity.' That's what it says at the top."

227

"Everyone said that," Mingo said. "A great curiosity."

Lark continued.

"It says Harry Moss remained black for thirty-eight years, after which his natural color began to rub off. It says his body is now all white, as fair as any white person. There are small parts of him that are still black but changing very fast."

"He was all white, my friend said. Go on. Read the rest."

"It says the wool is coming off his head, legs and arms and he is now growing straight hair like white people."

"My friend saw it for himself."

"This *is* some curiosity. But you didn't see him, did you Mingo."

"It costs a quarter of a dollar. So I was content to have others tell me about it. But I wish I had the money. For a moment I thought Master Preddy wouldn't miss a quarter of a dollar. But I came to my senses."

"This was almost as good as seeing, and it didn't cost you anything."

"Everybody was talking about it. Nothing else. The show came from Philadelphia. People there say he's as popular there as Thom Jefferson and John Adams."

"But I wouldn't pay one penny to see him, even if I had the money," Lark said. "I think he's like Frank. His skin's been burned off, that's all."

"The Lord can do anything. Why can't he do this? The Lord does good."

"Mingo, I would pay *more* than a quarter—a lot more—to see a white man who's turned black."

SIP, WHOSE ACHING BONES limited her ability to walk much further than to the edge of the woods, attended

Frank's meetings on the plantation. Lark would go with her, except if a circuit rider came through. Then she would go to hear the preacher with a reputation. Mingo didn't attend the meetings on the plantation; he went to Seaford each Sunday. Lark teased her brother about wanting to meet a girl there, and while he denied her charge, it was Fillis that he sat besides, it was her Bible that he practiced his reading and, he admitted only to himself, it was the thought of her, not the preaching, that brought him back every Sunday.

Gertrude hired out Fillis, her slave, for household work to a family near the Delaware border. Fillis kept part of the pay to purchase her freedom. The terms set for her manumission was not as high as Nicholas wanted but Gertrude thought it was a fair price. Fillis calculated that within five years she could buy her freedom, but the date was re-set each time she needed a physician or bought a new dress. She gladly gave to the preachers who passed through the county, never resenting the coins that she contributed to their upkeep so she could hear the glad tidings. Fillis all but gave up hope of reaching her goal when she had her baby.

On Sundays Fillis and Mingo were at Brown's Chapel, a fine building whose frame had already been increased since its completion in 1806 to accommodate a swelling congregation. When the weather was too inclement for Mingo to get to Seaford, he attended the plank cabin church on the plantation where Frank did the preaching reasonably well enough to fill the cabin with Young Man's Chance slaves and several free men and women who lived nearby.

Frank began all his sermons the same. "And the Lord said, I have surely seen the affliction of my people which are in Egypt, and have heard their cry by reason of their task-masters."

It may have been the only verse he knew, but it didn't matter. His storytelling kept everyone's attention and when he was done, the meeting continued outdoors with singing, clapping and praying that rolled through the woods like a storm. The meeting lasted into the night and ended in a ring of worshipper shuffling like a wheeling turning to the right until the voices after reaching higher, the tempo becoming quicker and the volume louder, the whirlwind slowly subsided and the worshippers marched to their cabins sweated and satisfied.

When news that Freeborn Horton, whose reputation was spread from Baltimore to Charleston, was preaching at Brown's Chapel, Gertrude approached Mingo.

"This Sunday I'm going to hear Rev. Horton. Master Preddy ain't going. So I want you to take me in the buggy."

"To Seaford?"

"Yes. How did you know?" Gertrude asked.

"Everyone hears Rev. Horton is preaching there on Sunday. I was planning on taking the buggy myself. It will save my feet some wear."

"You were planning to go?"

"Yes, ma'am. I go every week. I meet Fillis there. We go to Brown's Chapel together."

"You do?" Gertrude said. "You mean my Fillis?"

"Yes, ma'am. She's my wife and she's with my baby."

"I heard she had a child. But I didn't know it was yours."

"Yes. The baby Nan is mine."

Mingo nodded, afraid that he may have said too much.

"I promised to take Lark with me," Mingo said. "She wants to hear Preacher Horton."

"The buggy only takes two. She can walk," Gertrude asserted.

Mingo and Gertrude sat side-by-side in the two-wheel carriage as they rode to Brown's Chapel without a word.

Gertrude subscribed to the Presbyterian Church in Broad Creek with its weekly messages of hard work, honesty, loyalty and the promise of heavenly reward, the sober quality of a service of tempered preaching. She had little interest in the emotionalism that she heard pervaded Methodist meetings, but she wasn't going to miss out on seeing the famous preacher whose sermons, she heard, were delivered with such force that listeners lives were transformed by the words alone. The meeting places where he spoke lit with the glow of heaven itself.

Lark and Suthy, who had left before the sun rose, were already at the church when the mule and buggy from Young Man's Chance arrived. Lark walked from the square across from the chapel to greet them; Suthy continued to talk with friends.

Seaford had never seen such a crowd, not even on the first market day of the spring season or on Return Day in the fall. Slaves, free men and women, and twice as many whites again milled around on the streets and when the doors opened people jostled their way in to get the best view. Gertrude sat on the main floor where all the whites sat. Lark sat on one side of her and Mingo sat on the other. When Fillis arrived, Gertrude acknowledged her with a nod. Having seen her only a few times in the last many years, she wouldn't have recognized her. Suthy and his friend went to the balcony.

Born a slave in New Jersey, Horton's master encouraged him to become a Christian. Wanting to read the Bible for himself, he persuaded several congregants to teach him how to read. So moved by the book and the sermons, Horton decided to devote his life to bringing the word to others. He bought his freedom by the time he was twenty and had traveled the circuit for a decade, first as an assistant to a white minister, then on his own.

A small bald man appeared in the pulpit without introduction. He stood and seemed to grow taller. Quiet fell over the chapel. Then, without warning, there was a shout from the balcony and by the time Gertrude returned her attention to the pulpit, Horton, in a soft voice, continued, ". . . reason of their taskmasters, for I know their sorrows; and I am come down to deliver them out of the hand of the Egyptians."

Several more congregants murmured their approval.

"These words, my brethren, contain a short account of some of the circumstances which preceded the deliverance of the children of Israel from their captivity and bondage in Egypt."

When Gertrude turned to Fillis to see what was disturbing her, she saw tears flowing down her face.

"They were slaves to the kings of Egypt. Their work was dealt out to them in tasks, and performed under the eye of vigilant and rigorous masters. The least deficiency was punished by beating."

Mingo shifted in the pew. He heard the message in Frank's gathering but never in the presence of whites. And never with such certitude.

Horton's raised his voice only slightly, then lowered it again, causing many to lean in more closely. Interjections from the assembly were louder.

"Who can conceive of their measure of suffering?"

Gertrude was feeling faint.

"God didn't forget them. He saw their affliction. He heard their cries, every groan they uttered was recorded, every tear they shed was preserved."

Fillis began to sob. Mingo gave her his handkerchief. Gertrude reached for her hand and with that her head stopped spinning.

Scattered throughout the chapel were calls to the preacher, shouts to God.

"Clouds and darkness are round about him, but righteousness and judgment are the habitation of his throne."

Now Mingo joined in the chorus of encouragement.

"The common father of the human race has seen the affliction of our countrymen. He has seen the anguish which has taken place. He has seen the pangs of separation between members of the same family."

Fillis withdrew her hand from Gertrude's clasp. She stood up. A loud shout came from the balcony and Gertrude saw many standing, moving about, leaning over the railing.

The heat in the room was overwhelming, the light from Horton's pate blinding.

"We thank you that thou art no respecter of persons and that thou hast made of one blood all nations of men. Rend thy heavens, O Lord, and come down upon the earth; and grant that the mountains, which now obstruct the perfect day of thy goodness and mercy, may flow down in thy presence."

Mingo stood beside Fillis. They weren't alone. Others, white and blacks, stood as if being held aloft by the shafts of oratory. Something stirred in Gertrude but she didn't know what.

"We thank thee, that the sun of righteousness has at last shed morning beams upon them. May the nations, which now sit in darkness, behold and rejoice in its light and grant, that all those in false religions cast their idols to the moles and the bats of the wilderness."

Horton stepped out from behind the pulpit and walked from the podium to the floor. He looked at the congregants in the pews, then at those in the balconies on either side. After he let out the first line of the hymn, worshipers joined him in song: they stepped lightly on their right feet, swayed right and clapped, stepped lightly with their left feet, swayed left and clapped, keeping the four-beat pattern and Horton's soprano voice as strong as it had been all morning, filled with the same bittersweet hope as his sermon. One congregant took over the line from Horton, "When Jesus walked upon the earth," repeated it several times until others, catching the tune, joined in. The singers let out the second line and a chant rose. "Some said he was a spy," they repeated, until the hymn was entirely raised. Everyone but Gertrude, it seemed, had joined in, each adding their voice, embellishing the tune in their own way, a few ending with whoops and shouts. The chorus rose to a crescendo, then subsided and faded away. Horton closed with a poem.

> Lift up your souls to God on high
>
> The fountain of eternal grace
>
> Who with a tender father's eye
>
> Look'd down on Afric's helpless race.

> The nations heard His stern commands
>
> Britannia kindly sets us free
>
> Columbia tears the galling bands
>
> And give the sweets of liberty.

Amidst the stirring, Gertrude told Mingo they were leaving. Mingo wanted to stay with Fillis but didn't dare tell Gertrude. Mingo lightly touched his wife's sleeve and left her in the chapel, her eyes closed and her chin raised, unaware that Mingo was gone.

Gertrude never did learn that as the service continued into the later afternoon a support beam of right balcony loosened and split, pitching the platform forward. It hurtled a worshiper to his death. The white worshippers below, packed closely together, escaped with only minor injuries.

GERTRUDE DIDN'T SPEAK TO Nicholas for days after Brown's Chapel. At night Gertrude sat upright between her first and second sleep in an agitated state. She had disturbing dreams she couldn't remember. During the day she heard Horton's steady anguish: "The neglect with which their masters treated their immortal souls. The whip, the screw, the pincers, and the red-hot iron."

Finally she said to her husband, "My slave."

"Yes."

"She has too much religion."

"I worry about what religion is doing to our slaves, too," he said as he looked up from his ledger book. "I will talk to Frank. His meetings can't go on throughout the night."

"I am giving her her freedom," she continued.

Nicholas expressed his surprise.

"She doesn't bring you enough money?"

"I can't keep her," is all Gertrude said.

"This whole business of slaves is getting out of hand" Nicholas began. "There are more free Negroes than slaves here. I'm thinking of selling them all myself before slavery is abolished all together and we go the way of Pennsylvania. They will all be worthless. I'm in a terrible a bind. I can't sell them out of state. I'm being squeezed." Nicholas looked at the ledger. "Increase your take of her earnings, if she's not bringing you enough money." He said dismissively, "Or sell her if you like, Gertrude. She's yours to do with as you like."

"I'm *giving* her her freedom. She'll decide what to do with her life, not me or anyone else."

While she had inherited her from her father, Gertrude had little contact with Fillis before the Brown's Chapel meeting. She never visited the Maryland farm, leaving its operation to a tenant farmer. She mainly hired out Fillis to one household or another in the neighborhood on the Maryland side of the border.

Gertrude applied for a certificate of manumission and when it was accepted, she abrogated Fillis's latest contract. Fillis was a free woman. The letter she sent explaining the situation concluded: "Tell Fillis I wish for her a blessed life."

Her freedom came as a shock to Fillis.

"I's a free woman?"

"You are."

Fillis couldn't contain her joy. She burst into exuberant praise, clapping her hands and offering thanks.

"Miss Preddy wants you to bring Nan to her," her employer had told her.

"She doesn't know Nan."

She thought that perhaps there were other surprises in store. There were.

"Because she is hers and wants to have her at the plantation."

The freedom papers, she was told, were for her alone.

She was told to pack her things and leave the house, as she was no longer employed there. Fillis didn't know where to go and rejected the instructions to go first to Young Man's Chance. Miss Gertrude's gift was poison. But not knowing what else to do and longing to see Mingo, Fillis placed her belongings in a bedsheet. Although she was frightened of snakes in the swamps and wild boars in the forests, she was more afraid of encountering kidnappers on the road now that she was a free woman.

Fillis trudged for several days with the bundle on her back and often carrying her toddler, being taken in by freemen and slaves for food and shelter. One household gave Nan a clean dress. They stayed at another cabin for two days while Nan's fever subsided.

She didn't announce herself when she arrived at Young Man's Chance. She found an old man tending sheep.

"This is Mingo's girl?" the preacher asked.

He took mother and daughter to Sip's cabin. Everyone agreed that she and Nan should with stay Sip and Lark. For a week they stayed inside, the door and window shut when the Sip and Lark went to work at the main house. If Fillis heard Gertrude or her husband, she and Nan would hide under the bed until she thought they had passed.

"Stay with your aunties," Fillis told Nan each night as she left to be with Mingo in an abandoned shed—chinks in the walls, no furniture, cobwebs in every cranny. That they lay on the damp ground near the muck of the pigpen didn't matter to them. Soon the dark quieted the farm animals. All Mingo and Fillis heard were the swamp frogs, the screeching of a barn owl, the hammering of a woodpecker and the delirious singing of a mockingbird. Through the gape in the roof they watched shooting stars etch the black sky.

Fillis wanted Mingo to leave with her and Nan, to go to a place where everyone could be free.

"I can't run away," he said. "If I's caught . . . Look at Fortune."

"I'm not going without you."

"You'll have Nan. And when there is enough money, the two of us, we'll buy my freedom."

Fillis began to sob.

"There is no certificate for Nan."

Mingo was stunned into silence.

"How can I hide her? It will be worse that way. She'll be taken from me when she's found."

Mingo held her until she stopped trembling.

Each night they turned over the possibilities.

"I won't know what to do in the city. I've never been anywhere larger than Seaford. I'm afraid."

Mingo assured her that there would be many people to assist her in the city. The city was full of free Negroes.

Fillis did her best to distract Nan in the cabin. But the child clamored to go outside. Two weeks in the cabin was too long for a child. Finally it was decided: Fillis took Nan to Gertrude at the main house.

"Oh, you are Fillis."

Fillis didn't remind her that they had seen each other in Seaford.

"I've brought my child to you," Fillis said.

"Where is she?"

She said that a young woman named Lark saw her on the road and Nan was with her.

"I'm going to Philadelphia. When there is enough money, I'll purchase Mingo's freedom."

Gertrude stood in the doorway.

"Can I get you a glass of water, Fillis? Are you thirsty?"

"No, thank you."

"That's up to Master Preddy," Gertrude said. "You was mine. But not Mingo. He belongs to Master Preddy."

"The master must have the same spirit as you. You talk to him."

"Yes, I can."

"And Nan," Fillis added.

"The child?"

"Is she yours?"

"Yes," Gertrude responded.

"Won't you give her to me?"

"That wouldn't be good for her," Gertrude said without hesitation. "The poor girl. How will you be able to take care of her? Her life will be good here. I'll make sure of that."

"Then she can come with Mingo."

"Perhaps so."

"Let Auntie Lark take care of Nan until I get her."

"Yes," Gertrude said, wondering how Fillis could know anything about the woman she just met, but she let the question go. "Lark is good. She'll take care of the child. She's kind and loyal. She'll bring up a fine girl."

Gertrude looked at Nan's canvas shoes, a big toe sticking out of one.

"It's a long way to go. I'll ask Master Preddy for Mingo to take you in a cart."

On Sunday Fillis, Mingo and Nan went to Frank's meeting. It was the first time she attended a church with no whites.

Mingo took a sickle and put it under the seat of the carriage and drove Fillis to Philadelphia, being directed from the home of one freeman to another. Before Mingo left her in the city, Fillis found shelter in a boarding house run by a shroud maker, a free woman married to a cooper. An abolitionist paid her first month's rent for her.

Mingo and Fillis formalized their marriage at the First African Presbyterian Church.

"Our next child will be born free," Mingo said.

Fillis was shaking as though she was consumed with malarial fever, although her hands were ashen with cold.

"Nan," she cried. "Bring her to me soon."

Mingo rode back to the plantation anticipating the day when the family would be re-united. For the next two years Fillis and Mingo saved what they could to purchase his and their daughter's freedom.

Tangier

FRANK PREACHED on Freedom Day. The yearly occasion, on the 1st of January, marked the anniversary of the abolition of the trans-Atlantic slave trade five years earlier. Since blacks were excluded from participating in the Independence Day commemorations, slaves and free men and women from Delaware to New England shunned Fourth of July as a white man's holiday.

Frank led his small fellowship in rejoicing. The day was dawning, he said, when everyone would be a free person.

The old man, his voice a rasp that contained smoldering embers, mixed biblical verse with his own story of having been born a slave and was now alive to see the great liberation coming.

"No more will anyone be born in bondage," he said, as he leaned on his cane and raised his head heavenward. "Every child born today will know the sweets of liberty."

From the main house the Preddys could hear the songs issuing from the log cabin church.

Mingo remained subdued, afraid that the preacher was going too far in drawing the picture of freedom; Suthy called louder than anyone when Frank told the story of the Jews and Pharaoh. Lark rocked and swayed, her eyes shut tight when the singing began. Vergie struggled to stand erect on her gossamer frame. Benjamin smiled. Nan played with a doll as she sat beside Lark. Fortune and Paris preferred whiskey in their own cabins.

Sip—her grave was set under a pile of stones next to the ramshackle church. Her limbs had become so twisted that she could barely walk even with a staff. One night when she went to relieve herself in the weeds, she stumbled on a log, hit her head on a rock and died.

"And remember Sister Sip," Frank said. "She's been wagging at the hill so long, it's about time she cross over." He began to sing—

> My father, how long
>
> My father, how long,
>
> My father how long
>
> Poor sinner suffer here?

Benjamin and Mingo added their voices to the chorus—

> And it won't be long,
>
> And it won't be long,
>
> And it won't be long,
>
> Poor sinner suffer here.

Frank—

> My father, how long
>
> My father, how long,
>
> My father how long
>
> Poor sinner suffer here?

Suthy sang loudest of all—

> And it won't be long
>
> And it won't be long
>
> We'll fight for liberty
>
> When the Lord will call us home.

Frank concluded in the same deliberate voice with which he began.

> Today I don't feel weary
>
> and nowadays I ain't tired.

O glory hallelujah

Just let me in the kingdom
while the world is all on fire.

O glory hallelujah

And keep the ark a-moving
while the world is all on fire.

O glory hallelujah
"On fire, on fire, on fire."

Shortly after noon they lit a bonfire in the cow pasture and in the dim winter sun they roasted an old ox, crabs, Indian corn and drank apple and pear brandy. There was ring dancing and storytelling. Fortune joined them. Paris was there, too. Everything smelled good that day.

Sparks drifted upward from that the fire that crackled after sunset when William arrived on his horse.

"Douse the fire," he ordered, as he looked down on the celebrants. "Get back to your cabins."

A large gathering of slaves after dark was a dangerous thing, his father had told him. The German Coast uprising along the Mississippi was still fresh in his mind.

DESPITE EVACUATIONS BY leeches and cold-water soakings, an infection in Fillis's inflamed thumb spread unabated and killed her before Mingo had the chance to visit her again. In a letter from her employer, Mingo also learned that she had also been with child.

He was responsible for his wife's death—he should never have left Fillis in Philadelphia. He should have taken Nan away from Young Man's Chance and leave servitude behind. Thousands of blacks lived as free men and women in the city; they wouldn't have been discovered. Or even if they had, there were many whites and black there that would have defended their right to remain free from bondage.

He was a coward. Worse, it was he who encouraged her take work with a woman who dealt with the dead. Fillis hadn't wanted to take the position as the Negro woman's assistant sewing shrouds, but Mingo insisted. He was eager for them to start their freedom account.

"She's yours now, Lark," Mingo said to his sister.

"Yes. Of course she is," she assured him.

She suspected where this was leading. There were rumors that slaves around the Chesapeake were fleeing to British ships.

"I've leaving. I'm going get enough money to buy all of our freedom—mine, Nan's, yours. All of us, Lark."

"Be sensible, Mingo. All of us will contribute for Nan's freedom. Each of us can put something in for her. We'll get the money somehow."

"When? When will that be?"

"I know where it is kept in the main house."

"You'll be whipped for sure."

"We'll get it for her."

"And me? If I stay here, I'll be like Frank, waiting to be buried in the condition I'm in now. But I ain't going to be a slave all my life and neither will my daughter be."

"You saw what happened to Fortune."

"I won't be returned. The British control the Chesapeake. You heard what they've done there. They run up the water as they please. They are in charge."

Lark shook her head in disbelief.

"They'll take me and give me my freedom. They made a promise."

He took a folded paper from his pocket and showed it to Lark.

"These papers are all over the eastern shore. I got this one yesterday."

"I heard about the raids and the running. There's talk."

She read the proclamation slowly.

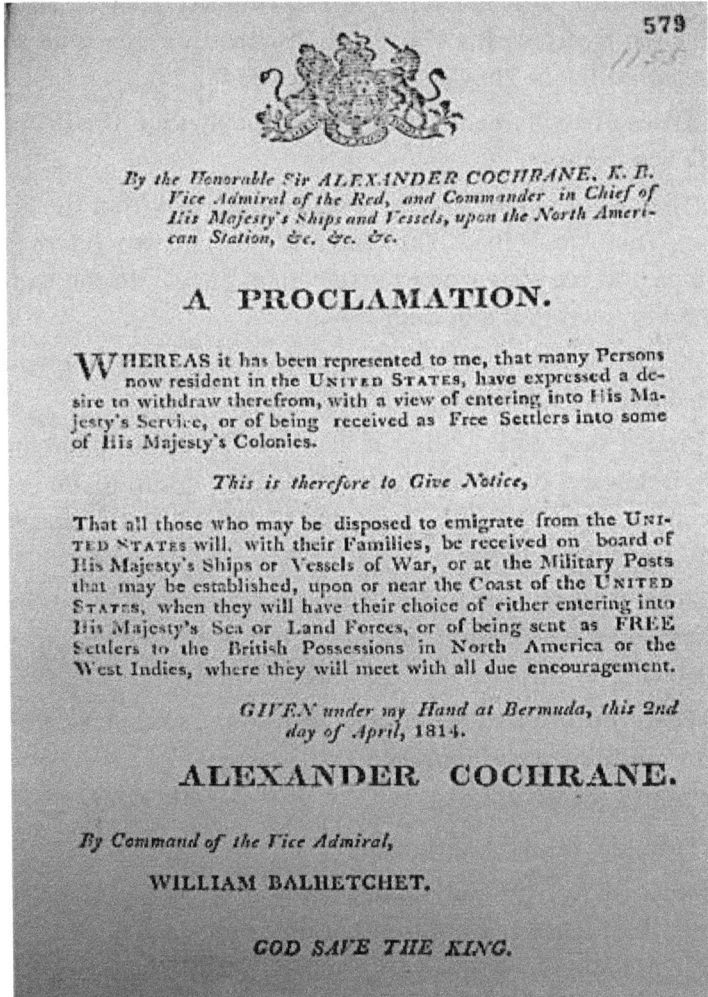

579

By the Honorable Sir *ALEXANDER COCHRANE*, K. B. Vice Admiral of the Red, and Commander in Chief of His Majesty's Ships and Vessels, upon the North American Station, &c. &c. &c.

A PROCLAMATION.

WHEREAS it has been represented to me, that many Persons now resident in the UNITED STATES, have expressed a desire to withdraw therefrom, with a view of entering into His Majesty's Service, or of being received as Free Settlers into some of His Majesty's Colonies.

This is therefore to Give Notice,

That all those who may be disposed to emigrate from the UNITED STATES will, with their Families, be received on board of His Majesty's Ships or Vessels of War, or at the Military Posts that may be established, upon or near the Coast of the UNITED STATES, when they will have their choice of either entering into His Majesty's Sea or Land Forces, or of being sent as FREE Settlers to the British Possessions in North America or the West Indies, where they will meet with all due encouragement.

GIVEN under my Hand at Bermuda, this 2nd day of April, 1814.

ALEXANDER COCHRANE.

By Command of the Vice Admiral,

WILLIAM BALHETCHET.

GOD SAVE THE KING.

"Many've already fled," Mingo said.

"You know yourself what good promises are from white people. It's not a promise but a trick."

She told him that those who have run away were whipped like dogs and kept in hard labor. The sick were thrown overboard.

"They'll sell you to the Caribbean."

"Americans are spreading these rumors. They're afraid that too many slaves'll join the British. But this time the British will win. They'll keep their word."

"Delaware will free us soon. More quickly than the British will win the war."

"They want to destroy the Americans so bad from the last war. They won't lose. They already burnt down Havre de Grace and plunder wherever they like. They'll do the same to every town that's in their way."

"If the British win," she argued, "then you'll get your freedom without having to run away."

"And if they don't? What if they don't? I'm not gambling on Delaware doing us right, Lark. I'm running for my freedom. I'm not waiting for some good luck to fall on me. I'm choosing for myself."

Lark, wiping her hands on her dress, looked at her brother. He was right, she knew, but she wanted him to stay with her, to stay with the baby.

When the sun had set, Mingo went to the women's cabin. Nan ran to him and jumped into his arms.

"You be good," he said.

"You, too, Mingo," Lark said.

Mingo didn't tell Nan that he would be gone for a long time. He hugged her and put her down on the floor.

In the middle of the night, with nothing more than a jacket, shirt, trousers and shoes, he walked in marshes, shadowed creeks, found shelter in houses of freemen and slaves' cabins; he subsisted on shellfish, berries and fruits, walking into Maryland, hearing that the British were gathering runaways on an island called Tangier, in the Chesapeake.

Several blacks were gathered on the pebbled shore. A young woman, her eyes wide with fright, who was holding an infant reminded Mingo of Young Man's Chance. He nearly turned to return to the plantation when they were hustled onto a canoe hidden in the rushes. Mingo sat down.

"Wait," the mother called. "Don't go yet. I've left something on the shore."

The woman placed the infant on the floor of the canoe and waded in the shallow water and disappeared as she ran into the darkness.

"Let's go."

"No. Wait."

The waves lapped against the dugout. Frogs croaked louder than any sound heard during daylight.

The woman had been swallowed in the gloom of the marsh.

One rower poked the other with the paddle and the canoe slipped out into the deeper waters of the bay. The two black men paddled to Tangier with three runaways and a sleeping infant wrapped in a shawl. Mingo picked up the baby to keep it dry. As soon as they set foot on the British occupied island, they would be free.

MINGO LANDED ON THE SANDY and mosquito infested island, one of the "crowds of refugees of color, of all descriptions, ages, sexes and conditions," as described by Admiral George Cockburn, commander of the Chesapeake Squadron.

The hundreds of runaways received seamen's clothing to replace the tatters with which many arrived. Cockburn ordered the old clothes burned to prevent disease. But the issue was to serve another purpose: to induce slaves to leave their masters for Britain's hastily constructed Fort Albion in the Chesapeake. Mingo received a seaman's slop of a duck waistcoat, check shirt, tall hat and mattress. The quartermaster decided Mingo's trousers and shoes were usable. Mingo traded with another refugee, his hat for a brown scarf, which looked like Nan's walnut-dyed blanket.

Elation gave way to a sensation that Mingo had not experienced before. For the first time Mingo felt the pangs of hunger. The refugees received two-thirds of a seaman's allowance of corn, rice, bread or flour; women were given half and children one quarter of the British sailor's food allotment.

Chosen by the refugees to speak for them, Mingo complained to one of the fort's officers.

"This food ain't enough to live on." He held the baby in his arms as he addressed the sailor. "The child won't survive on so little."

"Where its mother?" Captain Ross asked. "Why are you bringing it here?"

Mingo told him that the child wasn't his. The mother had abandoned the child.

"Boy or girl?"

"Girl."

Ross sat behind a crude desk. He lifted his pen, then put it down. He walked from behind his desk and looked at the child.

"She's healthy?"

"So far."

"Give the child to the sergeant," he directed.

Mingo tightened his hold.

"Don't worry," he assured Mingo, the captain's tone suddenly turning gentle. "Every Negro is a free person. If the mother is found, she'll have her child returned. But until then, she's better off with me, in my quarters.

"If not?"

Ross was taken aback by the boldness of a black man. But he responded kindly. "And if she doesn't appear, when my service ends here, I'll bring her to England. My wife and I . . ." he stopped himself. "Well, this child will bring us happiness."

Mingo loosened his grip. In England she would be a servant, not a slave. And that was better than remaining in America. Mingo watched the child being taken from the room, uncertain once again whether he had made the right choice. What did he know of the captain's real intentions? The soldier could just as easily sell the girl and pocket the money. Yet something about the officer's demeanor eased his conscience.

Mingo returned the subject back to the rations.

"Don't complain. You get what we can give you. First, this is a military fort."

"All dead men are free," Mingo countered.

"I see why you were chosen to speak for the Negroes," Ross laughed. "A free man can also return to where he's left."

That choice Mingo wasn't going to make.

The next day, Ross addressed the refugees at the parade ground. He told them he didn't have more food to give. His troops needed to be fed first to carry out their duty. Everything was being done to ensure there was no starvation. He explained that when his sailors arrived on the island it was desolate. They built everything they now see: the quarters, the barracks, the cooking places, privies, the garden, the wet ditch, the roads and the bastion with two redoubts. Nothing grew in the sandy and salty marshes when they arrived, the captain said. Land had to be cleared and when the first crops are harvested, it still wouldn't be enough to feed two hundred sailors and as many refugees. All their foodstuffs were confiscated from American farms on the mainland and everything was redistributed. A recent raid on the Rappahannock captured two schooners, 250 barrels of flour and sixty sheep. The marines also brought with them more slaves, another 130 mouths to feed.

"What you have been given ought to content you, if it were in your nature to be content," Ross ended churlishly.

Later that week Rear Admiral Cockburn supplemented the refugees' diet with fish.

Each night canoes and small boats with runaways arrived at Tangier, from the eastern and western shores, from Virginia and Delaware, every day the island becoming more crowded, the food rations becoming proportionately meager. The number of refugees continued to grow every day.

By day Mingo labored at building the infrastructure of the fort. The labor was relentless, far more arduous than what he faced at the plantation. There was little time to rest and he was under constant supervision. He sometimes felt weak from a lack of food.

At night he dreamt about Young Man's Chance—the friends, the food, the familiar grounds, Nan's aroma. Then the dream goes wrong. There is Fortune and a sizzling iron; there is Nan whose crying he cannot control. He is carrying her and he is bitten by a pit viper. He drops her in the dark waters of the cedar swamp. He sees Fillis in the trees but his feet are stuck in the mire.

When he wakes his resolve to remain a freeman is reinvigorated. He calculates how he will secure his daughter's freedom, his sister's, his friend's.

THE CAPTAIN SUMMONED the young male refugees to the parade ground.

"You pretend to be bold," he addressed them. "But who amongst you is ready to join us in any expedition against your old master?"

When Ross added that there would be additional provisions for any able-bodied blacky who would join the Colonial Marines, Mingo stepped forward.

The first test for the black recruits was the go ashore, and infiltrate plantations, spreading the word that freedom awaited them at Tangier. If they proved themselves on the mission, he said, upon return they would receive increased rations, a uniform and a weapon.

Mingo and his new friend, Kennedy, were deployed to the Virginia mainland, an area unfamiliar to Mingo. Kennedy had been a slave around these headwaters, so Mingo depended upon his knowledge of the terrain. The two went from plantation to plantation, never straying far from shore, talking to slaves about the freedom waiting for them, encouraging them to flee to the British fort where a new life was awaiting, all the while gathering information about the preparedness of the Virginia militia.

Mingo and Kennedy remained a week spreading the word and reconnoitering between the Potomac before returning safely. Some infiltrators were caught by Americans and weren't seen again. The black marines who did make it back had proven ability and loyalty sufficiently to be issued arms and uniforms, and to undergo military training.

Mingo enjoyed a full stomach for the first time in months. He didn't care much for the stiffness of his uniform, while others delighted in the finery. Neither did he look forward to combat but if it helped liberate others from bondage, he would do so willingly.

Twelve days after the Second Corps of Colonial Marines was formed. Mingo and Kennedy, part of the first company under the direction of Ross, rowed eastward across the bay most of the night with scores of Royal Marines, all in uniform.

Not more than three miles from their destination, they were spotted by the Americans when their barges ran aground in the shallow water. The lookout sounded an alarm bell that woke the Americans to the fact that they were under attack. With thirty other Colonials, Mingo climbed out of his boat and sloshed through the marsh until he reached dry ground. Two tenders, a sloop and a schooner under Cockburn's command had arrived behind them, their cannons and rockets providing cover for the black troops. The Marines gathered and charged Rumley's Gut where Mingo and Kennedy encountered ten Americans. Twenty Virginia militiamen arrived and took up positions in the pinewood, surrounding the Marines on three sides.

Cannon fire and rockets from barges that had been maneuvered into the creek continued the bombardment as four hundred Royal Marines debarked to join the Colonials, allowing the ex-slaves to break free, burn barracks, capture a field gun, and rob and pillage a planter's house.

Later the Marines and a reinforced militia faced each other one hundred yards apart, each with their back to the woods. Mingo heard a thud and saw Kennedy drop his musket and fall to his knees. Blood slowly stained the shoulder of his Marine jacket. When a bugle from a barge sounded the retreat, Mingo was overcome with relief. He put down his musket, removed a cloth from his haversack and bandaged his comrade's wound. With Kennedy able to walk on his own, Mingo wrapped a dead Colonial in a blanket and dragged the body back to a launch.

Pleased with the Colonial's showing, Ross told his commander that the "newly raised Black Corps gave a most excellent specimen of what they are like to be, their conduct was marked by great spirit and vivacity, and perfect obedience. Though one of them was shot and died instantly, it didn't daunt or check the others, but on the contrary animated them to seek revenge."

With the enthusiasm the navy felt for the black marines, he was soon sent on raiding parties around the bay: St. Leonard's Creek, Lower Marlboro, Magruder's Landing, burning or confiscating thousands of hogsheads of tobacco, returning with pigs, sheep, horses, oxen and furniture. And slaves—hordes of women and children and a few men— trailed the Marines back to the launches.

Cockburn came to rely on his black marines as his white troops began to desert, disappearing into the Maryland and Virginia countryside to seek a piece of land in the Piedmont or mountains, a sweeter life than theirs as sailors. The Colonials numbered over one hundred and in the height of summer, they raided St. Clements Creek, Machodoc Creek, Hamburg and Chaptico. On one plantation they freed two dozen slaves who were chained to trees.

WITH SO MANY RUNAWAYS in Tangier, the fort's commander ordered the refugees to board a couple of ships anchored in the bay. While Mingo believed the British promise that they were being taken to Canada, Kennedy was afraid that those who chose to leave were going to a worse fate—re-enslavement in the Caribbean. As proof Kennedy submitted that the commander of all the British forces in the war was himself a slave owner.

"Would you take the chance?" Kennedy challenged Mingo. "If I saw the ship sailing south instead of north, I'd kill the pilot."

"I'm sorry I volunteered for the navy," Mingo responded.

"And remain a slave?"

"No. A laborer on the island. That would have been better."

"And starve."

"At least I won't die from a bullet."

"Neither will I," Kennedy laughed.

Before the next raiding party, Kennedy was laid down with a fever, so weak he unable to lift his rifle. He remained in the barracks while Mingo donned his uniform once again, packed his haversack and cleaned his rifle. As he set a building on fire in Washington city, Mingo doubled-over from stomach cramps. Unable to stand up, a white Martine reached to set him on his feet. Mingo vomited on his comrade; bloody diarrhea ran down his leg into his boot. Mingo was put on a stretcher and carried back to the ship. Hundreds were bedridden at Tangier, stricken with the illness that wracked them with chills and shakes. Within a short time, a quarter of the Royal and Colonial Marines and many of the refugees were dead.

When the fever had finished burning its way through the fort, Mingo and Kennedy, with the remaining decimated Marines, were deployed South, to Georgia, where they joined forces with the black West Indian Regiment and Royal Marines.

Kennedy thought they were going to be sold in a slave market when they arrived and talked about seizing the ship.

"Then what? Do you what to do?"

"Someone does."

"Not a Colonial. And no white will join in a mutiny."

"When we see land, I'm going to jump over."

"You a fool, Kennedy. You'll be seized like a cur dog and treated worse than one."

Kennedy took part of the invasion of the sea island. The opposition to the British assault of Cumberland Island was light. Mingo never fired his musket. But Kennedy, who was standing next to the commanding officer, had a hole blown in his head by a sniper's bullet.

The reaction of the blacks in Georgia to the British was even more overwhelming than in Maryland and Delaware. Nearly every slave on Cumberland Island put down their tools and chose freedom with the British.

Mingo was given the duty to guard the manager of a cotton plantations on the island. For thirteen days, he stood by the door to the prisoner's hastily built shelter of wood and palmetto leaves, and listened to the complaints and bewilderment of the slave owner issuing from within.

"And you, blacky? Are you a free Negro?

Mingo didn't answer.

"A slave then."

The manager rambled on about his Negroes willingness to try new masters.

"I'll never get over the baseness of you ungrateful Negroes. I tried everything to make you wretches comfortable. It's all nonsense and folly."

Mingo tried not to listen. But when he gave him his food or emptied his chamber pot, he had no choice.

"To treat you Negroes with humanity is like giving pearls to swine. It is throwing away value and getting insult and ingratitude in return."

Mingo moved aside from the makeshift cell so the prisoner couldn't see him.

"Listen to me, blacky. I can't fathom why you want to throw in your lot with the British. But I can tell you this. As soon as I am released from this jail, I will find them all and persuade them to return." Between spoonsful of grits he said, "Those animals, I will rule them with a rod of iron."

The manager didn't get his wish. Death from disease spared three hundred refugees the manager's iron rod.

PROVISIONS ARRIVED FROM BERMUDA to feed the runaways and troops. On it return trip to its base in the Atlantic, more than 1,500 runways sailed with them, the British having promised that as soon as they were able, the Negroes would be settled in Canada as free people. Mingo sailed with them as a Marine.

There was no more military action for the Marines. Mingo spent more than a year at the naval base in Bermuda. With the war's end the Colonial Marines were disbanded. He thought about Young Man's Chance and reasoned that his best bet was to take the offer of land in Trinidad. With five hundred other former-Colonials, he arrived in the British colony off the coast of South America.

In the undeveloped southern reaches of the island, the former Marines were organized into villages. Each was given a pot, a hoe, a cutlass and a hatchet. Mingo, who before being discharged had been promoted to corporal, was selected to be a constable for several of the villages under construction. In a church he took an oath of loyalty to the Crown and swore to be responsible for the behavior of those placed under his guidance.

Settlers paid a quit-rent for the privilege of working eight hours a day on sixteen acres of land. Once Mingo cleared the designated wilderness of thick tropical trees and strangling vines and prepared the earth for farming, he received a pass so he could work outside Second Company, the name of his assigned village, so he could earn extra cash.

Mingo kept to the stern moral code laid down by the Baptist missionaries. Giving up liquor was a difficult stricture to abide by but mostly he followed the strictures the preacher laid down. He brought to Second Company the discipline he had seen in Tangier thereby bringing it success while other Colonial villages failed. But as constable, the enforcement of two of the colony's laws was lax: he overlooked the rule about settlers not conducting business with slaves;

neither did he try to apprehend runaways from Trinidad plantations.

After a difficult start and several seasons, Mingo's farm prospered: corn, plantains, pumpkins, cassava, and potatoes enough for his table and the market. He had eggs from his chickens and smoked meat from his pigs. A year later he married another refugee from the Chesapeake who arrived widowed and with two young children.

Each day his life as a slave seemed like a dream. He could scarcely remember the faces of his friends. He wondered what had become of Nan. For a while he sought out information from America, but information of the larger world arrived irregularly, if at all.

None of the letters he sent home were answered.

WILLIAM

Two Good Farms

ALTHOUGH Gertrude inherits Young Man's Chance after her husband's death when the gig collapsed on the Georgetown Road and broke Nicholas's ribs, she has no desire to run the plantation and turn its operation over to her son William. Since the accident, Gertrude leaves the house only on a Sunday, to attend the somber Presbyterian wooden chapel in Georgetown. Aside from conversations with an occasional visitor to the plantation, her remarks are reduced to issuing instructions to Lark and Nan and exchanging news with her son at the dining table. Gertrude's two daughters have married, one to a man from Boston and moved to London, the other marrying one of Outerbridge Horsey's sons in Wilmington.

William had been with his father the day of the accident. Nicholas had gone to Georgetown to visit a lawyer to amend his will, to add William now that he was near the age of consent and to stipulate that each of his slaves was to receive their freedom at thirty years of age or for those now adult, in ten years after the date of the will.

William has gone to buy a scythe for the farm. Not far from home, he feels the gig lurch from side-to-side.

"Not the road, William," Nicholas says, gripping the reins more tightly as he peered over the side of the gig. "That's the wagon. When we get to Georgetown, you take a look."

There is more than business that brings them to the county seat. It is the day two men, Brereton and Griffin, are to be executed for a murder that has taken place not far from Young Man's Chance. This wasn't an ordinary killing but one involving people so notorious that Governor Haslett himself offered a reward for the capture of the culprits.

The gang operated out of Patty Cannon's house, a two-story frame building with Delaware claiming one portion and Maryland another. From this house, far from the nearest neighbor, the gang planned and kidnapped freemen and freewomen, a rapidly growing population. With out-of-state slave sales forbidden, the gang fetched a decent enough price to keep themselves happy.

That day William and his father quarrel once again over manumitting the slaves on Young Man's Chance. They sit side-by-side in the jouncing carriage as Nicholas let his horse amble to the county seat.

Nicholas has come to the opinion, one pushed by Gertrude, that all their slaves should be manumitted. This has strained the relationship between father and son until every discussion about the running of the plantation is filled with acrimony.

"Slavery is over, son," he tells William. "There's no future in it. One way or another, in my time or yours, it will be gone."

William points to the growing demand for slaves in the Carolinas and along the Mississippi.

"You're wrong. It's far from finished."

"In Delaware, I'm telling you."

"But not on our plantation."

"We can't keep them from freedom any longer. Every day there are more and more free darkies."

"That's my point," William says. "That means that every day our slaves are worth more, not less. They're a scare commodity and getting scarcer."

The gig continues to wobble.

"How much does a slave cost today?" William demands to know.

"It depends," his father answers.

"And one between sixteen to thirty-five years old. How much is he worth?"

"I'm not certain . . ."

"Well, I know, so I'll tell you. One hundred fifty dollars," he shouted, repeating the number. "That's how much. And how much does a yoke of oxen cost?"

"About $20," his father says, his vexation beginning to show.

"And an acre here in Sussex? I know that, too. One dollar. So a slave costs one hundred and fifty times what an acre does. Every nigger is worth two good farms from this hundred."

"The numbers you give are meaningless, Nicholas. Something is worth something only if you can sell it. But you can't sell slaves out of state and few in Delaware are interested in purchasing any," Nicholas responds. "The number of free blacks is increasing every day. You're figuring like an ignorant man."

"And you know what the going price is for buying their own freedom?" Nicholas persists, ignoring his father's criticism. "Two hundred dollars."

"I'm not going to ask that of them. No one on Young Man's Chance has that kind of money. No one will be free at that rate."

"Have you joined the abolitionists now, just giving them their freedom?" asks derisively. "That's mother's doing. Women can indulge in pieties and fancy talk. But you have a business to manage. Let the ladies and preachers dream."

"Liberty is in the air, William. We can no more stop it that we can prevent water from running downhill."

William responds sharply, "You have no more right to free the slaves as you have to set fire to your own barn, not if your neighbor's barn is to be destroyed by it."

"Don't lecture me, William," Nicholas interjects.

"Free niggers are all Tories," William continues. "They don't love America. They'll run away at the first chance. Tell me, where's Mingo? Do you think he's the last?"

"Shut your mouth, son!"

"I'm saying that I will inherit something of value," William continues. "Not a worthless farm. You may be ready to give it up, sell it piece-by-piece. Give away your chattel. But it's not just yours to do with what you want. It's going to be mine someday and it'll be worth something when I get it."

"I decide who will inherit Young Man's Chance. I'll determine what is going to happen to it, not you. You have nothing to say about what I do with the farm or with my slaves, do you understand?"

William wants to call him a fool but thought better of it. Once the farm is his, he will make his own decisions about the property.

"Jackass," Nicholas says under his breath.

When they arrive in Georgetown, a great concourse of people already has gathered by the jailhouse awaiting the appearance of the condemned men. Roped together, the two prisoners dressed in execution clothes follow Reverend Dodge to the street, their faces indifferent to their impending fate. Facing Brereton and Griffin, the clergyman begins to read from the Book of Proverbs.

"The wicked flee when no man pursueth; but the righteous are bold as a lion."

The milling ceases, the chatting stops, the crowd turns its attention to the minister's words.

"Better is the poor that walketh in his uprightness, than he that is perverse in his ways, though he be rich."

One of the Negroes who has come to watch interjects his approval.

"He that covereth his sins shall not prosper: but whoso confesseth and forsaketh them shall have mercy."

Brereton and Griffin smirk. Having been arrested and released before, they anticipate a pardon before the day's end.

"A man that doeth violence to the blood of any person shall flee to the pit; let no man stay him."

There should have been one other to face the gallows, but after Patty Cannon had been charged, the state's attorney entered a nolle prosequi motion on her behalf because of her sex and she was set free, a controversial decision since most were convinced that Cannon was the ringleader and was the most vicious of the crew.

EVERYONE IN BROAD CREEK Hundred knew the stories about the gang's activities. A handful said they were rumors; everyone else had no doubt as to their veracity. Cannon's house was isolated in a deep forest, a part of the neighborhood without another structure.

Everyone, black and white, free and slave, feared the gang that carried out their illegal business unabated. The men kidnapped local freemen and freewomen from streets in the county or lured those who lived upriver and believed the blandishments that Cannon was part of an abolitionist society that escorted free blacks to new homes in the North. Brereton and Griffin gave the Negroes small gifts, treated them kindly and chatted with them as they rowed downstream back to the house where Brereton's mother-in-law waited. When they arrived, the dupes were chained and taken to secret places in her house—the attic, the basement, a room hidden behind a wall.

The woman was more fearsome than the men. No one in the hundred disputed the tale of Cannon having smashed the head of a black child against the table and having tossed the still-alive toddler into the flames of the fireplace.

The gang functioned with impunity because emancipations from the Abolition Society had given up trying to bring back kidnapped blacks. It was expensive and nearly always fruitless. Laws were complex and unenforceable across state lines. Even when a victim was returned and allowed to testify, finding lawyers willing to take the case proved impossible. In one case, Lydia Smith testified that she was held in leg irons for five months with ten others in Cannon's attic. She had seen men severely whipped who insisted that they weren't slaves but freemen. Some victims died.

"What did they do with the bodies?"

"I never saw. But I could hear digging in the cellar."

When the sheriff investigated her charges, he found that the basement was on the Maryland side of the border and had no warrant to search it. Bribes, threats and intimidations had done the gang no good this time. They had gone too far. Even the bought lawyers and politicians didn't come to their aid.

Those who attended the trial reported the same thing: free Negroes kidnapped by the gang were conveyed by covered wagon to be delivered to a waiting ship at the headwaters of the Nanticoke River on the Chesapeake. Sometimes buyers came to Cannon's house to purchase blacks rather than shipside wanting to assurances regarding the quality of the those they were going to purchase.

One day two slave-purchasers arrived at the Cannon house, where. they went to the hidden places to examine women, men, children; they determined whether they were clever—a liability; they examined them to see if they were lame—a bad investment; they asked questions to decide whether they were surly—too great a risk. They kept those whose shoulders slumped and looked away.

The buyers spent most of the day settling on the price of the Negroes, one by one, a child, a woman, a young male.

"We'll pay you when the niggers are put on board the ship in the bay," Ridgell said. "You'll get your money then."

"A down payment," Cannon demanded.

One trader removed a leather pouch heavy with silver and gold coins and gave her $50.

While Cannon entertained the buyers with apple cider and toddies, Griffin and Brereton left the house. They went to the main road, which they blockaded with logs taken from the forest.

"They knew the slave buyers carried a large sum of money," a friend told Nicholas. "They planned to kill and rob them. That way they'd have the money and the kidnapped Negroes."

Having finalized the purchased and having detained them long enough with her diversions, Cannon said good-bye to the two men. They mounted their waiting horses and rode down the path for a mile to meet the road to Laurel.

As soon as they left, Cannon grabbed a musket, took a shortcut to the rendezvous with Brereton and Griffin. She waited with them in ambush. Upon reaching the barrier, the traders dismounted to remove the roadblock when reports of guns echoed in the forest. The traders crouched, drew their pistols and returned the gunfire. A bullet tore through Ridgell's jacket.

"I don't know why they left," the second trader said when questioned by the judge. "But they did. Before they robbed us they fled."

"Did you see them before they were gone?"

"A good look," he said. "They jumped up straight in front of me and looked right at me. They were no more than twenty yards away. I was sure they were going to come for us. But they turned and ran into the forest. The same three I met at the house."

"And then?"

"When I knew they were gone, I put Ridgell on my horse and continued to Laurel. He died there that next morning."

"Anything more?"

"Yes. I want you to return my $50."

THE PREDDYS STOOD IN the crowd that included militiamen from the middle county. At the Kent sheriff's request, fifty citizen soldiers from Captain Dill's company and another twenty from Captain Kolloch's had been called as witnesses to the hanging. The militiamen leaned on their muskets as the convicts ascended an ox-cart. Brereton and Griffin were secured against the cart's sides and as the cart began to roll, the soldiers, with scores of others joining them, began a procession to the gallows a mile away.

"When the wicked rise, men hide themselves: but when they perish, the righteous increase," Rev. Dodge concluded with a gentle closing of his stereotyped edition of the Bible.

"I don't want to watch," William said as the cart lurched forward. "I'm going to stay here."

"You should see what happens to offenders," Nicholas said. "They deserve what they get for killing a white man."

"And that other offender, the nigger thief?" William scoffed. "He goes back to Georgia to continue his business."

"He deserves the lash and his ears cut off, I agree. Like the law says he should. I don't like it that he goes away free. But there would have been no conviction of these criminals without his turning approver. Besides, he won't be back here anytime soon."

"There's money to be made, so he'll return. Each year a nigger is worth more."

Nicholas began to follow the train behind the execution wagon while William stayed behind. He walked several blocks to the farm supply store to purchase another scythe but found it shut. Neither he nor his father had thought that businesses in town would be closed because of the execution, as Nicholas also discovered when he went to his lawyer's office after the hanging. The door was locked. The lawyer had gone to celebrate the end of the gang's existence.

While waiting for his father to join him for the return journey to Young Man's Chance, William circled the gig, looked at the hubs and axle, and ran his hand around the wheels to locate the cause of the rough ride to Georgetown. He found a badly cracked felloe plate and several broken spokes caused by it. He wasn't going to use the gig again until it was fixed.

William walked to the wheelwright's shop but it, like nearly every establishment in Georgetown, was closed. The freeman who owned the shop had also gone to watch the miscreants die.

William stepped up into the gig's seat to wait for his father.

"No scythe?" Nicholas asked as he glanced at the back of the gig.

"Closed."

"I can't get my lawyer to help me out, either," Nicholas said. "He doesn't want to do any work today. He told me to come back next week. Let's go home."

About to tell his father about the faulty right wheel, he kept quiet instead. William climbed down and put his hand on the horse's flank.

"The scythe. We need a new one," William said. "I'll stay and get buy it tomorrow. You can send for me."

"You should have seen those men," his father said."
Just before the rope was pulled, Brereton, I think it was
Brereton, he turned to the executioner and spit in his face.
Griffin laughed until he saw Brereton swinging and flailing.
Kicking violently like he was trying to run away, Griffin's
toes barely touched the ground. And then Griffin swung
and it was over."

"They got what they deserved."

"Yes, they did," Nicholas said.

Nicholas reached into the gig box and removed corn pone
and boiled ham. He poured cider into a tin cup.

"Come on. Get up. We're going home."

"No. I'm staying. You go."

Nicholas picked up the horse's reins and whip.

"I'll have Suthy fetch you tomorrow."

Anywhere but Here

WORKERS ON YOUNG Man's Chance heard there was a black man who owned of a shipyard in Massachusetts. Paul Cuffee had visited Baltimore in 1813 and stories about him spread quickly amongst slaves and free blacks. One story, which Negroes thought too fantastic to be true, was that he owned the schooners, barques and brigs that plied the north coast with all-black crews.

William, like other whites in Sussex, never heard of the black businessman until after the second war with the British. Cuffee came to their attention when the US Senate voted to underwrite his proposal to settle free blacks in Africa. When the House of Representatives didn't provide the funding for the venture, Paul Cuffee, using his own money, brought thirty-eight blacks, free of charge, to the British colony of Sierra Leone.

William heard about the Negro mariner from his cousin, David Morgan. They sat in a cook-shop next to Kaminsky's Tavern, the streets filled with scores of blue wagons with their white canvas canopies looking like land-bound ships, bell-collars jingling as teams of horses buried their heads in oat-filled troughs. This area of Baltimore resounded with the bellowing and grunting of cattle in stable yards awaiting the slaughterhouse. Stagecoaches came and went. There were taverns and booking offices, cabinet shops and dry goods stores, teamsters and seamen, merchants and clerks, horses swapped and sold. More than one churchman needed to be led home by his parishioners.

Morgan managed Deptford and Sons, a Howard Street flour company that bought grain from wheat-growing regions to the north, processed it at a water mill at one of the falls in the countryside outside the city and sold the milled grain to planters in the British Caribbean.

Conversing over pickled oysters and beer, Morgan brought up the benevolent society for Negroes set-up by Cuffee after his visit to the city.

"I don't know what you're talking about," William said.

"The colonization plan."

William remained puzzled.

"This news didn't reach you in Sussex? But you should know about it. Something must be done about our free Negroes. You see that it's a problem, don't you?"

William hadn't given it much thought. Sussex remained a stronghold of slavery with fewer freemen than anywhere else in the state, a county nearly isolated by swamps not yet drained and untouched pine forests, a location that looked South, not North, for discernment about such matters.

Morgan explained it some, then went to a counter across the room and removed *Niles Register* from a disorderly pile of broadsheets.

He read to William from an article that concluded with a quote from Cuffee's visit a couple of years before. "*I have for these many years past felt a lively interest in their behalf, wishing that the inhabitants of the colony might become established in truth, and thereby be instrumental in its promotion amongst our African brethren.*"

William shook his head.

"The darky needs to be locked up," he said. "What he's promoting is seditious."

Morgan was taken aback by William's reaction.

"No. It's serious. Think about it, William. This man Cuffee is the richest colored man in America and wants to take his brothers back to Africa."

"Rubbish," William said. While he knew that there were Negroes who had acquired some education and wealth, he knew of no one that had succeeded more than modestly.

"Not at all. He has more money that any of us in this room tonight. It's our Christian responsibility to care for them and what better way is there than by returning them to their own country?"

William was dubious and let him know with a snort.

The remarks caused him to reflect on his own education in the schoolhouse without windows, a hole cut at one end of the roof to let out the smoke from the brick and clay fire pit on the ground. All he could remember from the three months of early education was taking a canoe across a rapidly flowing branch where the schoolmaster taught the pupils to pronounce words. 'Ponger,' the schoolmaster said. 'Not porringer. Ponger.' He remembered Dilworth's spelling book but, more vividly, his father discouraging him from reading any books on his own. 'It takes up too much of your time,' is what he recalls him saying.

Much of William's education came from his mother. She instructed him from the Bible, as the scriptures had been banned from schools. At his mother's urging he attended the Great Laurel Camp Meeting. White and black, slaves, and free men and women gathered under tent made of bed-quilts, blankets and sheets.

William disliked the shouting, jumping, jerking, screaming and sinking to the floor in an unconscious state, the rolling of heads like a broken millwheel before throwing themselves on the ground and writhing as if in pain. Most unsettling to William was the singing that came not from the head but from the chest, a sound unlike any he had heard before.

After dark bonfires cast dancing shadows of possessed spirits; pine needles sighed in the dark.

Expecting disturbance from those who disapproved of the evangelical fervor, the Methodists erected a small building

271

built on a slab to serve as a jail. It held two men for breaking brandy bottles, overturning tables laden with cakes and trampling food thrown onto the sodden ground.

William told his mother he wouldn't go to a meeting or church again. He called it nigger madness.

Gertrude encouraged her son to kneel in prayer before bed but William refused, fearing the devil would take him, a vile hypocrite.

"He met with Mr. Madison in the White House, let me tell you."

"With the past president?"

"Yes."

"Maybe Mr. Madison and this darky should have been in the building when it was burned."

"And this man, Cuffee, he has the ear of Congress as well."

"He does? Well then, tell me the names of those from my state who have met with him and I will make certain I vote for their opponents the next time. Only a Federalist would want to get Washington involved in this. We'll take care of our problems. What are they doing taking my money for schemes like this? Let the states decide where the money goes."

"How do you think the Cumberland Road got built? It has been a boon to the Chesapeake. It was Mr. Jefferson's idea. To spend national funds."

"But not on the welfare of niggers. Not one cent of my taxes."

"No one is taxing anyone, William. Calm down. They are only listening . . ."

"To foolishness."

"Mr. Jefferson put this idea forward. So maybe it's not so foolish."

William remained quiet as he let Morgan carry on the conversation without interruption. There were things he knew little about. He wasn't going to express an opinion that would appear witless.

Morgan walked with William to the harbor to show him the ships being built there.

William wanted to know if Morgan thought there was money to be made in purchasing stocks in the shipping companies. He hinted that his plantation was in financial straits and had recently sold one tract he owned in Maryland.

"They can't build them fast enough. There is a vast demand in England for this kind of ship—Baltimore clippers. Look at them. They're the fastest ship on the water. England's engaged in big business with China. There's big trade in opium, I hear. And tea. The quicker they get their things from one place to another, the greater the profit."

Morgan took out a small metal box from his pocket, flipped the lid open and offered a pinch of snuff to his cousin.

"My company is now sending flour to the British. And we are opening negotiations with the Portuguese to send flour to Brazil."

They walked around the harbor. Morgan pointed out the Mud Machine, a mechanical dredge and a new kind of ship, a steamboat christened *Chesapeake*.

"There's money to be made by selling mud," he said.

They continued walking along the harbor and marveling at the many ships being built. Morgan returned with William to his saltbox home. The house, two-stories in front and one in the back, had a central chimney and the outside was coated with mortar and coarse gravel. Behind the house stood a smoke shed where cured hams hung. In the kitchen garden were cabbages, beans and herbs.

"I'm selling this house. There is a brick one I'm buying that is more fitting," Morgan said as William joined his cousin's family at the table for supper. The cousins finished their meal with whiskeys and tobacco, and continued their talk about investments, General Jackson's Indian war in Florida and the realignment of political parties.

"Did the doctor see you today?" Morgan asked.

Knowing Baltimore's reputation for leading in the area of medicine, William came to the city, he said to Morgan, to see a doctor about his stomach ailment. Morgan recommended Grafton Marsh, a graduate of the College of Medicine of Maryland. William had seen Marsh in his home that morning.

During the conversation, William revealed that he had another illness that concerned him.

"I need to come back to see him if the condition don't improve," William explained. "He said that there is something new that he could try on me, if I need to see him again."

Morgan didn't ask for details.

William puffed on his pipe and when it had burned to the bottom of the bowl, turned the pipe over and knocked the dottle into his palm.

"Do you mind if I play?" he asked looking at a violin, one less crude than Suthy's, which was propped against a wall.

"If you know how."

"Reasonably well. One of my slaves taught me."

William picked up the instrument and placed it under his chin. He plucked the strings, tightened the tuning pegs, and then sawed 'The Girl I Left Behind Me.'

> The hours sad I left a maid
>
> A lingering farewell taking
>
> Whose sighs and tears my steps delayed
>
> I thought her heart was breaking

Stopping after struggling to sing to William's playing, Morgan said, "I'll be buying a fortepiano in the new house."

"The next time I'm in Baltimore," William said, "I'll consider getting one for my household, too."

William went to sleep in a chair downstairs by the Franklin stove, all the bedrooms above being occupied by the couple and their four children.

BEFORE HIS TRIP TO HIS cousin, William had tried local concoctions: balsam honey, red pills, medicinal snuff, the juice of roasted onions, a poultice of snakeroot. But when these remedies failed to alleviate his condition, he went to Baltimore. The prescription given to him there worked for a while—a spoonful of ground cubebs taken three times a day with sufficient water, but when the pain flared up again, William resumed taking Marsh's prescription. Eager to rid himself of the pain, he forgot to take the powdered pepper on an empty stomach and developed tears in his rectum.

After an early April snowstorm, William made the trip to see his cousin again. During this visit, William found Morgan in a new home, a three-story brick rowhouse on Bridge Street. In the house stood a five-octave piano built in Baltimore. After inquiring about its cost, William decided against buying one for Young Man's Chance. While the sale of the property in Maryland and the recently improved economy helped William's financial situation, he was prudent with his money. Perhaps sometime in the future, "if I had a daughter," he thought. A trip every so often to Baltimore would have to do. He promised that he would bring his betrothed the next time.

"I'll see Dr. Marsh on Thursday."

"This must be a bother."

"More than you know," William responded.

Morgan suggested they go to the theater on Holliday Street, several blocks from his home.

"It's in a beautiful new building."

"I remember it from last year. The big white building."

"Yes," Morgan said. "Let's see a play tonight."

After a bit of hesitation, William admitted that he had never seen a performance.

"I don't think I'll enjoy it very much," he said. He imagined the delirious camp meeting.

"No. It's not like that at all."

He told William that he attended an astounding event in November. He talked about the scenery and the costumes.

"No one will forget that night," Morgan said. "Wait. I'll get the notice."

Morgan pulled a book of remembrances from a shelf full of books and opened it to a page with a newspaper clipping.

"at the Baltimore Theatre, Saturday evening, will be presented a performance in commemoration of the gallant repulse of the enemy from Baltimore. After the drama and farce there will be a grand military and naval entertainment, the conclusion of which will be as follows:

A New Song,

written by a gentleman of Maryland, the second time here—'The Star Spangled Banner,' by Mr. Hardinge. An entire new scene, representing the bombardment of Baltimore the night previous to the retreat of the enemy by land and water. The view is taken from Hampstead Hill, and exhibits Fort McHenry illuminated by the fire from the enemy's bomb vessels, which discharge a rapid succession of shells (accurately represented by machinery), some bursting in the air, etc.; to the right a detachment of the enemy's force under the fire of Fort Covington; on the left the gun-boats, hulks, and Lazaretto; in the distance the main body of the British frigates. The scene painted by Mr. Grain, marine painter. To conclude with a dance in honor of the commander and defender of the fort."

"I can't promise anything as boggling as that. Tonight, there will be two plays. I've heard that the same song is sung at every performance. Come, William. You need to see a play before you leave. It's the thing to do."

William modestly declined.

Morgan suggested the museum, several buildings away from the theatre. William had never heard of a museum and didn't ask for an explanation.

"When I get back from Brazil, I'll commission a portrait. Perhaps from the famous Mr. Peale himself. There are indications that I'll be made partner at Deptford."

William congratulated his cousin.

"You can see many of this gentleman's fine paintings in his museum."

William expressed no interest in viewing portraits.

"There's more," Morgan continued. He told him about the skeleton of a mastodon and a chandelier of fifty burners lit by "carbureted hydrogen gas."

With each item mentioned, William felt more keenly his lack of education and backward ways.

"Which shall it be, the theatre or the museum?"

William changed the subject.

"Since my last visit," he said, "I've been considering our conversation about the problem of free Negroes."

They talked about President Monroe's signing of the bill that admitted into the union Maine as a free state and Missouri with slaves. The discussion turned to Charleston's new law that required slaves to wear identification tags.

"To distinguish them from freemen and runaways," Morgan explained.

"That would be helpful," William said. "But why not have every black wear one? That way there wouldn't have to be passes and such."

"All the more reason for colonization, don't you think?"

After leaving Marsh's home the following day, William didn't tell Morgan about the silver nitrate treatment that he received but he did ask his cousin, without further explanation, for some items that the additional prescription called for. He wanted to attend the monthly meeting of the American Colonization Society and wanted to begin his treatment immediately. But he didn't show Morgan the surgeon's written instructions:

The patient should stand over a slop-pail, holding a small basin brimful of very hot water in his left hand. With the right hand he should lift up the penis by the skin of the upper part, and just allow the lower surface to come in contact with the fluid, which must be of such a temperature that the patient cannot bear the contact of it for more than an instant at a time. When there is uneasiness about the perineum, he should roll up a piece of rag, flannel if possible, into a ball about the size of a walnut, tie this firmly to a small piece of firewood, dip the ball in almost boiling water, dash off the drops, and press it against the perineum; or sit lightly down upon a sponge, just taken out of boiling water and put on a cane-bottomed chair over a slop-pail.

BY THE TIME HE RETURNED to the plantation, William had decided to devote time to promoting the movement of Negroes to Africa. By his estimation there were over four hundred slaves within twenty miles of his plantation. It was obvious from his own observations that the number of free Negroes in the county must have matched, if not exceeded, that number.

The picture was the same across the border in Maryland. Free colored men and women were everywhere, engaged in every enterprise and demanding their rights as citizens. The Jew Bill, as Morgan called it, was being debated in the Maryland legislature. If Jews, so few in number, were given all the liberties of citizenship, how much more difficult it would be to deny them to Negroes.

What he had seen in Baltimore shook his confidence, a city full of freemen and freewomen mixing with slaves and whites. He wasn't moved by his cousin's philanthropic impulses, which he disdained; William doubted that slaves would remain docile while their brethren were off experimenting with freedom.

William dismissed Thom Jefferson's notion that the emancipation of blacks was written in the Book of Destiny. Colonization had nothing to do with emancipation, he thought, but with ridding the state of rabble-rousers. William wasn't an abolitionist but a realist. Useless and pernicious free blacks were a dangerous source of discontent amongst slaves. And with the General Assembly repealing the law prohibiting the migration of free black to Delaware, the situation could only worsen.

William did agree with some of Jefferson's argument and printed an expurgated version to distribute as he traveled from plantation to plantation hoping to form a local chapter of the African Colonization Society: *"It is certain that the two races will never live in a state of equal freedom under the same government, so insurmountable are the barriers which nature, habit and opinion have established between them."* to form a local chapter of the American Colonization Society. He disagreed that ACS's position that the plan be carried out with a Negro's consent. You didn't ask whether a criminal wanted to go to jail.

When recruiting Methodists, William touted the program as a philanthropic scheme, "the most glorious enterprise of private benevolence." He argued that bringing Christianized free blacks to Africa would civilize the continent.

He offered a different argument for the kindhearted: "Our blacks themselves will be put in a better situation if they leave. Only in Africa will they truly be elevated and their rights secured." He added, "The more you improve the condition of these people, the more you cultivate their minds, the more miserable you make them in their present state. You give them a higher relish for those privileges which they can never attain, and turn what we intend for a blessing into a curse."

To those impervious to the voice of duty or benevolence he asked, "Are you willing to abandon your county and have it taken from you? "We need to whiten America."

At that end of each outing, he returned to Young Man's Chance, not only exhilarated by his solicitation but also finding the rides useful in creating new business possibilities.

Gertrude didn't want to hear about colonization. She favored gradual manumission, not removal.

"Then what?" William challenged. "You freed your slave and look what it led to. Your actions deprived me of my slave Mingo. A runaway."

Gertrude didn't answer this time or any time after, and there was no more to their conversation. Each preferred the quiet that pervaded the house.

Lark brought them their supper. When they were done, Gertrude retired to her room to read the Bible and reproductions of sermons by her favorite preachers. They would help her interpret her dreams, understand the source of her maladies and keep her away from the Devil.

Lark returned to her cabin while Nan cleared the table and washed the dishes.

William poured another glass of apple cider and took a plug of tobacco. He then went to the kitchen, instructed Nan to boil water. When steam began to rise from the iron pot, he removed a piece of flannel from the cupboard and lowered his trousers. Nan held her master's penis in one hand and with the other wiped away the secretions with the cloth. As she bent in front of him, William clenched her hair in his fist, flinched, and sighed.

Topsy-Turvy

THE SUN DISAPPEARED one day in February. Along the Atlantic Coast crowds gathered in streets with pieces of smoked glass and turned their gaze heavenward to witness the greatly anticipated eclipse.

In Boston, business was suspended. In Richmond, "*every person was star gazing, from bleary-eyed old age to the most bright-eyed infancy.*" Newspapers reported that unlike previous solar events that produced fear and foreboding, this eclipse would be met with sufficient scientific knowledge that witnesses would see it as a marvel of nature.

But it wasn't so for everyone. One correspondent wrote:

> An old shoe-black accosted a person in front of our office, the day previous to the eclipse, and asked him if he was not afraid. For, said he, with tears in his eyes, the world is to be destroyed to-morrow; the sun and moon are to meet and a great earthquake was to swallow us all! —Others were seen wending their ways to their friends and relations, covered with gloom and sadness; saying that they intended to die with them.

Neither giddy excitement nor anticipatory anxiety gripped Young Man's Chance. Perhaps if William had read *Hitchens' Improved Almanac* as many did in the upper counties, they would have expected the eclipse. But the obscured sun caught everyone on the plantation by surprise.

When the sun was blocked on the cloudless day, worked stopped. Nearly all fell as silent as did the barnyard animals. Birds, too, ceased their chatter, as night creatures came awake. In the shadowed darkness, a voice often heard at church meetings said, "Her sun has gone down while it was yet day. She was ashamed and confounded."

When daylight reappeared, William didn't insist that the workers return to their chores. He had no thoughts about the cause of the eclipse, only an unidentifiable feeling like a vaguely remembered dream.

At the supper table later that day, a stabbing pain, as fierce as a cramp, struck Gertrude. She dropped her cup and pressed her palms against her eyes as the pain radiated to her ears and jaw. It felt as though a grinding wheel was crushing her temples.

James and Anne bolted in their chairs and stared at their grandmother. The girl began to cry.

"Nan," Leah called to the kitchen. "Get the mistress a cold cloth."

Nan grabbed a piece of cotton cloth and dipped it in the tub of water. She took the compress and placed it on her mother-in-law's forehead.

"Our Negroes," Gertrude said as Nan patted her eyes and wiped her forehead. "Our Negroes."

Nan picked up her head and eyed William sharply for a second longer than propriety permitted, he thought. She looked away as William's reddening face began to prickle.

Gertrude's pain began to abate under Nan's hand.

"Don't worry about them, mother," William said.

What Gertrude meant was that the mid-day darkness was a sign and the stabbing pain an admonition for holding slaves. She wanted to tell this to William but she couldn't rally the strength. She began to shiver and Nan helped her out of her seat and brought her to her bedroom.

"Is grandma going to die?" James asked.

"Not now," William answered.

"I'm going to the parlor," Leah said, telling the children to follow her.

William sat in the room alone as he lit one of his ten-for-a-cent cigars.

SHORTLY AFTER THE DAYS of preternatural darkness, William talked to his neighbor Purnel Dickerson. Dickerson told William that he had one slave that he wished to be rid of.

"If I could sell him, I would," he confided. He said Nathaniel had been born deaf and dumb. "He is ignorant but he readily converses with signs of his own. The nigger is intelligent and possesses a great deal of mechanical ability. He is a good hand and workman."

"I'm not in the market."

"I was hoping."

"But, Dickerson, I don't understand why you would want to . . ."

"He is even-tempered with everyone except with me."

Dickerson said that he had gone to Georgetown to buy implements for his farm. He was driving home in his wagon drawn by a yoke of oxen while Nathaniel walked behind.

"I suddenly felt much weight at the end of the cart. I turned to look and saw that he had climbed on to the tail of it."

Dickerson said that wagon was already heavy with the pieces brought from a furnace store and the oxen grew tired from Nathaniel's added weight. Dickerson directed him to alight.

"He paid no attention. I told him several times. Finally, after I raised the ox goad in his direction, he did get off. He made foul noises that left no mistake that he was in an angry mood. He muttered and mumbled as he walked beside the cart for about a half-mile." Dickerson refilled his whiskey glass. William declined. "When we reached a bridge, he shook his fists at me and jumped up on the bench beside me. I threw off my coat and we seized hold of one another. He threw me to the ground. I think he might have killed me if someone hadn't come along and pulled him off me."

"He is a bad one," William said.

"Yes, he is with me. But mostly he is mild. And as I said before, he is a good worker."

Their conversation wandered into different, more trivial matters but they returned to once again to Dickerson's slave. Dickerson sketched out an idea.

With the spiking price of slaves, Dickerson thought he could fetch a good price for him.

"Being deaf and dumb is an advantage. He's as solitary as an owl. He's not going to conspire with other slaves. At twenty-five years old, he's at his prime."

What happened to the kidnappers at the gallows the day he was with his father remained vivid in William's mind. But this was different. It wasn't kidnapping a freeman but the sale of lawful property. While disposing of a slave outside of Delaware was illegal, William saw the law as a violation of a person's right to dispose of property as they saw fit. He had a right to ignore such an infringement upon his liberty.

For his part in helping a friend he would receive a decent cut of the deal.

On the arranged day, Dickerson told Nathaniel that they were going to buy lumber. Dickerson had arranged for the slavers to place a log across the road and when Nathaniel went to remove it, the buyers would emerge from the woods and abscond with him.

William was to do no more than hide in the woods so later to testify that Dickerson tried but failed to beat off the kidnapper.

As Nathaniel bent to shove the tree limb aside, the slave-buyer approached from behind. The club missed Nathaniel. Nathaniel stood up and kicked the assailant. Dickerson stood up in the wagon, afraid to intervene; William kept his distance behind a tree. Nathaniel took the slave-buyer's club and pounded the assailant on his face and chest.

Nathaniel looked at Dickerson, let out a bark and ran into the brown swamp water, disturbing a giant heron that gave a reverberant squawk, screeching *frawnk, frawnk, frawnk, frawnk* as it took flight, its head tucked in, the long legs trailing behind like a blue-gray arrow, the deep wingbeats roiling the air above the heads of William, Dickerson and the dead slave-buyer.

Dickerson lost his slave and William his fee.

THE JULY MORNING began shrouded in what appeared to be mist from the marshes. But by nine the gray turned a sickly blue and remained that way until sunset turned the western sky crimson; the same the next day and the day after that. This wasn't swamp fog but something more like drifting smoke from fall fires, a luminescent haze. But there was no sting in the nostrils or burning eyes, no smell at all, only a fine layer of dust visible on black skin. Some said it was the swamp having a bad dream. The current of warm air that wafted through the plantation was a clear sign that ha'nts were on the loose.

Gloom hung over the plantation for most of the week. The scientific explanation for the bluish-green atmosphere didn't appear until fifteen years later, when Quinn Thornton wrote in a scientific journal:

Mount St. Helens mountain was in a state of eruption in the year 1831. With the exception of a slight red, lurid appearance, the day was dark, and so completely was the light of the sun shut out by the smoke and falling ashes, that candles were necessary. The weather was perfectly calm, and without wind; and during several days after the eruption, the fires, out of doors, burned with a bluish flame, as though the atmosphere was filled with Sulphur.

First the midnight dark at midday, then, five months later, days infused with grayish blue light—these were awful events that many took as signs to be deciphered. While everyone knew that the obscuring of the sun, not once but twice, was portentous, on Young Man's Chance there was no agreement regarding the nature of the lesson they contained.

No uncertainty remained in the minds of others. A black man's hand twice obscuring the sun was a vision clear enough to a black person imbued with the Holy Spirit. For more than a month, insurrectionists struck, gathering arms and horses, freeing slaves from Virginia plantations and recruiting more than seventy to the cause of freedom.

"Whites are being slaughtered in Virginia," Dickerson said as they sat around a tavern table.

William said, "We need funding for colonization. To remove them. They're a noxious weed."

His companion disagreed.

"Where will we get black labor if all the freemen were gone?" Jobs Quillen, a business owner said. "I need to have them for hire."

William wiped his hands on his trousers.

"I can't afford to let them go," William said. "But it's becoming a burden, I admit."

"Do what I've done, William," Cornelius Adyelot interjected. "Free the adults but keep the children. That will keep them around."

William drained his whiskey.

Adyelot continued, "They won't leave. Then you work them as tenants. Pay them what you want, enough to keep them out of the almshouse."

"The other legislation they've instituted," Dickerson said, "it can't come soon enough. These coloreds need to be kept in line. Let's make sure the Assembly doesn't allow more trials by jury for freemen. If they commit a crime, they lose the privilege of being a freeman. Then send them to a place where they have no attachments."

"To Africa," William laughed. "Where they can never come back."

The wind shifted and the nauseating odor from a tanyard drifted into the room. The men drew their handkerchiefs to their faces.

DREADING THE SPREAD OF sedition to Delaware's blacks, William received word from the state assembly that militia drills were being re-instituted. Not since the late war with Great Britain had anyone on Young Man's Chance thought about armed conflict, but William was convinced that defending one's property against insurrection was a just cause. He had his musket ready and would gladly drill with the Georgetown Minute Men if called upon.

The leader of the Negro uprising remained at-large throughout late summer and into autumn, hiding in the marshes, eluding frantic efforts to capture him. Whites in Delaware's lower hundreds were alarmed by rumored gatherings of blacks to commit murder. Suspicion followed every Negro, free or slave, even those known to William since childhood.

On the second Tuesday in October William anxiously set out from his plantation to vote with a pistol at his side. Suthy wanted to ride along but William refused. Better to rely on his own vigilance than to be alone on an isolated road with a Negro, he calculated.

William's anxiety was alleviated with his uneventful trip. Even the contentiousness of the elections between Democrats and Whigs that divided friends and neighbors, hundreds and counties, cleaving the state in two, was a welcome diversion from brooding about wayward Negroes.

William milled around the table with a dozen others preparing to cast his vote. He picked up his party's ballot, marked and folded it and was ready to stuff it in the wooden box when a man rushed into the room raising the alarm: "Blacks are on the uprise! Blacks are on the uprise! On the Nanticoke River," the messenger managed to say as he regained his breath, "a rebellion. They are rebelling. There is a rebellion under way."

The room went quiet.

More than a thousand blacks had taken up weapons, he said, whites were being murdered and a horde was rampaging, destroying everything in its path. The messenger reported that whites positioned themselves on both banks of the river at Seaford.

"They are engaged in a bloody defense," he said.

White families had fled to the deep forests for protection; others stood their ground, guns loaded, curtains drawn, doors bolted.

"Protect your families, men."

The building emptied. Many immediately took off for their homes. Having come alone, William was fearful about his trip back to the plantation.

A clerk picked up the ballot box and walked towards the door.

"What are you doing?" William demanded.

"Hiding the box until it's safe to return."

"You can't do that."

The clerk continued to the steps.

"Wait," William said. "I'll help you." He added, "Just to make sure you don't tamper."

William followed the clerk to his two-room log house at the edge of town. They emerged a couple of days later when the immediate threat dissipated. Still leery of crossing the country alone, he sought out someone to accompany him back to Young Man's Chance. A freeman, whom he recognized as a tenant farmer near his plantation, asked for a ride.

"I'm not going that way," William lied. "I have business in Dover."

Later he found someone looking to go in his direction. William didn't charge this white man for the ride, grateful as he was for the protection the stranger provided.

A week later the truth emerged: there hadn't been an uprising at all. The hysteria had been set off when a group, believing that blacks were going to attack, took up positions on either side of the Nanticoke. They then engaged in a mock battle with one another, firing shots from one bank to the other. Some of the men pretended to be wounded. Hearing the shots and seeing men fall to the ground was enough to cause panic.

Although the black uprising turned out to be unfounded, white citizens still felt beleaguered. After all, fifty-one whites had been murdered in Virginia in a diabolical crusade. No citizen in the lower hundreds disagreed with the newspaper account that *"no crime in the whole range of human enormity as heinous as this."*

William traveled throughout the area with a petition he had initiated to "proceed to the immediate disarmament of the emancipated Negro. It is the indispensable duty of the legislature to disarm free blacks for only then can the state prevent such a catastrophe as has transpired in a sister state." He easily gathered signatures from his neighbors.

"That infernal villain Turner was a preacher," Dickerson said. "There's something wrong with how these niggers carry out their religion. Religion is to save the soul, not incite revenge."

His neighbor's comments agitated William. Since Frank's death, he was ignorant of his slaves' religious meetings. He knew they gathered each Sunday, but he didn't know who the preacher was nor the nature of the sermons.

"I don't worry about our darkies meeting. We have good boys preaching in this hundred. But outsiders, that's different. They're agitators, wolves in sheep's clothing."

"More the devil than a wolf," William added.

At Dickerson's suggestion William drew a new petition. This one stressed that there needs to be an end to "*all nocturnal assemblies, of our coloured population, under any pretense whatever.*"

"You need more," Dickerson said as he looked over the draft.

William appended the petition to include the demand that "*the ingress of free blacks into this State, upon the plea of preaching, be also made unlawful.*"

The governor, in Dover, acknowledged the concerns raised by William's petition. A new law, passed the following year, satisfied William—free blacks would need the endorsement of at least five white citizens in order to be issued a permit to possess firearms; more than twelve free blacks couldn't meet after ten o'clock unless in the presence of at least three white citizens; and a monetary award was given for each warrant issued for an offense.

RELIEVED BY THE NEW Negro codes, William felt expansive. He traveled to a nearby town and carefully sorted through the pile of clothes in a general merchandise store. He walked silently around the store, looked at the farm implements, then placed a pile of cigars on the counter.

"I'm looking for a girl's dress," he said to the merchant.

William found a calico dress near the rocking chair. He also took an apron, headscarf and a pair of women's shoes.

"And trousers for a child," he added.

William also bought a doll for Ann and for James a toy soldier.

"Your boy would like this." The owner showed William a wooden toy about the size of his hand. When he showed him how it worked, William was amused and added it to his purchases.

Upon returning to the farm, William first went to Nan's cabin.

"I brought these," he said as he held out a small bundle.

Nan assumed a stony silence. She kept her hands by her side as she stood beside her table.

"Some clothes. For you and the boy."

Sharper, a child the color of willow wood, crouched against the wall on the dirt floor. A shaft of sunlight came through a chink in the ceiling. Sharper hid his face behind his hands.

Nan said nothing.

"Take his gifts," Suthy had once said to her.

She would do with these what she had with the others: tie a stone around them and drop them in the swamp.

291

William put the package on a stool, leaving the clothing for her and the child.

In the big house Leah asked where her husband had gone for the day.

"I've gotten these for the children. Here, Ann, come get it," he said, giving her a cloth doll. "Look," William said, pulling the doll's dress up and turning it upside down. The movement covered the white face and revealed a black one. "Two dolls in one. It's topsy-turvy."

Ann took the doll from her father and pulled the dress up and down, a black and a white figure joined at the waist. She turned it over and over.

William let out a guffaw and then handed a toy soldier. James fingered it and put it down.

"Don't you like it?"

"I do, sir," he answered, leaving the toy on the floor.

"Well, I have something else that will amuse you, then." William gave his son the three pieces of wood joined together end-to-end. As the merchant had demonstrated, William showed James that by holding the toy by one end, the three blocks seemed to cascade one over the other. He turned it over and he did it again

James eagerly grabbed the toy that his father said was called 'Jacob's Ladder.' James tried to make the ladder descend but was unsuccessful.

"It was business," William said.

"You were just at Nan's cabin just now," she said.

Leah's disapproval bothered William.

"Yes," he said, "I told her that she could use the kitchen from now on. Without your supervision."

"There was never a need to worry about her."

Leah's solicitous feelings towards his slaves bothered William. He couldn't understand how she didn't share his apprehension. Perhaps he shielded her too much; ignorance may be bliss, he thought, but it was also foolish.

"She's a decent girl."

William expected to hear Leah's appeal for manumission. Instead, the family ate quietly, William not asking a question of his children, as he sometimes did. James and Ann were eager to leave the table as soon as they finished. Leah went to the parlor to sew.

William took a bottle of laudanum from the sideboard and poured it into his apple cider. His testicles ached and were swollen.

William pinched tobacco in his pipe, then put it aside for a pinky-size cigar. When he finished smoking, he picked up a violin and played a popular tune. He mixed another glass of laudanum and cider. Since the cholera outbreak, the drug was more widely used than ever. He kept a considerable supply on the plantation, as he expected it would have to be used soon.

He positioned himself by the window and sat motionless looking out into the blackness. Leah found him sitting upright in the chair the next morning, his eyes opened but neither asleep nor awake. She shook him by his shoulders to rouse him from his torpor. William was uncertain whether he had been asleep or awake throughout the night.

The Well's Gone Dry

THE WELL AT Young Man's Chance had gone dry and no one knew why, although Nan had a hunch. Years ago her auntie had told her that one night she had seen the well crank turning and the bucket of water coming up all by itself.

"The handle," Lark told her, "was going 'round and nobody was there turning. The dipper lifted off the well wall and went as high as where a human mouth would be. Then the treetops started making a terrible noise like the leaves themselves were alive and moaning. Cold beads of sweat were on my forehead. And then, like that, everything went back to the way it was. I knew it was Hany doing it."

Water sufficient for drinking and cooking was available on the far side of the north thicket but this required laborers leaving aside more essential tasks. William concluded that it was time for a new well. After weeks of futile digging in the sandy soil by Suthy and a freeman hired for the work, William sent a letter to Bruno Daniel, a dowser in Lewes Town, one noted for having uncovered treasure from a Spanish ship marooned offshore a century before. William was willing to pay the high price for his talent, but when the water-witch didn't offer a guarantee that water would be found near the houses, William employed a different water diviner from Maryland. The black man held his forked stick in front of him, walking around the houses as if being led by an invisible mule with James and Sharper trailing behind.

"Here," he said, as the tip of his willow rod vibrated and pointed to a patch of ground by one of the abandoned cabins.

"You're certain?" William asked. "I'm not digging on speculation."

"You'll pay me the whole only if there's water."

"And I'll pay you nothing if there ain't," William insisted.

Daniel shook his head.

"That's not the contract we agreed on."

"Nothing's written."

"It's your word that you gave."

"Yes, it was," William said. "My word."

Both knew that Daniel's word was nothing against that of a white man.

"I want half for what I've already done."

William insisted that he would give him his $10 only if there was water.

As they stood there each waiting for the other's rejoinder, the point of the witching stick, still quivering, began to rise.

"Keep that from pointing at me!" William cried.

"It does what it needs to," Daniel said as he struggled to keep the stick away from William. "I'm not its master."

When William agreed to the original terms, the rod calmed down and pointed to the ground once again.

"This is where I'm to dig?" William asked again.

The water-witch said nothing. William gave him a $5 gold coin. The switch stopped quivering.

Daniel thanked William for his generosity and said, "I'll be back in two days to collect the rest." He reached into his pocket and took out a black bundle tied with snakeroot, shook it enough to make sure that William saw it.

Digging began soon after Daniel left. When the workers hit damp soil, William ordered them to stop. He piled shoveled dirt over the dark earth and left it that way until the water-witch returned the following week, his black pouch dangling from his side.

"There's no water here," William insisted. "You've robbed me of $5."

The dowser looked down into the freshly dug pit.

"There's water there. You need to dig a little deeper. I know it's there."

Suthy and the two little boys looked on from the front of Nan's cabin.

"I can dig some more," Suthy volunteered.

William ignored him.

"You owe me $5."

"Get off my property now if you ever want to get off at all."

The dowser grasped his pouch and waved it in front of William.

"There will be justice," Daniel said.

Suthy took the two boys away. That night he told them a tale:

> The animals and the creatures all be familiar with one another, so it's not long before Brer Rabbit, and Brer Fox, and Brer Possum goes to work together because the well's done gone dry. They had a big day's work in front of them so they brings their perishables along. They lumps all their vittles together and in that big pile is the butter Brer Fox brings.

> Not long before Brer Rabbi's stomach begins to growl and pester him. The butter Brer Fox brought sits heavy on Brer Rabbit's mind and his mouth waters every time he remembers it. He wants a nip of that butter bad, so he lays his plan.

> 'Here I is, I's coming' he says, like something is calling him, and he sallies around back to the food pile, and he stays there until he gets a bit of butter. Then he

saunters back to work with the others.

'Where you be?' says Brer Fox.

'My children were fetching after me and I go back to see what they want. I find my old woman's pretty sick.'

They work until the butter tastes so good in Bret Rabbit's mouth that Brer Rabbit shouts out, 'Hold on, children. I'm coming for your momma.'

And he puts off like he's going see his sick family. He eats some more butter and when he gets back Brer Fox asks him where he's been.

'My old woman is sinking fast,' Brer Rabbit says.

Brer Rabbit says he hears hisself called again and off he goes. He licks and he scrapes until there ain't nothing left but a few little drop on the bottom of the pot.

'How's your old woman this time?' Brer Fox asks.

'I'm afraid she's gone,' Brer Rabbit says, wiping away pretend tears.

When dinner time come, they get out their vittles but Bret Rabbit looked lonesome. Brer Fox and Brer Possum try make Brer Rabbit feel good. They rustle around getting out the vittles.

'Brer Possum, you run down to the well to fetch the butter and I'll sail around and set the table,' says Brer Rabbit.

Brer Possum lopes off after the butter and directly comes loping back with his tongue hanging out.

'What's the matter, Brer Possum,' he says.

'There's nothing but a few last drops of that butter in the pot. Looks like she's all dried up.'

Brer Rabbit looks solemn and he up and says, 'I suspect that butter melted in somebody's mouth.'

They go down to the water and sure enough, there's

nothing but a drop of butter. Brer Rabbit says he sees tracks all around and says after they all go to sleep he'll catch what stole the butter.

Brer Fox and Brer Possum soon drop off to sleep but Brer Rabbit rises up easy, put his long hand in the pot, runs back to Brer Fox and Brer Possum and smears Brer Possum's mouth with butter.

When Brer Possum wakes up, he says it sure looks bad for hisself and he is jammed up in a corner. He says he's innocent. Brer Rabbit says the way to catch the real thief is to build a big brush heap and set it up a fire. Then they each try to jump over and the one that falls in, that's the one what stole the butter. Brer Fox and Brer Rabbit both agree and when it got to blazing good, Brer Rabbit takes the first turn. He runs and jumps like a bird flying and easy clears way over to the other side. Then come Brer Fox. He jumps over but he got on fire. He is good but his tail burn off. Then come Brer Possum. He takes a running start, jumps no higher than a lowly ant and falls right in the middle of the fire.

"You can't stop there. What happened to Brer Possum?" Sharper asked.

"That was the last of Brer Possum. He be done gone like that water in the well."

"That's not right," Sharper said.

"What do you want?" Suthy asked.

"The rest of the story. There's more."

"No. There ain't no more," Suthy said.

"But Brother Possum didn't steal the butter," James protested. "Why did he get punished?"

"In this world," Suthy responded, "lots of folks got to suffer for other folks' sins. It's mighty wrong but that's the way it is."

"YOU NEED TO PUT A STOP to this," William said to Leah. "I saw James with the darky boy in the kitchen. He's always with Nan's boy."

"James likes him."

"I don't," William said. "I don't want our son near him. That boy's not right."

"I give them both some milk and rusk now and then. No harm in that. Besides, James needs someone to play with."

Several times William had told Leah he was afraid that the slave boy would infect James.

"He's cursed."

Leah thought for a moment.

"Maybe so," she responded. "Sharper's early birth wasn't a good omen."

"A bad sign," William said.

"And the pus and swelling around his eye. But it was gone before long. His eye was washed out and he's good now. Don't be so hard on him."

"Look at his hair." William stumbled for a second; he wished he hadn't said it. "No nigger should have hair like that," he continued.

"Yes," Leah said. "You're right. But that doesn't make Sharper an unsuitable companion for James."

"Our boy's discipline belongs to you, Leah. I won't interfere with that. But his welfare is mine. He's my son and one day Young Man's Chance will be his."

Domestic matters was Leah's domain and he wouldn't say any more about James or Sharper as long as they were children.

Leah took William's complaint as the opportunity to raise the matter of Nan's status.

"You didn't want to before," Leah said, "But I beg you to reconsider. Every day there are more free Negroes."

"That's a problem I don't want to contribute to. When there're funds to return them to Africa, then I'll consider setting her free. But not before."

"It's shameful. Having a slave."

"The shame is turning them loose. Then what, Leah? That would be the shame. Treachery."

"It's time to free her. It's only right. Let go of her."

"Examine your conscience," she said.

William's face turned lurid and he pounded the table.

Leah hoped that with manumission, Nan would leave the plantation.

Leah sipped her tea, broke off a piece of drop biscuit and swallowed. She began to cough.

"Get Nan!" Leah struggled to say as she tried clear the crumbs from her throat.

"You take care of James and I'll take care of the plantation," he said as he rose from the table with his cider and walked over to his chair by the window. "Drink some more tea," he added.

William pinched tobacco between his fingers and tamped it into the bowl of his clay pipe. He sat with it unlit until Leah left the room.

WITH THE MONEY FROM the sale of fifty acres of forestland, William built a one-room extension on the upper story of the main house. Leah had requested a bedroom of her own; her husband's crying out in his sleep prevented her from resting, she said. He said that her snoring kept him awake.

William readily obliged. He no longer had no more interest in sharing his bed with his wife than she had with him. They hadn't been intimate more than a half-dozen times since James' birth. There had been several failures— rejections and excuses, pains and repulsions—until neither desired the other.

When the room was complete, Leah asked her husband to improve Nan's cabin.

"A wooden floor, a window," she said.

"I have something better," William responded.

After many failed attempts to recruit new members to the colonization society, he concluded that the program was futile. Although hundreds of blacks had sailed to Liberia, William recognized that it wasn't a realistic solution to the growing number of free blacks in the state.

He placed a piece of paper on the table.

"I'm giving Nan her freedom," William said.

Leah's eyes brightened, but she remained doubtful. She put down her sewing and reached for the paper, but before she could unfold it, surprising her, William added, "Immediately. As of this moment she is free."

She sat back in her chair and placed her interlaced her fingers across her breasts.

"After what you've said, William. What made you change your heart?"

"I've not had a change of heart. Only a change of mind."

When Leah was next alone with Nan, she found her servant in distress.

"I should have thought you would be joyous," Leah said.

Nan burst into tears.

"It's Sharper," Nan said.

"What's happened to him? Is he hurt?"

"No, no. Sharper. He ain't free. Master freed me. Not my boy. Not my boy."

Leah put her hand out to Nan. Nan ignored the gesture. She wiped her eyes with the sleeve of her woolen shawl.

"What can I do?" she sobbed.

"I HAVE A RIDDLE," Suthy said. "I went down the road and I saw a rabbit. I pulled off its neck and drank the blood. What was that?"

The children waited for Suthy to give the answer.

"A bottle of whiskey."

The children laughed.

Nan wasn't amused.

"Whiskey and brandy ain't no friend to my kind," she said. Nan continued with a brief discourse the children often heard from her: "They killed my daddy and they troubled the mind." Nan looked at Suthy crossly.

"You're too serious," Suthy said. "You could do with more spirits than's just in the church."

The children found the spat amusing.

"I have one to tell one," she said.

"Yes," Sharper said. "We'll guess it this time."

"A riddle, a riddle," Nan began, "as I suppose." James and Sharper waited. "A hundred eyes and never a nose."

"Smoke!" Sharper exclaimed.

"I have another riddle," she said.

"No," James said. "Tell us a story."

Nan thought for a moment while she shifted her bandana away from her eyes. She felt her hair cut close to her scalp. She remembered her master's anger at her the day that she refused to treat his sores, when she would no longer touch him. He took the scissors himself and sheared her nearly to the skin.

"Tell us," James repeated.

Nan adjusted her headkerchief and began:

There is a widow woman out in the woods looking for things to make into potions and rubs. She got potions for every kind of ailments, from rumbling stomachs to red hot fevers. She got rubs for hurting feet, to fainting spells, and presses for sores in places that shouldn't be sore.

One day she says, 'Come up, stubborn root, let go of that ground. I want to make you into something useful.'

When she ain't looking, Hairy Man catch her from behind. He puts his ugly hands on Widow Woman's throat and is squeezing, getting ready to kill that poor old widow woman.

Getting up all her strength, the widow woman says nice, 'Hairy Man, I only ask for one thing.'

'What's you want, Widow Woman?' he says, his words as full of hair as his arms and legs.

'Just give me a few minutes to pray,' she tells him.

Hairy Man don't know what prayer is, so Widow Woman, she takes advantage to call her dogs. They come bounding from out of the trees and before Hairy Man can do even one thing, her dogs eat up Hairy Man. Sharper and James hugged each other in delightful fright.

Suthy looked at Nan and said, "Never despise a bridge that carries you over."

"Depends on what's on the other side," she said.

What awaited William on the other side was known to everyone when he died not long after drawing up his will. He was in his chair by the window with a half-pitcher of pear brandy and an empty medicine bottle that had been full at the beginning of the night beside him. His mouth and eyes were open, a sign that he had received his just reward.

Not more than a month later Suthy died from inflammation of the brain.

Changes

LEAH

Last Will and Testament

FOR THE FIRST time in her marriage, Leah is privy to William's business dealings and private thoughts. Piles of papers, personal correspondence and a notebook wait for her after she returns from the burial. The internment is in the Hooper graveyard, recently acquired by the Methodist Protestants who have removed their frame church from the Maryland line.

As Leah sorts through the bills stored in a box beside William's desk, to her great distress she discovers that many are unpaid. Her husband has accumulated a sizeable debt to merchants and innkeepers. She finds receipts from six general stores throughout the Chesapeake. Evidently, when credit ran out in one store, he patronized another.

While there are numerous receipts from a Dr. Carey, a Georgetown physician, for an unspecified treatment, these were always paid in full.

In another box, labeled ACS, is a notebook. She had often seen William writing in this book but she never had inquired about it. In the past, she would have thought of what she now is going to do as prohibited. No longer. She opens the book; the first entry is from the middle of the last decade. Page by page she reads about her husband's increasing disappointment.

How could they not see that colonization was the most sensible solution to an obvious problem? Did anyone have a better plan? Those that couldn't understand the wisdom of the program were fools, he wrote. *Even a blind man could see how removing free blacks would not only make the white* men's lives safer but would also protect the institution of slavery. *It was to everyone's benefit. Even the best darkies take up this most sensible plan. Some had already settled in Liberia.*

William made the same arguments repeatedly, his vehemence showing through with more strident and sharper language.

The more recent entries switch from frustration with others' lack of support for the worthy cause to complaints directed at the African Colonization Society itself. *"What the society is doing to him was more serious than his neighbors' obstinacy,"* he wrote. Ignorance he could forgive, ingratitude, never. He had gone to work on their behalf but his attempts to be compensated by the colonization society is ignored. He didn't want a fee for his service, only reimbursement for the expenses incurred in inns where he had eaten *"inedible fare and slept in conditions worse than that of a bondsman."* Without their recompense, *"I am at great financial risk,"* he wrote without an attempt to conceal his scorn. *"Their perfidy was more painful than the betrayal by free blacks."*

From letters written to his cousin in Baltimore, Leah learns that dozens of appeals by her husband to the ACS are unanswered. She uncovers but one letter, from the secretary of the state chapter who responds, thanking William for his untiring exertions on behalf of such a critically important cause. However, he reminds William *"you voluntarily undertook the recruiting efforts." He hasn't been deputized by the state chapter or by the national organization*, the correspondent noted. *All expenses incurred were his alone to assume.*

LEAH RECEIVED NOTIFICATIONS FROM creditors threatening to hire attorneys to protect and collect their claims. There was one letter from the keeper of the Knife and Fork in Bridgeville, stating that matters were already in the hands of a lawyer and that action would be taken if full payment wasn't received within sixty days. She had heard that creditors seized everything, even selling beds from under the sick and dying. One creditor took pots from the poor while food was boiling and emptied the victuals on a dung hill leaving the woman and her children crying for food.

A letter from William's lawyer confirmed her assessment of her financial position: Young Man's Chance was almost insolvent. If she didn't set matters straight immediately, according to law all but one-third of the estate would be sold off at an administrator's auction. She would also be allowed provisions up to the value of thirty dollars. As a woman she wouldn't face a debtors' prison, she was assured, but an almshouse loomed as a threat.

Her mind spun with anxiety. What would become James? And Nan? What about Sharper? Would he be taken and bound out elsewhere as an apprentice? She didn't know the law but the possibilities weighed heavily on her.

Troubled by the thought of being a debtor and frightened of being driven into destitution, even before reading the will in full, Leah set about righting her affairs. She had thought about writing to her brother for help, but she was afraid that he would take too long to respond to her letter. And then she was unsure about what assistance he would really provide. She didn't trust her in-laws or any lawyer and she thought that neighbors would try to take advantage of her vulnerability—she wasn't going to show him the precarious state of Young Man's Chance. Re-marriage, if it were to come at all, would arrive too late to save her.

At her behest an uncle in Trenton took Ann in.

Leah decided to sell a portion of the forest nearest the bog. This would still leave her with more acreage than the one-third she would receive if there were an auction. The mill, dilapidated as it was, could be rehabilitated and, she hoped, would make the property attractive. She had no doubt she would find a buyer at a good price quickly enough to stave off creditors eager to receive their due. She knew that rebuilt mills throughout the hundred were prospering using the newly invented process of kiln-drying corn meal. They now produced enough ground corn to be sent to the West Indies.

Word-of-mouth brought several potential buyers to the plantation. Her hand was stronger than she had initially calculated. She could sell off the parcels, receive enough money to satisfy the claimants and have a remainder.

After immediately settling what bills she could from the sale of a few pigs, a horse, and a buggy, she turned to her husband's private correspondence. A few were pleas from the Methodist Episcopal Church beseeching William to continue his subscription long since lapsed. He had joined to satisfy Leah upon their marriage, but he had no interest in the life of the spirit. Leah was free to do what she liked.

"I won't rent a pew to pay the salary of a useless preacher," he said. "I'll keep my $5 for better things. My Bible is all I need."

Leah didn't know why he needed even that since he never opened it.

During the first year of marriage, Leah attended Moore's Chapel every so often. One Sunday while Reverend Benson was engaged in the first prayer, a blind horse, running at full speed against the end of the church opposite the pulpit, forced its head through the weatherboard, knocking over the second-hand stove. Along with other worshippers, Leah rushed to the door.

When she told William about the incident, he laughed.

"It's not a horse's head in the wall that bothers me," he said. "What bothers me is the horse's ass in the pulpit."

For the rest of her life, many nights were visited by visions of being trapped in the parlor with the head of a black horse mounted on the wall, its eyes shining like lanterns that followed her around the room.

Leah also found a handful of letters from David Morgan. In these he referred to plays, museums and other amusements they had seen in Baltimore. Morgan also mentioned a physician who may have a cure for William's ailment.

When Leah finished Morgan's letters, she began to read the few that were from people unfamiliar to her. They were inconsequential renderings of ordinary events. After skimming through such trifles, Leah was ready to burn the entire batch. She called Nan to make a fire in the stove for her.

As she waited for the kindling to catch, she opened one last letter. Not more than a few sentences in Leah saw that this correspondence had been misplaced. It belonged with the business files. Relieved that there was no demand for money, it was merely congratulations for a successfully completed deal. Leah looked for the bill of sale, but it was not there. Perhaps it had been separated and put elsewhere. Uncertain whether it should be disposed of, she read it a second time. When she was finished, she felt uneasy. Something about it disturbed her. The details were vague in the way her husband's conversations with her had often been. Her discomfit prevented her from tossing the letter aside; she read it for a third time. She put it down and puzzled it through. As she glanced at the date again, the references became clear and her distress turned to disgust.

She remembered the day when William returned from a trip to Maryland that he had taken with Edwin Freeman, a hand hired for carpentry work around the farm. William seldom discussed details about his trips with his wife but this time he said he was bringing Edwin to a colonization society. Although not open to blacks, the meeting would benefit from hearing from a freeman directly, William explained.

"He will see the advantages of his migrating to Africa."

She remembered asking after he returned and no work was done on the cabin: "Where's the carpenter?"

"I didn't need him anymore," William responded curtly. "I don't know where he is."

The work for which the carpenter had been hired remained incomplete. She thought that William had decided that one of the slaves could finish putting in a floor and window in Nan's cabin. Leah gave the carpenter's absence no more thought, although the floor remained partially done and no cut was made for a window. Not until she saw the message did she give Freeman a thought.

With paining eyes, she read the letter one more time. Wanting to make sure she was correct, she went to old Suthy.

"Do you remember the freeman who worked on Nan's cabin?"

Suthy furrowed his brows. He said nothing.

"Do you know what happened to him?"

Suthy rubbed his balding head, his forehead furrowed in deep creases, his hands as rough as hide.

"Was he kidnapped?"

Finally he said, "Some say, Missus."

"Did Master William have anything to do with it? Is that what some say?"

Had William conspired with the notorious group of kidnappers from the hundred? That didn't seem possible since Patty Cannon had died in prison some half-dozen years before after having confessed to murdering more than twenty blacks whose kidnappings she had arranged. Leah thought the gang had ceased operations and the practice abandoned.

She repeated the question but Suthy remained stoic.

"Thank you, Suthy," she said.

Leah understood why there was no bill of sale: it would have been proof of his crime. William had sold the carpenter to a slave buyer. Without thought she begun to sing a hymn she often heard Nan sing: *The end will come, it will not wait, / Bond, yokes, and scourges have their date/ Slavery itself must pass away/ And be a tale of yesterday.*

MONTHS AFTER William's death, Leah received a letter informing her that her husband's will had been probated. She hadn't paid attention to will's details since she had been informed that she was the sole beneficiary and the lawyer had taken care of all the legal matters. There may be relatives who might contest the will, she had been warned, but, the lawyer assured her, that hadn't happened. No one bothered to lay claim to a piece of William's estate, one worth so little that it was too much bother to challenge its disbursement. Neither did anyone offer to help the widow with advice or monetarily. There wasn't a single letter of condolence.

The estate was now fully in her hands. She oversaw Young Man's Chance.

Sun streamed into the room. Leah watched Nan in the kitchen garden planted with beans, potatoes, turnips and cabbage. Behind the garden the milch cow bellowed on the ground she had trampled tight. Stacks of salt hay and corn fodder stood around tall poles.

In the envelope with the letter was her husband's will, which Leah had not seen before. When the lawyer had read it to her in his office, she was still recovering from husband's death; she scarcely remembered having sat listening to him reading the will to her. She unfolded the document and began to read:

In the name of God, I William Preddy of Northwest Fork Hundred Sussex County and State of Delaware being of sound mind and memory blessed be almighty God for the same to make and publish this my last will and testament.

1st I give and bequeath to my wife my real estate the dwelling house, garden and orchard together with the field or portion of land lying northwardly of the buildings running with the main road to intersect the line of Joseph Nichols then running said line up the boundary stone of the said Joseph Nichols and Anthony Wallace then running a line thence onward To the main road of the said starting place.

I allso give and bequeath to son James after he shall have attained the age of twenty one years all the remaining part of my real estate. I allso Will and bequeth to son James after my deseas my favourite gun which shall bee exclusive of the estate and my bondsman Sharper Preddy who shall not be manumitted before he shall attain the age of forty years.

In testamony whereof I hereunto set my hand and seal and publish and decee this to bee my last will and testament in presence of the witnesses named this eighteenth day of December in the year of our Lord one Thousand Eight hundred and thirty-five.

William Preddy

Witnesses:

Ralph Givens

Little Creek Hundred

Fletcher Rust

Northwest Fork Hundred

314

"I allso Will and bequeth to James . . ." she read again. What did this mean? She was now the proprietor within the boundaries as stipulated. James would take the remainder, a smaller portion she would learn, within seven years. She found the next provision loathsome—James would inherit Sharper, an unconscionable bequest.

Leah wrote to William's lawyer inquiring whether, despite the language of the will, she could manumit the slave. Was Sharper really left to James and was James then obligated to abide by its condition and not be able to free him for more than a decade? In his return letter, the lawyer apologized that he had since retired and Leah would be better served by consulting another lawyer. Leah talked to a neighbor who recommended his brother who had a law practice in Salisbury, across the state line in Maryland. This lawyer said that he was unfamiliar with Delaware's laws and couldn't give a definitive answer. However, he said—and she shouldn't take his remarks as legal advice but should consult a Delaware lawyer—it was his opinion that once she accepted the inheritance, the provisions bound her to the letter. Sharper, therefore, belonged to James and couldn't be freed until the stated time.

Leah didn't consult another lawyer. It was a senseless expenditure simply to hear what the first lawyer told her, she thought.

She read the will one more time, folded it and placed it between the pages of a cookbook, which after purchasing a copy of Mary Randolph's book of Virginia recipes she never opened again.

Child's Books

BOTH **BOYS** enjoyed Lydia Child's *The Juvenile Miscellany,* a magazine for *"the instruction and amusement of youth."* There were three volumes of the magazine that lay flat next to *The Frugal Housewife,* by the same author; a newly arrived but much used copy of *The Virginia Housewife* by Mrs. Mary Randolph; and the family Bible that stood propped upright against the north parlor wall.

Leah often read aloud to Sharper and James from the juvenile publication. After hearing a dramatic story, the boys enacted it as a play, not letting the obligatory moral ending spoil the diversion. They endured the stories and poems about girls, which were the preponderance in Child's magazine, and skipped over them when they looked through the magazine on their own. There was sufficient material in each issue to entertain—and, Leah believed, to instruct—that they looked forward to the bound yearly editions arriving in the post. They always found a few poems that appealed to them, which they committed to memory, reciting them to the Leah or a friend of hers when commanded, but mainly finding entertainment in them for themselves.

While James attended the district school by Joseph Horsey's land with twenty other children in one room, nothing he experienced there compared to reading the miscellany.

Without direct instructions from James, Sharper learned to read as he sat with his friend with the magazines—science, innovations, inventions, wild tales and stories from foreign shores all appeared on the pages. After one story about the second war against England, the friends argued whether it was the British or Continental navy that was superior; they both agreed on the advantages of steamboats over sailing ships that plied the two bays. They vowed one day they would become sailors, take to the seas, travel around Cape Horn and land on India's shores.

"I'll take you to Africa. Do you want to see your home?" James said, vaguely remembering his father's remarks about Negroes and their African home.

Sharper didn't know to respond to a nonsensical question.

They agreed that Old Hickory had been a great president, defeating the British in New Orleans, the Indians at Negro Fort, all the time with a bullet lodged near his heart from a duel.

They pored over illustrations of railroads. The line from Wilmington to Baltimore had opened in 1838 and they vowed that they would ride on the new line. A ferry steamboat carried the train across Susquehanna River, so they could satisfy both desires at once.

One poem in the magazine became their favorite. They dog-eared the page, returning to it many times. They took turns reciting alternating stanzas from "The Lame Horse."

Oh, I cannot bring to mind
When I've had a look so kind . . .

When not half so old as she
I was bounding light and free . . .

Speaking as the horse, together they declaimed—

And to-morrow is the day
Set for me to limp away

To some far sequestered place
There at once to end my race . . .

—breaking into tears before the final lines—

Gentle lady, when I'm dead,
By the blow upon my head,
That the hungry dogs and crows
May not mar my last repose—

Only bid them dig a grave. For the faithful, patient slave,
That will find his truest friend,
Him who brings him to his end?

Did the poem really end with a question? Or was it a printing error? They recited it with various inflections but never reached a definitive conclusion.

When they read about leather bottles used in Eastern Countries, they wondered if sheep could be substituted for goats. Following the article's description, they "pulled off whole the skin, and the places where the legs and tail were, were tied up." Leah was annoyed by untimely slaughter of the sheep more than the boy's careless butchery.

The boys hunched over the *Miscellany's* illustrated pages. Here was giant holding a rod. On its line dangled three men by their necks. The central figure, the large man, is wearing a yellow cap with a knob on the top, a red coat and green breeches, white socks and slippers. Two other normal-size men, also wearing clothes like the boys had never seen, are staring at the giant and running away.

"That's a head with a crown floating," Sharper said, pointing to an image placed between the red-coated man and little man in green clothing.

"And what's that behind the hill?" James asked. "Do you think it's a church? It looks like the top of a church."

"No, no. Your mother said they are Chinamen. There are no churches in China."

"Why not? Why aren't there churches there?"

"Because Chinamen are savages. Savages don't go to the church."

"They don't look like savages."

"Not the little men. They look like they could be Christians to me."

"The giant. He's a savage. He cut off the man's head."

"He cut off the head of the king. The king deserved to die."

They liked the first part of "Chinese Children," when Leah read it to them, but when they read it by themselves they stopped before the end, which read, "*When the children do not get their lessons well, or have done anything wrong, the common punishment is to lay them flat upon a form, and give them eight or ten stroke with a bamboo lath.*"

"What's a lath?" James asked when the boys were alone, not wanting to expose his ignorance before his mother.

"A whip. A big whip," Sharper guessed with complete confidence. "Like a slaver's."

"Not like your mother's switch," James said.

"No, much bigger," Sharper said. "I've never seen one, but I've heard. It's a whip so big it can skin you alive."

James believed him. He had never seen such a whip but had no doubt that it would be very large and lethal.

At the end of each issue were puzzles that challenged them. Sharper read this conundrum to James: "Why is a beggar like a baker?"

When neither could produce a satisfactory answer, they tried to make a dancing egg. They found a quill but not quicksilver and were defeated.

"I know the answer," Sharper said. "The beggar is like a baker because—he needs the dough."

"That's a good one," James said. "Kneads the dough like your mother does for the bread."

They argued about the moral of the anecdote called "Indian Justice."

> One Indian assaulted another, and a third person gave information of it. The judge ordered the sheriff to bring the parties before him. The officer went in pursuit of them, but returned without them.
>
> "Where are your prisoners?" inquired the judge.
>
> "I caught them," replied the sheriff.
>
> The judge asked, "What did you do to them?"
>
> The sheriff told him
>
> "I gave them fifteen lashes."
>
> "What did you give the plaintiff?"
>
> "I gave him fifteen, too."
>
> The judge then asked, "What did you give the informer?"
>
> "I gave him twenty-five lashes; for if he had held his tongue, we should have had none of this fuss and trouble."

James looked at Sharper and pointed to his head.

"You've got hair like an Indian."

Sharper's face grew hot. He would sometimes complain to his mother that his hair wasn't like hers or any other Negro.

"Don't wish for what you don't have," she scolded. She told him that it was his good fortune to have hair as beautiful as his.

Sharper referred to his hair again. He saw the vexation of other children as their mothers washed, picked and braided their hair.

Even if they didn't like a poem, they didn't mind it much. They would just ignore it. But Shaper disliked "Alvan, The Poor Little Burnt Boy" when Leah read it to them and said he didn't want to hear it again.

"What's the matter with you?" James laughed. "I think it's a good poem."

James returned to the poem without Sharper and had it memorized within a few days. One night, when they were in their bed and the candle blown out, he recited it aloud to Sharper.

"Sharper, the Poor Little Burnt Boy, by Miss Lydia Maria Child, from the New Series, Volume III," he began, substituting his friend's name in the poem's title. James had teased him with the poem before. But he said nothing, listening until James recited:

There came a wild, distressing scream—

A scream so fearful, that it froze

The heart, that listened as it rose.

A scream so dreadful to mine ear,

It fixed me to the spot with fear.

Another came . . .

"Stop, James! I don't want to hear any more. I don't like it."

"It's a good story," James said.

Sharper began to say more but dropped his protest. James always had the final word, especially when adults were around.

James continued:

I saw that boy, whose artless smile

An hour before could cares beguile;

That lovely boy, with trembling frame

Shrink from the fire's restless flame.

I saw that skin like lily pure,

Mid dark'ning cinders now obscure;

And I saw those eyes in beauty bright,

Close on the flame's terrible bright . . .

"Stop, James, that's enough," Leah said.

That night, when James slept in the main house and Sharper was in the cabin, he shook his mother awake. Sharper told her he was afraid. He had fallen into a fire and had been burnt.

"It's a warning, Sharper. Stay away from fires."

"Is it a fire that's made me black?" he cried. "That's what James said. He said that long ago there was a man who fell in and was burnt and that's why we're all black."

"I'm blacker than you," Nan said, placing her hand against his. "Some are the way they are and that's all there is to it. That's the way it is."

"But why you blacker than me and I'm blacker than James?"

"There's no shame in it," she soothed him. "Someday I'll tell you. Now you go back to sleep."

One day Nan asked the boys if they wanted her to tell them a story.

> In the beginning there is a pile of mud and God rolls it in his hands until he makes it a ball. He takes the ball and sets it down. And one day he makes the ocean and one day he makes the land and sky. There are fishes and terrapin and birds and so forth. And then he makes all the animals, even the snakes and mosquitoes. And he makes one man and one woman.
>
> God gets so tired from his making he sits down to rest on the seventh day.

James said, "I like this story, Nan, but I heard many times before."

"Just wait a minute. Don't be so impatient." She continued:

But the man Adam and the woman, they don't give him no time to take it easy like in the garden. The Maker, he gives him a hard time and he sends them out of the garden. They ashamed and they cover themselves with nothing but leaves they pick off the nearest tree.

Nan stopped herself and broke into song:

O Adam, where are you?

Adam, where are you?

Adam, where are you?

O what a trying time!

Sharper responded:

Lord, I am in the garden.

I am in the garden.

I am in the garden.

O what a trying time!

"I've heard this story before," James complained.

"Sure you did, James. All the world knows that story. But listen to the rest."

James fidgeted.

Everything be going good until the man Adam, and the woman Eve, they have children, two boys.

She paused again.

"Oh, there's something I forgot to tell you," she said.

When God make the man Adam and the woman Eve he makes them the color of earth. So the two brothers, Cain and Abel, they also made the same color as the man and the wife, the color of the earth out of which everything grow.

Cain and Abel, they don't get along so good. One day they get into a terrible fight, cussing one another and all that. Cain is jealous of Abel. His jealousy is so bad it overruns him. He is angry like a trapped forest pig.

Cain, he is so angry he pulls up a big rock right out of the ground and knocks Abel on his head and kills his poor brother.

She paused and looked at Sharper and James.

"Now here's the part you ain't heard before. Cain, who is done the killing, he gets so scared what's he done he turns white with fear."

Sharper asked, "Afraid of what?"

"What everybody's got to fear when they don't do right. He shouldn't have done that to his brother. You know that, don't you?"

When James finished his night prayers, he turned to Sharper and said, "I'm sorry."

"What for?" Sharper asked.

James turned to the wall and fell asleep.

EVERY SO OFTEN LEAH wished that Ann would return to Young Man's Chance. She recognized, however, that her daughter's New Jersey residence enhanced her future marital prospects. Still, she shared the concern expressed in *The Frugal Housewife* that Ann wasn't receiving a home education that would point her in the only direction in which the female heart could be happy. Ann, she feared, was being taught to "enjoy herself all she can, while she is single." Leah worried that Ann might have come to believe that indolence and vanity were necessary to happiness. She prayed that Ann would heed the book's advice to refrain from marrying for money. "Carpets, vases, sofas, white gloves and pearl earrings" weren't the sources of happiness. Duty was and extravagance was its enemy. How much Leah agreed with the epitaph by Ben Franklin: *A fat kitchen maketh a lean will.*

Leah aspired to be the housewife whose frugality would, as the book said, make her a "person of moderate fortune." She was not, after all, ashamed of economy and attempted to instill in Nan the habits of domesticity. The book's advice was sound, the homilies inspirational and the recipes fitting for a farmwoman.

CUSTARD PUDDINGS.

Custard puddings sufficiently good for common use can be made with five eggs to a quart of milk, sweetened with brown sugar, and spiced with cinnamon, or nutmeg, and very little salt. It is well to boil your milk, and set it away till it gets cold. Boiling milk enriches it so much that boiled skim-milk is about as good as new milk. A little cinnamon, or lemon peel, or peach leaves, if you do not dislike the taste, boiled in the milk and afterwards strained from it, give a pleasant flavor. Bake fifteen or twenty minutes.

With several buyers inquiring about the tract, Leah found herself in the unexpected and enviable position of choosing amongst several bidders. The demand for real estate was strong throughout the state. Two hundred acres on the river above Wilmington was rumored to have sold for more than $10,000. Tracts that sold for $10 per acre a few years back were now valued at five times that. Sussex was far less desirable than the northern counties but even there the demand for land had grown. And near the plantation a company with investments in woodlands in several states had bought a thousand acres of pine and oak forest to construct a factory to process planks, staves and shingles.

Turkeys took flight and geese hissed their alarm as a purchaser's agent came up the lane. Leah came to the porch to greet the buyer she had settled upon.

Leah had a contract drawn up by a lawyer waiting on the desk. Abner Taylor placed his hat on an empty chair. She and the agent reviewed the conditions and found them satisfactory.

"We need a witness," the agent said.

"Yes. I know. I see that here."

Leah left for a moment to return with Nan. She handed the pen to the agent.

"I can't sign before we have a witness," Taylor said.

"We have."

The agent looked around the room. He shrugged his shoulders.

"Nan will be a witness."

The agent smiled and shook his head.

"A Negro can't be a witness," he said.

"She's a free woman," Leah said.

"Only a white man can be a witness. Get a white man."

"There are none here."

"Then I will come back next week."

After the agent left, Nan and Leah resumed their weaving. When she mentioned the agent's name, Nan blanched.

"What's the matter?" she asked.

"There are bad stories about a man with that name."

Nan told her about a kidnapper who lived on the Maryland side of Reliance. Leah went to the box of papers she had stored in the attic. She found the correspondence to her husband that referred to Edwin Freeman. The signer was the same as the agent.

When Taylor returned, she asked Nan to bring them coffee and Indian cakes. Nan stood by the door. The agent broke off a piece of the hard cake and dipped it in the coffee.

"Do you have the witness?"

"I have," she said as she took out the contract and spread it on the table.

"Do you accept all the terms?" she asked.

The agent ran his finger down the two pages.

"Yes," he said. "It is fine. I'm ready to sign."

The agent looked around.

"The witness?" he asked.

"She is my witness."

"Mrs. Preddy," he said. "No japery."

"I am all seriousness," she said. "But since you find this woman unacceptable, I do have another witness for you."

"The other is here?" the agent asked scanning the room.

"Always."

"Where is he?"

"I know that you don't see him," Leah responded.

"Mrs. Preddy," he said with thinning patience. "No puzzles. The other witness."

"God is the only witness I need," she said.

The agent looked at her incredulously.

"God?"

"Do you need another?"

"For this sale."

"Is there a more perfect witness?"

"Yes, for contracts. Bring me a proper person."

"You are a wicked man," Leah reproached. "As God is my witness."

Leah picked up the contract, held it before the agent and shredded it. The pieces scattered on the hook rug. She inched closer to him, closer to him than she had been to any other man since her marriage.

"May the heavenly witness bring his righteous judgment down upon you. You are an evil man, Mr. Taylor. Evil."

The agent was puzzled.

"It's time for you to leave."

"Let's complete the deal," he said.

"There is only one place for you and it's not in my house. Nan," Leah said. "Give this devil's agent his hat."

HAVING FOUND THE *FRUGAL* *Housewife* instructive and knowing the boys' interest in the juveniles' magazine, when Leah learned that Lydia Child had published another book, she ordered a copy, expecting it to be another manual for household management. Not until the book arrived did she realize that *An Appeal in Favor of That Class of Americans Called Africans* had nothing to do with domestic economy but was an abolitionist's disquisition.

"Reader, I beseech you not to throw down this volume as soon as ou have glanced at the title," Child's wrote, as if reaching into Leah's home. *"Read it, from sheer curiosity to see what a woman (who had much better attend to her household concerns) will say upon such a subject."*

Having been piqued by Child's directness, she began the first chapter. She read no more than the first page to know that she had no interest in the history of Negro slavery. Chapter II held even less interest. What differenc did a comparative view of slavery in different ages and nations make? There was nothing in the book for her, she concluded. Better that Child's produced a new edition of the magazine for the boys' edification; Leah wanted further instruction on how to manage her domestic affairs.

Before closing the book, she looked at the contents. "Colonization Society, & Anti-Slavery Society, Chapter V." Here was a discussion that mattered to her. Perhaps through

Miss Child she could understand William's attachment to the ACS.

"*I discovered a lurking tendency to palliate slavery; or, at least make the best of it,*" Child wrote. "*I object to the Colonization Society, because it tends to put public opinon asleep.*"

'This book is putting me to sleep,' Leah thought.

She stopped reading half-way through the chapter.

"*We may at once agree to live together in mutual good will, and perform a mutual use to each other.*"

'Yes, that's all that is required.'

She was no closer to understanding her husband than before she opened the pages. But Miss Child had convinced her: she would remember to extend good will to her Negroes and to engage in mutually useful activities with all colored people.

Leah closed the book, glad that she had read that uplifting paragraph. Nothing more than good will was needed, nothing more than mutual respect required. She agreed. It was all very simple. If only men would listen and shut up.

She placed the book on the shelf where it remained unopened for years. Leah hoped that the author would publish more domestic books and edit more junvenile magazines. But that wasn't to happen. Child's bold and uncompromising abolitionist writings lost her subscribers to the *Junvenile Miscellany* and she never wrote another book for women and their domestic chores.

Salamanders

ABARREL-CHESTED man stood at the foot of the porch, the tallest person Leah had ever seen. He wore a woolen vest over an open-necked white shirt revealing a thick neck bulging with veins. Dust covered his trousers and his brogans were caked with mud. Flies buzzed around his mule's flanks.

He stood in the freshly swept yard.

"I'm here about the sale of the parcel, Miss," he said.

"Are you Mr. Jones' agent?" she asked the visitor who crushed a brimless hat in one hand and held the reins of the mule with the other.

"No, ma'am," he said.

"I had a letter from Mr. Jones. I was expecting Mr. Jones or his agent." She looked more closely at him and added, "I don't need any more laborers."

"I don't need work," he said.

"Then what do you want?"

"I came to buy the parcel," he said.

Leah said nothing.

"I'm Samuel Jones."

Leah didn't suppress her surprise as she stared at Jones, a man the color of a one cent coin. His midnight-black hair was speckled with gray patches, as though ash had fallen on his head. A beard covered his cheeks and chin like a woven carpet. Jones looked up at Leah who remained on the porch.

Jones said that he came from Wilmington, where he had seen her advertisement, to examine the parcel that had been advertised.

"I was expecting a . . ."

Jones completed Leah's thought.

"White man."

"Yes," she said.

"Most are tenants. Or are hired hands. Not many Negroes buy farms."

"That's right. It is unusual here," she stumbled.

Leah remembered years ago having overheard her husband mention Levin Thompson, the owner of acreage where Trussom's Pond emptied into Bald Cypress Branch. The black man owned more than 400 acres, spinning wheels and looms that produced quantities of linen and woolen cloth, two mills, and stands of timber when he died. Her father-in-law, she heard William say with some scorn, had borrowed money from Thompson and had been sued by the freeman to recover the loan. But it had been years since a black man bought property in the Sussex hundreds. The flow of freemen was northward, not southward.

"I'm not from here."

"So you've said."

Jones continued, "I'm wanting a piece of my own. This seems like an attractive place."

"You've been to Broad Creek before?"

"No, ma'am."

"What do you know about farming here? It's not the same as it is in the north. It's different."

That he hadn't farmed anywhere before he kept to himself.

"I liked what you said in the advertisement. I've come to take a look for myself."

It seemed a strange choice for a freeman to make, Leah thought—a forlorn part of the state, a backwater place compared to more prosperous north. And while elsewhere in Delaware there were more free Negroes than slaves, the sentiment in the southern hundreds favored the continuation of their peculiar institution. She didn't know more than a handful who advocated abolition and none who favored it forthwith. The previous year Leah had been solicited by her New Jersey relative to join the more than three hundred women in Wilmington who were petitioning for immediate abolition. Leah agreed that slavery was a burden oppressive both to master and slave, and a dishonor to the country. Before she could ask whether they were calling for immediate abolition, the legislature put an end to the matter. They denounced the women with unwarranted interference in subjects that more properly belonged to their fathers, husbands and brothers. Women should confine themselves, the legislature said, "*to matters of domestic nature, and be more solicitous to mend the garments of their husbands and children, than to patch the breaches of the Laws and Constitution.*"

Leah surmised that it was the asking price that attracted Jones. The county was still dominated by forests and swamps. The canal connecting the Chesapeake and Delaware Bays and expanding railroads in the north brought prosperity to New Castle and Kent Counties while Sussex trundled into the modern age.

Jones released the mule's reins and put his hat on the animal's back. He held up his hands for her to see, turning them from side to side. Half of his right index finger was missing; his knuckles were like hickory nuts. A scar ran down his left arm from his elbow to his wrist.

"I work hard."

"Yes, Mr. Jones," she said. She didn't need convincing. Unlike many of her neighbors, Leah never questioned the industriousness of Negroes. But why would a free Negro want to buy in this hundred? Negroes in the neighborhood were known to work with kidnappers. That he had come from New Castle to enter the dirty enterprise fleeted through her mind but dissipated as she said his name to herself.

"*He becomes poor who works with a lazy hand, but the hand of the diligent brings wealth,*" Leah quoted.

Not recognizing the biblical verse, Samuel thought himself forewarned.

Leah looked at his huge hands and then examined his face. She stared at him. Then to her chagrin she said, "I'm selling some acreage so I can keep the rest."

They stood outside, Leah eyeing the stranger. There was something about the man—the odd request, or his confidence, perhaps. She wasn't sorry she had revealed her position to him. She felt somehow relieved.

She continued to look down at him from the top step.

"Nan," Leah called.

Nan lifted her head. Sharper had just rolled the main house privy barrel to the garden and emptied its contents to be spread on the topsoil.

Leah summoned her again.

Nan put down the spade and walked to the main house. Sharper watched from a distance and then rolled the barrel back to be reset in the privy hole.

"Mr. Jones has come to inquire about the tract for sale."

Jones nodded.

"Would you like tea, Mr. Jones?"

Leah invited Jones into the front room. They sat across from each other, Leah in a rocking chair, Jones in a straight-back chair that wobbled as he sat. A carpet—"*an adornment irrelevant to the business in the farmyard,*" she had said to William as she unrolled it over the plank floor—

was the only piece of ostentation in the parlor, covered half the plank floor. Jones glanced at the books on the secretary.

"It's the only way to be my own man," Jones explained after telling Leah about his trip from Wilmington. "I depend only on my own diligence. I'm successful enough to save for a farm. I'm a mason by trade. I also am a carpenter and there are other things I can do with my hands."

"You've not been a farmer before?" she asked incredulously.

"No, ma'am."

"It's not easy."

"It's a skill and until I learn it, I'll be able to find someone to assist me. I'm good with my hands. I've learned a lot of skills."

"I hope so, Mr. Jones. You are right: it won't be difficult to find someone to hire. Many blacks are looking to be hired."

The more they spoke, the more Leah settled that she would complete the deal with him. She had Sharper hitch the buggy.

"Come along, James," she said.

James helped her into the buggy and took the seat beside her. Jones sat behind them with his feet dangling over the side. The three rode to the woodlands laced with rushing rivulets and runs. Jones walked amongst the towering trees as Leah sat on the carriage bench with her son. A pig rooted under an oak tree, a vulture took flight. Two nightingales sang their call and response.

A deer raised its head and bolted into the understory as Jones began a walk to survey the parcel.

"Where's the mill you advertised?" Jones said when he returned to the buggy.

Leah pointed to a tangle of trees and brush.

"Is there a path?"

"Go show him, James."

James jumped from the buggy and took the visitor to an opening in the woods he and Sharper knew well.

Water rippled around a crumbling and splintered mill. Jones examined the wheel with many missing blades. He looked beyond the ruin to tawny swamp waters.

"I like the parcel," Jones said when they returned to the house. "But I'm a bit surprised. I expected there'd be need *some* clearing. But there's little there that's ready for using."

Leah listened.

"There is also the part needs to be drained."

Each was absorbed in their thoughts.

"I'm sorry for having taken your time. It ain't possible for me to pay what you ask," Jones said.

"I can't lower it," Leah said. "It includes the mill. With the skill you say you have, you will put that back to work while preparing to farm."

"Yes. But the farm will be too small to turn a profit."

Nan brought them cider and pudding.

"I can't lower the price."

At the end of the day they had reached an agreement: Leah agreed to half the payment immediately and a quarter of his profits from the property until the remainder was paid in full. Jones felt confident that within a few seasons the property would be his.

Leah saw little risk on her part. She had no use for the tract, so even if he defaulted, she'd still own the property, have some money, and could offer it for sale again.

The following month Jones arrived with a mule-drawn wagon filled with building supplies and his tradesmen's tools. He gave Leah her money with which she paid off her debts and became a creditor herself.

Deducting the payment for his work the remainder of the mortgage, Jones hoped to own his own farm within two years.

WITH JONES' PURCHASE COMPLETED, Leah could now hire hands to increase her own tillage. Nan had moved into the main house, leaving Sharper to occupy the slave cabin alone, while Jones, after attended the meeting at the African Methodist church a few miles away, became a regular Sunday visitor to Young Man's Chance. Sharper liked being with him and while they were together, Jones, now called Uncle Samuel by Sharper and James, taught him how to use his carpenter's and mason's tools.

"You don't go the church," Samuel observed.

"No," Sharper responded.

"You and your mother can come with me."

"I don't think I'd like it," Sharper said.

"Which chapel have you been to?"

Sharper had never been to a church. His mother's attitude towards religion was much like Leah's: daily Bible reading was sufficient for salvation. The rest was distraction and vanity.

"There is a different spirit when the preacher brings the word down. Reading the Bible is good. But singing lifts the spirit higher. It's like leavening to bread."

He added that it was good to be with others who could help one another with their journey over troubled waters.

"*Private prayer is the true essence of vital piety,*" Leah said. She had read the sermon in *The Frugal Housewife*. "He can go with you, if he likes. But a sincere prayer is the desire of the heart. And the prayers I know in church ain't sincere and the desires ain't pure."

Samuel encouraged Nan and Shaper to join him.

"It's not much," he said, "not like churches in Wilmington."

"I've never been to Wilmington," Nan offered.

"Maybe someday I'll take you with me."

"I want to go," Sharper said.

Nan told Sharper to be quiet.

"The church here, even here it's full of spirit. Most times an un-ordained Negro preaches but sometimes there is an authorized circuit rider."

One Sunday Samuel took Sharper to his church, a congregation that met in a frame building hardly bigger than Sharper's own cabin. James wanted to come along and Leah saw no harm in it. It was much as Jones had described.

By the end of the day, Sharper agreed with his mother that salvation was an inward journey taken alone while James was swept up in the enthusiasm he witnessed. But he wouldn't attend without Sharper and it was the last time he sat with Negroes for worship.

A few thought Nan had given Sharper the farmer's surname, believing that she and Jones had become more than visiting neighbors. But it was Leah, now known as Widow Preddy, who called him Sharper Jones, desiring to erase her late husband's relation to the boy.

News from the larger world came primarily through Jones whose source was other Negroes at church or his occasional visits to Seaford and Laurel. Politics didn't interest Leah. She didn't know who held office or what disagreements were about. Democrats, Whigs—they were all the same to her, men bound by their own interests pretending otherwise. While others looked forward to going to Georgetown on Return Day, when residents from throughout the state came to hear the election results and to celebrate, she declined. She thought things would be better if everyone simply minded their business instead of bothering the conscience of others. Hypocrites, she thought. *'Why behold the mote in your brother's eye but consider not the beam in your own eye?'*

She listened to Samuel's stories about people.

One Sunday evening, sitting in front of James' cabin with both boys present, Samuel related a story:

"A court was sitting in Georgetown," he began. Sharper liked the way Uncle Samuel told his tales, leaning forward, his voice rasping and as strong as he was tall, his feet planted firm on the ground. "It was a criminal case they was hearing. People assembled in the courtroom ready to watch the trial, making the room full of anticipation. The room was buzzing like hornets. Until the judge came in. The judge, dressed in his robe and his wig falling to his eyes, stepped into the room. And everything became hushed. The judge, he was ready to begin the trial."

"You saw a trial with your own eyes?" Sharper asked.

"No. I was told. But the person telling me the story swore it was true. He said I could read up on it in the Georgetown newspaper and the whole account is there. It's true story I'm telling you."

James urged him to continue.

"He—the judge—opened his mouth and before his first words could tumble out there was an awful flash of lightning. The thunder was so loud that the town shook." Samuel stamped the floor with his bare feet. "A horse broke loose and ran off. No one knows where he went. Dogs slid into ditches like snakes. Birds flew up into the black sky."

He stopped. The boys looked at him. Nan picked up her knitting.

"That's not the end," he said.

"What happened next?" James wanted to know.

"Lightning came down like that," he said, waving and wiggling his arm at the boys, "and struck the courthouse. Bam! Lightning ran down the rafters and cracked the building in two."

"The building fell down?"

"No. It stood there. But it was in two pieces. Two pieces leaning against one another. It's useless. And I don't think it will stand long. As the Bible says, '*If a house is divided against itself, it cannot stand.*'"

Nan knew the next line, which Samuel didn't quote: '*And if Satan is divided and rises against himself, he cannot stand; his end has come.*'

"That's a good story," James said. "Now I have one to tell. Not a story. A conundrum. If the building is sundered, is it one building in two pieces or is it still one building?"

Sharper ignored James' riddle.

"What happened to the prisoner?"

"Something terrible, Sharper. Something terrible. The prisoner and twelve others who were witnessing the trial were set on fire. They kept on burning. The fire was so hot the buttons on their clothes melted off. The rich men with watches—their watch cases and silver dollars melted in their pockets."

"How dreadful," Nan said.

"Yes. But those you think would be dead because of the heat, the other twelve, they weren't dead. They're alive. Some saved by bleeding or other means of resuscitation."

"Even the prisoner was saved?"

"No. I said the other twelve."

"What happened to the prisoner?" James asked.

"The prisoner," Samuel said, "received a just judgment from heaven. The kidnapper was left in smoke."

"Kidnapper?" Leah asked.

"That was the charge."

"He was burnt up right there in the courthouse?" James asked.

"Nothing left but ashes."

"What did this kidnapper look like?" Leah wanted to know.

"I wasn't there."

"What was his name?"

"I don't know," Samuel said.

But Leah knew immediately; she knew who he was with her whole heart.

"It was God's finger that came down into that room," Samuel continued. "In his mercy, he spared the others. But that one he sent right to hell before everyone for them to see the retribution. There was nothing but smoke and ashes, smoke and ashes and a terrible smell."

A wave of nausea swept over Sharper. His hand went over his mouth to prevent his puking. James pointed at Sharper and laughed.

"Is it two buildings or one?" James asked again.

"What's the difference?" Sharper responded to James in irritation. "The criminal got his just judgment, just like Uncle Samuel said."

Nan listened to Samuel's story.

"I have a story, too," she offered. "This is about salamanders."

Jones looked at Nan as if he had heard the story before.

"Salamanders are cold creatures. That's why they like to stay by a bog furnace. You have a furnace going, Mr. Jones?"

"It's burning every now and then."

"This furnace that I'm telling about is in Millsboro. That's what I heard. In Millsboro down the other side of swamp."

"There's one there," Samuel interjected, building on Nan's introduction. "The fire never goes out in that one."

"Never?" James asked.

"Not ever."

James objected that a fire must go out some time.

"The sun's a big fire and it ain't never goes out."

"That's different. A fire here on earth, it has to go out some time. The big forest fire that burnt down the trees in the marshes, well, that fire went out. Not soon. But it went out. So I think . . ."

Sharper shook his head and said, "I want to hear the story."

> One day there be dozens of salamanders hanging by a furnace, walking around and around. They be like buzzards circling waiting for slaughtered pigs' leftovers. Like ants waiting for sweet honey to drip. They got nothing else to do but watch that hot stove glow day and night, night and day, day and night.
>
> The fire in the furnace is a iron-making furnace, it is so hot. Salamanders, they looks at the furnace with bulging, envy eye and they is imagining the warm they will feel all up in their cold bodies.
>
> It gets colder and colder and they feels colder and colder. Their heads is freezing and their feets is like ice and they don't feels their tails no more. The leaves lose their green on the maple tree, then brown leaves shake on the oak tree and snow is falling little cotton lint.
>
> Then salamanders decides they can't stand the cold no more and just mope after a hot fire. Winter is just beginning, Christmas be waiting to happen and already it be freezing so bad salamanders thinks their feets will stick to the ground. They stares at the fire, they looks at it this way and that and they is tempted, wanting to stop shivering and shaking.

But the furnace, she is sitting on top of red-hot crackling wood with flames making dancing shadows on the wall. Salamanders have enough. The first one moves his four feets fast and scrambles over the red-hot wood. Salamander runs over the burning wood like it ain't burning at all, like it's nothing more than August dirt in the field. He gets to the furnace, leaps up and dives right into the bubbling metal. The second salamander sees this and he do the same, then another sees that and he leaps in and then another sees that and he do the same thing, one after another, all the salamanders rushing over the burning wood and jumping into boiling furnace.

Problem is this—

Nan pauses for a long minute—

So many cold creature jumped in that their cold selves puts the fire out and the furnace owner, he gets angry. And there is another problem. The problem is this—

This pause seemed longer than the first—

For salamander, before the fire is out, there ain't but nothing left of them, just ash that goes up with the leaping flames.

Samuel waits to make sure that Nan is finished with the telling before says, "That's a true story she's telling. I heard it myself from those that witnessed it, watching salamander jumping in one right after another."

"Like the lightning in the church?" James said scornfully.

Samuel laughed.

"They're both true."

"I don't believe you," James said.

"You believe the stories you read in your magazine," Samuel said.

"I'm going to see for myself one day. You going to come with me, Sharper? I'm going to see if there's two churches standing there or just one."

"You don't need to see everything yourself to know it's true," Sharper said. "You didn't see yourself being born but you're here, ain't you?"

"But you can't believe everything that's said. That ain't right. You got to verify it for yourself. There are true stories and made up ones. You need proof. Like the experiments in the Miscellany, Sharper. I wouldn't believe you could make an egg dance unless we had tried it for ourselves."

"You're mixing up things. You ain't never seen a locomotive or a steamship, have you? But you know they exist."

"Because everybody knows about them. If enough people say so, then it's proof. Uncle Samuel's but one person."

"Is the lame horse real?"

"That's different. There's locomotives and there are made up stories."

Samuel interjected, "I heard it from someone else. So that makes two. You've heard it from your mother, so there's you and Sharper now that knows about it. That's a lot of people already. And you tell it to others and now there's more."

Sharper looked at James.

"That's what I'm trying to say, James."

"Maybe so," James responded. "But don't you want to see for yourself if it's two buildings or one?"

"If it's two," Sharper said, "by the time we get there both parts will have fallen down and there won't be any standing. Not one building or two."

"Thank you for the good story, Nan," Samuel said. "Salamanders are cold blooded creatures. They can make you cold just by looking at them."

James and Sharper agreed that they liked both stories, but James continued to protest.

"Why did Uncle Samuel say that Aunt Nan's story was true? Everyone knows that salamanders can't leap. They scamper across the ground. They can't any more jump than a snake. You know that, Shaper, don't you?"

"Just because you ain't never seen them jump don't mean they can't."

SAMUEL

Wise Choice

DURING HIS FIRST year in Sussex, Samuel builds a one-room, windowless log cabin constructed from fallen trees, a dwelling that would make-do until he could build a more suitable dwelling.

He repairs the long-neglected gristmill to working order. On trips to neighboring towns, he takes orders from merchants and shopkeepers for items he expects to begin crafting by the end of the following summer. In appreciation of Leah's assistance, he presents to her an oak chair he has made. He clears an acre to plant corn and vegetables and digs a cooler pit.

"Why are you putting that down there?" Sharper asks as Samuel places in the cellar pieces of iron and shards of glass to protect against malevolent spirits.

Samuel doesn't answer but Sharper guesses. His mother, too, has buried blue beads outside the door of the old cabin.

Sharper teaches Samuel how to catch birds, game and fish. Although he uses James' gun when he hunts with his friend, Sharper doesn't know whether he can use the musket without its owner being present. Rather than risk being arrested for possession of a firearm, Sharper shows Uncle Samuel how to catch muskrats by baiting a trap with the animal's gland. Sharper finds resin in a pine tree's broken knot, smears the birdlime on a twig and rubs it on a perch where he has seen a bird sit.

"There," Sharper says. "We got one."

A wren, the size of a child's fist, churrs in the pine tree as it tries to free itself from the sticky perch.

"If I get that hungry," he says, as the bird's cry filled the grove, "I'll go back to Wilmington."

They leave the desperate bird on the branch and go to tong for oysters.

At the end of the first season there is sufficient silage for his mule. Nan puts up vegetables for him and he has some produce for the cooler. Leah provides him with cured meats the first winter in exchange for the oysters, shad and sturgeon he has fished from the tidewaters.

Throughout the winter, when the paths aren't too muddy or the weather too bitter, he visits the Preddy farm. The first time he brings Nan a terrapin, Sharper shows him how to step on the back of the reptile to get it to extend its neck from under its carapace. After cutting off the head, Sharper uses an ax to break the bridge connecting the upper and lower parts of the shell. Nan and the other Negroes at Young Man's Chance enjoy terrapin but she has never prepared it for the Preddys. Leah says she is repulsed by the odor of its fat. Once when James returned to the main house with the smell of the reptile on his clothes, Lean forbade him to be around when the vile dish was being prepared. Nan and Sharper, now the only blacks living on the plantation, are happy to share the meat with Samuel.

By the following summer the corn crop is plentiful enough that Samuel buys a dairy cow and there is enough flour from the mill for him to sell.

Samuel completes his payment to Leah. With a portion of the money, convinced by a premonition that her farm should be covered with fruit trees, Leah plants apple and peach saplings although she knows it would take several years to realize a return on the investment. Her neighbors think she has made a serious mistake, one that will benefit them when she will be forced to sell. The land isn't right for fruit trees, they think, but her dream has convinced her otherwise. It takes a few years to prove her correct. In the meantime, she brings a couple of calves to begin a livestock herd. Swine are a constant nuisance but the salt pork and ham they provide are necessities.

Samuel teaches Sharper the use and care of carpentry and masonry tools. Leah employs Samuel to work around her farm and over the course of several months, with Sharper's help, the two replace the dilapidated fence that has collapsed and has been nearly reduced to compost. They erect a sixty-by-sixty foot post-and-rail fence that encloses the farmyard to keep out rooting pigs. He repairs the smokehouse and builds a new tool shed.

The old well is replaced and new pits for the human waste are dug. As for James' cabin, Samuel concludes that it was beyond saving.

"I can build another," he tells Leah.

Leah says that there was no reason for that. Sharper can join Nan in the main house, if Samuel would add an extension. Sharper can sleep in the new side room. Samuel repairs the loom and soon Nan sews women's apparel and begins to save money to purchase Sharper's freedom.

Samuel uses scrap wood from the cabin for the construction of a worm wood fence to demarcate, for the first time since its purchase a century earlier, the boundaries of the plantation. Before winter the improvement of the main house is complete.

"Your parcel was surveyed before the sale," Leah tells Samuel, "but it may be wise for you to erect a fence for your property, too."

Samuel agrees. But there is no hurry, he says. It will have to wait. Other matters are more important. Leah admits that she wants to sell a few more acres but hasn't received any other solicitations and, as far as she hears, interest in acquiring land in the hundred has tapered off.

James complains to his mother that he wants to work with Samuel and Sharper, but Leah has hired a teacher to instruct him in bookkeeping. Some are made to work with their hands, she says, and others with their heads. Hard work will come to naught if not managed properly. When Young Man's Chance becomes his, he had better be versed in good business management and not employ strangers.

CERTAIN HE HAD MADE the right decision in buying the Sussex tract now that he had become self-sufficient, Samuel decided to return to Wilmington to bring his wife to the parcel he christened 'Wise Choice.'

Before leaving his farm for the city, Samuel dusted his summer shoes, placed a clean shirt in a gingham bundle and tucked his working ax under the seat of the wagon. He patted the pocket of his cassimere jacket, the woolen coat his finest article of clothing he owned, to make sure he had his freeman's pass and climbed onto the buckboard to set out north, choosing the road that took him past Young Man's Chance.

When he reached the entrance to the plantation, he guided his mule up the lane to the main house. There he hitched the wagon to the picket fence. Leah, who was in the kitchen garden, went to greet him. Nan came around from the back of the house where she had been doing laundry.

Sharper and James were gone for the day in the woods.

"I came to this neighborhood alone," he said to the women. "It wouldn't have been right to take my wife from the city and bring her here if I couldn't succeed. It's a hard life. But it's time for me to get her."

"It's a long ride to Wilmington," Leah said.

In the past Samuel had alluded to his family. Leah assumed his wife had died; she never asked him about her.

Despite the many hours he had spent with Nan, she knew nothing about his life up north. Nan thought that it was up to Samuel, a freeman in a slave state, to raise the topic about his past life and until he did, there must be a good reason to keep it concealed.

"I remember the roads here. It will be easier this time, knowing where I'm going and what's waiting at the other end."

"What about your children, Mr. Jones?"

"None of my children live there any longer," he said.

"Come in," Leah said to him. "Sit with me a little before you go."

Leah doubted he would return to his farm, that he had really come to make the parcel gainful and now having done so would sell it for a profit in New Castle County.

As Leah sat and pointed to his own crafted chair for Samuel, she turned to Nan and said, "Prepare tea for Mr. Jones and me, Nan."

"Yes, Missus. Maybe Mr. Jones would like coffee."

"Mr. Jones?"

"Yes. Coffee."

"I'll have tea for myself, then."

Nan left to boil water on the kitchen stove and upon returning set down on the table two white cups.

"Join us, Nan," Leah said as her servant poured the tea for her. "Get a cup for yourself."

Samuel glanced at Nan, who cast her eyes downward.

"No, thank you missus," Nan replied. "I prefer to stand."

The third chair in the room was the one with the splintered seat.

Samuel turned away.

Nan removed her headscarf, fussed with it, and then retied it around her hair. She turned to look towards the

351

kitchen. She held her left thumb in the fist of her other hand, slowly twisting it back and forth.

"I insist," Leah said.

Leah walked to the shelf to remove a cup.

"Sit," she said, raising her finger to the chair with the broken spindles.

Nan continued to stand as Leah placed the cup on the barrel next to Nan. She poured the tea for her. She removed a cloth cover from a jar on the table and sat down again. Samuel stirred honey with the bone handle of a knife.

"Take some honey in your tea, Nan," Leah said as she spooned some into her cup.

Nan placed herself next to the door, carefully folding her frock under her.

"You're going home for your family," Leah said.

Nan stared out the doorway.

"Yes. For my wife."

There were no children to be gotten, he explained.

His wife, he said, lived in the city, near her parents.

"It's time for Rachel and me to be together again."

"Who will care the farm while you're gone?" Leah probed, doubting that Samuel planned to return.

"My hired man will be there but there's nothing much to do, just small things. I've told him that he can get Sharper if he needs to. I've taken care of everything."

"How long will you be gone, Mr. Jones?"

Samuel sipped the remainder of his coffee.

"I expect no more than a week."

"One week?"

"Maybe two."

"There's much to do?"

"Rachel needs time. Coming down here requires . . ."

"I know," Leah said.

Samuel rose to leave. Nan moved their cups to put by the wash bucket. She hadn't touched her own tea.

"Good-bye, Nan," he said as he extended his hand.

Nan kept her back to him. She had no more faith that he would return than Leah.

"I'm going out, Missus," Nan said. "I didn't finish my work when Mr. Jones came."

Samuel leaned over Nan's shoulder and said he would see her in a week. She didn't respond and walked out back.

Samuel followed Leah to the front of the house. He unhitched the mule.

"Mr. Jones," Leah said. "I've never been to Wilmington."

"It's a big place," he said.

"Is New Jersey far from there?"

"Just the other side of the bay."

"Can I get there from Wilmington?"

"The bay's wide but I heard there are steamboats that go across."

"I have a daughter in New Jersey." Leah put her hand on the plank seat beside Samuel. She didn't know why she said what she said next. "Wait. I want to go with you."

"It's a hard journey," he said. "It may not be proper, with me and a buckboard for you to be riding in. We can't make it in one day. Two at best. I hoped to start out earlier. Maybe I can make it as far as Dover before it gets dark. About half way to New Castle."

Samuel presented a few more worries.

Leah dismissed his concerns and went to her room to pack some of belongings. When she opened her husband's portmanteau, a whiff of mildew struck her. She brought the leather bag to the window to examine it for mold. Finding none, she placed in it a few items and buckled it closed.

Samuel took the bag from her and secured it on the back of the wagon next to his own bundle.

"We need to be going."

"Yes," Leah said. "Nan's out back. I have to tell her that I'm leaving."

Leah walked around the house to where Nan was hanging the wash under the noon sun.

"I'm going to visit my daughter in New Jersey, Nan."

"Yes, Missus Preddy," Nan said as she pegged bed sheets to the clothesline. "Miss Ann's been gone a long time. She must be a woman by now."

"Yes, I suppose."

Leah held one end of her bedsheet for Nan to peg.

"I'm going to see her now."

"How are you going to do that? She's far."

"I'm going to take a steamer from New Castle. I've never been on a boat. But Mr. Jones said there are ferries that cross the bay."

"Like in the boys' magazine."

"I'll find out," Leah said. "Mr. Jones has put my bag on his wagon."

"How are you getting there?"

"With Mr. Jones. I'm riding with him."

"Oh," Nan let slip. "He's leaving now, ain't he?"

"Yes, he is. It's a long trip. He says we have to leave now if we want to make it to Dover."

Nan wiped her wet hands on her checkered apron.

"I can't wait for James to get back. Say good-bye to him for me, Nan."

"When will you be back?"

"A week. Mr. Jones said no more than two."

"You know he ain't coming back."

"Why do you say that?" But she knew why.

Upon returning to Samuel, she began, "Mr. Jones . . ." and, once again surprised herself when she concluded, reaching her hand out to his, "Help me up."

Without Wind or Water

SAMUEL UNBUTTONED HIS jacket as Nan called out for him to wait. She had gone to the kitchen and quickly put Indian slapjacks and apple pie in a basket to give to him and her mistress.

Leah turned, took her valise from the back of the wagon and placed it between herself and Samuel. She then reached for Nan's basket and placed it on her lap.

"Let's go, Mr. Jones," she said.

As the wagon rolled down the main road to Dover, moving in and out of the dappled light, Leah wrapped herself in a shawl, her hair secure under a cap and bonnet.

The two barely exchanged a word. When it began to drizzle, Samuel pulled his hat down to his ears. Leah sat unperturbed.

Thoughts about his wife absorbed Samuel—how would she greet him; how she would receive the news about moving to a farm; how had her appearance changed? He worried about a life with her where there were as many slaves as free Negroes, where slave catchers and kidnappers continued their business.

Qualms about leaving for Wilmington with a black man filled Leah's mind as the day lengthened. She had under-estimated the arduousness of the trip. Samuel had been right, she thought. Hazards of all sorts presented themselves. While public improvement abounded in the northern two counties, only after reaching Dover would the journey proceed on graveled roads. Until then it would be corduroy lanes and paths through forests and open land, and there were many creeks to cross without the aid of bridges. Several times Samuel stopped to tighten a wobbling wheel or to adjust a slipped harness.

Nan's food remained untouched.

Each rustle in the underbrush, every movement in the woods startled Leah. She regretted not having learned to use a gun. Samuel's hammer and the ax she saw on the floor under the seat provided small comfort.

"We can't go further," Samuel said as night approached. The gray sky was turning black. "There's a house I know not far up the road from here. We'll put up there for the night."

"There must be an inn where I can stay," she countered. "I won't stay in a stranger's house."

"No, Missus Preddy. There ain't no inns. None until Dover."

"Then let's go on to Dover." she urged.

Samuel shook his head.

"Missus Preddy," he said, "no respectable woman stays at an inn alone."

She thought about the ax and wondered if it hadn't been for Samuel's protection after all.

"To Dover," she demanded.

"It's not possible. It's too far. I can't drive the wagon in the dark."

"If you go faster, Mr. Jones."

"I can do all the whipping and shouting I want, Missus Preddy, but this mule ain't going to go any faster no matter what I do."

Leah conceded as much.

"We can't be out much longer. It'll be night soon. Even the mule will be blind."

He wanted to say that he had wished to leave earlier that day; that they could have reached the capital if she hadn't delayed him; that he couldn't understand why she needed to go in a hurry. Instead, he repeated the necessity for stopping before they would have to stop on the road for the night.

"I forbid you to stop, Mr. Jones, before I can find a proper place to rest," she said.

Samuel didn't reply.

When they reached a rail fence, Samuel turned the wagon down a path towards a brick and stone two-story dormered house, its chimneys on either side of the roof silhouetted against the gray sky.

"Where are you taking me, Mr. Jones?"

"This is people I know. They'll take care of us."

As Samuel drew the wagon to a halt, Leah realized that this wasn't a makeshift 'colored house' common amongst freemen but a home of a prosperous family.

When a white man appeared at the door, Leah tried to contain her surprise.

"Samuel?" the man asked.

"Yes, Mr. Hanson. It's me."

"You have someone with you," he said, as he peered into the darkness.

"Yes," Samuel said. "Widow Preddy."

Leah sat stiffly on the bench seat and remained mute.

Samuel continued, "Widow Preddy's the one I was going down to Sussex about buying the tract from."

"And what happened?" Hanson asked.

"I bought it and it's mine now. She sold it and has been good to me."

"Welcome, Missus Preddy," Hanson said as he walked to the buckboard.

Leah remained silent. She felt for the ax with the heel of her shoe.

"She's going on to New Jersey. She's a daughter up there."

"And you, Mr. Jones."

"To Wilmington. To get my wife. The farm's been fruitful."

"Then it's time to multiply," Hanson joked. "Come in."

Samuel alighted from the wagon.

"Mary'll make supper for you. Watch your step, Missus," Hanson said as he extended his hand to help Leah from the buckboard. "You must be hungry."

"And tired," she said.

"We'll have something for you shortly."

Leah hesitated before following Hanson into the house, but when a smiling white woman appeared wiping her hands on her apron and addressed Hanson as her husband, Leah's neck muscles relaxed.

Samuel sat easily next to Hanson. The aroma of fried fish wafted into the room. When plates were put in front of Samuel and Leah, Hanson said grace.

"Missus Preddy," Hanson said. "You can take the bedroom upstairs with Mary whenever you're ready to retire. Mr. Jones and I will take to the loft for the night."

"There must be an inn nearby," she said.

"Not for miles," Mary Hanson said to Leah's distress. "Come with me."

Mary led Leah up a winder staircase to the upper floor. In one corner a ladder led to the loft.

"You need a night's sleep, Missus Preddy," she said, putting the candle down on the table beside the bed. "I'll join you when I finish in the kitchen."

Leah fell asleep with the candle still flickering. She felt the bed jostled, heard whispers and faint footsteps in the stage before complete blackout. She awoke the following morning to the honking of Samuel's mule. The valise, which she had forgotten to take from the wagon, was on the floor next to the bed. From below she heard Mary and her husband talking and she smelled bacon and coffee.

Light filled the room. She pulled the curtain aside and for the first in days she saw a clear sky. From the upper window she watched Samuel examine the wagon. He patted the mule on its rump, said something she couldn't hear and walked into the house.

BEGINNING IN HIS FIRST WINTER in Broad Creek Hundred, Samuel began writing letters to Rachel apprising her of his success in Sussex, ending each missive: *"I will rest content only when you join me at my side."*

While Rachel read the scores of letters he sent over two years, she put each away without reply. She had made her opinion known before her husband left. She wouldn't plead any longer. Any response, she reasoned, would only encourage him—she wasn't going to leave a city to become a farmwoman.

When, years before, she first told her parents that she intended to marry a tradesman, Rachel's parents disallowed it. They wanted an educated man, not someone with a rudimentary knowledge of reading and writing, someone recently released from bondage.

"Father Spencer was born a Delaware slave," Rachel responded, referring to the founder of her father's independent black church.

"Yes, he was," Charles Chandler agreed. "As were the reverends Absalom Jones and Richard Allen. But they didn't continue to think like slaves. Look at what they have done. Father Spencer, like the others, has made something great of himself."

"Samuel may not be a gentleman but he thinks like a freeman. He will make something of himself, too."

"You don't have to wait. There are elevated men for you to meet at the church."

"I know them."

"And there ain't one for you?"

"Not one that my heart has taken to."

"Give your heart time to mature. You're yet a girl."

"At least meet him," Rachel begged. "There is so much goodness in him that I see. You will see it for yourself."

Though Samuel prayed in the Methodist Episcopal church, where a parishioner had bought him his freedom and taught him his trade, he had no objections to worshipping with Rachel at her church on French Street when she invited him to join her there. While he understood the appeal of being free from the interfering and sometimes-unjust hand of a white association, he had always participated in a congregation where both Negroes and whites attended. Only once had he been slighted at church— during a service that became so crowded the minister asked the colored worshippers to vacate the balcony for the whites.

"I talked to the man you brought to see me," Chandler said to his daughter. "I can't approve of him, Rachel."

"Don't you like him?" Rachel said in astonishment.

"He is a sincere man."

"Then why won't you bless the union?"

"You said that Father Spencer was born a slave. He follows the spirit and is a light in the darkness. He is a beacon to the world. But this man Samuel ain't following him in the pulpit, is he?" her father stated.

"Everyone is called to serve in a different way, as you do. His work is with his hands to make and mend."

"I offered him to be an apprentice with me as an undertaker. I understand that it may not be for him. So, I told him I would take him as a clerk in the store and, if he proves himself, I will make him a partner when the time comes. 'Chandler and Son.' I would like that. But he refused that, too Rachel. It is an arrogant man who refuses assistance."

"He went to church school," Rachel insisted. "He can read and write. He's not a laborer or a waterman. He's skilled."

Her mother stopped her and reminded Rachel that her father was a vestryman and represented the African Union Church in the Association for Moral and Mental Improvement.

"Your father is secretary of the benevolent society," she said. "You need to marry someone of standing. We go upward, Rachel, not backward."

For many months her parents mounted reasons why other men were more suitable. But Rachel wouldn't be dissuaded. She only wanted Samuel. No longer able to deny Samuel's upstanding character and Rachel's desire for him, they relented.

After the wedding, at which Father Spencer officiated, the Chandlers introduced Samuel to their colored acquaintances. Samuel's skill and probity meant he never lacked for work, going from one recommendation to another, eventually hiring others to work for him in his expanding trade. After much soul-searching, he decided to hire slaves as well as freemen, employing only those who sought to purchase their freedom. He ensured this by putting a portion of their salary in escrow, releasing the money when they had accumulated enough to buy their way out of slavery. More than once he put in his own money to hasten their manumission. More than two decades later, having buried all his children, Samuel decided to leave his trade behind.

"I've found a tract that I want to buy," he told Rachel.

At first Rachel thought Samuel was land speculating, a risky but sometimes profitable venture.

But it wasn't a turn on an investment that interested him.

"We are going to live there, a new home for us," he said. "I'm going to farm."

She accepted Samuel's explanation about wanting work the land, but when he told her that the parcel was in Sussex—swamp infested; a county that looks to Virginia, not Pennsylvania; a region in where Negroes matter no more than livestock—she had no response.

None of his explanations convinced Rachel that life there could be better than that which they had known for decades.

In the city she had a proper social life, diversion for a cultured person. Her parents needn't say it, she took on the duty willingly: as their only daughter still residing in Delaware, she would care for them. If he bought a farm in New Castle County, that she could accept but not what he proposed.

Nothing she could say, no inducements by her parents made a difference. He left with the understanding that if within two years his venture wasn't successful, he would return to Wilmington. Rachel agreed but left unstated because she herself was unsure what she would do if he did succeed.

VISITS TO PHILADELPHIA and New York, the African Union Church's women's benevolent association, friends, entertainments—none assuaged Rachel's loneliness. That many black women were without men in their households held little comfort for her. She had known the grace of marriage and the consolations of a fine husband: the warmth of his body, his soft snoring that lulled her to sleep, the smell of his skin, the feel of his hair, the bitterness on the tongue—his leave-taking had been long enough.

Rachel thought the optimism she detected in his letters

was as a kindness to her, to salve her anxiety. Now that he was at home she was certain that he was going to tell her that he had abandoned his farming venture and had sold the mill and farm for a profit, that he would resume his life in Wilmington.

His announcement the day after his return stunned Rachel into silence. Samuel, she knew, was a thoughtful and headstrong man. Her reasons opposing his decision, no matter how heartfelt, would be futile.

She hoped her father would be convincing. Chandler had come to see his son-in-law as in upright person worthy of respect. He, like Rachel, had thought that Samuel had gone to Sussex as an investment.

"I look around and I see that every purchase," Samuel said—"a pound of groceries, a yard of linen, a vessel of crockery ware, the very provisions we eat—all are products of the white man. And every purchase here is from the white man. But I've made a place where I can truly be free."

"There is my dry-goods store that will give you enough money to be your own man."

"And there a few other shops, too, that colored men own. But who are we, really? Coachmen and cooks and waiting men. The decision makers and the owners of the manufactories . . . "

"Yes, the white man," Chandler interjected. "I agree. They control industry and enterprise. But you know for yourself the progress we have made. And soon there will be more. The vote. And abolition."

"Stay near Wilmington," Chandler said. "The silk industry is where you can make money enough for the independence you seek. Brother Garret sold cuttings in the ground for $7500. His purchaser sold them for another $10,000, the third for $12,000."

"It sounds as though I missed the time to buy."

"If you don't have enough, I will lend it to you. The price will only go up." He turned from Samuel and called to his wife. "Vivianna, bring us coffee." Vivianna and Rachel retired to the kitchen. "My dry goods store is the only one for coloreds. The business can only prosper with the coming of abolition."

"I know that."

"I have no son to give my businesses to. I buried them all myself," Chandler said. "You have been a fine husband to my daughter. She couldn't have done better. But it ain't right for you to be apart."

"That's why I've come to get her."

"But her life—your life—would be better here, amongst free Negroes. Where you are, down in Sussex, Samuel, no black man is safe. No free Negro should be staying. Life is better for you here where there is a great movement for abolition."

Samuel responded, "Maybe so. There's been talk for so long that I suspect some won't live long enough to see it."

"Have faith," Chandler urged.

"I bring my faith wherever I go. I've just finished paying my debt for the farm. I'm not taking on another."

Chandler made a final appeal.

"I was there the day Father Spencer assembled us and he preached the first independent service. June 1813, nearly thirty years" Chandler said. "He rang a new freedom bell and it's chiming today. You can feel it every time he preaches, you can feel it." He looked Samuel in the eye. "You have strong hands, son. You have a good soul, but you are stubborn. You can say you are steadfast and you are right about that. You have observed the sanctity of marriage and have been a strong father to your children, but you are still headstrong. Why do you want to return to the seat of bondage? Stay here with us."

Rachel's adamancy was unacceptable. A wife's place was to follow her husband, but her stubbornness equaled his own. If she wouldn't come with him, he said as they lay together, he would go back without her.

LEAH HADN'T GONE TO New Jersey after all. Her visit to a lawyer extended over several days and there wasn't enough time to see Ann and be back in time meet up with Samuel for the return journey.

"I don't know if you can legally do this," the lawyer said. "It is an area of the law that I don't know. I'll have to do some research."

She came back that afternoon but he still had no clarity. He was busy with more pressing matters, he explained, but he would consult with someone in the city more knowledgeable than he.

"Come back tomorrow afternoon, Mrs. Preddy. Perhaps I'll know then."

Leah returned on three consecutive days. By then it was too late to take the boat to New Jersey.

"I'll write to you, Mrs. Preddy when I find out," he said. "But I don't think it matters one way or the other."

"It's not right."

"No, it's not right at all. It's against the conscience. But I've been told by those who know that a bill is being introduced this month and this time they have the votes. I don't see that it makes any difference whether *you* free the boy or not. It will be done by the Legislature. We will be rid of the scourge. But if you want me to continue, Mrs. Preddy, I will. It's your money."

Leah paid the lawyer for his services. The next day she met Samuel and they rode back to Broad Creek Hundred together.

"I thought I would meet Mrs. Jones," she said.

"Oh, it was quite a surprise to her, coming to Sussex. She's always lived in a town. But she'll be joining me soon. She just needed some time, that's all."

Samuel began to hum to the rhythm of the mule's pace.

"What's that?" Leah asked.

"Some song I know."

"Stop. I have a headache."

"It'll make the time go quicker. Besides," he added, "the spirit won't come down without a song."

"Then sing it," Leah said. "If it will make the time pass quick, sing."

> Samuel's mills a-grinding
> Samuel's mills a-grinding
> Samuel's mills a-grinding
> Samuel's a-hay
> Built without a nail or hammer
> Built without a nail or hammer
> Built without a nail or hammer
> Samuel's a-hay
> Runs without wind or water
> Runs without wind or water
> Runs without wind or water
> Samuel's a-hay

Given a letter of introduction by the lawyer to a family in Dover, they stopped at the house before sunset. Leah was invited in.

"Is there a place where a colored man can stay?" Samuel asked.

The householder knew of none.

"If your Negro needs food, there's a place for him in the kitchen."

"And to sleep?" Leah asked.

"There's the root cellar."

Samuel told Leah he wasn't hungry.

From the window of her bedroom Leah watched Samuel brushing his mule. He climbed onto the bed of the wagon, reached into a bag and removed something to eat. He then emptied a burlap sack and covered himself with the bag.

Leah climbed into bed but couldn't fall asleep. Next to the billowing curtains snapping in the breeze she saw beams of light streaming from the eyes of a black horse whose head protruded from the wall.

An Auction in Dover

AFTER HIS MOTHER AND NAN died in a kitchen fire, James looked through the family papers. It was upon finding his father's will tucked between the pages of a cookbook and finding no papers to undo his inheritance of Sharper that he realized that his friend had never been given his freedom. James went to a local lawyer to have a freeman's pass drawn up for Sharper. The lawyer at first demurred, but a generous Christmas gift overcame his objection to backdating the document.

"For you, Sharper," James said to his friend, handing him the paper. Ashamed of his father's meanness and mother's oversight, he added, "I found it amongst my mother's belongings."

The two young men were on their way to see Uncle Samuel. Sharper pulled the wagon to a halt as a terrapin ambled across the dirt road and slid into the brackish water on the south side.

"That terrapin reminds me of a story Aunt Nan told us."

James remembered listening to the tale sometime after turning the soil for spring planting. They were in the field with Nan and Samuel not far from the barn, on one of the first warm days of spring. The waters were flowing again; life was coming out of its hibernation and moving about in the greening woods.

When Nan finished her telling, James recalled Samuel saying, "It's not always so."

Nan disagreed but James couldn't recall the nature of her objection.

James asked Sharper if he also remembered the incident.

"Yes," Sharper said.

"How Samuel disapproved," James declaimed.

"Did he?"

"He was cross with your mother."

Sharper said James got it wrong: it was Samuel who told the story, not his mother.

When they rested, about half-way to Dover, James asked Sharper how well he remembered the tale.

"Better than who you think told it to us," Sharper said.

"Tell it then. I want to hear it again. Even if you're wrong about who's the teller."

Sharper thought for a while.

"I'll tell it as I remember it."

"I won't stop you if you don't get it right."

"Do you remember it well?"

"Hardly."

"Then I'll tell it."

One day long ago there are two kinds of creatures, one that lives on the land and the other that lives up in the sky. On Earth there is turtle calling hisself Tappin and up in the sky Eagle flies above the clouds.

Tappin has six children and they all be demanding food. They's hungry, so hungry their stomachs stick out and their hair is orange like a peach. There is no food for them to eat because a bad drought has come down on the land. Tappin's ears is paining with all that screaming of six hungry children.

No one remembers the last time it rained—no rain for months on end, then one year, then two with just a few teasing drops. There is no food, so all six children be howling for food to fill their swollen stomachs. But there ain't no food because there's only hunger everywhere.

"You're as good a story-teller as your mother," James laughed. "When did you get to be so good?"

"Don't know," he says and continued the telling.

Eagle, though, he is flying way up there in the sky. He has no cause for crying; he got but two children and he can fly so good that he crosses the ocean to get his food to bring to his children.

Tappin be seeing all that Eagle and his children gets to eat, so he calls up to Eagle.

'Eagle,' he says. 'I got a favor to ask of you.'

'What's that, Brother Tappin?'

'My children is hungry,' Tappin says. 'They gots nothing to chew on but some clay dirt. I see you got a whole lot of feathers. So, I am asking you to give me some of your feathers. And you could teach me how to fly.'

'You is a good Tappin, so I'll help you out.'

Eagle got lots of feathers, so he won't miss but the three he gives Tappin. Tappin asks if three feathers enough to make him fly, seeing that Eagle's body all over is covered with feathers.

Eagle says that's Tappin's doing, whether he fly or not, but just to be merciful he gives him one more feather, making four all together, one feather for each corner of his tappin body.

Tappin, he thanks Eagle and sticks two on each side, front and back.

'Now start flapping,' Eagle instructs Tappin.

Tappin is flapping as hard as he can and starts rising above the earth. He flies out over the water with Eagle and they fly to go to where Eagle gets his food. But one-by-one the feathers Tappin stuck on come off and Tappin starts falling from the sky right down towards the ocean.

'Stupid Tappin,' Eagle says, 'that's not how to fly.'

Eagle swoops down and catches Tappin. He tucks him under his wing.

'This smells real bad here,' Tappin complains.

So, Eagle lets go and Tappin falls into the water. He goes down deep until he reaches the underworld below.

"Remarkable. How do you remember all the details, Sharper?" James said in amazement.

Sharper didn't tell him that the story was common amongst Negroes.

"Every story is an embellishment," is what he said instead.

"There's more to the story, I remember. Ain't there?"

"Yes. It's when Tappin reaches the underworld, the king asks Tappin what he's doing there. Tappin says that things on earth are terrible.

Tappin says to the king, 'King, there's no food for me and children. There's nothing I can find anywhere. But Eagle, he has only three children and he crosses the ocean and they's never wanting.' He begs, 'Please, king, give me something to feed my children.'

The king being an obliging king gives Tappin a dipper and tells him whenever he wants food it will be there in the dipper.

'What vittles you want, Tappin?' the king asks.

And as soon as Tappin names the foods that is in his mind that's making his stomach rumble, there it is in the dipper. All the creatures of the underworld shows up, it smell so good, and there is bacon, fish fry and biscuits, apple pie and melons to be feasting on.

Tappin comes up from the deep sea.

'Come on, children,' he calls but there is nothing in the dipper. No matter what he does the dipper's empty.

Tappin goes back to the underworld king and says, 'King, there ain't nothing in the dipper. Fix this dipper up.'

The king says to Tappin, 'You take this cowhide when you want something.'

Tappin, he says he wants bacon, fish fry and biscuits, apple pie and melons, but instead of the dipper providing all this fine, delectable food, the cowhide beats the land children until the children falls down.

Tappin calls the king up from the underworld.

'King, come up here to help me and my children,' he says all helpless.

But the cowhide keeps beating and beating. It don't stop beating no matter Tappin's begging and crying.

Tappin makes hisself a coat of sand and lime to cover up good. But the cowhide keeps beating and beating. It never stops beating.

James waited and then asked, "Is that the end? A story never ended like that. Sometimes a lesson came at the end. I don't remember what it was with this one, but it didn't end like this."

Sharper laughed and said, "You're right. That's not the end. There's never end to some stories, they just go on and on."

James had a perplexed look on his face.

"All right. Here's more, if you like."

Tappin, he has beat marks on his shell. That's why whenever you see a tappin its shell has marks all over his hard back. And it's why you won't ever find a tappin in a clean place. He's under leaves or he's dug hisself under mud. And maybe just once in a while you can find tappin sunning hisself on a log.

"Is that how it ended or are you just making it up?"

"I told you, some stories never end. But the part about Tappin's shell, that part's true."

"I remember Samuel said something like, 'It's not always so.'"

"Did he?"

"Why would he say that?"

Sharper scratched his wisp of a mustache with his thumbnail.

"I tell you, it wasn't Nan who told the story but Samuel. But anyhow, why don't you ask him when we see him?"

"I want to know what you think."

"How should I know?" Sharper responded as they climbed back onto the buggy. He took the reins.

"Let me," he said to James.

JAMES REFUSED TO BURY HIS MOTHER next to William in the churchyard and instead interred her alongside Nan in the woodland section of the farm. Samuel had offered a few words of consolation and said a prayer as they put the bodies in the ground. He erected two crosses that he had made.

Before the calamity he had been a regular visitor to Young Man's Chance and while his sleeping in the room with the women on many occasions didn't cause the boys any concern, it was a topic of gossip in the hundreds. But after the women were put into the ground, Samuel ceased visiting. It took the boys a while to notice; they were busy maintaining the farm that had grown under Leah's care.

James saw Uncle Samuel a couple of times at the general store the year following the fire, while Sharper met him only once, at a camp meeting in Maryland. But when they heard about his trouble, they didn't hesitate to set out for Dover.

They knew the circumstances of his arrest, but they couldn't believe it. Not once had they suspected Uncle Samuel was capable of the kind of unlawfulness with which he was charged. If he had been arrested for the possession of a gun, James would have vouched for having given the rifle to him himself. The sheriff would understand that with the threat of kidnappers it was reasonable for Uncle Samuel to have a gun for protection. It was illegal, James would argue, but if there was culpability to be ascribed, blame him, not Samuel Jones.

Uncle Samuel didn't even use the gun when they went to hunt. James would testify that the rifle probably hadn't been fired since he gave it to him and he would be surprised if Uncle Samuel even knew how to load it. James would pay the fine and assume responsibility for his supervision. James didn't know if anything he would say would help Samuel, but would eagerly vouch for his good character and ask for clemency from the court.

They found Samuel in the county jail, having been arraigned, charged and declared guilty. He had been convicted of having aided slaves in their escape.

James and Sharper visited Samuel in the Dover jail.

They gave Samuel a bar of soap, knotted jumbals baked especially for him, and a clean shirt.

"Is it true?" James asked as the three stood in the cell.

"Yes," Samuel said.

"What happened?"

"A slave owner in Broad Creek reported me to the sheriff. It wasn't his slave I was taking. Another slave I helped was caught on a steamboat and returned. He talked to his wife and she was the one that let slip that it was me that was aiding those coming up from Virginia."

"Who was this fool?" Sharper asked in anger. "Let me know. Just tell me and I'll get her right."

"She was careless but she didn't mean no harm."

Sharper could barely contain himself.

"Give me her name."

"Don't be foolish," James said.

"James right, Sharper. That won't do any good. It's the evil law that needs to be changed."

"Helping a Negro run away ain't helping," James said.

"Not to change the law. Maybe it's not. Maybe you're right about that. But it's helping those to get to freedom. Until the law's changed, it's helping a few. Because you can't help everyone doesn't mean you don't help no one."

"It's not for me to do. Not to break the law."

From the conversation, it became clear to Sharper that James knew nothing about the network running from Seaford and Laurel and Millsboro up through Delaware that brought slaves north. He began to wonder how his friend could continue to live in such ignorance. Yet he himself had not known that Samuel's house was a depot or that he was an agent. Why hadn't Samuel entrusted him with such knowledge? He began to wonder if Samuel saw in James something that he had been blind to, something obscured by their friendship.

"What are they going to to do with you, Uncle Samuel?" Shaper asked.

Samuel interlaced his fingers, drew in a breath and then spoke slowly with his eyes shut tight.

"I'm being put up for auction."

"What?"

Sharper couldn't speak. Finally, he said, "They can't do that, can they? Can they?"

"Yes, they can. I'm being auctioned for seven years of servitude."

"They can't do that," Sharper said again, clenching his fists.

James leaned against the jail wall.

"They convicted me on two counts: the aborted trip and the successful escape of two from Maryland Shore. They said I'm lucky not to be hanged. What I did was almost as bad as murder is what they said."

"What they've done is worse than murder," Sharper said.

"Listen, boys. When I heard the sentence, I said to myself I wish they had sentenced me to hang. Nothing is worse than being a slave. Then I thought, I've helped others escape bondage. It is better to be alive and flee . . ."

"What were you thinking of, Uncle Samuel? You can't break the law just because you don't agree with it." James said.

"What law are you talking about, James?" Sharper said glowering at James, suppressing an anger that he couldn't express to a white man, not even his best friend.

"The Delaware law. The federal law. You know."

"There's a higher law than that," Sharper continued more calmly. "Uncle Samuel may be breaking one law, but it's to abide by another, one higher. Slave-owners are the ones guilty of a crime."

James thought for a moment, then said, "But they can't sell you out of state. The law won't allow that."

"With a court order, they can. I don't know what they are applying here," Samuel said.

"What difference does it make where you're a slave?" Sharper said.

"Stop it, boys. You two didn't come here to fight with one another," Samuel said. "You came to give me your well wishes, didn't you and I thank you for that."

"I had no idea, Uncle Samuel," James said. "I thought it was because of the gun that you got arrested."

"See, James," Sharper said. "You break the law. too, when you have to."

"Everyone breaks the law now and then. But there's little laws and there's big laws and this was very big. There's a difference."

Sharper interrupted James.

"What can we do, Uncle Samuel?"

Samuel put his hand on Sharper's shoulder.

"Pray and act. Pray and act. You two have been good boys. I trust you'll figure out what to do. Pray and act."

"Abolition is coming soon, Uncle Samuel," James said soothingly. "There'll be no more slaves. Even if . . . ."

Samuel placed his other hand on the top of James' head while the three fell silent.

"I'm done praying," Sharper said as they left the jail.

FROM DELAWARE, Maryland Shore and Virginia, men came for Samuel's auction. After serving ten months in prison and having been fined $500, he was now up for sale. The unusual nature of the case had brought few bidders but many spectators to Dover. Who would want a man born a slave but now free, a farmer and a felon whose crime undermined the right to private property, the foundation of liberty upon which the nation rested?

"Stay here. Don't come with me," James said to Sharper. "Do you really think you'll be safe with all those slavers and their agents? Besides, if you was with me, that would raise suspicions. What are this Negro and white man doing together?"

James convinced Sharper that it was prudent for him to keep his distance from the auction site.

"I won't go with you to the auction, James, but I have to go with you to bring Uncle Samuel back."

After their visit to Samuel, Sharper and James had devised a plan: they would purchase Samuel themselves, then manumit him. Between the two they had pooled four hundred dollars, more than the going price for a man past his prime. James considered it a loan that Samuel would repay over time.

Sharper sat by the elm tree in the public square, near the State House while James went to the yard behind the jail. Samuel was brought out with chains around his wrists and looked far more worn than when he and Sharper had seen him. Samuel loomed over the warden and the auctioneer.

The auctioneer invited bidders to come forward to examine Samuel.

"Stop. You can't do that here," the warden said. "This ain't Carolina. Samuel has fallen on hard ways and he will be sold, as the law demands. Leave him alone."

"How is the buyer to know what he's getting?"

"They will bid for him just as they see him standing here, nothing more. What they do with him once he's theirs is between them and their conscience, but as long as he is in my charge, you will do as I say."

"Be reasonable. I need to get the best price."

The auctioneer leaned into the warden and handed him a fistful of coins.

Potential buyers approached Samuel and examined the soles of his feet. They looked for lice. They pinched his skin and tested his arms and legs. They opened his mouth for inspection.

The bidding began at $50.

James: "Sixty."

The Virginian countered with $90, the man from Wilmington $100.

James: "One hundred twenty-five."

Others raised the bid to $250. At $300, James and the man from Wilmington remained in the bidding, the others having dropped out.

When James met up with Sharper, he was without Samuel.

"I was certain no one would bid more than the $400," he said. "Everyone around me said that he wasn't worth more than $200. But the man with the top hat from Wilmington kept driving up the price until I didn't have any more money. He bought Uncle Samuel for $500."

"You could have done something."

Sharper had never been so angry with James. If only he had gone to the auction with him, things would have turned out differently.

"What? There was no more money. At least he 's staying in the state. He couldda gone south."

Sharper's animosity towards James lasted for months, until they received a letter from Uncle Samuel.

> *My Dear Sharper and James,*
>
> *I am writing to you from my home in New York. When you last saw me, James, you lost your bid. I think you must have meant to buy my freedom and I am grateful to you for the gesture.*
>
> *As you can imagine, when I was sold to Mr. William Hardcastle I was in great distress. I thought again about ending my life. When the shackles were removed, I thought I would run, although I knew I would soon be caught. But when Mr. Hardcastle placed me on the*

carriage without irons, I was too tired to jump. From the start, Hardcastle treated me different than what I expected. He gave me food and drink and I fell asleep. He put a blanket on me to keep me warm.

He brought me to Wilmington where turned me over to Mr. John Hunn. I knew of John Hunn from reputation but I had never met him before that day. Mr. Hunn is an abolitionist. To my astonishment, Mr. Hardcastle was an agent of the Abolition Society posing as a slave buyer. John Hunn would have been recognized in Dover. That's why they hired Mr. Hardcastle to do the bidding for the Abolition Society.

You should know that I was assisting runaways since Missus Leah and Nan died. I didn't plan for it but it just happened like things sometimes do. There's a plan that you can't see. God put me to use in my grieving. One day someone shows up at my doorstep and asks me to take care of two sisters running from Virginia. He gave me the name of a white family in Cantwell Corner and I brought them there. More were brought to me and I took them to other places in the Sussex and Kent where they were taken in. They were passed on from house to house, but I didn't know where they went to after that. They were on their way to freedom and I've been told that some get as far as the Canadas.

When I was in Wilmington with Mr. Hunn, I talked to my wife Rachel. Before we could decide what to do, the legislature passed a law for aiding a slave to escape a second time 60 lashes. Rachel agreed to join me if we went north. We are now residing in Weeksville, a community of free Negroes near Brooklyn. I am happy to be returned to my wife but I do miss the farm. I know I'll never see it again. I won't be seeing you boys in this life again either.

James, would you be so kind to send me the deed. I will arrange for the sale of Wise Choice from here. I can use the money.

May God bless you both.

Ever Your Uncle SAMUEL

Separation and Union

SHARPER

Stand in the Storm

FROM **GEORGETOWN** to Slaughter Neck and now on the wide beach, the wooden frame lighthouse sending its beam across the bay; his having moved at night from one house to another, one way station to another, safe-haven to safe-haven, and, at last, he's at the water's edge.

Horseshoe crabs have come ashore to spawn; the air is thick with the gable and stench of shorebirds feasting on the roe. Pipers, red knots and dunlins scatter as runaways, their feet nicked and bleeding, step on the tens of thousands of the ancient creatures that cover the beach. The refugees hold on to one another as they slip on the bird droppings. Wading into the lapping bay the band climbs out of the chilly June water and onto the sloop.

For two nights they have waited until the wind calms before the black pilot risks the trip to New Jersey. Two others are from Sussex and three are Maryland slaves. No one asks Sharper, a freeman, why he chooses to flee. On the far shore where the sun rises all believe lies sanctuary and salvation.

SHARPER HAD CONSIDERED the route through Blackbird to Wilmington and onto Philadelphia, but the Christiana incident was still on his mind. Although the resistance was several years past, Sharper believed the Negro self-defense association killing of Edward Gorsuch, the Maryland slaver and his posse that broke into William Parker's house to reclaim four slaves, made that network inherently more dangerous than the one through New Jersey.

When he was directed to Ben Webb's house, his first stop on the freedom road, Sharper recognized the operator's name, one bandied about with scorn by whites in southern Delaware. The epithets attached to the man were legion: 'amalgamationist' 'niggerite' and 'nigger thief.' At the general store in Laurel, he overheard others declaim for him to hear, he was certain, that Negroes couldn't trust him, that Webb tricked Negroes into thinking he was helping them flee. He detained them at this home with false hope so they would work for him without pay. When the work was done, he would call the marshal to return them to their owners.

Sharper placed his trust in those who dismissed such stories and who, instead, directed him to the Webb house.

As Sharper sat at the table for dinner on his first night of his passage, his only meal since leaving the farm, Webb bowed his head and quoted Deuteronomy, "I will not deliver unto his master the servant that hath escaped. Amen."

Listening to him, Sharper remembered Uncle Samuel and admired this man who didn't shrink from the prospect of a $1000 fine, months of imprisonment and enslavement.

A white woman, whom Sharper took to be Webb's wife, two other white men and a black woman were present around the table. When conversation turned towards the dangers Webb faced, he dismissed the concern.

"The penalty is small compared to that faced by this brave woman," Webb said, gesturing to the Negro woman at the table, her high cheekbones reflecting the candlelight, her hair parted in the middle and pulled tight, her mouth slightly pouted, as though ready to speak. "She is journeying in the opposition direction. From the United Canadas to Maryland. She made this journey twice before."

"For kin?"

"Her seventy-year old parents she's already brought to freedom. The last time she passed through she had her niece and her two children."

Whites in Sussex talked about Canada whenever near enough for blacks to hear depiction of the bleak country—snowdrifts as high as horses' heads, so cold that fire freezes, lakes frozen over until July. Sharper knew better from the boys' magazine; others knew that if whites were so intent upon diminishing Canada, it must be a promised land.

Sharper wanted to ask this woman if it were true that she had been there and that she planned on returning with her family, but she looked too tired to engage him and he let her go.

Rising to retire for the night, she spoke for the first time.

"Mr. Jones, there is one of two things you have a right to," she said firmly, "liberty or death. You is making the right choice. I see you ain't a boy no more. But God gave you strength in your limbs so you should be free." She reached into the folds of her dress and withdrew a small pistol. "You'll be free or die." She waved the pistol in front of him, then put it back in her dress and left the room.

When all were gone but for Sharper and Webb, the agent said, "From boyhood up to my manhood I've been taught that it is my duty to struggle for freedom. And you, Mr. Jones, are as desirous of freedom as I am. Duty, therefore, impels me to help you."

"Thank you," Sharper responded.

"You will find a bed in the adjoining room. In a few hours, before the sun rises, you'll leave." Webb gave Sharper a crude map and a pocket compass. "I'll give you the name of the person in Slaughter Neck in the morning. I won't write it down. If you be caught . . ."

"I understand."

"Do you have a weapon, Mr. Jones? Some of us ain't inclined to carry arms. But if you do, remember, slaveholders won't hesitate to kill you."

"I only have these," Sharper said, holding out his hands for Webb to see. "They have always served me well."

A magazine stood next to the bed, the page turned back: "If you come to us, and are hungry we will feed you; if thirsty, we will give you drink; if naked, we will clothe you; if sick, we will minister to your necessities; if in prison, we will visit you; if you need a hiding-place from the face of the pursuer, we will provide one that even bloodhounds will not scent out."

Webb roused Sharper before the roosters crowed. He handed him a bundle with food and a pair of shoes.

"I can do little more for your deliverance than pray, Mr. Jones."

"I bless you both and wish you a safe journey, Mr. Jones."

She handed Webb a small package.

"Tell the gentleman what to do with this," she said to Webb.

The door opened and Sharper saw the Negro woman from the night before step into the dark without a word.

The woman turned left on the road and disappeared; Sharper walked east, trying to remember the directions from the map he had been given.

"TAKE THIS," SHARPER SAID to the woman. "I was given this bread at the last stop. It has laudanum in it. Use it if you need to ease your child to sleep."

He heard only the susurration of water washing over a thousand horseshoe shells. The freedom seekers slept against one another for warmth, shared provisions and rationed drinking water.

Was the crossing taking Sharper to the land of liberty or were those preachers right who said that there is but one hope, O Lord, and it is reserved for heaven? Sharper prayed that shrouded night before the skiff set sail towards the distant lighthouse at Cape Island.

The asylum seekers huddled together as the pilot, a free black man, arranged the passengers to balance the single-sail boat. They pushed from the shore soon after dark and when the Delaware sand dunes receded into the distance, a humming filled the darkness, a melody Sharper knew from the camp meetings. He remembered the gatherings that lasted throughout the night, the pine knots burning on a fire table covered with dirt, the crackling wood gathered from the woods, the air filled with the smell of resin. Sharper watched a child who lay on her mother's lap rise and fall with each breath. The lantern light from New Jersey grew brighter as the skiff tacked across the bay. When one passenger began to sing, Sharper joined in the melody. A single voice sang, "My ship is on the ocean." He joined the response, "We'll anchor bye and bye." Again, "My ship is on the ocean." "We'll anchor bye and bye."

The voyagers' voices created a soft but urgent chorus:

> Stand the storm
>
> It won't be long
>
> We'll anchor bye and bye
>
> Stand the storm
>
> It won't be long
>
> We'll anchor bye and bye

The singing rose as the verse was repeated a dozen times, but grew softer still, then ceased all together as the long journey brought exhaustion and consternation. The sail billowed and snapped. The child trembled in the cold; she couldn't be consoled. The mother took the bread that Sharper had given her, soaked it in her saliva and fed it to the child. A man declared that he would jump into the water before returning to slavery. The pilot put his hand on him for reassurance.

Sharper wondered whether he had miscalculated. The soaring price gotten for Negroes brought South emboldened slave-catchers making every trip outside Young Man's Chance a genuine risk. While the Fugitive Slave Law strengthened the claws of slave-catchers everywhere, life in a slave-free state had to be better than that in Sussex where capture of runaways and the disappearances of free Negroes was common. But now, sitting in an open boat rocking in the broad bay, not a star to guide them, a stranger at the till, Sharper had second-thoughts about choosing to travel the underground instead of taking his chances in daylight with his freeman's pass.

As the skiff approached the New Jersey shore, Sharper heard the call of roosters; the sky began to brighten to a leaden day. The boat scraped across the bay's bottom and came to rest as the pilot furled the sail. The skipper pointed to the land and the passengers stepped onto the beach, waiting for their instructions. The dampness weighed heavily on them, wheezing and coughs issued from each passenger.

A thin black man in plain clothing approached the boat and handed a package to the pilot. He then helped turn the boat and pushed it back into deeper water. The sail unfurled again and the skiff headed back to Delaware.

"Welcome to freedom," a man awaiting on the shore addressed them. "This is the beginning of a fresh life. And to start, I've brought food for you." He kneeled and opened a bundle that he had placed on the ground beside him. "Take what you need." The voyagers remained silent and not yet relieved. "Don't be concerned. You'll be at a house on your next stop on your journey, wherever that may be, in a short while. Some may even choose to stay here in Cape Island. If there are any who want to remain, let me know. You can see a few of the hotels from here. During the summer, Philadelphians come here for their recreation.

Now the town is preparing for them; the hotels can use workers, both men and women. If you are literate, let me know. Meanwhile, there will be fresh clothes for you at the safe house. You'll receive instructions to the next stop."

Chills ran through Sharper and his body began to tremble. He hunched under his blue blanket coat; it couldn't warm him. Despite his hunger, he couldn't bring himself to eat.

As the group followed the man along the beach towards buildings built back from the strand, Sharper began to stumble,

"Do you need assistance? If you can't go any further, wait here and I'll fetch someone to help."

Not wanting to be alone and exposed in an unknown place, Sharper rejected the offer. After a few more steps, he collapsed.

"Come, help."

One refugee lifted Sharper to his feet.

"There's a cave over there."

Too weak to resist, the two men placed Sharper in the small opening that faced the ocean.

"I'll be back soon," the rescuer said.

The biting wind blew in from the ocean.

SUNLIGHT AWAKENED Sharper in a room unlike any he had been in before. For the first time in years, his eye ached and he placed his palm over it to calm its twitching. Bare except for a bed and chair, the room was no bigger than the master's bedroom in the main house at Young Man's Chance. Patterned paper partially covered the walls. The room smelled from turpentine, paint and cleaning fluids.

The man who had met him on the beach entered the room.

"You're awake. Good. You slept all day yesterday."

"Who are you?"

"Harris. Garret Harris. I brought you here. You don't remember?"

"No."

"I put you in a cave . . ."

"I remember."

"I went to get assistance and then brought you to here."

Sharper looked at him skeptically.

"I have clean clothes for you."

One shirt and a pair of trousers were folded on the chair.

"The others chose to continue on. They left last night," Garret said. "You weren't fit to leave."

The window was ajar and. Sharper heard the pounding surf and smelled the salt air.

"What was your destination?"

"New York. I am looking for Samuel Jones. He was a freeman caught helping slaves escape."

"Like you."

"Not like me. I'm a freeman myself. But in southern Delaware, it sometimes don't make any difference whether slave or free."

"But you said Jones was caught."

"He was auctioned. An abolitionist bought him and Uncle Samuel is now in New York."

Garret said that the Samuel Jones incident was well-known amongst railroad operators.

"Unfortunately, the abolitionist who bought and freed him was brought to trial himself. He was fined $4500 for aiding runaways contrary to the federal law. I understand that he is bankrupt."

Garret told Sharper they were in the Mount Vernon Hotel.

"I thought it was best to keep you by yourself until you recovered. There are no guests now. In July they will be coming from Philadelphia. We're getting readied for them. I'll take you to a Negro boardinghouse today, but before you leave, you may want to take a bath." Garret pointed to the room behind the closed door. "If you want to stay in Cape May Island, I can arrange for work here. There's a summer resort called Banneker House for the colored elite, but I work here."

Sharper listened.

"This hotel is maintained mostly by black men and women. The chambermaids, the waiters, the workmen. Come the end of June, there'll be a hundred of us. I work here year-round. Keep the grounds. And you. Can you do sums?"

Sharper nodded.

Garret thought for a moment, then said, "Me, I'd stay for a while. Comes September, you can go to New York with enough money you'll need to sew another pocket in your trousers."

Never having used a tub, Sharper declined to bathe before leaving with Garret. His benefactor took him down a long hallway to the office where a white man sat behind a large desk. Garret introduced Sharper to the secretary and after a few questions, the clerk offered Sharper a job. Sharper considered Garret's advice and took the work.

Throughout the spring and through the month of June, Sharper took inventory—plates, saucers, cups, cutlery, glasses, tablecloths, napkins—for the dining room seating 3,000 guests in what was advertised as the world's largest hotel. The work was easier than farm labor and the pay better. Garret brought him to the game room and taught him how to play games in the billiard saloon. Sharper enjoyed the camaraderie of the boardinghouse and Garret's friendship.

Occasionally he thought about James and having left him without a word, just disappearing. Soon he would write to him, he thought, and explain why he needed to leave as he did.

Many dreams disturbed him, his sleep troubled by apparitions. In one, his feet are mired in a bog while barking dogs pursue him, buzzards watch from a tree limb; in another, iron turns blistering red in a forge as a white man holds him fast.

One warm mid-week afternoon, as the sun hovered long in the blue sky, Garret stripped to his underwear and ran into the ocean as Sharper watched from the shore.

"Come on," Garret encouraged Sharper as the water rose and fell from his chest to his knees. He raised an arm and scrubbed his armpit.

"It's too cold," he called to Garret. "I'll bathe inside."

"Where you can roll your jelly in a little heat, I know" Garret laughed.

"I want to live long enough to see summer."

The boardinghouse, Sharper learned, mostly served as a stopover for runaways. Next to the rooming house stood Stephen Smith's summer cottage. A slave until 28-years old, Smith lived in Philadelphia, and now owned a coal and lumber company and held extensive real estate in that city and the Cape. As one of the wealthiest blacks in the country, represented as being worth $200,000, with a stud of horses and teams, Smith underwrote much of the cost of the illicit operation in the area.

Smith built the African church, which Sharper attended intermittently, when Garret roused him from his one day of rest.

"He and his partner Whipper use their railroad cars carrying lumber and runaways," Garret told Sharper as they listened to the preacher.

Although remnants of slavery existed in New Jersey—an old slave sat next to Sharper in church—and the fear of slavecatchers was real, the tone and direction of conversation in the Cape wasn't like what he had heard in Delaware. Few white men defended enslavement, he had heard no one resort to the Bible for justification. Since the half-century old law freed everyone born a half-century earlier, nearly every black lived as a free man and woman; the very air felt different. The question for Negroes wasn't whether slavery had any future but the method by which it should be expunged.

"We must be prepared at all times to meet the scoffs and scorns of the vulgar and indecent," the preacher sermonized, "the contemptible frowns of haughty tyrants and the blighting mildew of a popular and sinful prejudice."

The message was no surprise.

"If amid these difficulties, we can but possess our souls in patience we shall finally triumph over our enemies."

If the preacher hadn't been born a slave, Sharper would have found an excuse to leave.

"But among the various duties that devolve on us, not the least is that which relates to ourselves. We must learn on all occasions to rebuke the spirit of violence, both in sentiment and practice. God has said 'vengeance is mine, and I will repay.'"

Sharper remembered the woman in Delaware. The gun.

"Whoever for any cause inflicts a single blow on a fellow being violates the laws of God and of his country and has no just claim to being regarded as a Christian or good citizen."

At the tavern that night, as they sang and danced, drank and loved, Garett said, "Spare the rod and spoil the child. Who here hasn't felt a mother's rod? Do you believe she ain't a good Christian? Her duty was to raise you properly. The blows you received were righteous. It can't be right that our duty is to rebuke a single blow."

Sharper said it was vengeance that was unchristian.

"To protect yourself . . ." Sharper began.

"Yes, and bring the innocent to justice, protect them against unjust violence. Is justice an unchristian cause? Tell me Sharper."

Sharper put out his hand to quiet his friend.

"The truth, Garret, is I don't know much about what's Christian or not. I didn't come here to discuss these heavy issues. Come on. Play your banjo. We'll worry about the world another day."

BY THE FIRST WEEK IN July, many of the 500 hotel rooms were occupied. Sharper began to think he shouldn't have left the farm. His fears were exaggerated, he thought; he had never encountered a kidnapper himself. These thoughts were prompted by two unexpected factors: he worked from dawn until after dusk, mostly in the basement storeroom. He never thought he would miss the smell of the turned earth, walking bare-footed on the forest floor covered with smooth pine needles, the sound of an owl's hoot or sighting a terrapin while trapping with James; he preferred earth under his nails and callused hands to ink stains.

Steamboats from New York, Philadelphia, Baltimore, Washington and Southern points brought a thousand visitors a day to the cape. Sharper grew uneasy surrounded by so many white people and his anxiety multiplied when, for the first time since arriving in New Jersey, the demise of slavery wasn't taken for granted. Who was resorting, who was a slavecatcher? Sharper was glad that his tasks kept him far from the guests, but he found himself thinking about Uncle Samuel again.

There was a parade on the Fourth of July, with orations and night skyrockets. Hotel workers kept to their duties caring and cleaning for celebrants. The next night, in the boarding house section of town, a hundred Negroes gathered in the African church. The preacher spoke for an hour.

"Though the right to be free has been deemed inalienable by this nation, from a period antecedent to the Declaration of Independence, yet a mental fog hovered over this nation on the subject of slavery that had well-nigh sealed her doom, were it not that in the Providence of God a few noble spirits arose in the might of moral power to her rescue."

Sharper stood next to Garret by the towering oak tree.

"If they continue their injustice towards us, let us always decide that their reasoning powers are defective. In every case of passion that presents itself, the subject is one of pity rather than derision, and in his cooler moments let us earnestly advise him to improve his understanding, by cultivating his intellectual powers, and thus exhibit his close alliance with God. And in conclusion, felt it always be our aim to live in a spirit of unity with each other, supporting one common cause, by spreading our influence for the good of mankind, with the hope that the period will ultimately arrive when the principles of universal peace will triumph throughout the world."

As the gathering began to disperse, Garret stepped forward.

"On this glorious occasion," Garret said cuttingly, "I want to ask, what is the Fourth of July to a slave? We may be freemen, but what about the others? Abel," he said to the hunched man leaning on a cane, "will you ever see freedom? How long must the others wait for the blessings of liberty, those where each day the ropes are tightened and the lashes more frequent? What are we celebrating when our brothers and sisters remain in chains? I have here the answer, given by someone whose tongue is greater than mine and whose courage puts me to shame. Here's what he said when he was invited to celebrate this wonderful day last year. Telling white men what this glorious day means to the slave."

Garret unfolded a paper taken from his pocket. He read as he faced the gathering, his face pressed close to the clipping.

> *I answer, a day that reveals to him, more than all other days in the year, the gross injustice and cruelty to which he is the constant victim. To him, your celebration is a sham; your boasted liberty, an unholy license; your national greatness, swelling vanity; your sounds of rejoicing are empty and heartless;*

—he paused, took a breath and continued—

> *your denunciation of tyrants, brass-fronted impudence; your shouts of liberty and equality, hollow mockery; your prayers and hymns, your sermons and thanksgivings, with all your religious parade and solemnity, mere bombast, fraud, deception, impiety, and hypocrisy*

Garrett stopped, looked over the crowd and concluded—

> *a thin veil to cover up crimes which would disgrace a nation of savages.*

Sharper remembered the crime against Uncle Samuel. That night he and Garret sat on a jetty. The glow of gas lamps from the New Atlantic, Mount Vernon and other hotels faintly illuminated the strand.

"Do you fish, Sharper?"

"Not in the ocean, never."

"How about next week?"

A thousand stars filled the sky; water sloshed in the shingles.

"What you said today got me thinking. I can't stay here any longer," Sharper said.

"If you ain't safe here, you'll feel threatened everywhere. If you're going to go, go far. A delegate to the Cleveland Convention has made treaties with eight African kingdoms. Someone named Redpath has arranged to send coloreds to Haiti. New York's not far enough for you."

"It's not that. All these slaveholders here, I don't like it. But what you said, it got me thinking about Samuel Jones again. It's him I've come to see."

"So, you want to go to New York."

"Yes. I want to find him."

"Patterollers are everywhere, Sharper. You gotta watch your back when you surrounded by whites."

Sharper didn't need the advice, remembering many variations of a song he heard in Little Creek Hundred—

> *Run, black boy, run, patteroller'll catch you*
> *Hit you thirty times and swears he didn't touch you.*
>
> *My old master promise me*
> *When he died he set me free*
> *Now the old man dead and gone*
> *Left this black boy to shelling corn*
> *Run, black boy, run*

"Why not stay the summer? The hotel ain't finished yet. There's much to do here. You'll have work for the entire year."

"Maybe so."

"And I can use your help on the railroad," Garret told him.

Sharper stayed through August. One night he went with Garret to meet refugees on a skiff from Delaware. They stayed at the boarding house and at the house next door; they were gone the next day.

After taking inventory at the end of the season, Sharper packed his belongings and left Cape May Island, following one station to another: Springtown to Snow Hill to Timbuctoo; walking, hiding, secreted on a train, riding in carriages and wagons; taken by rowboat across Arthur Kill to Sandy Ground, his first stop in New York, where black oystermen welcomed him in their village.

Somewhere between the boardinghouse and Staten Island, Sharper's identification papers had disappeared, perhaps the night he slipped and fell into a swamp in the pinelands, a loss that he would have thought perilous before crossing Delaware Bay but now was merely bothersome, like his twitching eye.

The View From Crow Hill

DRESSED IN MILITARY BLUE, the Hannibal Guards, New York's volunteer colored company, marched across Hunterfly Woods' open field to the music of fifes and drums at the annual celebration of Haitian independence, on grounds owned and occupied by the black inhabitants of the village.

"They most certainly look like men today in their uniforms," Isabella, her white cuffs showing from under the sleeves of her cotton print dress, the hat ribbon brushing her neck, commented to Sharper. "They look like they're ready for battle."

"They do seem to enjoy themselves," Sharper responded.

Ten cars on the Long Island Rail Road brought revelers from downtown Brooklyn; others arrived by omnibuses from Flushing, Williamsburg and more distant places; steamboats ferried New Yorkers, while those from nearby came on foot to the annual celebration.

"Have you thought of volunteering?" she asked.

Sharper snickered.

"If you were younger," she said.

"You serious?"

"It's question. Yes. Would you?"

"I never thought about it."

"You have now."

Sharper's mood quickly soured.

"Then I'll give you an answer, Isabella. First, can you tell me what is it that they are defending?" Before she could respond, he continued, "It's not for their own country, for independence. It will be for the cotton merchants' who buy from slavers. That's what they would be fighting for."

There wasn't any argument Sharper could present that she hadn't heard at her own home. But Isabella had come to love Sharper and let him have his say.

"Do you know that the New York State Militia has rejected these lads from its service?"

"Yes," she said, "but that will change. if the time comes for that. If there's war."

"What will they be fighting for? Not for black men's freedom or a woman's dignity. The country is two-faced and we'll always be outsiders."

She hadn't come to the festivities for such talk. There needed to be some time away from the daily concerns.

"I'm more American than any slaver."

"Try to tell that to them and see where it will get you. Can you vote? Can I?"

Isabella knew the arguments as well, perhaps better, than her beau. Her father was, after all, an abolitionist who was at one time a fierce opponent of emigration but now maintained that full rights for Negroes in America was a forlorn hope.

As the guards marched closer and the cheers of the onlookers grew louder, Sharper and Isabella dropped their squabble. They stood with shoulders nearly touching as they watched the young troops parade and drill on the sunny afternoon in Weeksville.

When the parades ceased, they walked amongst picknickers, bought a nick-nacks from Negro vendors, saw several other parades and listened to orations by blind abolitionist William Johnson; the principal from Colored School No. 1; Rev. George Hogarth; and, lastly, Isabella's father, Junius Morel.

Sharper and Isabella strolled over to the game played by men wearing sporting uniforms.

Sharper had thought that after the picnic he would approach her father and ask for her hand. His plan was to purchase a small tract near Crow Hill. Lots near the Citizens' Union Cemetery, the Negro burial grounds, had been put up for sale. Since arriving in New York he had worked at New York restaurants and dug graves at the cemetery. Recently he worked at Crow Hill at one of the ropewalks, as a porter and keeping track of the hemp inventory as steam-powered machines spun the material into ropes for sailing ships. What Sharper found most foul was smell from the rat-rendering and fertilizer factories that ground the bones of pigs, cows and horses. And he hated the caws of the thousand crows that descended on the hill every day.

By now he had saved enough for the modest purchase of land, making him, a property owner. He would then become an eligible voter and full citizen.

As they sat on the grass, Sharper told Isabella of his intentions and why he would now have to drop them.

"I had the money and I go to pay them. Then they tell me they won't sell to me. Because I'm colored, they say."

Isabella reached for Sharper's hand and placed it in hers.

With the crack of the bat and jeers from the crowd, the long silence that had fallen between them was broken.

The loss of the game by the Weeksville Unknowns to the Henson Base Ball Club did nothing to dampen Sharper's spirits. If he were a few younger, he would have wanted to learn to play the game himself. With one bad eye, though, he knew he would never equal the prowess of those in the field. He was content to watch, puzzle the rules and applaud the skills of the black base-ball players.

"Did you enjoy the game?"

"I don't understand it much," she responded. "Tell me, why did he run around in a circle?"

"A woman can't understand . . ."

"Appreciate," she interrupted.

". . . appreciate the game."

"But I do like watching just the same. Some day you may want to explain it to me."

They found the Bethel congregants under the shade of an oak tree. The women had prepared the food and spread blankets on the grass.

After several jigs, a fiddle began to play a slower song, repeating the melody a couple of times. A woman began to sing.

"I don't know this song," Sharper said as he leaned into Isabella and whispered.

"It's a parlor song that is popular. Would you like to come to the next gathering to hear it again?"

Sharper nodded.

"I think I should like that."

When the song reached the second verse, Isabella and a few other women joined in:

> Let us pause in life's pleasures and count its many tears
>
> While we all sup sorrow with the poor
>
> There's a song that will linger forever in our ears
>
> Oh, hard times come again no more.

All the women, now standing and swaying, their bonnets tied under their chins, sang the chorus:

> c'Tis the song, the sigh of the weary
>
> Hard times, hard times, come again no more
>
> Many days you have lingered around my cabin door
>
> Oh, hard times come again no more.

HARPER HAD WANTED to be a citizen before beginning a family, but he questioned his reasoning when the picnickers dispersed. Why should this racial law stand in the way of his love? Why should he, a black man, be a property-holder to vote, a requirement not levied on white men? Clearly she would agree to be married to him. He resolved to approach her father soon.

After taking Isabella home, he went to the plot behind her house to gather vegetables to bring to his room. If he relied upon the largesse of others, marriage would wait, he thought, as he placed greens into a sack already filled with nuts and berries he had picked earlier. In the evening cool, he placed the bag over his shoulder and began to walk to his residence near the railroad tracks.

"You," the policeman called. "What's that you got in your carpet-sack there?"

Sharper's body tightened, as if ready to bolt. Uncle Samuel—that's why he had come North, why he had made his way to Weeksville (*"Yes, a Mr. Jones stayed here; his name wasn't Samuel but John. Left last year. Yes, with a wife; I can't remember her name; no, not Rachel. Fifty, about fifty, I'd say. He never told me and I didn't ask; the South, maybe, from the way he talked. Very, more than six feet, enormous hands, everyone remarked on his hands; broad chest. White hair, close cropped, no beard. Light-skinned. Don't know for sure, but I think maybe he said Elmira; somewhere in New York."*) Sharper didn't know his way through the tangle of brush, deep gorges or the way around Suydam's Pond to safety of a house elsewhere.

The police officer walked over quickly and pointed to the bundle. Sharper dropped the sack and opened it.

"Yours?" The officer with a brogue that Sharper had begun to identify with the police and thugs.

"Yes."

He looked at the produce.

"Where's your garden?"

Sharper said he rented an apartment and didn't have a lot of his own. He had gathered the nuts and berries at festivities at Hunterfly Woods; the vegetables came from a garden where had been given permission to take it by the owner's daughter.

"Darky, you can get fifteen days in the Flatbush Penitentiary for this," the policeman upbraided him.

"Take me to the house where I got this. The owner will vouch for me."

With Sharper standing beside him, the policeman rapped on the door.

Morel opened the door. Isabelle's father stood with his shoulders back and his chin jutting forward slightly. The jacket he had worn at the festival was removed but he still had on the checkered pants, white shirt and flowing silk necktie. The parlor light faintly illuminated the stoop. After a few words were exchanged between Morel and the policeman, Sharper saw Isabella and an older woman appear behind Morel.

"I told him to take the greens what he needed," Isabella said to her father, as the policeman emptied the sack's contents on the steps.

"The berries and nuts?" The question was directed at Isabella.

"We were the event today," she said. "We went to the woods to gather these."

"If you are saying you ain't accusing him of nothing, you can have him," the policeman said. "I don't need to take him in, if that's what you're saying."

"Yes, no need to do that," Morel said.

"There is one thing, though. There's a five-dollar bond needed to release him to you," the policeman added.

Morel stared at the officer. Sharper was a near stranger to him; he didn't know if he were a freeman or runaway. Slave catchers found the jails easy pickings.

"I saw you earlier today at the grounds with my daughter, didn't I?" Sarah Morel asked as she moved out from behind her husband.

"We were together, mommy," Isabella answered for Sharper.

"And I believe I see you at Bethel, don't I?"

"Yes, ma'am."

"Wait here," Morel said to the policeman. He returned shortly with the cash and handed it to the officer. The policeman didn't count it.

"Keep yourself out of trouble," the policeman said to Sharper as he waved a stick in his face. "Don't go digging in a place that ain't yours."

"Not bad advice from a white man," Morel said to Sharper as the policeman disappeared in the dusk.

Sharper thanked Morel and turned to leave.

"You aren't going," Sarah said. "Stay here for the night. When the sun comes up, you can leave. Isabella, fix him a bed in the parlor."

This wasn't the first time strangers stayed at Morel's home, Sharper learned. The Committee of Thirteen arranged for safe houses for hundreds seeking freedom, and Morels on several occasions used their own home as a refuge.

"As my esteemed colleague, Mr. Dalany has said," Morel addressed Sharper, "we are all slaves in the midst of freedom. We each choose whether we shall fly or whether we shall resist. He's right, of course. But today, dear fellow, isn't a day for choosing but celebrating. You don't need to do either tonight, Mr. . . . ?"

"Sharper Jones," Isabella interjected.

"Sharper," Morel repeated thoughtfully. "Well, I think, Mr. Jones, whichever course you choose, you need to consider changing your name. I told the census taker my name was Joseph Merrill, born in the West Indies, which is not true, of course. We can't be too safe from anglos, Mr. Jones. But for now, just rest. Just rest."

He had changed his name once before, he thought, but he wouldn't do it again. This was the name his mother had chosen and he would keep it. He had been arrested by the Irishman without offering his name. Whatever the additional risks he willingly assumed.

Before the lamp was extinguished, he glanced around a room far more modest than some others he had seen since leaving Delaware but one with the indicia of an educated family. Books and newspapers were neatly stacked one on another, from the floor to the windows. He stopped at a book still smelling from ink. The *Isaac C. Hopper: A True Life.* The author's name—it seemed familiar. L. Maria Child, but gave it no further thought. Inside was a familiar quote: *I was a father to the poor: and the cause which I knew not I searched out.*

Copies of newspapers—from Brooklyn, Boston, New York, and a half-dozen other places he never heard of—were amassed by the fireplace. The bold type at the top essay in one caught Sharper's attention: ARE YOU A MAN OR ARE YOU A BLACK MAN? Until then, the question had never entered his mind.

Sharper laid down on the ticking Isabella had placed on the parlor floor for him. He fell asleep with his arm draped over magazines at his side.

> *Flames lick his feet. He darkens to the color of cinders. His lank hair tightens into a tight mat.*
>
> *A voice says, 'And I saw those eyes in beauty bright, close on the flame's terrible bright.'*

James?

The more he tries to dampen the fire, the hotter it grows, the more scorching the flames. Something frizzles.

'Put it out, James. Please put it out.'

Where is he?

He is lost in the woods. He runs into black swamp water. A copperhead slithers by. The hammering of the woodpecker is deafening.

It still hurts.

A lighthouse beam shines and there is laughter on a distance shore.

'It's a joke. Can't you take a joke? It's a good story. Come on, burnt boy.'

Everyone else is laughing.

BELLE HADN'T NEEDED TO PLEA with her father. Morel readily agreed to his daughter's marriage to Sharper. One Sunday their union was blessed, followed by a Sunday School celebration, an event which was reported in the *Christian Recorder* by Morel himself, although he referred to himself in the third person and made no mention of the wedding.

> Four beautiful trees, tastefully hung with books and presents for the lovely children, graced the altar. The little ones being seated, the pastor opened the services, then addressed the scholars, then they sang, led by one of their own number. Mr. J.C. Morel, an old and experienced teacher of public schools, addressed them, illustrating the scientific process of evaporation in his peculiar and happy manner; the boiling of the tea kettle, being the example of the mode of evaporation, the sticking of your finger in the molasses, that of

adhesion, &c., then came the crowning of the queen of the school, a lovely, modest, and gentle little creature, who was presented and crowned with a beautiful white wreath, by Mr. Morell, and the scholars were rejoiced to greet their fair queen. After this came the distribution of presents. It was pleasant to see the children with smiling faces and sparkling eyes, receiving their books and presents as tokens of good conduct, they seemed happy in knowing that they have someone who cares for them. After this part of the exercises, they all retired to the basement, where the teachers had prepared amply for the comfort of the little ones.

Since Sharper had experience as a clerk, his father-in-law employed him at the new publicly-funded Colored School No. 2. Although he would make no more than the eight dollars at month he had been earning, Sharper seized the opportunity to leave noisome the vapors of Crow Hill.

It didn't take long after beginning his tasks at the school educating two hundred pupils before Sharper learned the lessons incidentally and within two years could understand even the most difficult texts in the Morel household, an apartment stuffed with abolitionist material, newspapers articles and proceedings from organizations and speeches by and about Morel himself.

Sharper and Isabelle were given an apartment on the upper floor of the row house. The family ate dinner together whenever Morel wasn't detained by his civic activities. He would sit with Sharper in the parlor, the two sharing cigars, Morel never without his silk tie, always proper even when away from the women.

"I'm really not from the West Indies," Morel told Sharper one evening. "Despite what everyone believer. Nor am I from North Carolina, as I sometimes claim. I'm from South Carolina. Truth be told, son, my mother was a slave and my father a planter." Lifted his chin and let out a puff of smoke. "Much like you, I suppose."

Sharper let the idea settle. Sharper wouldn't pry and Morel didn't continue or ask Sharper about his own background. Instead, he gave Sharper a copy of the *North Star,* an article signed Junius of Cedar Hill.

"A small cover," he explained. "You can read it if you like. This is the true story."

The piece explained he had been born on a slave plantation called Pembroke Hall. He left South Carolina on the *Olive Branch,* a ship captained by a colored man and whose crew was white.

> Captain Rial offered the first intelligible prayer that I ever heard. My father sprinkled and crossed and blessed, and he read prayers out of a large book in Latin and French, and kissed and caused me to kiss the picture in the book, but what of all that—what did I know about it? But when I heard Capt. Rial pray, I was amazed and lost in wondering.
>
> That prayer brought forcibly to my remembrance that I had often witnessed sufferings and stumbling and heard efforts made to pray as I have knelt down on the damp earth floor of the slave cabin, in the quarters where on the earth was spread a mat made of a species of flag, over which were a few rags and shreds. This we called a bed. Often at the side of such bed I have knelt down with a group of other little slave children, girls and boys, all in a State of nudity, while some kind old "auntie or uncle," groping in the thick mental darkness was aiming to instruct us in the Lord's prayer. Ho! the place, the group, the scene and the trembling embarrassment with the language of the instructor are so deeply engraven on the tablets of my heart's

memory, that neither space nor time nor place nor the change of position nor any other change saved reason or death can even obliterate it.

The following morning, at the breakfast table, Morel asked, "Did you read the article, son?"

"Yes, sir."

"You've seen such depredations yourself, I'm certain" Morel declared.

Sharper wouldn't say that his experience was different. He understood the truth of Morel's comment.

"I seldom talk about these personal matters. But you should know them about me. I've kept much of this from Belle, too."

"I know a little, poppa," his daughter said.

"I never told anyone what I'm going to tell you. Some things are best forgotten. Yet I can't expunge this incident from my memory."

Morel started and stopped several times, adjusting his tie, until he said, "I witnessed a husband, a man from a nearby plantation, forced to lash his wife because she refused the advances from a white man."

They waited for Morel to continue. He sat still with his hands folded on the table.

Breaking the silence, Sharper asked, "Do you hate the white man?"

Morel's mood shifted and his face lightened.

"Not hatred. Never hatred."

"But what you've witnessed with your own eyes," Sharper said.

"You've seen the white children in the school, son. They have equal facilities elsewhere, but they choose to come to me because they are treated with kindness." He explained that the Brooklyn School Board of Education was bothered by the attraction of the Colored School. "Those white men say it is unhealthy for black and white students to have an intimate relationship. They once ordered all white children to leave and enroll elsewhere. I've ignored them, son."

This was another example of her father's courage that Isabelle admired.

"Children are different than adults," Sharped said.

"Well, I'm going to hire a white woman as my assistant. I said this many years ago. You women have heard it: human rights aren't to be defined by either sex or by complexion."

Another night, as they sat in front of a fire, drinking coffee, Sharper, wearing the trousers from his teaching suit, raised the matter again.

Morel took a cigar out of a box resting on a mahogany table, touched a piece of lighted wood to the tip of the cigar and puffed until it glowed.

"Don't you think a white teacher lacks sympathy for colored children? Would she visit any of them in their homes?" He took the cigar proffered by Morel. "Could she love them?"

"I'd say most Caucasians are cold and treat us like ciphers. You are right about that. They don't have real sympathy for the colored man. I hate anyone who is unjust and cruel, son, no matter what race. Once there was a colored man near Pembroke who hunted runaways with a pack of dogs. I despised him."

"There also were white men who helped me on my way," Sharper said. "But . . ."

"And there are some righteous anglos," Morel continued. "I don't condemn a race. I work on committees with them every week. I saw a kidnapper beating a slave on the street. A man in a broad-brimmed Quaker hat put himself between the slave catcher and the poor man. That Quaker, who I later learned was named Isaac Hopper, was the first white man that I saw who pitied the colored man."

"The man who is the subject of the book in your library," Sharper noted.

"Yes. His daughter and her husband are keepers of our cause to this day. As I hope you will be."

"I plan on being a good husband," he told Morel.

"A good husband is a good man. And a good man does good for his and all people, son."

WITH ISABELLA CARRYING their child, Sharper thought about his own boyhood.

"*Dear James,*" he wrote for the first time since going north. He explained why he didn't tell him that he was leaving or where he had been, but now that he was settled in New York and had a wife, he wanted to let him know that he was safe. "*If at all you should have been worried be assured that all is well.*" Then, paraphrasing his father-in-law, he concluded, "*Perhaps when this great abomination with its tender Christian and republican cruelties are behind us, we shall see each other again.*"

Sharper made no mention of his initiation into an abolitionist family.

Pilgrim Fathers

CORNEILIUS DIED BEFORE his first birthday, the same year that consumption took Sarah Morel. The next child's grave marker read 'Baby Jones, one day.' Barcella cut his finger and died of tetanus before he was three.

When Isabella gave birth to Martha, it was uncertain whether Belle had any more chance of survival than did the Union, if Mr. Lincoln were elected.

"One of my colleagues," Morel told Sharper, "one of the Thirteen, is a physician. We sometimes meet in the back room of his pharmacy."

The physician, James Smith, opened the windows wide for circulation, gave Belle purgatives, bled her and fumigated the room. He ordered Sharper to stay away until the fever passed.

"You know, Junius, if your granddaughter is left without her mother, I will care for her at my Colored Orphan Asylum," Smith said to his colleague. "I'm sorry there's nothing more for me to do."

Many attributed the survival of mother and child to prayers

During Belle's recovery, black New Yorkers followed the fate of the captain of a slave ship seized by the African Squadron off the Congo coast.

"No slaver is ever convicted," Morel said scornfully to his son-in-law. "Not one—captain, crew, owner. Not one responsible for this abomination. There's no reason to think this will be different from any other time. Nine hundred on board. It's beyond imagining. So many. And there won't be a conviction, I assure you."

Sharper listened as Morel placed the *Daily Tribune* on the side table. The *Erie,* the newspaper reported, had been put up for auction by the US government.

"They'll sell the ship and nothing more. In forty years that the slave trade has been a capital crime. Not one, son, not one conviction. The government's always on the side of the pirates, not the side of black men and women. Of course, they won't hang him. Worse is done daily and see what action has been taken."

"Mr. Lincoln will be the difference," Sharper interjected.

"We'll see."

"He'll turn over a new leaf for the colored folks."

"*If* the slaver chooses to stay around for the trial. He's let out every night to gad about. Why does he return each morning? I ask. It's simple. Because everyone knows full well he'll be acquitted."

Sharper disagreed and Morel suspended his discourse, hoping that Sharper was right.

The *Erie's* owner and master had been held in the Eldridge Street jail since August. But after the inauguration of the new president, the Democrat-appointed judge and prosecutor were replaced by Republicans. Gordon found himself confined to the Tombs for a half-year before facing a new prosecutor now intent on enforcing the law.

"You'll see," Morel said, when the trial ended in a hung jury. "Even with the weight of the Republicans behind them, the government doesn't have the heart to hang a white man."

But the prosecutor wouldn't let the case go. He brought a new trial several months later and this time, after deliberating for thirty minute, the jury returned a guilty verdict.

Morel called the family into the parlor and read to them the comments of the judge as they were printed in the afternoon newspaper.

> **Think of the sufferings of the unhappy beings whom you crowded on the *Erie*; of their helpless agony and terror as you took them from their native land; and especially think of those who perished under the weight of their miseries on the passage from the place of your capture to Monrovia! Remember that you showed mercy to none, carrying off as you did not only those of your own sex, but women and helpless children.**

> **Do not flatter yourself that because they belonged to a different race from yourself your guilt is therefore lessened—rather fear that it is increased. In the just and generous heart, the humble and the weak inspire compassion, and call for pity and forbearance. As you are soon to pass into the presence of that God of the black man as well as the white man, who is no respecter of persons, do not indulge for a moment the thoughts that He hears with indifference the cry of the humblest of the children. Do not imagine that because others shared in the guilt of this enterprise, yours is thereby diminished; but remember that awful admonition of your Bible, 'Though hand join in hand the wicked shall not be unpunished.'**

Sharper felt hopeful, but his father-in-law sounded less sanguine.

"Read this carefully, son. Does Judge Shipman say we are equal to the white man or are we the race to be shown mercy? Which is it, compassion or justice? I know which it is for me."

Sharper wasn't sure on which side Morel really stood. He was equally uncertain about his own answer.

There was more conversation about Gordon, until January, when a letter reached the Morel household.

"Are you prepared to watch the execution, son?" Morel asked. "The government has sent invitations to certain individuals. I received mine today."

Sharper didn't know what to say except to ask, "Are you going?".

"None that I know want to attend. I'll arrange to have it passed on to you."

Pain pierced Sharper's eye.

"No, sir. Knowing about it is enough."

"I'm glad, son. The hanging is just, but it isn't a time for celebration. Let God be the witness, not black men."

When Morel brought home the March 8th edition of *Harper's Weekly,* he sent the others out of the room and asked Sharper to sit down.

"We both need to hear this. We didn't need to see a man die on the gallows but we should know about his final moments. Sit down, son."

Morel took a cigar from the box, twirled it in his fingers and placed it unlit on a tray.

The man was not sober—that is, so powerful had been the effect of the poison he had taken in an attempt to kill himself the night before that in order to keep him alive till the necessary moment, they had been obliged to give him whisky enough to make an ordinary man drunk three times over. He sat lollingly in the chair, gazing listlessly around, while the Marshal, with unaffected emotion, read to him the death-warrant.

After this he looked around with a senseless smile, asked for some more whisky, which was kindly given him. The procession was then formed,

> Gordon stalking with a bravadoish air, upheld by the Marshals, toward the scaffold.
>
> To a casual spectator it would appear that exhausted by mental or physical suffering, Gordon was making a great effort to walk manfully to his fate. As it was, however, he had just sense enough left to endeavor to follow out the suggestion of the well-meaning deputy, who told him to die like a man, and to walk to the rope, so that no one could accuse him of fear. When he reached the scaffold, he said, "Well, a man can't die but once; I'm not afraid." The cap was drawn over the whitened, meaningless features, the noose-knot was carefully adjusted under his ear, and he stood, an unthinking, careless, besotted wretch waiting for he knew not what, when with a jerk he went high in air, and fell to the length of the rope, still senseless, still unfeeling, still regardless of pain or pleasure.
>
> The body swayed hither and thither for a few moments, and all was quiet. No twitchings, no convulsions, no throes, no agonies. His legs opened once, but closed again, and he hung a lump of dishonored clay.

Morel picked up the cigar and lit it. He looked at the crackling logs in the fireplace and said, "The devil has gotten his due."

BEING A MOTHER OF AN INFANT didn't prevent Belle from resuming her community activities, not with the patriotic fervor sweeping the black communities following Lincoln's victory.

The Morels, like all their neighbors, hung a flag from their parlor window; from Brooklyn to Jamaica, Union banners fluttered atop roofs; red-white-and-blue bunting festooned the streets of Negro neighborhoods.

More than ever Belle wanted to lend her efforts to the causes that had engaged her before.

Sharper had other ideas: he wanted his wife to devote herself to her motherly duties. She countered that every hand needed to be lent to fight for justice.

She asserted, "Doesn't Father say that women's rights are human rights?"

"Yes, he does. But children also have the right to their mother, don't they?"

"Of course," Belle retorted. "But the meetings of the Abyssinian Daughters of Esther aren't far from here, at Mary Wilson's crockery and clothing store, on Atlantic Avenue," she said, as if Sharper knowing that Mary's husband was a member of the Thirteen would be enough to clinch the argument.

They settled on a compromise: she would meet the women at Mary's store only if it weren't feasible for the women to get together at her home.

The need to respond to the world around them became more compelling as it seemed that an economic catastrophe would befall New York and Brooklyn because of the Republican victory. Prices for goods plummeted as the South no longer bought New York's garments; hotels, once filled with Southern businessmen and vacationers, remained empty. Men, unable to find work, joined the army out of desperation. Dozens of young black men from Brooklyn volunteered to serve. In the early months of the war, the army accepted them as paid workers. Shortly after they were also accepted into the military but they weren't issued muskets and bullets or made officers.

By the fall, when the prospect of protracted war sunk in, the economy recovered as quickly and as sharply as it had fallen. Clothing and arms manufacturers couldn't keep up with the demand created by outfitting Union soldiers. Carriage-makers sold ambulances and military wagons as fast as they could be assembled, shipyards overflowed with activity. Several Weeksville men worked at the docks and the Hospital Annex at the Naval Shipyard.

While the war brought modest prosperity to Weeksville, mainly providing menial jobs in the region, it also brought an intolerable stench, a putrid smell emanating from Crow Hill's fat-rendering facilities. Operating 24-hours a day to process the carcasses from the New York's horse market, a trading center that bought and sold 100,000 horses the first year of the war, breezes that used to bring the scent of the salt air now brought a smell so foul that residents walked about with handkerchiefs to their noses.

The Daughters of Esther voted to continue their benevolent work with the burial society, but also considered several other recourses. Just the previous year Belle refused to participate in Elizabeth's fundraiser. She wouldn't endorse Elizabeth and her husband's support for John Brown's purchase of arms for an insurrection.

"You are all talk," Brown had accused abolitionists. "What we need is action—action!"

It wasn't that Belle disagreed with the necessity for action. It was clear to everyone that words were insufficient to soften the stonehearted. Neither did the commercial halls of sugar, tobacco, cotton and indigo have room for conscience. Belle also accepted that good works alone could never overturn the muck of slavery.

But the call for rebellion amongst slaves wouldn't lead to the death of slavery but to the deaths of slaves.

"What he is calling for is suicidal, Elizabeth. If wants to be a martyr, let him choose it for himself. But don't bring us along with him."

"He needs money, Belle, to do battle with that ugly foe, slavery."

"But a slave insurrection can't succeed. You must know that. It will only cause Southerners to become more brutal. John Brown is badly mistaken in thinking otherwise," she said.

But with the country at war, Belle had come to accept Brown as a hero. She, like every colored person of her acquaintance, agreed with Frederick Douglass's remark that Brown's "defeat was the hour of his triumph."

Still, Belle resisted Elizabeth's entreaties to throw their efforts behind the war. Belle shared her father's sentiments and stood behind the young men, who were being criticized by white abolitionist for not heeding the call to arms.

"*War is a reality*," her father wrote in defense of the scant number of black volunteers for the Union army. "*While there is no lack of patriotism amongst us, we won't leave our homes and families at wages of $25 per month, to fight rebel white men, with the prospect of dog's death should they be captured, all for that sum, without bounty at that.*" Morel noted that while New York found segregated street cars illegal, blacks still faced humiliation on them. "*There's no beauty or enough glory of dying for the privilege of riding in the Jim Crow car in 6th Avenue, or standing with the driver on 4th Avenue is not a sufficient compensation.*"

"You and your husband's involvement with the Colored Orphan Asylum is unsurpassed. I think we should continue with those efforts," Belle asserted.

Elizabeth countered that their charitable works could include both causes, but Belle convinced the other women to concentrate on the children's asylum, the stone building in New York that housed more than five hundred children. To stimulating giving, they decided to invite Elizabeth Greenfield, the Black Swan, to sing at an event they would organize in New York.

"Do you think we can entice her to travel to New York?" Bell asked. "I don't believe she has left Philadelphia in a number of years. She sings in her church but not elsewhere. It's a pity. I have never heard her but I understand she was magnificent."

"She sings like no one I've ever heard. I was present at her performance she gave years ago." She reminded the gathering that after performing for an all-white audience at Tripler Hall, the Black Swan apologized to the black community for what she had done and provided a benefit concert for the Home of Aged Colored Persons and the Colored Orphan Asylum.

"So, she might agree," Belle said.

"I understand she does occasionally perform benefit concerts, although they all have been in Philadelphia. I think that perhaps we may be able to entice her," Elizabeth said. She added that her husband, the minister of the Siloam Episcopal church, would prevail upon the Baptist minister of Greenfield's church to at least speak to her.

WITH THE ASSISTANCE OF MALVINA SMITH, whose husband was the doctor at the asylum, and other colored women from New York and Brooklyn, the Daughters' brought Greenfield from Philadelphia for the benefit recital. It had taken months to organize. By the time of the concert enthusiasm for war turned. The Union called Antietam a victory, but the slaughter of the Irish brigade left many calling it something else. The battle of Fredericksburg couldn't be called anything than what it was: a defeat for the Federal troops, not a battle but butchery, more than twelve thousand Union casualties. And when Lincoln issued the Emancipation Proclamation, the *New York Weekly Day Book* wrote that it degraded Irish laborers "*to a level with Negroes.*" Archbishop John Hughes said that "*we Catholics,* *and a vast majority of our brave troops in the field, have not the slightest idea of carrying on a war that costs so much blood and treasure just to gratify a clique of abolitionists."*

Taking the better part of winter to organize, the concert took place the summer after Lincoln's proclamation of emancipation of slaves in the rebellious states; the lottery conscription of white men for the army had just begun. Leading New York abolitionists, Republicans and older children from the asylum filled the 1,600-seat auditorium at Henry Garnet's Shiloh church.

Frances Harper, who had traveled with Greenfield for benefits in the past, opened the afternoon recital by reading her well-known poem.

> Make me a grave where'er you will,
> In a lowly plain, or a lofty hill;
> Make it among earth's humblest graves,
> But not in a land where men are slaves.
>
> I could not rest if around my grave
> I heard the steps of a trembling slave;
> His shadow above my silent tomb
> Would make it a place of fearful gloom.
>
> I could not rest if I heard the tread
> Of a coffle gang to the shambles led,
> And the mother's shriek of wild despair
> Rise like a curse on the trembling air.
>
> I could not sleep if I saw the lash
> Drinking her blood at each fearful gash,
> And I saw her babes torn from her breast,
> Like trembling doves from their parent nest.

I'd shudder and start if I heard the bay
Of bloodhounds seizing their human prey,
And I heard the captive plead in vain
As they bound afresh his galling chain.

Accompanied by piano and violin, Greenfield sang a medley that began with Beethoven's cavatina "Adelaide," included an aria by Verdi and the ballad "When Stars Are In The Quiet Skies," and ended with "Old Folks at Home," presenting the first verse as a soprano and the second as a tenor. Those who had heard Jenny Lind perform agreed that the Swedish Nightingale had nothing over the Black Swan.

With their spirits lifted by the inspiring and financially successful recital, the concert-goers emptied onto the streets where private carriages awaited. The Joneses had gone to the concert with the Gloucesters, but since Elizabeth and her husband were staying with the Garnets for the weekend, Belle and Sharper took the horse-drawn street car with the distinguishing pale green light to Grand Street Ferry.

At the ferry slip a group of white men, dressed in dockworkers' clothes, glared at them. Nearby stood a blindfolded man who pulled out an envelope from a drum shaped wheel. The person in the top hat took the envelope from him and removed a piece of paper.

"Thomas Quinn!" and received another envelope. "Timothy O'Brien, Dennis O'Neill, William Sweeney, Patrick Campbell," he called after removing the name from the envelope.

A dockworker pointed to the Joneses and jeered.

"What did they say?" Belle asked, afraid of the mean looking men. Four months prior Irish longshoremen refused to work with a newly employed black man. A mob set upon black laborers on berthed ships; others roamed the streets in search of Negro cartmen and porters, ceasing their rampage only when routed by the police.

"Something about the draft. Just ignore them," Sharper responded.

"Kill the damned niggers!" another man in the crowd taunted, waving his fist at the couple.

The men remained across the street as a soldier stood beside the draft wheel. Sharper helped Belle board the ferry as it pulled away for the Williamsburg shore.

"One of the men at work said to me the Irish spirit for the war was dead," Sharper told Belle as they stood on the deck, the East River cooling them on a muggy July afternoon. "He didn't want any part of it any longer. They're being cut down like wheat on the battlefield. He said that he didn't have $300 to buy a substitute, like those 'hypocrite abolitionist,' he said. 'What are we fighting for?' is what he said to me. If the slaves are free, they'll flood North and take their jobs, he said. 'Why am I going to fight while you Negroes aren't part of the lottery,' he said. He was angry at the president. He said he had Negrophilia."

Sharper watched the ferry approach the Williamsburg slip.

"I like this man, Belle. He's been nothing but good to me. But I'm afraid of what might happen."

A BLACK FRUIT VENDOR and a nine-year-old boy were the first to be attacked; the mob then stalked uptown to the Colored Orphan Asylum.

At 4 PM, on a muggy Monday, as sick children rested in their beds, babies slept in the nursery and pupils sat at their school desks, the rioters converged on the four-story building.

A lone white man standing on Fifth Avenue castigated the marchers.

"If there is a man among you," he chided, "with a heart within him, leave those poor children and help them."

Not moved by the stranger's plea for mercy, the mob turned on the stranger, long enough for the superintendent and matron to gather the children and usher them out the back door.

"About four hundred entered the house at the time, and immediately proceeded to pitch out beds, chairs, tables, and every species of furniture, which were eagerly seized by the crowd below, and carried off," Elizabeth reported at the Daughters' meeting the following week. "When all was taken, the house was set on fire. The firemen arrived quickly but they were too late. They couldn't control the fire. The building is completely gone. Ruined."

"What about the children?"

"The matron and superintendent rapidly conducted them out the back yard, down to the police station. They were kept there without harm. They couldn't be returned to the asylum, of course. They are now on Blackwell Island."

Belle told the others that in Weeksville they knew few details about the massacre in New York. They thought that they were soon to be attacked by a mob from Jamaica.

"We shut the doors to our homes and businesses, boarded up windows. We took whatever we could find for protection: pitchforks, shovels, knives, hammers, guns. But nothing happened. The gang never came. Or maybe there wasn't a gang at all, only a rumor."

Belle said that the day after the riots erupted, Mary Lyons, with her husband and daughter, stayed with them for a day after their home had been vandalized and her husband's seamen's outfitting store had been destroyed.

"All they had was the clothes they were wearing. They left the next day to take a ferry from Long Island to New London," Belle explained. "Mary said they would never return to New York."

The conversation returned to Elizabeth. They agreed that how everyone from the asylum arrived safely at the stationhouse several blocks away was a miracle.

But Charles Jackson received no such sanctuary: he was beaten and nearly drowned; nor did Jerimiah Robinson whose body they threw into the river; nor had William Williams whose chest they crushed, whose breast they stabbed, and whose body they smashed with paving stones; nor had coachman Abraham Franklin, dragged through the streets and hanged from a lamppost, then dragged once again, this time by his genitals. Chopped fingers and toes were kept as trophies. These names, these facts would come to light later. Now news came word of mouth.

Elizabeth said that she, her husband and two others were sequestered in the Garnet house for several days, too frightened to go to windows to look outside. But they could hear crowds and church bells, fire engines racing through streets. The smell of smoke seeped through the windows, which they kept shut despite the heat. On the third day, Reverend Garnet went outside.

"We told him not to go out. With his missing leg, he wouldn't be able to flee. He scowled and waved his cane at us. He said he needed to see things with his own eyes. He put on his pegleg and left. When he came back—I'd never seen a look on anyone's face like that before. I don't know how to describe it."

Elizabeth looked away from the women and sat still for what seemed to Belle to be five minutes before she continued.

"The reverend said, 'There were marauding bands dancing and howling around flames of burning buildings. There was a black man hanging while a demon in human form . . .' he could barely utter the words. He asked the women to leave the room but I could hear him from the next room anyway. The demon cut off pieces of the hanging man's flesh and offered it to the mob. He cried, "Who wants some nigger meat?' I was so sickened myself by what he said," Elizabeth concluded, "that I fainted and took to the bed for a day. I'm sorry."

She began to cry.

"I'm sorry that I'm telling this to you."

When military units that had been redeployed from the South to New York quelled the riot, one newspaper reported seventy-four dead, another put the number at 1,200. Three thousand blacks were left without shelter; Brooklyn's colored population swelled with those who permanently decamped to the city.

When the breadth of the event became evident, Sharper told his father-in-law that he was joining a self-defense association.

"In the Eighth Ward they defended themselves. They made the place too warm for the rioters."

Morel listened while Sharper continued a bit longer.

"It's remarkable," Morel said with an element of sadness that his children had never seen. "Whatever we think, our relations with whites is like a bubble on the ocean. It is destroyed by the first fierce storm that blows."

"Then you approve of being armed."

"We've seen where violence on our part has led us in the past. We are peaceable men." He laughed. "Just ask Mr. Lincoln. He thinks we're so peace-loving he won't give us arms to fight for his Union."

Belle walked in their conversation.

"Let us talk," Sharper said to her.

"No, stay if you want, Belle."

Martha wandered in behind her mother. Her grandfather picked her up and put her on his lap.

"In Flushing a group went to the Catholic priest. They told him that if the Irish threatened them again, they would burn two Irish houses for every one of theirs. And they would kill two Irish men for every colored man killed by them."

Belle listened to her father.

"Are you advocating vengeance?" Belle asked.

"I'm saying that if white soldiers won't or can't protect us colored folks, I'm with Mr. Douglass; it's time we had sable soldiers who will do it."

"But we don't have Negro soldiers."

"We will soon enough."

"Until then I'm with those in Flushing. I'm not going to let them take my family."

Morel dandled Martha and placed his hand gently on her head.

"Yesterday," Morel began, "I was at a meeting with the relief committee. Blacks and whites. Rev. Garnet said that when the committee completed its charitable work what the community needed was protection to obtain an honest living."

"Yes."

"The committee's chairman agreed. He talked about justice. Then he asked us to trust the white man as a friend. I could hardly suppress a snort. He talked to the whites there and said that there was no escaping the black man. 'They sit at their tables, they follow us to our chambers when we retire,' he said. 'What shall be done with the negro?' He asked. What should they do with us. That's what he wanted to know."

Belle reached to take Martha from him. The girl made it clear she wanted to remain with her grandfather. Morel kissed her on her cheek.

"But don't be rash or foolish, son. Before you stock up on ball and powder, we must study the use of arms for self-defense."

Sharper shook his head at Morel's moderation. "I'm not going to let this happen to us. Americans took up the fight two times against the British, to claim their liberty."

Morel took Martha off his lap, stood and rubbed the small of his back. He walked across the room.

"I agree with you there, son. Looking to the past for guidance is a good rule. But you need to know where to look. And how to understand what it is you find."

He walked to the window and drew in a deep breath.

"The example I look to is the pilgrims leaving their home to start again in colonial New England. And the Germans who left their homeland to come to start over again in New York. Why shouldn't the colored man follow in the example of the pilgrim fathers?"

Martha pulled on Belle's sleeve. She asked for a biscuit.

"Better than defending yourself here may be to hew out a nationality and reputation for yourself. Someplace where the accursed prejudices of the whites don't predominate over law and justice. Mr. Douglass says if colored men can enlist, they will disprove the slander and insults hurled at us. It will put us on a plane of common equality when we will be seen as nobly defending the liberties of our own country. I'm not convinced."

Sharper was taken aback by his father-in-law's pronouncement. In the past he was known as one of the strongest opponents of colonization.

"Are you serious about leaving?"

"The headquarters of the African Civilization Society has moved to Weeksville. I don't know if leaving . . ."

"To go where?"

"Honduras. Or where Negroes are already masters of their own fate, Liberia . . ."

"Which you once rejected."

"When it was a white man's scheme. Circumstances change. This is now under our control. Everything needs to be reconsidered."

"Will you go? Elsewhere?"

"Emigration isn't for everyone. I am simply asking you to consider every option, son. There is the Southwest. Canada. Taking up arms doesn't seem like the best option to me. We want homes more than anything else, owners of lands, houses and stocks. We must be equal to others in possessions and intelligence. I'm convinced so there will be mutual dependence and independence on both sides. Then there will be respect."

Morel rubbed his hands together.

"We can't expect this in the large cities of the North because our poverty and ignorance of commercial relations disqualify us to enter into the contest with any hope of success. We'll never be able to compete successfully in the big cities, get on equal footing. Rear Martha in industry and cleanliness, son, where she can feel that she is entitled to the same degree of respect and consideration as any other surrounding her."

Belle hadn't said a word during her father's discourse. When she and Sharper were alone, she said that she wouldn't leave her parents. But if he they were ready to migrate with them, she had no objection to starting over somewhere else.

JAMES

Lincoln's Toe

WHEN THE railroad opened a station in Laurel three years ago, connecting Sussex to Kent & New Castle, everyone had great expectation that the line would finally bring us out of our isolation. What little prosperity occurred was brought to an abrupt halt by the outbreak of the war. The carriage roads remain sandy, oxen still draw plows, & grains are still sown by hand, cut with sickles, & cradled just as they have always been. Our hundred is still the jest of the state.

Readymade clothes are hard to come by as I imagine they may be with you as there so many men requiring uniforms. I must rely upon homespun flax & wool for all my needs. I haven't had a pair of store-bought boots in two years. But I do have enough to eat. I subsist on my own meat, berries, vegetables, fruit, & flour. Of all the things I can't get, it's coffee I miss the most. I've resorted to sweet potato cubes as a substitute.

Although no battles have taken place near here, the war's effect weighs heavily in the hundreds. Many have it worse than I do. At least I resisted the temptation to invest in bonds, which are now worthless. I stopped counting the bankruptcies & abandoned farms. In this woeful picture, there is one bright spot for me. I thank my mother for the foresight in having planted fruit orchards. The trees are producing high-quality peaches, & the demand for the peaches from Northern canneries is more than I can meet.

James ends his letter by apologizing that he has taken so long in responding to Sharper and hopes his friend won't be as tardy in answering as he has been. Two months later, upon receiving a half-page response from Sharper, James writes again. He refers to the beginning of the war.

When Sumter fell, Southern sympathizers in Seaford fired their guns. There was a Democratic militia company in town, but a Union company was immediately formed. The Unionists pledged their fortunes & lives to the Star-Spangled Banner. Flags were raised & before the end of the year each town had its company of loyal men. They refused the order from Gov. Burton to transfer control of federal military equipment from Union men to Democratic secessionists.

I have bought pistols, a rifle-musket & bayonet for my own protection. Many of those in the vicinity around here are Southern sympathizers. Sons of some of the prominent citizens in Sussex have enlisted in the Confederacy. Negroes are terrorized by nocturnal visits. The Willow Grove Negro meetinghouse was burned last August. Secessionists stole muskets from the armory of the McClellan Home Guard in Smyrna. Supplies & medicines ship down the Nanticoke to be smuggled to Virginia by water.

At the last election fifty Federal soldiers were at each of the voting places in Kent & Sussex. An Englishman appeared in front of me without his naturalization papers. A soldier commanded the inspector to take his vote or he would smash ballot-boxes and the whole damned concern. But when I wanted to cast my ballot, the soldier in charge demanded that I take an oath of allegiance. I protested. One soldier raised his bayonet & said he wanted to" kill the damned secessionist." I asked for a Republican ballot & I agreed I would take the oath only because I valued the right to vote.

I am loyal to the Union, but its tyranny to require an oath to vote. The next week I was arrested under suspicion that I was smuggling quinine in fruit cans from Seaford to the Confederacy. Sergeant Johnson of New York was there with a private soldier in a Delaware regiment. One had a sabre & a musket. The sergeant had a revolver. They took me to the Laurel jail where I remained for the night. I was released in the morning. There was no talk of my taking the oath. I asked the jailer where I could send him some of my peaches for providing me with lodging for a night without charge. He looked astonished & didn't laugh.

Though the legislature has passed an act to prevent illegal arrests like this, the governor ignores the provisions of the state law & sides with the Federal marshals. Such is what happened to my friend Warren Rust, a school teacher. He is an advocate of State Rights which made him obnoxious to the Radicals. I don't agree with him on most political matters, this being one of them, him being a Democrat & all, but when I was arrested he wrote a letter to the Gazette against my detention. He questioned whether we lived under tyranny & oppression. During school hours two soldiers came for him without a warrant. They ordered him to dismiss school. They placed him in a dearborn & drove him to Felton Station.

My friend explained this in a letter to his wife he sent from New York, where he is in a military prison on an island in Brooklyn. I feel a duty to visit him. We haven't seen each other in a long time. I hope you will welcome me. I plan to come North in the near future.

BELLE HAD LEARNED ABOUT Sharper's life on Young Man's Chance as her husband related anecdotes from his boyhood, but when Sharper told Belle that he had written to James Preddy, she was taken aback.

"We were raised together," he said. "Like brothers. I never held any animosity. We worked the farm together. He paid me my wages. There was no cause for complaint."

Sharper didn't mention James' first letter and that he had thrown it away. He decided to tell her about the second.

"I received a letter from James Preddy," Sharper told Belle, holding a piece of folded stationery in his hand. "He's asked for my help in locating someone he knows. He says that he's in a military prison in Brooklyn."

"He wants you to help him find a Confederate soldier?" she asked incredulously.

"No. He says he isn't a soldier."

Sharper read the letter to her.

"Will you help him?"

"I'm suspicious that his friend is not as innocent as he says."

"You don't trust him?"

"James won't lie. It's his friend who may be lying. No one gets locked up for no reason."

Belle's eyes narrowed and she shook her head slightly.

"Well, no *white* man gets locked up for no good reason," Sharper agreed. He was uncertain about Rust's arrest.

"But Preddy believes him?"

"I don't know."

That night, in bed, as Sharper kissed her neck and ran his hand along her thigh under her cotton nightgown, Belle asked, "What will you do?"

Sharper kissed her as he reached for her breast. He thought briefly, then said, "No harm in locating him."

She stroked Sharper's flaxen hair and pulled him closer to her.

When through Morel's contacts they discovered that Rust was being held at Ft. Lafayette, on a reef in New York

Harbor, Sharper wrote to James. James responded with a telegram, saying that he would arrange to come to New York the first Sunday of the following month. Sharper told him where they would meet.

Sharper's right eye, covered with a patch, ached as he waited at the windy ferry slip for James. His sight had so deteriorated in that eye that it was best kept shut. He buttoned his jacket tight.

Was this James? he wondered, as a man with a valise, his hat pulled low, stepped onto the pier, his gait more deliberate than Sharper remembered, his steps nearly a shuffle.

"Sharper?" the passenger said to the earth-tan who stood erect with his hands behind his back.

James had grown older, Sharper thought, with deep creases from his cheek bones to his mouth and lines as dark as charcoal etched in his forehead. When his boyhood friend removed his hat, the wind mussed his thinning hair. Sun glistened on his bald spot.

"I've never been so cold as I was on the ferry," James said. He quickly put his hat back on. "It's good to see you again, Sharper. I dearly miss you."

"Yes," is all Sharper said as they walked away from the pier.

The two boarded the Long Island Rail Road, alighted at the stop near Sharper's home and walked to the house. James put his valise down in the parlor.

"This is my wife, Belle," Sharper said. "And my daughter, Martha."

Belle acknowledged the visitor with a curtsy.

"Bring Mr. Preddy coffee," Belle told her daughter. "He looks like he would like a hot drink You would like some, wouldn't you, Mr. Preddy?"

"More than you can imagine, thank you," he responded.

"And open the venetian blind, Martha. Let in some sun to warm the room."

Martha, staring at the visitor in her house, adjusted the blinds. Despite her grandfather's association with white abolitionists, this was the first Anglo she had seen in her home.

"Martha!"

The girl went to the kitchen and after awhile returned with a pot of coffee, milk and a bowl of sugar.

"Where are you staying, Mr. Preddy?" Belle asked, as she poured coffee into a white cup.

"At a boardinghouse he said," Sharper interjected.

"Yes. I hope you will help find one for me," James said.

"There are several Downtown that are suitable," Sharper offered.

"Will you be having supper with us?" Belled asked.

James looked at Sharper.

"Yes, he is, aren't you, Mr. Preddy?"

James ate little.

"I'm so tired from the trip," he said.

After dinner James presented Sharper with a package wrapped in paper. Martha looked on eagerly.

"A book," she said.

"Yes," James said. "When your father and I were boys, we liked adventure stories. So I thought he would like this one, a true story. I bought it in a Philadelphia bookstore on my way here."

Sharper handed *Arctic Explorations* to his daughter. Martha thumbed through the pages, looking first for the illustrations, just as her father had once done. Sharper looked on with her.

"It's all snow," is what Sharper said and he slowly sang: "O the winter O the winter, O the winter soon be over children."

Martha put the book down. This was a boy's story, she thought, and lost interest.

Belle insisted that James stay for the night. James sat by the fireplace. As he warmed up, he removed his jacket. He furiously scratched a red mark above his thumb.

"That." he said, as he saw Martha looking at his reddened finger. "I chased after a hog that ran off, but instead of me catching it, when I got into the woods, I was bit by a bat when I brushed against some leaves." James covered his hand in shame.

"Don't be rude, Martha," Belled chided her daughter who was staring at the stranger. When Martha had gone to bed, Sharper asked James about himself and the war.

"I didn't want to enlist. There is no one to care for the farm." He said that he had never married. As for the military, he said, "My name was enrolled but I wasn't called. But when we heard that Rebel forces were on the way towards Washington, we were alarmed. A party came to my neighborhood recruiting men to protect the state from the Rebels. We heard that Baltimore and Washington had fallen to the Confederates. It wasn't true, of course. But we didn't know it then. The Rebels were expected to be at Wilmington any time. So I joined. There was hardly enough time to receive a uniform. The scare passed. The emergency infantry was disbanded and I was mustered out in 30 days."

"There is my wife and daughter," Sharper said. "And as long as colored men's names aren't in the draft, I won't consider being part of the military. To preserve the Union for what? For whose benefit, James? Yours? Certainly not mine or my family's."

WITH A LETTER IN HAND signed by the U. S. District Attorney, who Morel had induced to intercede, James rode several horsecar lines to reach Ft. Hamilton, the command center for the fort in the bay. The guard escorted him to an office in a stone building in an inner courtyard. A lieutenant examined the paper, glared at James.

"You look nervous, Mr. Preddy."

"I am sir."

"You sound like a Southerner."

"I'm for Delaware."

"Then what's your problem?"

"I'm reminded of my service with the Delaware Seventh," James dissembled. "Memories."

Delaware troops had a high reputation amongst military men, having fought at Antietam, Fredericksburg, Chancellorsville and Gettysburg.

"The paper is in good order. I'm not going to ask why you're visiting that bastard. You know, the prison is across the channel, at Ft. Lafayette."

"Yes, sir, I know that."

He quickly examined James' carpet-sack filled with tins of biscuits and a wool sweater.

"Corporal, accompany this gentleman to the wherry." He turned to James. "You can see the traitor. The pass is for one hour."

James slung the bag over his shoulder as he followed the soldier down a flight of steps to the water's edge. James stepped on to the small steamer and was conveyed across the channel. A quarter mile in the harbor stood the casemated fort bulking three tiers high. James debarked and was led through the gate into the sandstone and brick fortress. The corporal delivered James to a cheerless Colonel Burke.

"You will meet the prisoner in the courtyard," the colonel instructed.

The grating of heavy iron doors echoed in the hall. There was the sound of shackles rattling. Rust was brought to James. The two met outside in the dank enclosure. Rust wore a light jacket worn thin at the elbows.

"Welcome to the American Bastille," Rust said, as James handed the prisoner the woolen sweater. "I feel like a cat in a strange garret," Rust said. In reaching to pull the sweater over his head, he revealed a suppurating cut. He thanked him for the visit. "When I heard the whistle from the steamer when it approached, wouldn't let myself be disappointed again. I had nearly given up hope that I would ever see anyone on the outside again."

James gave his friend several dollars when Rust said that if they wanted to eat anything palatable, they needed to pay for it.

"I won't bother you with the details, James. Needless to say, they would rather we were dead. Why they just don't kill us outright us I don't know. We will all be dead under these conditions."

"Can't you take the oath of allegiance?"

"Kiss Lincoln's great toe? I will leave with my conscience or I will leave on my back."

They had walked from one side of the yard to the other, following the sun.

"It's good to see sunlight," Rust said. "There are so many here that we are confined to our chambers all day. There is only a small hole for air. No candles are permitted."

Rust took an envelope from his trouser pocket and handed to James. "I composed it hoping that one day I could give it to someone. I was afraid that if I sent it from here, it would never reach its intended reader. It's an appeal for my release."

"I assure you, it'll be delivered," James said as he put the letter in the carpet-sack.

James showed the letter to Sharper when he returned to the house.

> *Fort Lafayette*
> *New York*
> *Feb. 13,1864*

To Hon. Abraham Lincoln, President of the United States:

Sir: I have been prisoner in this fortress for eleven months this day. Until this hour I am unadvised of any charge or charges against me, or of any special cause why I was arrested. My position is most painful and mortifying. In regard to my actions touching the questions at issue, I have nothing which I desire to conceal. I am a citizen of the State of Delaware, by profession a school teacher. The story of my private life, or of my relations, of blood, or social, cannot interest you just now.

From you, as Chief Magistrate and Executive of my Government, I have the right, respectfully, to demand justice. As a citizen, I would fain appeal to your humane and Christian sympathies. I am incapable of crime, or of pre-meditated wrong. I now respectfully request that I may be permitted to communicate personally with some one in whom you may confide, who shall be empowered to set me at liberty, in the event that he shall be satisfied that there is no just cause for my further detention. I trust that my motives in this communication will not be misapprehended.

The welfare of my country, and her restoration to unity, peace, and prosperity, have been the burden of my highest aspirations. I am not a criminal, begging for mercy, but a free citizen demanding justice, to know wherefore I am accused, and who is my accuser, to be confronted with witnesses against me, tried by the law, and by it be convicted or acquitted.

I have the honor to subscribe myself with due respect,

Warren Rust

"HE'S A DECENT MAN, Sharper. His wife is distraught and the children at his school are deprived of a good teacher. What has happened to him ain't right. I'm convinced he's innocent. He's nothing more than a school teacher taking a stand for liberty."

"Not for mine, if he's a Democrat."

James let Sharper's comment slide.

"What do I do with the appeal? If I post it, I don't think there's a chance in hell that it will get to the proper place."

"Let me take it."

James was reluctant to hand it to him.

"I found him for you, didn't I? I think my father-in-law will deliver it well."

"He's an abolitionist. Will he really do that?"

"I don't think you have a better idea," Sharper responded.

Sharper brought the letter to his father-in-law.

"What should I do with this? I told James I would give it to you. But I'm inclined to throw it away."

"I can't know what this man Rust thinks of Negroes or the war," Morel said.

"The restoration of peace and prosperity," Sharper said. "You know what he means by that."

"Do *you* want to war to continue? And don't you want better times?"

Sharper said he didn't want to help any white man who didn't stand for the cause of black liberation.

"You don't have to stand for him to stand for something that's right. If we want the government to deal straight with us, it must be straight with everyone. At least he is deserving of a trial."

Morel passed the letter on to the chairman of the Republican party in Brooklyn. Within a month he received word: Secretary of State Seward had written to the commander of Ft. Lafayette directing him to discharge Mr. Warren Rust on condition that Rust take an oath not to travel into any insurrectionary state, and not carry on any communication in the United States or any other country with persons disloyal to the Federal Government.

James didn't think Rust would agree to the stipulations. But it made no difference. Typhoid killed Rust along with fifty-three other prisoners before he could decide.

"THAT WAS THE KEY—one main reason for leaving, to talk to him, to understand him better. He risked his own freedom to help others."

"But why did you leave the way you did? You just disappeared. I didn't know what happened to you. No one did. No one had seen or heard from you."

"Well, yes, James, maybe I should have come to say good-bye. Something just took hold of me and I needed to go. But tell me, do you miss Uncle Samuel?"

"I've often thought about him myself," James said ruefully. "That terrible day, the last time I saw him. I've had night terrors about the auction."

They spoke deliberately, the silence broken by the jangle of a horse and cart, the whistle from the railroad, Martha's voice through the open window. They looked up as crows swooped across the clouded sky.

"His farm was sold last year, you know," James said.

"How did he arrange that?"

"I don't think he did. He wanted me to send him the deed to the farm. But when I went to the get a copy, the clerk told me that it wasn't on file. I protested and they escorted me out. I think it was confiscated."

"Who took it?"

"No one came to live on it, so I don't know. But selling it off is part of the scheme set up by the governor to get Northerners to invest in the state. Agriculturists, manufacturers. To improve the state."

"For the white man."

James shook his head.

"No, no, no. The governor's son died a Union man at Gettysburg. Our Senator, Bayard," James said contemptuously, "accused the governor of wanting to exterminate the white race. The governor's despised by the Democrats."

"Was Uncle's farm bought by a black man?"

"I don't know. No one's living there. I would have bought it myself, if I had the money. I've heard that it's being resold, though, to a Philadelphia lumber company interested in clearing the forest."

"Stephen Smith?" Sharper asked. "Is that who bought it?"

"I don't know anything about the sale except what I'm telling you. Only hearsay. But, say, Sharper, in his letter

Uncle Samuel said he was living in Weeksville. Did you find him?"

"I asked about him and thought I'd found a trace of him. But I'm not sure it was him who lived here. There was a Jones who came here from down South at about the time Uncle Samuel would have arrived, but people knew him as James. They said his wife's name was Mary. Was that her name?"

James shrugged.

"He stayed for only a short time. It could be him. I described him and they said it could be."

"Are you still seeking him?"

Sharper thought for a moment, his questioning visible on his brow.

"I haven't thought about him much since then."

Martha came out and joined the two men on the front steps.

"What are talking about?" Martha inquired.

"Someone we once knew in Delaware. Someone dear to us both."

"Is he dead?" she asked. "Did he die in the war?"

"No, not in the war. He's too old for that."

Martha asked a few more questions about Samuel.

"What happened to the Jones who lived here?" James asked. "Do you think it was Uncle Samuel?"

Sharper told him that he heard that Jones removed from Weeksville saying that he was going upstate, to Elmira. When Sharper asked his father-in-law about Jones, Morel said that Mr. Jones had been part of the underground.

"I think he wanted to be more helpful by being closer to Canada. I think it's him, Sharper. I think that's Uncle Samuel, I'm sure of it."

They remained on the steps until the cold brought them back inside. Belle brought them coffee.

"I think we should find him," James said. "How far is this place from here?"

When he was alone with Belle, he told her about the auction. After listening, she said, "You loved him, didn't you?"

"Yes. It's the reason why I left Delaware."

"Then you should try to find him."

"I can't just leave. What about you and Martha? The school?"

"You will never rest unless you see him again. It's only in New York. Martha and I will be fine. Go."

Sharper kissed her.

"For only a short while," he said. "I love you more."

Dust of the Earth

THE TRAIN CHUGGED THROUGH glens and mountain passes, the broad-gauge rail line hugging the upper Delaware River as the men traveled through the rugged country to Elmira. Before pulling into Port Jervis, a glistening black horse on the far side of the rapids kept pace with the passenger train, its head turned as though looking at the second carriage where the two men sat.

Sharper woke his dozing friend.

"A horse has gotten loose," he said.

James stood up to look over Sharper's shoulder. The horse turned and disappeared into the deep woods on the Pennsylvania side of the river.

The passenger in the rattan seat in front of them said that he must never have seen a bear before. It wasn't a horse.

"I know bears and I know horses. What did you see, James?"

"No doubt. It was a horse, no question," James responded empathically.

Beyond Sparrow Bush and Pond Eddy, the train stopped briefly at Shohola Station. A bag of letters was offloaded. What appeared to be a coffin was placed the rear carriage of the train. One passengers boarded with the box. Whatever chatter there had been ceased as the train pulled away from the platform. Throughout the compartment they heard whispered: "accident," "soldiers," "prisoners."

The train proceeded slowly, no faster than a walking pace, the cars snaking around bends and blind curves, the whistle a constant blast resounding in the ravines.

At King and Fuller's Cut, the women on the train looked away, the men removed their hats. Peering from the window they could see scrubby growth beginning to take hold on a long trench the width of a body, a fresh wound beside the tracks. Twenty yards away two dozen small Union flags leaned against fresh wooden crosses.

Hushed, broken conversation resumed as the train resumed its crawl.

"A thousand Rebs were being transferred from a prison camp down south."

"A bunch of prisoners escaped during the crash. Still not caught. Keep your eyes peeled for them."

"Head on with a coal train coming the opposite direction, I heard. The engineers couldn't see each other around the bend."

"These flags are flying over our boys, from the Invalid Corps—our boys. Fifteen dead, I heard."

"More," another added.

Sharper and James had difficulty piecing the story together. They wouldn't ask.

The train crossed the Chemung River. From their window they saw what seemed to be a thousand A-tents and dozens of barracks along the river bank; many more buildings were being erected.

"Do you want to join me?" asked an alighting passenger.

James stumbled on the train steps and Sharper caught him by the arm before he hit the ground. James coughed as the fetid air drifted from the prison lagoon used as the camp latrine and garbage pit.

The din of hammers and saws filled the air.

"No," Sharper responded.

"We're looking for a friend," James explained.

"You and *him*?" the passenger asked incredulously, looking briefly in Sharper's direction.

"Yes," Sharper said. "Me and him."

"Maybe your friend is one of them up over there." The passenger pointed to a wall across from the depot, ignoring Sharper. On a rampart scores of men, women in their walking dresses, and children pressed shoulder to shoulder looked on to an event on the field.

"I've come to see this for myself."

"Is it a county fair?" James asked. "A game? I heard about base-ball"

"They play that game in many prison camps. But no. Here the prisoners are the sport," the passenger laughed. "The traitors are arriving thicker than mosquitoes in a summer swamp. Every day they shuffle in by train. The Union can't keep up with all the Rebs they're catching down in Virginia, so they are sending them up here."

Sharper tugged at James' coat sleeve, urging him to leave.

"Must be meal time, that's what they're watching, feeding prisoners," the passenger said. "I've been told they eat rats. It's only 10 cents to go up on the viewing stand for the entire day."

James looked at Sharper.

"Ten cents more than I want to spend on watching dogs," Sharper said.

"If you're lucky, you can see one hung by his thumbs."

A church bell rang, then another.

"Horseheads!" a gig driver announced. "All going to Horseheads!"

"Pine Valley! Mills Landing!" another called from a larger conveyance parked across the avenue.

Stagecoaches waited in front the Brainard House Hotel.

"Ithaca," a stagecoach driver announced.

While the men decided what to do, a commotion erupted across the street. A neatly dressed tall black man, berating another, raised his hand and hit his adversary, knocking him to the ground.

"You good-for-nothing." He rebuked the younger black man and severely kicked him with several blows.

The older man lifted his opponent from the ground and, grabbing him by his jacket lapels, drew him up close.

"Get out of here! If I see you again . . ." he slapped him across the face and shoved him away.

None of the many witnesses intervened to stop the altercation.

As the humiliated man ran off, the tall man, straightening his jacket, placed his hat in his hand and crossed the street.

Sharper and James approached a stage driver and asked after a Samuel Jones. The driver suggested they check with the hotel clerk. The clerk knew Jones and told them his house was on the main road north of the hotel. As they stepped into the street, they were accosted by the black man who was entering.

"Sharper?" the man asked in astonishment, as he examined Sharper's eyepatch to make sure he had the right person. "Is that you, Sharper?" He looked at Sharper's companion. "And you James?"

James looked at the elderly black man.

"I can't believe it. Lord have mercy!" The barrel-chested man dusted his jacket and stared at the two men.

Sharper and James looked at the gentleman in front of them. This man's pate reflected the sun, but he wore the same tight beard they had once known so well. Although he stood slightly stopped, he still towered over them. His narrow eyes, egg-shaped head, broad chest—

"Uncle Samuel?" Sharper stuttered.

"Yes. Yes, that's me," the man said, his voice cracking with emotion. "Same person. Different name."

"Uncle Samuel!" Sharper exclaimed, doffing his straw hat.

"I call myself John now, since coming North. But it is me. And if you please, call me by that name you know me by."

James stood astonished. Sharper reached for Samuel's arm.

"Are you all right? You look all right," James said.

"I'm fine, boys. I may be older, but . . ." Samuel stopped and looked at both men carefully. "What are you doing in Elmira?"

James said they had coming looking for him. Later they would provide the details that had taken them on the journey.

"Who was that man? A thief?" James asked.

"No," Samuel said. "Well, yes, in a way. A liar and a thief."

He explained that the man he had just given a beating to came to Elmira pretending to be a runaway.

"A few others have done this before. They're scoundrels, taking advantage of the goodwill of people. They bring shame to us." He began to declaim his displeasure, but shifted his remarks. "But enough of this. What are you doing here?" he began again in amazement. "I can't believe it. Sharper. James. My, oh my, oh my."

"So you are safe!"

"Yes. And with my wife. We've been here for several years."

They stared at one another. Tears trickled down Samuel's cheeks. James placed his hand on Samuel's shoulder while Sharper took the old man's hand in his.

"Then you must come to my home with me," Samuel insisted.

"A hotel will do," James said.

"No it won't. Not for the two of you. Come with me."

James and Sharper followed Samuel several blocks north from the prison camp on the river, to the home of the man they knew as Uncle Samuel.

THREE STEPS LED TO THE porch of the weatherboard house beside the Baptist Church. Tall windows framed either side of the door of the yellow building.

Samuel invited the men to sit.

"Rachel," he called as he went out back. He told his wife that two men he had known as boys in Delaware had come to visit and would staying for several days. Accustomed to visitors, Rachel quickly began preparations for their stay.

"Yes, that was me in Weeksville," Samuel said in answer to Sharper's question. "My wife and I remained for only a short time."

Sharper and James sat on a cushioned sofa in the living room. Rachel brought out plates, cups and saucers for sassafras tea, and butter for the dozen Johnny Cakes. Modest furniture filled the main room; a hooked rug covered the floor in front of the fireplace against which rested a musket.

"Today is fish day," Rachel said as she joined the men. She straightened her apron and fixed her gray braided hair neatly on her shoulders.

Samuel insisted that the companions stay for at least a couple of days. James weakly protested; Sharper readily agreed.

"Rachel came with me to Philadelphia," Samuel explained, as his dunked his cake into his steaming tea, "but that was too near to Delaware for me. I went north and people told me about a black man's village in Brooklyn. The underground was well organized there. When I arrived, there was a lot of talk about emigration and colonization. Rachel was against going to Liberia, so I thought about Canada, where I could live free and not live in fear each day that I would be sent back down South. So, I packed to go to where the law would protect me, not threaten my dignity."

Samuel told them that when he reached Elmira, he decided to stay.

"I could do a lot of good here," he said. His big hand enclosed the cup as he lifted it to drink. "There were others on the railroad to work with: Mr. and Mrs. Langdon, Dr. Smith and his wife, and others. Some who weren't part of the railroad sided with us. The judge defied the law when a caught woman was brought to court by the slavecatcher and the judge ignored the Federal law and secured her freedom. That's when I began to arrange for people to take the 4 o'clock train out of Elmira. Hide them in with the baggage. Most made their way to Niagara Falls and crossed to St. Catherines. Across the border."

Samuel didn't tell them that he had arranged passage for nearly 1,000 runaways nor that many stayed with him and Rachel, in the addition he had built onto the rear of the small house.

Rachel encouraged the visitors to take more cakes.

"A few stayed around this neighborhood. Most went on. 'O, old master don't cry for me, For I am going to Canada where colored men are free.' But Rachel and me, we stayed. A Mr. Still, an abolitionist, gave me land in the Adirondacks—not just me but many of us—so I could be a property-owner and vote. But the land's not good for living on." He put down his cup of tea. "Which reminds me, James, I wrote to inquire about my farm down there, to get my deed so I could sell it."

"Oh, I wrote back. But I never heard from you."

"I never received a letter from you. I must have already been away from Weeksville when it arrived."

"I did inquire. But no one could find the deed."

"Must have been confiscated," James said.

"No matter," Samuel replied, as if used to dealing with deceit. "I don't need the money. There's enough to be made here."

He told them that the house belonged to the church.

"I'm the sexton. I've always used my hands and even today I'm good at it. I keep the church in good making and repairing. I also get paid by the city when there's a fire and I ring the church bell as the alarm."

This didn't seem like a lucrative enterprise to the companions.

"I also bury the dead."

At dinner, Sharper broached the subject of the gun.

"I organized a society for the purpose of protecting ourselves against slave-catchers prowling through. We're encouraged to keep them for our self-protection."

"Did you ever use it?"

"No. But one time I did think I was going to need it. It had to do with four escaped slaves from Maryland. One of them was an old man not in good health. They didn't stay in Elmira but went to Canandaigua."

"Canada?"

"No, a town in New York on a lake north of here. Well, many months after we put them on the train, the old man came back with a white man. He was being kidnapped and taken back to slavery, we thought. Sandy Brandt, Jefferson Brown and me, we went down to the Brainard House Hotel where they were. A large crowd gathered. I had my gun with me. There must have been a hundred of us, real angry, demanding that the old man be released."

"You got back his freedom," Sharper said.

"The story ain't so straight. The sheriff came to keep order. Brandt, Jefferson and me, we went into the hotel with the sheriff to rescue the old man. We talked to him. He said that he hadn't been captured by Mills and he wasn't being forced to return to Maryland. He had written to Mills, his master, asking him to come get him. He *wanted* to return with Mills. It was his choice to return to slavery."

"He had to have been forced into saying that," Sharper insisted.

"He convinced me. The others, too. We all believed him. He said he couldn't take care of himself up here. He was too old. The other three he came with all left for Canada. He was alone. And he said he never felt such cold before. I know what he means about that. After talking with him, all of us decided that he was a sincere man, I had no doubt.

"We went outside to tell the crowd what we found out. But it didn't matter. They weren't going to let anyone go back to being a slave, even if that was his choice. It was a near riot. A bunch trooped to the train station to make sure they didn't board. They were going to rescue him no matter what. That's when I was glad I had a gun."

"You always told good stories, Uncle Samuel."

"This one is a true one."

"Then what happened to the old man?"

"Never saw him again. The sheriff had taken Mills and the old man out the back door and took them in his carriage to the next station, Southport, to wait there. The train stopped at Elmira but the old man and Mill didn't get on. That's when we realized the trick. A few ran after the train as it pulled out of the depot but they couldn't keep up. It crossed the bridge and was gone."

"What did you think, Uncle?"

"I feel sorrow for a man who thinks slavery is the best life he could have."

Later, after their dinner of cabbage soup, perch fried in lard, stewed apples and countless reminisces, James and Sharper continued the conversation as they lay side-by-side in the extension.

"I don't want to talk about it no more," Sharper said.

He pulled the coarse blanket to his shoulders.

"I miss you, Sharper," James said. He turned on his side and looked at his companion in the dim room. Sharper continued to look at the ceiling without a word. James touched Sharper's cheek. Sharper could feel his warmth breath on him. He brushed his forehead with his lips and placed his leg over Sharper.

"Stop, James. We're not boys any longer," Sharper reproached his companion, pushing James' leg aside. "Be a man."

James turned his back to Sharper. James' fever rose again, his muscles felt weak, and his feet and hands tingled. James hardly slept but when he did, it was filled with confused, roily dreams.

THE FOLLOWING MORNING, a spade over his shoulder and carrying a pot of ink in his other hand, Samuel walked a short way with the two men to the cemetery. They stood surrounded by dozens of freshly dug graves. Shortly after they arrived, a military wagon drawn by one horse stopped in front of them. Coffins piled in three rows of three on the back bed of the wagon were lowered to the ground. A corporal handed Samuel papers and several cardboard boxes containing belts, buttons, letters, regimental badges and other personal items.

"So many deaths in the prison?" James asked.

"More and more. They're now brought here most every morning. With the weather turning soon, there's bound to more sickness."

"How can there be so many dead?" Sharper asked.

"Let me tell you: there was a dog in the camp to keep the rats down," Samuel said, "but the dog was killed by one of prisoners because having rats around was better than having nothing to eat."

"But the soldiers have rations."

"Not these soldiers, Sharper."

James bent over to read the inscription on the cross on the grave next to him.

"These are Confederates!" James exclaimed.

"Help me with this," Samuel said.

Samuel looked at the number on a coffin, found the paper stuffed in a bottle with the corresponding number and the description of the items associated with the body. Samuel then inscribed the name, rank, regiment in a meticulously kept book—Pvt. William Franklin, 59th Virginia Infantry. Next, he took one of the many urns resting on the ground and put the soldier's belongings in the container.

James stepped forward and helped Samuel lower each coffin into a separate pit. On top of the freshly dug graves Samuel placed the urns.

Before leaving the cemetery, Samuel stood at the foot of the last grave he covered and offered a short prayer: "The day is past and over, the morning bright. The toils of day are over. We thank Thee heavenly father, What'er I do, things great and small."

"How could you, Uncle?"

"What should be done, Sharper?"

"Bury them, if that's what you want to do. But me, I would let them rot and be eaten by dogs. They're not men."

"They are."

"They're wolves in men's clothing. If you want to bury them, do it. But not like this. They don't deserve any honor."

"I understand you, Sharper. We've known many bitter things, the two of us."

"At their hands."

James shifted uncomfortably, then stepped away from the conversation.

"That I don't know about these men. I also bury Union soldiers. And what do I know about them? There are abolitionists amongst them, but many didn't have the money to pay their way out of the draft and have no count for us any more than the ones you despise." Samuel reached for Sharper's elbow. "Many of the prisoners at the camp have violated every commandment of God and conscience. But not all, Sharper. There are those that got dragged along, foolish perhaps or maybe they had no choice. Maybe some were caught up like the old man I told you about yesterday."

"You're more forgiving than me," Sharper said. "It's not the same as that man. He was too scared and didn't know what else to do."

"Some of these soldier, too, they're too scared to think for themselves or to hear their conscience speak to them."

"Why are you apologizing for them? No one's forced to put on a uniform and pick up a gun to defend slavery. If they were forced, then they're cowards. It's better to die yourself than enslave another human being."

"I have this verse in mind to keep my own honor: You know it?" Samuel began to recite: "'And many of those who sleep in the dust of the earth shall awake, some to everlasting life, and some to shame and everlasting contempt.' They arrive covered up, they can't tell me anything. I can't converse with them. Who believed what? Who was a decent man and who was craven? I can't tell them apart, so I honor them all, not to overlook those who are deserving. The Lord will sort this out, not me, Sharper. I can't judge and neither can you."

Samuel didn't tell them that when he began his duties at the cemetery, he came across a soldier named John Rollins, from the neighborhood of his own birthplace. Samuel wrote to contacts there and learned that Rollins had been the son of the overseer on the plantation where he had been born. He remembered him as a pleasant boy and now was arranging to have him buried not in Elmira but at his home in Virginia.

On their return to Samuel's home, James took Samuel's shovel from him and carried it. He asked how he could do such hard work, digging the graves and all.

"My hands hurt," Samuel acknowledged, "but the burying soothes my pocketbook."

Sharper and James looked at Samuel in surprise.

"What?"

"I get paid for this duty. $2.50 for each one I bury. There are thousands in the camp, being replaced every day. One comes in to Hellmira on his own two feet and another goes out on his own back. I calculate that at the rate they are turning over, by the end of this war I'll be a rich man."

Later, after they reached the house, had eaten dinner and retired to the living room, James asked Samuel to tell them a story.

"Preaching is the stories I tell these days."

Sharper joined James in the entreaty.

"We can't go without a story."

They recalled a few he had told them.

Samuel massaged his brow. After a long pause, he leaned forward in his chair, planted his feet firmly on the floor and began.

One day Brother Cat and Brother Rat, they finds a big piece of cheese in the kitchen cabinet. The two never be friends but they not be enemies either. So they steal a big piece of cheese together but they can't agree on how to divide it.

They call on Fox to judge between them.

Fox, he agrees. He come and look at the cheese.

"Wait," he says to Brother Cat and Brother Rat. "I gwine be right back."

Fox, he run off and come right back carrying a scale. He set the scale down and put the cheese on it. He take out his knife and cut off a big piece.

"This piece is for the judge," Fox say and put it aside.

Then he weigh the cheese again and he cut off another slice.

"This piece for the judge," he say again.

He done this two more times and by then he take most the cheese.

When he hold it up his knife again to cut another piece, Brother Cat and Brother Rat, they both call out, "Hole on, Judge. This thing is wrong. You are going to to take all our cheese and leave us none."

Fox, he is very vexed and he holler at them, "Out of here. You both are lying thiefs, and you going tell *me* how to do justice? Good for you I only take the cheese and let you go with your lifes. Be grateful I don't kill you both."

With that, Brother Cat and Brother Rat, they leaves.

Then Fox laugh and eat up all the cheese by himself.

The following morning Samuel walked with his visitors to the train station. As they stood on the platform, he turned to Sharper.

"God gave you strength in your limbs so you should be free." He told him that he could arrange for property in the mountains, but it was wilderness of never-ending winters with snows higher than the tops of houses, a place he himself had chosen not to live. "But a young man could maybe make a go of it, Sharper."

Whether he could support himself and family on a farm in the Adirondacks didn't matter to Sharper.

"A black man isn't made for country with so much white in it," Sharper joked. "In Sussex there's milk, some sweet, some sour stirred in with the coffee."

They talked about the war, which they all agreed had come to favor the Union.

"Slavery'll soon be done with," Sharper said. "I'll be able to live my life in peace and quiet. Unmolested."

"Don't let your optimism drag you like a greasy bone in a dog's mouth," Samuel said.

James quiet, at a loss for words, leaned against the station wall.

"The war's going to end and the abomination will end with it. But for treating us like men, that's only a hole in the cooking pot of hate. The hole'll be plugged up before the hate's drained."

James leaned forward and said, "Then why are you staying? You could go to Canada."

"Yes," Samuel said thoughtfully, his eyes seeming to have gone distant. "I sometimes think about going, more when I first got here than now. But I'm useful, serving God and men. I don't know if I can do both in Canada. Listen to what I say, boys. Emancipation is nothing without respect and only you can give it to yourself by giving it to other people, dead and alive. Cutting leg irons off is only half the emancipation."

The two returned by train to New York in thoughtful silence. As they waited for the ferry in Jersey City to take them across the Hudson, James said to Sharper, "I don't understand one thing, Sharper. Why did the cat and the rat just let the fox get away with it?"

Sharper slowly shook his head.

"It's an old story, James. But you don't understand nothing, James. Nothing."

HIS FATHER-IN-LAW'S ADVICE was no different than Uncle Samuel's: a free man needs to be free from others, to rely upon himself and God by returning to the soil.

"I was at the annual meeting of National Convention of Colored Men just recently," Morel said to Sharper after his son-in-law's return to Weeksville. "We passed a resolution calling on our men to settle the public land. I support the sentiment. There's no gain to be made by remaining in the cities."

"You're here," Sharper responded.

"I've often thought of leaving. But I've concluded that I can do more good at my school. It is the only place where colored and white children sit down together, where there's no difference in what they learn, where the education colored and white children get is equal."

"But you think I should take Belle and Martha to a farm."

"Believe me, if I was younger, I would seize the opportunity. Owning your own land where you smell the dirt that's yours is best way to be a free man. The yoke of slavery may soon be broken, but there's more that keeps a man down than shackles and whips."

And there was James beseeching Sharper to come back to Delaware where they could take up the farm together.

"It is all but certain that the ordeal of this war will soon come to an end," he wrote from Young Man's Chance. "The farm can use you. Peaches have much potential and with your assistance I believe this can be the most prosperous farm in the hundred. I beg your consideration and look forward to having you join me."

Perhaps his father-in-law was right. What was he to do in Brooklyn? He could continue at the school, but as a self-educated man he would never be as successful there as was his father-in-law. Sharper examined his hands, which had grown soft. Self-reliance, as Morel urged, was the freedom he sought.

"I've never lived on a farm," Belle said. "There is much I like about city-life. But Father has persuaded me that owning your own land is an honorable thing."

"Then you also think that I should return to Delaware."

"There are other places. Long Island. There's a village that's a stop on the railroad, an hour away. Black farmers and proprietors live there."

"No. If it's farming that I'm returning to, then I'm going home."

Belle said she would go wherever Sharper decided to take the family.

"Think about Martha," she said.

Sharper suggested that their daughter could be left with her grandfather until she finished school. The Morels didn't object to the idea.

"Sharper needs to be his own man," Morel told his daughter. "Let him do what he thinks best. A new world is borning, Belle. It's at hand. Can't you feel it?"

Belle thought about what she would be losing but stifled her concerns. It would do no good. Sharper had made up his mind.

Deferring to her father's judgment as she often did, she told Sharper she would stand with him, whatever he chose, she said, her body quivering, her eyes swollen red and raw.

"I need to see for myself," Sharper said. He would go to Delaware and if the prospects were promising, he would bring Belle down to join him.

"Where's Father going?" Martha asked when they watched the ferry cross the river to Manhattan. "When will he be back?"

"Soon," Belle said. She hugged her daughter. "Let's go home and help grandma. And you need to get ready for school tomorrow." She took her by the hand and walked to get the train back to Weeksville.

The Lame Horse

THE QUESTION IS SIMPLE.

"Did you kill Mr. James Preddy?"

"Yes sir," Sharper says.

"You needn't say anything," Sharper's defense lawyer advises him. The lawyer turns to the judge. "I am entering a plea of not guilty, your honor."

"What did he say?" Acting Judge Ben Sturgis asks the state's lawyer.

Sturgis struggles to take down the recording himself in these irregular proceedings.

"Speak up, boy," the prosecutor insists. "The court wants to know. Did you kill Mr. Preddy?"

"Answer Mr. Fisher," the judge, demands, ignoring Sharper's previous response and the lawyer's interjection of 'not guilty.'

Sturgis had before him a signed confession that had been solicited the day of the shooting. The sheriff convinced Sharper that if he wrote what had happened, the justice would look favorably on it. Sharper had nothing to hide and, distraught, put his signature to the document without reading it.

The coroner's inquest, also before the judge, corroborates Sharper's description of the murder.

Sharper's counsel speaks up again and is overruled by the judge. The lawyer remains quiet for much of the rest of the proceedings.

Although Sturgis received his law degree three decades earlier, he has practiced his profession in a desultory fashion, accommodating those who seek him out for small matters. He prefers overseeing his farm and practicing the life of the gentry that had been passed down to him. Men more ambitious and younger than he had left the hundreds, to join as military officers with one side or the other. Two of his sons, both killed in combat, had been officers in the Confederacy. He keeps his criticisms of the Union to himself.

With those more qualified than he to act as judge—and there should have been a total of three to hear a capital offense—, Sturgis presides over the case that should have been heard in a Court of Oyer and Terminer. Everyone agrees that given the inevitable outcome that would be an unnecessary expense and inconvenience. Still, the citizens of the county want to present some semblance of propriety and good order. With little persuasion, Sturgis agrees to provide the stamp of legality, glad to enforce justice and the law as he knows it.

THE DEBASED CONDITION OF *the farm shocked Sharper when he had returned to Young Man's Chance—buildings in disrepair, fields gone to weed, implements rusting and broken. Scarcely an animal roamed the grounds, the land untenanted, except for James. Only the orchards seemed cared for and as far as Sharper could tell, the peaches were James' sole source of income.*

The creeks and sandy lanes, the forest sounds and swamp odors, knowing the best place to put down his net, the time to sow and the time to reap—all this he had deeply missed.

But Sharper's father-in-law and Uncle Samuel were only partly right: it wasn't just a matter of owning land that made a person free; it was also a question of numbers. In the lower county, there were so many Negroes that he could feel at ease and take it up as his own. Shaper had forgotten what it was like to be surrounded by so many Negroes. Once he left the train in Laurel, he realized how much he had missed Young Man's Chance and Wise Choice. Even in Weeksville, an island in a white sea, he had often felt estranged.

Not Haiti, not Canada, not Liberia or Sierra Leone, not the beckoning West but the southern hundreds; not a black or white man's land but his *land, a man's.*

A COURTROOM HAS BEEN HASTILY assembled; no one thinks it is necessary to travel to the county seat to find a proper venue. The general store will do. Windows are cracked open to allow for circulation. It is cold outside, as this had been the first winter in recollection when chamber pots froze over, although the first spring flowers have already made their appearance and the sounds of mockingbirds can be clearly heard. A pile of wood rests next to the unlit cast iron stove.

The justice sits on a stool behind the wooden counter. A candy jar and cuts of tobacco and cigars are pushed to one end; cough drops, salt, sugar and medicines occupy the cubbyholes behind him. On the floor are washbowls and pitchers and against the wall rest farm implements. Horsewhips hang suspended from the beams. The room smells mostly from cured tobacco leaves.

Before the war, the room would be packed for a trial such as this. Today, except for Sturgis, Fisher, and the defense attorney who stands next to the accused, the bailiff brought in from Mud Creek, and the store's proprietor, the makeshift courtroom is empty.

The prosecutor repeats the question.

The defense attorney objects that the prosecutor is badgering the defendant. He is overruled.

No jury had been impaneled. Sturgis makes some notes that he would submit if he ever receives such a request but he expects none. Everyone is too exhausted, too consumed with what comes next, how to recover, how neighbors are to reconcile. The colored folks stay at home. They, too, are worried about what comes next.

Having recently finished his apprenticeship with a lawyer in Dover and needing the experience, Fisher has agreed to serve the court without a promise of a fee for his time. The experience of defending a client, even as a case in which the conclusion is as forgone as this one, is worthwhile for him since he had no military experience to bolster his resume.

Lawyers, like everything else except summer mosquitoes, are scarce in the state's southern counties. Perhaps if there were some question of fact, some ambiguity surrounding the death, some matter of law, there would be an effort to find proper representation for Sharper and someone to take the record and file it amongst other county documents. As it is, the region has become depopulated over the last several years, as the war dragged on and most men had gone away and many women gave up the farms to move in with relatives in the towns. Court records are a mare's nest, so not having one for this case is of no concern as far as Sturgis is concerned.

"I did," Sharper responds, repeating what he had said earlier in the week.

"With this gun?"

Sharper looks at the revolver.

"It seems like the one," he says.

"Is this the one you used to shoot Mr. Preddy or isn't it? Answer the question without equivocation, Sharper."

Sharper stares at the gun held by the lawyer whose left leg had been amputated at the knee. Although he is only a few years older than Sharper, Fisher looks like he is nearing old age; his thin hair is white and heavy skin droops under his eyes. Sharper doesn't know him. The prosecutor has been brought in from Red Lion for the trial.

"I think so."

"Is this or isn't this the weapon you used?" the justice with spiked eyebrows and unruly hair asks from the high stool from behind the counter. He cupped his ear to hear.

"I want to be truthful, sir."

"Yes."

"But I'm not certain that this *is* the gun. I want to answer the question you asked. There are a few pistols in the house. They look much alike to me."

"Yes?"

"To be precise, sir, it looks like it, though, this one."

The judge wobbles on his stool as he leans across the counter to look at Sharper and says, "Mr. Fisher, we have gotten what can, I should think, from this wretched boy. Would you please move on?"

Sharper means to tell the court in his own words why he killed James but he isn't asked. No matter. Whatever he would say, it won't matter. No reason is mitigating. Every house is a home of desolation; the losses are too many to innumerate.

Sharper doesn't dispute the truth of the accusation.

"I am a free man," he says to his lawyer, "but I am guilty of the skin that I ain't in power to control."

"What did he say?"

"Nothing, your honor."

He says to Sharper, "It is best to keep quiet."

"WHY YOU'VE COME, Sharper?" James asked angrily.

"What?"

"You've runaway. Why do you want to come back here? What do you want?"

Sharper was nonplussed by James' questions. Only two months before, when James left New York, he had encouraged Sharper to purchase a farm near Young Man's Chance. And the previous day, when Sharper arrived, James had greeted him warmly and talked excitedly about their joint venture.

James reached up and pressed his hand over his own throat as he swallowed hard. Sharper hadn't paid attention to the dark circles that ringed James' eyes. Sharper looked at his friend's arm festering with blisters.

"What are you saying, James? You encouraged me . . ."

"Burnt Boy, my faithful, friend," James said in an unctuous voice. "My beloved darky."

James muttered incoherently: freedom papers; Wise Choice; a sale; a lame horse.

"Something's wrong in your head. You don't make sense, James. I'll get a doctor."

'**WHO SHOT YOUR LEG OFF,** Mr. Fisher?' Sharper wonders as he looks at the prosecutor standing before him, but he knows the answer wouldn't matter, either, whether the shooter was young or old, defending his home or severed by a cannonball because that's what happens in war—shoot when ordered, stand and be shot at.

Fisher has a few more questions for Sharper. Sturgis asks several. The court won't let Sharper testify in his own defense—blacks can't testify against whites, according to the law and Sturgis has determined that's exactly what it would be if Sharper is allowed to speak.

The trial lasts less than an hour and concludes before noon. Being of sufficient capacity, reason and intelligence, Sharper is found guilty of first degree murder.

JAMES PICKED UP A GUN that had been resting on the table. He began to raise it.

'Don't run. Don't scare him. Avoid eye contact.'

Sharper slowly turned his body sideways. He glanced at the door but remained fixed to the spot. He hoped James wouldn't smell his fear or hear his frightened heart.

"Kill the lame horse. Come on, you bastard. Shoot me." James held the gun at his side.

He motioned to another pistol that lay on the counter. He told Sharper to take it.

"You remember the lame horse don't you, Burnt Boy?"

Sharper wouldn't respond.

"You won't steal my farm. You come like you're a free man. But you're not. Just a darky. You think you can do whatever you want. You can't."

James continued to rant without sense.

"The Almighty has drawn the line of distinction between the black and white races" James wiped the corners of his mouth. He squeezed his eyes shut for a moment.

"You're not going to impugn my honor. I assure you, it won't go unchallenged. Pick it up. The gun. It's loaded." Sharper didn't move.

"Sable brother, I won't let you insult me any longer. Pick up that gun." James wiped the spittle from the corners of his mouth. "I'll walk over there. And you'll take your paces to the other wall. I will count to three and we will shoot."

Sharper finally blurted, "You want to duel?"

"Like a gentleman."

James turned his back to Sharper, took several paces across the room and turned around to face his old friend.

Sharper had remained unable to move.

James held the gun in his swollen hand and pointed it at the ceiling.

"One."

"Stop it, James!" Sharper blurted.

The door was too far.

"Faithful, patient slave, pick up your gun."

"Put yours down, you fool."

"Two."

"This isn't a proper duel. Where is you second? We need seconds."

"Three," James said as he lowered the gun and pointed at Sharper.

Sharper grabbed the pistol on the counter and squeezed the trigger.

SHARPER IS TIED TO a post and the sentence is carried out the following morning. He is strung from the loblolly pine beside the stable down the street. The bailiff arranges the noose and hoists Sharper from his feet. He cuts him down after Sharper stops kicking. The body lays on the ground until after noon, when many turkey vultures circle in the gray sky.

The hundred's farrier and blacksmith brings his wagon around to the side of the barn and without help lifts the stiffening body onto the bed. He drives the corpse to Cypress Swamp where he dumps it to decompose in the brackish water.

Before the war there would have been other witnesses to the hanging, a crowd from the surrounding neighborhood eager to see a malevolent Negro swing. No doubt there would be an article in the Georgetown newspaper, most likely on the front page, and maybe even a mention in Philadelphia's *Public Ledger.* What would have been an incident of considerable note before the war goes by without notice.

Two deaths unmourned, one placed in a shroud under a headstone at a church near Horseys Pond, the right thing to do however nominal Preddy's religious observance may have been; the other body eaten by fishes in water stained the color of honey by the tannins of rotting trees.

Justice Sturgis remembers reading in a law book the case of Catharine Bevan who had murdered her husband in New Castle, in 1731. Tied to a stake with a rope around her neck, to be consumed by flames after being hanged, the kindling at her feet spread quickly and, as he recalls the passage, a fire "broke out in a stream directly on the rope around her neck, and burnt off instantly, so that she fell alive into the flames, and was seen to struggle therein." A crowd, described as both eager and fearful, witnessed the scene.

Sturgis believes Sharper deserves no less a punishment than Bevan's but thinks better of it. Such barbarism, once common but now eschewed by decent people, has resurfaced on the battlefield. Death isn't anything to celebrate no matter how heinous the crime and however deserving of the gallows the evildoer might be. As an Episcopalian, Sturgis believes that the Christian thing is to swiftly bring down the sword of justice, thereby letting others know that such violations would not be tolerated, not even under the calamitous circumstances as had descended upon them, but it will be done without display.

While Sturgis only has contempt for those churches and ministers in his denomination that have declared for the

Confederacy, he isn't an abolitionist himself. His warrant is simple: maintain the union and everyone's proper place in it.

The war has let loose demons thought to be long banished and the magistrate will do what is in his power to keep the threads of civility from coming thoroughly unraveled. Charity could be restored when peace returned, if he does his duty. A guilty verdict, a quick hanging and prompt disposal of the body without the benefit of clergy—that much is in his power.

On Sunday Benjamin Sturgis and his wife are driven in his carriage to the Christ Church, where he worshipped his entire adulthood.

The priest prays: "O God, from whom all holy desires, all good counsels, and all just works do proceed; give unto thy servants that peace which the world cannot give; that both, our hearts may be set to obey thy commandments, and also that, by thee, we being defended from the fear of our enemies may pass our time in rest and quietness; through the merits of Jesus Christ our Savior."

Abner drives Sturgis and his wife home in their carriage immediately after the service. Before retiring for the night, Phebe sits in the glow of a kerosene lamp, places the concertina on her lap and sings: "'Tis the song, the sigh of the weary/Hard times come again no more."

"Such an echo of sadness," Sturgis says. "Can't you sing something more cheerful?"

Phebe folds the sheet music, places the concertina in its resting place and retires to her bedroom.

Sturgis removes a copy of his will from a storage box and reviews it; he recalls the will that his father had left: Abner and Hessy, who were children at the time, were given the opportunity to choose their own master upon their master's death. They had chosen Benjamin Sturgis.

Sturgis revises his will: upon his death, Abner and Hessy are to be emancipated and are to receive his ewes, cows, two horses, household goods, his favorite gun and all his acres. The two have been with him his entire life and have served him for more than thirty years. It is right that they join the other Negroes in Delaware who are free.

FUNDS TAKEN FROM PREDDY'S *estate paid for James' burial. With no heirs to inherit the farm, this seemed a reasonable disbursement after the auction was completed and all the creditors paid. The farrier, who had transported Sharper Jones' body to the swamp without charge, demanded payment for his service. Mr. Fisher can't be located.*

Most of the congregation of the local church dispersed after the war and the abandoned building collapsed from neglect. During construction of a highway a half-century later, a worker came upon a stone with an illegible inscription. Taking Preddy's gravestone as a mile marker from an old road, the worker tossed it into the pile of rubble in a ditch that eventually got covered over with creeping vines.

Delaware's 900 slaves were emancipated soon after the end of the war, but it wasn't until 1901 that the Delaware Assembly ratified "certain amendments to the Constitution of the United States," and removed slavery from its own books. Four years later, it abolished the use of the pillory, the last state to do so.

At the turn of the millennium, during construction of the Plantation Assisted Living at Willow Grove, a backhoe uncovered the foundation of an 18th century house. Less than a hundred yards away, two female skulls buried under a midden of oyster and clam shells are uncovered. There is a trough with bones from several individuals—a burial pit for slaves, archaeologists surmise.

Where We Started

Remnants of the once extensive cypress swamp are now a state park, home to the worm-eating warbler and the brown-headed cowbird.

BIBLIOGRAPHY

Although this is a work of fiction, several anecdotes related in the book are based on real events. Below are the sources that help make the novel as accurate as possible. However, as in any creative work, I have taken liberties by altering some of the places, people, and dates.

Abrahams, Roger D., *Singing the Master: The Emergence of African American Culture in the Plantation South*, New York: Pantheon Books, 1992.

Allen, William Francis, C. Ware and L. Garrison, *Slave Songs of the United States*, New York: A. Simpson & Co., 1867.

Bell, Howard H., "The Negro Emigration Movement, 1849-1854: A Phase of Negro Nationalism," *The Phylon Quarterly*, Vol. 20, No. 2, 1959, pp.132-142.

Berlin, Ira, *Slaves Without Masters: The Free Negro in the Antebellum South,* New York: The New Press, 1974.

Bruce, Susannah Ural, "Summer of Irish Rage, *America's Civil War*, March 2009.

Child, Lydia, *The Juvenile Miscellany, Vols. II. III*, Boston: Putnam & Hunt, 1829.

_____. *The Frugal Housewife,* Boston: Carter and Hendee, 1830.

———. *An Appeal in Favor of That Class of Americans Called Africans.* Boston: Allen & Ticknor, 1833.

Clark, Ellen McCallister and Emily L. Schulz, *Delaware in the American Revolution: An Exhibition from the Library and Museum Collections of The Society of the Cincinnati,* Washington, D. C.: Anderson House, 2002.

Crimmins, John Daniel, *Irish-American Historical Miscellany: Relating Largely to New York City and Vicinity, Together With Much Interesting Material Relative To Other Parts Of The Country*, New York: private publication, 1905.

Dalany, Martin, R., *The Condition, Elevation, Emigration, and Destiny of the Colored People of the United States, Politically Considered*, Philadelphia: published by the author, 1852

Dalleo, Peter T., "The Growth of Delaware's Antebellum Free African American Community," http://www1.udel.edu/BlackHistory/antebellum.html

David, Johnathan C., *Together Let Us Sweetly Live: The Singing and Praying Bands,* Urbana and Chicago: University of Illinois Press, 2007.

David, T. J., *A Rumor of Revolt: The "Great Negro Plot" in Colonial New York*, New York: The Free Press, 1985.

De Cunzo, Lu Ann, *An Historical Archaeology of Delaware: People, Contexts and Cultures of Agriculture*, Knoxville: University of Tennessee Press, 2004.

Douglass, Frederick, "Oration, Delivered in Corinthian Hall," Rochester: Lee, Mann & Co., July 5, 1852.

Drimmer, Frederick, ed. *Captured by the Indians: 15 firsthand accounts 1750-1870,* New York: Dover, 1961.

Essah, Patience, *A House Divided: Slavery and Emancipation in Delaware, 1638-1865*, Charlottesville: The University Press of Virginia, 1996.

Foner, Eric, *Gateway to Freedom: The Hidden History of the Underground Railroad,* New York: W. W. Norton & Company, 2015.

Franklin, Benjamin, *A Narrative of the Late Massacres, in Lancaster County, of a Number of Indians, Friends of this Province, by Persons Unknown, With Some Observations on the Same*, 1764.

Geiser, Karl Frederick, *Redemptioners and indentured servants in the colony and commonwealth of Pennsylvania*, New Haven: The Tuttle, Morehouse & Taylor Co., 1901.

Glasse, Hannah (By a Lady), *The Art of Cookery, Made Plain and Easy; Which far exceeds any Thing of the Kind yet published*, London, 1747.

Gibbs, Jenna M., "Columbia the Goddess of Liberty and Slave-Trade Abolition," *Sjuttonhundratal*, Vol. 8, 2011.

Hancock, Harold B., *Delaware During the Civil War: A Political History*, Wilmington, Delaware: Historical Society of Delaware, 1961.

_____. *Liberty and Independence: The Delaware State during the American Revolution*, Wilmington, Delaware: Delaware American Revolution Bicentennial Commission, 1976.

_____. "William Morgan's Autobiography and Diary: Life in Sussex County," *Delaware History*, 1980.

Harris, Joel Chandler, *Uncle Remus: His Songs and His Sayings*, New York: Appleton, 1902.

Harris, Leslie M., *In the Shadow of Slavery: African Americans in New York City, 1626-1863*, Chicago: University of Chicago Press, 2003.

Hatfield, Edwin (ed), *Freedom's Lyre: or, Psalms, Hymns, and Sacred Songs for The Slave and His Friends*, New-York: S. W. Benedict, 1840.

Herman, Bernard L., *The Stolen House*, Charlottesville: University Press of Virginia, 1992.

Horigan, Michael, *Elmira: Death Camp of the North*, Mechanicsburg: Stackpole Books, 2002.

Houston, John W., "Reports of Cases Decided in the Court of Oyer and Terminer and the Court of General Sessions of the Peace and Jail Delivery of the State of Delaware," Wilmington: Mercantile Printing Co., 1920.

Jones, Absalom, "A Thanksgiving Sermon, preached on January 1, 1808," originally published by the St. Thomas

African Episcopal Church, Philadelphia. Electronic edition, Tucson: Antislavery Literature Project, Arizona State University.

Joyner, Charles, *Down by the Riverside: A South Carolina Slave Community,* Urbana: University of Illinois Press, 1984.

Kelley, Sean M., *The Voyage of the Slave Ship Hare: A Journey into Captivity from Sierra Leone to South Carolina,* University of North Carolina Press, 2016.

Lepore, Jill, *New York Burning: Liberty, Slavery, and Conspiracy in Eighteenth Century Manhattan,* New York: Alfred A. Knopf, 2005.

McGruder, Kevin, "A Fair and Open Field: The Response of Black New Yorkers to the Draft Riots," *Afro-Afro-Americans in New York Life and History,* Vol 37, 2013.

MacNeill, G. Swift, *English Interference with Irish Industries,* London: Cassell & Company, 1886.

Marshall, John A. *American Bastile* [sic]: *A History of the Illegal Arrests and Imprisonment of American Citizens During the Late Civil War,* Philadelphia: Thomas W. Hartley, 1871.

Masur, Louis P., *1831: Year of Eclipse,* New York: Hill and Wang, 2001.

Mehlinger, Louis R., "The Attitude of the Free Negro Toward African Colonization," *The Journal of Negro History,* Vol. 1, No.3, June 1916.

Miller, Kirby A. et al. (eds.), *Irish Immigrants in the Land of Canaan: Letters and Memoirs from Colonial. and Revolutionary America, 1675-1815,* New York: Oxford University Press, 2003.

Mittelberger, Gottlieb, *On the Misfortune indentured Servants,* http://www.let.rug.nl/usa/documents/1600-1650/gottlieb-mittelberger-on-the-misfortune-indentured-servants.php.

Newton, John, *The Works of the Rev. John Newton, Vol. IV*, New–Haven: Nathan Whiting, 1824.

Puckett, Newbell Niles, *Folk Beliefs of the Southern Negro*, Chapel Hill: The University of North Carolina Press, 1928.

Rediker, Marcus, *The Slave Ship: A Human History*, New York: Viking, 2004.

Rupp, Daniel L., *The History and Topography of Dauphin, Cumberland, Franklin, Bedford, Adams and Perry Counties*, Lancaster, PA: Gilbert Hills, 1846.

Russell, Daniel, *History of the African Union Methodist Protestant Church,* Philadelphia: Union Star Book and Job Printing and Publishing House, 1920.

Scharf, J. Thomas, *History of Baltimore City and County, From the Earliest Period to the Present Day,* Philadelphia: Louis, H, Everts, 1881.

_____. *History of Delaware 1609-1888, Vols. 1 & 2,* Philadelphia: L. J. Richards & Co., 1888.

Siebert, Wilbur H., *The Underground Railroad from Slavery to Freedom*, New York: The Macmillan Company, 1898.

Sippel, Peter, (editor) "The Quaker Homiletics Online Anthology, Section Two: The 18th Century," http://www.qhpress.org/quakerpages/qhoa/18th.htm

Slavens, Chris, peninsularoots.com

Shomette, Donald G., *Shipwrecks, Sea Raiders, and Maritime Disasters along the Delmarva Coast, 1623-2004*, Baltimore: The Johns Hopkins University Press, 2007.

Smith, Gene Allen, *The Slaves Gamble: Choosing Sides in the War of 1812,* New York: Palgrave Macmillan, 2013.

Stewart. A. T. Q. *The Shape of Irish History*, Montreal: McGill-Queen's University Press, 2001.

Strausbaugh, John, *City of Sedition: The History of New York City During the Civil War,* New York: Hachette Book Group, 2016.

Switala, William J., *Underground Railroad in Delaware, Maryland and West Virginia,* Mechanicsburg, PA: Stackpole Books, 2004.

Thompson, Peter, *Rum, Punch & Revolution: Taverngoing & Public Life in Eighteenth Century Philadelphia,* Philadelphia: University of Pennsylvania Press, 1999.

Tolles, Frederick B., "Quietism versus Enthusiasm: The Philadelphia Quakers and The Great Awakening," *The Pennsylvania Magazine of History and Biography,* Vol. 69, No. 1, January 1945.

Turner, C. H. B. (compiler), *Some Records of Sussex County Delaware,* Philadelphia: Allen, Lane & Scott, 1909.

Watson, John Fanning, *Annals of Philadelphia, being a collection of memoirs, anecdotes, & incidents of the city and its inhabitants from the days of the Pilgrim founders,* E. L Carey & A. Hart, New York, 1830.

Wellman, Judith, *Brooklyn's Promised Land; The Free Black Community of Weeksville, New York,* New York: New York University Press, 2014.

Weslager. C. A., *Delaware's Forgotten Folk: The Story of the Moors and Nanticokes,* Philadelphia: University of Pennsylvania Press, 1943.

Whipper, William, "Non-Resistance to Offensive Aggression," *The Colored American,* September 1837.

Williams, William H, *Slavery and Freedom in Delaware, 1639-1865,* Wilmington, Delaware: S R Books, 1996.

Wright, Donald, *African Americans in the Colonial Era: From African Origins through the American Revolution,* Wheeling, Illinois; Harlan Davidson: 1990.

Young, Henry J., "A Note on Scalp Bounties In Pennsylvania," *Pennsylvania History: A Journal of Mid-Atlantic Studies,* Vol. 24, No. 3, 1957.

Other Titles by Arthur Dobrin

1. Angles and Chambers: Poems
2. Being Good and Doing Right (ed.)
3. Business Ethics: The Right Way to Riches
4. Convictions: Political Prisoners—Their Stories (co-author)
5. Ethical People and How They Get to Be That Way
6. Ethics for Everyone: How to Improve Your Moral I.Q.
7. Gentle Spears: Poems
8. Getting Married the Way You Want (co-author)
9. Lace: Poetry from the Poor, the Homeless, the Aged, the Physically and Emotionally Disabled (ed.)
10. Love Is Stronger Than Death
11. Love Your Neighbor: Stories of Values and Virtues
12. Malaika: A Novel
13. Religious Ethics (ed.)
14. Salted With Fire: A Novel
15. Saying My Name Out Loud: Poems
16. Seeing Through Africa: Personal Essays
17. Spelling God With Two O's: Inspirational Notes
18. Spiritual Timber: aphorisms (online publication)
19. Sunbird: Poems
20. Tea in a Blue Cup: Poems
21. Teaching Right From Wrong; 40 Things You Can Do To Raise a Moral Child
22. The God Within
23. The Harder Right: Stories
24. The Lost Art of Happiness
25. The Role of Cooperatives in the Development of Rural Kenya (monograph)
26. Kwamboka's Inquiry
27. This Red Land

www.ingramcontent.com/pod-product-compliance
Lightning Source LLC
Chambersburg PA
CBHW020450270326
41926CB00008B/547